D0906076

INFLATED

*How Money and Debt
Built the American Dream*

2/9/11

*To Rep Scott Garrett with
the best regards of
the Author.*
ROW

R. Christopher Whalen

WILEY

John Wiley & Sons, Inc.

Published by John Wiley & Sons, Inc., Hoboken, New Jersey.

Published simultaneously in Canada.

For general information on our other products and services or for technical support, please contact our Customer Care Department within the United States at (800) 762-2974, outside the United States at (317) 572-3993 or fax (317) 572-4002.

Wiley also publishes its books in a variety of electronic formats. Some content that appears in print may not be available in electronic books. For more information about Wiley products, visit our web site at www.wiley.com.

Library of Congress Cataloging-in-Publication Data:

Whalen, R. Christopher, 1959–
    Inflated: how money and debt built the American dream / R. Christopher Whalen.
      p. cm.
    Includes index.
    ISBN 978-0-470-87514-8 (hardback); 978-0-470-93371-8 (ebk);
    978-0-470-93370-1 (ebk)
      1. Debts, Public—United States.   2. Inflation (Finance)—United States.
3. Money—United States—History.   4. Monetary policy—United States—History.
I. Title.
  HJ8101.W43 2010
  332.10973—dc22

                                                     2010028553

Printed in the United States of America

10 9 8 7 6 5 4 3 2 1

For Pamela

Voici mon secret. Il est très simple: on ne voit bien qu'avec le cœur.
L'essentiel est invisible pour les yeux.
 —Antoine de Saint Exupéry, *Le Petite Prince* (1943)

I do not think it is an exaggeration to say that it is wholly impossible for a central bank subject to political control, or even exposed to serious political pressure, to regulate the quantity of money in a way conducive to a smoothly functioning market order. A good money, like good law, must operate without regard to the effect that decisions of the issuer will have on known groups or individuals. A benevolent dictator might conceivably disregard these effects; no democratic government dependent on a number of special interests can possibly do so.

—F. A. Hayek

Denationalization of Money,
Institute of Economic Affairs (1978)

Contents

Preface

W hat is the American dream? The historian and Pulitzer Prize winning author of *The Epic of America*, James Truslow Adams, is recognized as the first American to define the concept:

The American Dream is "that dream of a land in which life should be better and richer and fuller for everyone, with opportunity for each according to ability or achievement. It is a difficult dream for the European upper classes to interpret adequately, and too many of us ourselves have grown weary and mistrustful of it. It is not a dream of motor cars and high wages merely, but a dream of social order in which each man and each woman shall be able to attain to the fullest stature of which they are innately capable, and be recognized by others for what they are, regardless of the fortuitous circumstances of birth or position."[1]

Adams's observation was as much a reflection on the nation's past as it was asking about its future. Adams published his book, *Epic of America*, in 1931 during the Great Depression. His world view was more egalitarian and libertarian than the corporate perspective, which today governs much of American life. Adams expressed hope for a world that was not merely defined by commercial standards but comprised of a society where individuals were free to pursue their own definitions of liberty and success.

In the twentieth century, the concept of the American dream can be said to trace its roots back to the promise of "life, liberty and the pursuit of happiness," the most famous line in the Declaration of Independence. Simply stated, when the immigrants who built the United States came to this country, they expected to be able to achieve a level of personal freedom and material security that was substantially better than that which was available in other nations of the world. Today's Americans as well as the thousands of immigrants who come to the United States each year still have that same promise in mind.

Americans as a whole view themselves as reasonably prudent and sober people when it comes to matters of money, though the choices we make at the ballot box seem to be at odds with that self image. As a nation we seem to feel entitled to a national agenda and standard of living that is beyond our current income, a tendency that goes back to the earliest days of the United States. This book examines this apparent conflict by reviewing our nation's past from a political and financial perspective, with an emphasis on the portions of the narrative prior to the decade of boom and bust.

Events such as the Gold Rush of the 1840s, the Civil War, the creation of the Federal Reserve System, and the two World Wars, are examined in the context of the changing definition of the aspirations of a nation. Whether taming the frontier in the 1800s, fighting poverty in the 1930s or bailing out private banks and corporations in the twenty-first century, successive American governments turned debt and inflation into virtues in order to make ends meet, a choice not unlike that made by leaders in many other nations of the world. But Americans have taken the tendency to borrow from the future to an extreme and in the process made it a core ethic of our society. In pursuing the American dream today without limitation, we have made our tomorrows less certain.

The rejection of any practical limits on expenditure is a view particularly encouraged by the generations of Americans that have come since WWII and the subsequent half century of Cold War. By virtue of the sacrifices of the past, Americans believe that we are somehow exempted from the laws of gravity as regards finance and economics. We speak of our "special" role in the global economy even as we repeat the mistakes of Great Britain, Rome, and other ancient civilizations whose financial systems have come and gone. The same popular delusions about inflation and debt that have affected societies in the past are also present in America today.

By highlighting the work of some of the great economists, historians, and researchers of the past two centuries, I've attempted to tell the unique American story of money and debt from a layman's perspective. And by describing the use of the printing press and credit as enduring features of the American dream, the story of a nation that is just two centuries old, I hope to illuminate these issues and thereby encourage a broader national discussion about the future of America's political economy and our place in the world.

Acknowledgments

This book is the synthesis of several decades of conversations and research on the topic of politics and finance. The dialogue began with my parents, Richard and Joan Whalen, who taught my brother Michael, sister Laura, and I to think and write independently. I especially want to thank my father and fellow writer Richard J. Whalen for his suggestions regarding this book and about life over the past half century.

There have been many other teachers and editors who have taught me to write and to think about the political economy. Karl Pflock and Terry Hauser at *Legislative Digest*, a publication of the Republican Conference Committee of the U.S. House of Representatives, introduced me to the world of political journalism and the *Chicago Manual of Style*. Congressman Jack Kemp, who chaired the committee in those days, will always symbolize the optimism and the hope for a brighter future, which are the American dream.

Great journalists and editors such as Robert Bleiberg, Tom Donlan, and my other friends at *Barron's* taught me how to write editorials. James Lucier, Sr. at *Insight on the News* likewise made me a better writer through vigorous editing. My political mentor John Carbaugh was one of the most effective Washington political operatives of his generation and supported some of the research reflected in this book. Robert Novak called John Carbaugh his best source ever. He was my good friend.

Martin Mayer, Alex Pollock, Alan Meltzer, Bill Greider, Anna Schwartz, Bill Janeway, Paul Volcker, Ed Kane, George Kaufman, Murray Rothbard, Robert Higgs, F.A. Hayek, Roger Kubarych, and Nouriel Roubini are a few of my personal influences when it comes to matters of economics and money. Some of these people I've known for decades, others more recently or through their writings, but all have shaped my understanding of money and debt.

Former colleagues from the Federal Reserve System and Treasury have contributed greatly to my understanding of the nuances of finance and economics, including Walker Todd, Richard Alford, Terry Checki, Roger Kubarych, Joseph Mason, Bill Arzt, Brian Roseboro, Jim Martin, Gerry O'Driscoll, Alan Boyce, Greg Zerzan, Chris Laursen, Thomas Day, and Robert Eisenbeis, as well as other current and former employees of the Fed and Treasury I cannot mention by name—what we refer to as the *Herbert Gold Society*.

Over the past decade, the comments from the readers and interview subjects of *The Institutional Risk Analyst*, have also influenced my thinking on money and finance. Collaborating with my friend and business partner Dennis Santiago has informed my view of the workings of the global financial system and also on the limitations of analysis.

Many colleagues on and off Wall Street have tried to teach me the business of finance with varying degrees of success. Alan Schwartz, Gerry Stanewick, John Crudele, David Setchim, Joe Calvo, David Weild, Joan McCullough, John Liscio, Charlie Biderman, Mark Pittman, and Bill King have been just some of my friends and colleagues over the years when it comes to understanding the markets.

Some of my fellow travellers who work in and around the money markets and share their views, perspectives, and insights include James Lucier, Jr., Henry Smyth, Lenny Glynn, Josh Rosner, Robert Arvanitis, John Crudele, Chuck Gabriel, David Reilly, Marshall Auerbach, Richard Leite, Jay Cook, Frank Leitner, Joseph Engelhard, Sylvain Raines, Scott Frew, Ann Rutledge, Dawn Kopecki, Matthieu Royer, Susan Webber, and Barry Ritholtz. There are many more and I thank them all.

My friend David Kotok and all of our colleagues who attend the annual fishing trips to Leen's Lodge in Grand Lake Stream, Maine, deserve thanks for the discussions we have shared over the years. David bears chief responsibility for spurring me to take on this project and for the introduction to the good people at John Wiley & Sons. Special thanks to Laura Walsh, Stacey Fischkelta, and their colleagues at John Wiley & Sons for making this project a reality.

I owe a special debt of gratitude to Jack Tatom, Martha McCormick, and their colleagues at the Networks Financial Institute of Indiana State University. Jack's interest in my work and sponsorship of research and published papers in many of the areas that are covered by this book made this project possible. I have included some of the material from previously published papers with the permission of Networks Financial Institute.

Special thanks also to Nouriel Roubini for taking the time in mid-August to write the Introduction for this book. I look forward to working with Nouriel on other projects we have in process over the months and years ahead.

My longtime friend and Washington consultant Robert Feinberg reviewed early versions of this book and provided comments. Our discussions over the years about the nature of power in Washington and its evolution are reflected in this book. He has been proactively proofreading and commenting on my work for more than a decade, a true sign of friendship.

Ad majorem Dei gloriam

Introduction

C hris Whalen is one of the leading independent analysts of the U.S. banking and financial system. In a world where too many sell-side analysts of the financial sector are not truly independent, Chris represents a fearless beam of enlightened and independent light who avoids the usual self-serving spin that is presented in so much Wall Street research. In this book he also emerges as a leading historian of the U.S. financial system and of the complex nexus between banking/finance, politics, and fiscal policy. This tour de force of the financial history of the United States is also a political history and sovereign fiscal history of the United States.

Whether you agree or not with Chris' views on the state of U.S. banks, which reforms of the system of financial regulation and supervision are appropriate, the risks that large monetized fiscal deficit imply in terms of future inflation, and risks of a crash of the U.S. dollar, he is always thought provoking, a master of details of financial history and presenting lateral and contrarian thinking that challenges the conventional wisdom. You may believe—as I do—that the greatest short-term risk facing the United States is deflation, as a slack in goods and labor markets implies seriously strong deflationary forces. But Chris correctly points out that large and monetized fiscal deficits eventually may cause, in the medium term, a rise in expected and actual inflation as they did after the Civil War and World War II. Indeed, the temptation to use a moderate and unexpected inflation tax to wipe out the real value of public debt and avoid the debt deflation of the private sector is powerful, and history may repeat itself—even if the short-term maturity of U.S. liabilities, the risk of a crash of the U.S. dollar and associated runaway rising inflation, and the related risk that the United States' foreign creditors may pull the plug on the financing of the U.S. deficit may constrain these inflationary biases.

Similarly, Chris stresses the role of poor fiscal and monetary policies and botched regulatory policies in triggering recent and not so recent financial crises. But financial crises existed well before there was a central bank causing moral hazard distortions through its lender of last resort role, before misguided regulation and supervision of banks, and well before there was a significant role of federal fiscal policy in the United States. Indeed, my recent book, *Crisis Economics: A Crash Course in the Future of Finance* (The Penguin Press HC, 2010) shows that financial crises and economic crises driven by irrational exuberance of the financial system and the private sector—unrelated to public policies—existed for centuries before fiscal deviant sovereign and central banks distorted private-sector incentives.

Markets do fail, and they do fail regularly in irrationally exuberant market economies; that is the source of the role of central banks and governments in preventing self-fulfilling and destructive bank runs and collapses of economic activity via Keynesian fiscal stimulus in response to collapse in private demand. The fact that these monetary policies and fiscal policies may eventually become misguided—creating moral hazard and creating large fiscal deficits and debt—does not deny the fact that private market failures—independent of misguided policies—triggered asset and credit bubbles that triggered a public rescue response. Market solutions to market failures don't work because in periods of panic and irrational depression markets fail given collective action problems in private sector decisions. Still, there is a long-standing debate about whether bubbles and the ensuing crises are due to poor government policies (the traditional conservative and Austrian view) or due to market failure requiring policy reaction (the liberal and Keynesian view). Chris takes the Austrian view but the Great Depression experience shows that too much Schumpeterian "creative destruction" leads to uncreative destructive depression. On the other hand, the Japanese experience of the 1990s also suggests that keeping alive zombie banks and companies can lead to persistent near depression.

The most fascinating parts of this great book are about the historical similarities in U.S. financial history:

- Cycles of asset and credit booms and bubbles followed by crashes and busts;
- The fiscal recklessness of U.S. states that leads to state and local government defaults;
- The temptation to socialize those state and local government losses, as well as the losses of the private sector (households and banks) via federal government bailouts;
- The recurrent history of high inflation as the solution to high public deficit and debt problems and private debt problems both after wars (Civil War, World War I, Vietnam War, and possibly now following budget-busting wars in Iraq and Afghanistan) and in the aftermath of asset and credit bubbles gone bust;
- The historical resistance of U.S. state, local, and federal governments to raise enough taxes to finance an increasing public demand for public services and entitlements that cause these large fiscal deficits, and the schizophrenia of an American public that hates high taxes but also wants public and social services—the trouble being that you cannot have at the same time public spending like in the social welfare states of Europe and low tax rates as under Reagan— at least the Europeans are willing to bear high taxes for the public services that they demand instead of living in the delusional bubble that both the government and the household sectors can live beyond their means, piling on more private and public debt.

The recurrence of financial crises—especially in the last 30 years (three big bubbles gone painfully bust since the 1980s) after a long 50-year period of relative financial calm following the reforms of the Great Depression—leads to the question of why these crises keep occurring in spite of attempts—after each crisis—to better regulate and supervise the financial system. Here I would like to develop a point that is only half fleshed out in Chris's analysis of U.S. households and governments living beyond their means and piling public debt on top of private debts; it is the role of rising income and wealth inequality in these financial crises.

Indeed, in the last 30 years there has been a large increase in income and wealth inequality in advanced economies. This rise is due to many factors: winner-take-all effects of an information society; trade integration of China, India, and other emerging markets in the global economy; knowledge and skill-biased technological innovation; rise in finance and increased rent-seeking and oligopoly in financial markets.

This increase in inequality led to a "keeping up with the Joneses effect": households in the United States and Europe could not maintain their living standards and spending and lifestyle goals as wages and labor incomes rose less than productivity, with the share of income going to capital and to the wealthy rising.

This rising inequality is the root cause of the American household tendency to spend beyond its means that Chris correctly bemoans in this book. Indeed, this inequality led to alternative policy responses in the Anglo-Saxon countries versus the social welfare countries of continental Europe. In the former group (United States, United Kingdom, Ireland, Spain, Iceland, Australia, and New Zealand) the response was one of democratization of credit that allowed households to borrow and spend beyond their means: the boom in mortgage and consumer credit (credit cards, auto loans, student loans, payday loans, subprime loans, and so on) led to a massive increase in private household debts that found it matching in the rising leverage of the financial sector (banks and shadow banks). This financial system leverage was abetted by reckless financial deregulation—repeal of Glass Steagall, non-regulation of derivatives, explosion of toxic financial innovation, rise of a subprime financial system, explosion of the shadow banking system. Since households, and the country, were spending more than their incomes, all of these Anglo-Saxon countries run large current account deficits financed by over-saving countries (China and emerging markets, as well as Germany and Japan). The explosion of private debt and foreign debt eventually became unsustainable, and led to the financial crisis of 2007 to 2009.

In continental Europe, the response was more that of a social welfare state: the governments spent more than their revenues and increased budget deficits and public debts to provide households with semi-free public services—education, health care, social pensions, extended unemployment benefits, and other massive transfer payments—as the slow-growing incomes did not allow private spending to grow quickly enough. This increased public debt was absorbed by households that maintained positive savings rates as the government was spending (dis-saving) massively, as well as by banks and other financial institutions. So the financial system piled on public sector assets (government debt) rather than claims on the private sector (as in the Anglo-Saxon countries).

In one set of countries you had an initial rise in private debts and leverage, while in the other group a rise in public debt and leverage. However, when private liabilities became unsustainable in the Anglo-Saxon countries—leading to an economic and financial crisis—you eventually had a massive re-leveraging of the public sector for three reasons: automatic stabilizers, counter-cyclical Keynesian fiscal stimulus to prevent the Great Recession from turning into another Great Depression, and socialization of the private losses. This third factor put many of the debts of the private sector (especially banks and financial systems, but also households and non-financial corporations) on the balance sheet of governments, as the fiscal costs of bailing out the financial system became very high. At the end of this cycle, the Anglo-Saxon countries ended up with large budget deficits and stocks of public debt as the democratization of credit and massive releveraging of the private sector (households and banks) became unsustainable.

Now we have problems of combinations of large stocks of private debts and public debts in most advanced economies: household debts, bank and financial system debts, government debts, and foreign debts. That is why crises will continue and we will have an era of economic and financial instability: households will default when their debts are unsustainable; governments will default when their debts are unsustainable; and banks and shadow banks will be insolvent because they are full of bad assets, including claims on the private sector in Anglo-Saxon economies and claims on the public sector in the social welfare state economies.

Thus, the problems of Greece and the Eurozone are only the tip of an iceberg of large private and public debts and leverage in most advanced economies. This implies a new normal of—at best—slow growth in advanced economies for the next few years as households, financial systems, and governments need to deleverage by spending less, saving more, and reducing their debts. At worst, if these deficit and debt problems are allowed to fester, we will get households defaulting en masse, governments going bankrupt, banks and financial institutions going bankrupt as their public and private assets go sour, and countries going bankrupt with more economic and financial instability. So the coming financial instability and economic crises, with the twin risks of deflation followed by inflation will be driven not only by the unwillingness to rein in—via proper regulation and supervision—a financial system run amok. They will also be driven by the deeper economic and social forces that have led to income and wealth inequality and a massive rise in private and public debts given the stresses of rising inequality and globalization of trade and finance.

So we can unfortunately say goodbye to the Great Moderation and hello to the era of financial instability/crises and economic insecurity. Chris provides us with a fascinating and deep financial history and road map of how we have gone through repeated cycles of great moderations followed by asset and credit bubbles leading to financial crises driven by excessive debt and leverage in the private sector (households, banks, corporate firms) leading to excessive public sector debt accumulation—via socialization of private losses—that leads to twin risks of outright default (usually by U.S. states) or use of the inflation tax through monetization of fiscal deficits (at the federal level).

The philosopher Santayana once said: "Those who cannot learn from history are doomed to repeat it." This deep study of U.S. financial history may help policy makers to avoid repeating the mistakes of the past; even if—in thoughtful Marxist spirit—one could argue that powerful economic, financial, and, thus, political forces drive these repeated cycles of boom and bust that study of history alone cannot prevent.

—Nouriel Roubini

Nouriel Roubini is professor of economics at the Stern School of Business at New York University and chairman of Roubini Global Economics (www .roubini.com).

Chapter 1

Free Banking and Private Money

In his December 1776 pamphlet *The Crisis*, Thomas Paine famously said, "These are the times that try men's souls." He then proceeded to lay out a detailed assessment of America's military challenges in fighting the British. But after the fighting was over, America faced the task of creating a new, independent state separate from British trade and especially independent from the banks of the City of London. The story of money and debt in America is the chronicle of how a fragment of the British empire broke off in the late 1700s and supplanted and surpassed Great Britain in economic terms by the end of WWI. Though Britain for centuries was the dominant economic system in the world, America would come to lead the global economy by the early twentieth century.

The English pound was not the first great global currency, nor will the dollar likely be the last. Mankind has been through cycles of inflation and deflation more than once, going back to before Greek and Roman times. The story of money in each society is a description of the ebb and flow of these states in economic as well as social terms. The latest version of this repeating narrative features a still very young country called America, which has used money and the promise of it to build a global economic empire, but one that may now be in question after almost a century of relative stability.

When the 13 colonies reluctantly declared independence from Great Britain in 1776, the young nation had no independent banking system and no common currency, even though most colonists knew the political and financial traditions of Europe. The Articles of Confederation the infant nation adopted in 1777 did not even give the central government the ability to levy taxes to retire the war debt. European banks and governments met the capital needs of the young nation via loans and even provided what limited physical means of exchange were available aside from pure barter. Pawnbrokers were the predominant source of credit for individuals, and businesses obtained commercial credit from banks, mostly foreign. Foreign coins and some colonial paper money were in circulation, but barter was the most common means of payment used by Americans from the start of the nation's existence through the Civil War.[1]

Sidney Homer and Richard Sylla wrote in the classic work *A History of Interest Rates*:

> The American colonies were outposts of an old civilization. Their physical environment was primitive, but their political and financial traditions were not. Therefore, the history of colonial credit and interest rates is not a history of innovation but rather a history of adaptation.[2]

The first American government had no credit and was dependent upon private, mostly foreign banks and wealthy individuals for financing. Upon winning independence, the colonies formed states and issued colonial currency. Bonds were issued when possible, with individuals and even the government of France subscribing in the earliest days of the young nation.

The Bank of North America was established in Philadelphia by the Continental Congress in 1782 and became the first chartered bank in the United States. Creating a new bank under the control of the American government was an effort to gain some independence from private banks and also from foreign states.

David McCullough's Pulitzer Prize-winning biography, *John Adams*, presents several scenes where the ambassador of the new American government went literally hat in hand to the capitals of Europe seeking hard currency loans to finance the most basic needs. The tireless Adams was able to secure from foreign banks huge sums that sustained the colonial war effort. But as Adams knew too well, his family and other Americans suffered horribly due to inflation and scarcity in those early years. "Rampant inflation, shortages of nearly every necessity made the day-to-day struggle at home increasingly difficult," McCullough relates. "'A dollar was not worth what a quarter had been,' Abigail [Adams] reported. 'Our money will soon be as useless as blank paper.'"[3] This need was acute since the U.S. government lacked the power to tax or the means to collect it. Nor would the American people tolerate higher taxes, because of the unhappy experience with Britain. The leaders of the American revolution had led a political revolt against unfair taxes, thus they were not in a position to then raise taxes to pay for the war.

Adams was neither an apologist for debt nor for inflation. He believed that having a national debt was a good thing because it created relationships with other nations that would help the infant nation survive and grow. In his prolific correspondence with Thomas Jefferson, Adams showed the sharp contrast between on the one hand wanting to create a constituency among financial powers for America's national debt while on the other hand expressing his opposition to having private bankers and banks. In fact, Adams advocated creating a single national bank to serve the needs of the country, with branches in the individual states. Adams wanted to prohibit the states from chartering banks themselves and to have one single, national institution, perhaps under public control. Ron Chernow wrote in his excellent 2004 biography, *Alexander Hamilton*, that Adams viewed banking "as a confidence trick by which the rich exploited the poor." He quoted Adams similarly saying that "every bank in America is an enormous tax upon the people for the profit of individuals," suggesting that one of the more conservative founders of the United States would have preferred banks to be run as a giant collective, not-for-profit utility. Adams differed significantly from Alexander Hamilton on these issues, even though like Hamilton he also was of New England mercantilist stock. Hamilton was a great advocate of private banks and debt, and believed that that finance was the key both to state power and economic growth. Chernow confirms that Adams wanted one state bank with branches around the nation, but no private banks at all.[4]

The charter of the Bank of North America lapsed in 1790 and two years later, the State of New York chartered The Bank of New York, which is the corporate predecessor of the company now known as Bank of New York/Mellon. Supported by New York's powerful merchants, the bank was first organized in 1784 and was led by Hamilton, a New York lawyer and Revolutionary War general who became the first Treasury Secretary and a future leader of the United States. So important was the Bank of New York to the local economy that much of the region's commercial activity was financed by this single institution for decades as the number of banks and thus competition grew slowly. The formation of the bank was not just a financial event, but a very significant political milestone as well that greatly elevated the power of New York.[5] There was no real money nor any payment system in existence for the country. All trade had been financed by English and other foreign banks up until the Revolutionary War. Now the United States had to create a new financial system to replace these relationships, a process that would take more than a century.

The demise of the Bank of North America came as a political battle raged over whether the federal government should assume the debts incurred by the states and cities during the war against Britain. The final agreement from the southerners to support the assumption of state debts was tied to the compromise over moving the location of the capital city from New York to Philadelphia temporarily and eventually to an entirely new capital on the Potomac River to be called Washington. But this "compromise of 1790" engineered by Jefferson and Hamilton did not deal with the issue of a national bank.

The Bank of the United States

President George Washington chartered the First Bank of the United States in 1791. This was the government's attempt at creating a permanent central bank of issue for the infant nation. Madison and Jefferson opposed the bank, but Adams ironically led a sizable majority in the

Congress that favored the measure. McCullough described Adams's views on banks and economics in *John Adams*:

> Adams not only put his trust in land as the safest of investments, but agreed in theory with Jefferson and Madison that an agricultural society was inherently more stable than any other—not to say more virtuous. Like most farmers, he had strong misgivings about banks, and candidly admitted ignorance of "coin and commerce." Yet he was as pleased by the rise of enterprise and prosperity as anyone. . . .[6]

The First Bank of the United States had just a 20-year charter. While it was a bold and novel innovation, the bank only provided credit to established merchants. During the presidency of Thomas Jefferson, the agrarian and other interests not served by the Bank successfully pushed for the establishment of state-chartered institutions to serve the need for credit of a very rapidly growing nation. The state-chartered banks also created alternative sources of political power in the states. The First Bank's charter was not renewed due to the intense attacks by the advocates of Jeffersonian cheap money principles, who taking the lesson of King George III and his taxes, rightly feared that a "central bank" would be dominated by the central government. Even or, worse, it could be dominated by the bankers and merchants in New York and New England commercial centers such as Boston.[7]

In 1811, the First Bank of the United States was resurrected by the New York merchants who controlled it and chartered anew by the State of New York. Today the successor to that corporation is known as Citibank N.A., the lead bank unit of Citigroup Inc. Now two of the largest banks in the new nation were located in New York. This point was not lost on representatives of the other states in the union and especially the Jeffersonian faction in the Congress, who represented agrarian interests dependent upon New York banks for trade credit

The decision not to renew the First Bank of the United States left the United States to fight the war of 1812 against Britain with no means to finance the military struggle, much less the general operations of the federal government. Then Treasury Secretary Albert Gallatin, who was no advocate of public debt, made careful plans to borrow up to $20 million via the First Bank to finance the war, but instead was forced to seek loans from abroad because the First Bank was disolved. Along with Hamilton, Gallatin was one of America's first great financial geniuses, and a talented bond salesman to boot. He is memorialized by a large marker in front of the Treasury building in Washington, having also served as Commissioner for the Treaty of Ghent, as well as minister to both France and Great Britain. Because America's position with the nations of Europe was that of debtor and former colonial possession, Gallatin's financial expertise was invaluable. His role recalled the invocation of Hamilton and also of Adams of the virtue of increasing the number of nations willing to hold the American government's debt.

As the nation reeled from the financial disaster of the War of 1812, a heated debate continued in the Congress regarding the need for a common currency and a new bank of issue for that currency. Notes issued by banks in New York, for example, could not be used at face value to settle debts in other states. The problem of the scarcity of adequate medium of exchange had existed since colonial times and often made it difficult for creditors to secure payment from customers, even if the customer wished to pay! By 1814, the federal government itself was unable to pay its bills and was on the brink of financial collapse. Treasury Secretary Alexander Dallas was forced to suspend payments on the national debt in New England due to a lack of hard currency, a necessary move since all Treasury debts had to be paid in gold or silver. Following the capture of Washington by the British in that year and the default on the national debt, the United States was on the verge of financial and political dissolution.[8]

The creation of the Second Bank of the United States was the American government's next attempt at establishing a central bank, an effort that came only after significant political debate and negotiation. Many Republicans fought the resurrection of the Bank of the United States, fearing that its size and ability to do business across state lines would give it monstrous political power that would prove uncontrollable. There was also a strong suspicion by representatives of southern colonies that the Second Bank would be controlled by New York business and financial interests. But after the destruction of the Federalist Party following the War of 1812, the Republican majority in the Congress eventually chartered the Second Bank of the United States, albeit with very limited powers.

The first time the measure to create the Second Bank came up before the Senate in February 1811, it was defeated by the tiebreaking vote of Vice President George Clinton of New York, who was empowered to cast the vote in his role as presiding officer of the Senate. He justified his action because the "tendency to consolidation" reflected by the proposal for a national bank seemed "a just and serious cause for alarm."[9] The subsequent proposal to charter the Second Bank was not passed by the Congress until 1815, but then was vetoed by President Madison. A year later the Congress reconsidered the matter. This time, the bill passed the Congress and President Madison signed it into a law.

The late Senator Robert Byrd, the West Virginia Democrat who was one of the longest serving members of the body, wrote in his 1991 history of the Senate that the early debates regarding a central bank "were far from over and would surface again within the coming decades to alter significantly American political history." Byrd also notes that coincident with the authorization for the Second Bank, the Congress for the first time dared to provide themselves with an annual salary. Previously, members of the Congress had been paid $6 per day or about $900 per year. Wartime inflation had greatly reduced the purchasing power of this per diem compensation, so the Congress voted itself a $1,500 per year annual salary. The decision was a political disaster and led to the defeat of two-thirds of the members of the House in the following election.[10]

Ironically, many Republicans who supported the Second Bank considered themselves heirs to the libertarian legacy of Thomas Jefferson. When they finally supported the proposal, however, they were following the plan of Alexander Hamilton of New York and other supporters of a strong central government and the virtue of private banks for supporting economic expansion. These same Republicans, who essentially held a one-party lock on the Congress during that time, opposed funding for interstate roads and canals, and even the railroads, to help the struggling economy. The Republicans of that era doubted that the central government had the power under the Constitution to fund internal improvements, yet they did support the central bank. The fact was that the United States was changing as fast as it was growing and with that change was losing many of its libertarian attributes. The nation's founders, whether federalist or anti-federalist, found the process bewildering. Susan Dunn, professor of Humanities at Williams College, wrote:

> Jefferson and Madison's Republican Party championed the enter-
> prising middling people who lived by manual labor. But the
> year before he died, Jefferson felt lost in a nation that seemed
> overrun by business, banking, religious revivalism, "monkish
> ignorance," and anti-intellectualism . . . The Founders' revo-
> lutionary words about equality, life, liberty, and the pursuit of
> happiness, along with their bold actions, had unleashed a dem-
> ocratic tide—one so strong that within a few decades many
> of them found themselves disillusioned strangers living in an
> egalitarian, commercial society, a society they had unwittingly
> inspired but not anticipated.[11]

Following the creation of the Second Bank of the United States, the American economy grew rapidly and more private banks were created, but the largely powerless federal government provided vir- tually no finance to support this growth by funding public improve- ments. The Congress preferred to leave this task instead to the cities and states which, naturally enough, turned to borrowing rather than taxation to finance economic growth. By 1840, the total debt of the states amounted to some $200 million, a vast sum by contemporary standards given that total U.S. gross domestic product or GDP was just $1.5 billion. Much of this debt was issued by banks chartered by the states and was held by foreigners.[12]

Though the Founders had made provision under the Commerce Clause of the Constitution for trade between the states free of tar- iff, there was no provision for a common currency or banking sys- tem tying the nation or even the individual states together. A similar problem is evident today in the European Union, which has a com- mon currency, the euro, but no real economic integration. To provide some liquidity, state-chartered banks issued various forms of notes to the public in return for some future promise to pay in hard money— that is, gold. There was no common means of exchange nor any back- stop for banks, which from time to time needed emergency infusions of funds. Panics occurred when public unease about particular finan- cial institutions, companies, or the markets caused deposit runs on individual institutions that could grow into a general financial crisis that affected regions or even the entire country. Crises of just this sort would become the hallmark of the U.S. economy for the next century.

In 1809, for instance, the Farmer's Exchange Bank in Gloucester, Rhode Island, failed—one of the first significant bank failures in the United States. There was no Federal Deposit Insurance Corporation or Federal Reserve System to provide support or even organize the orderly liquidation of the bank. This task fell to state and local authorities. The demise of the Farmers Exchange Bank illustrated the types of financial schemes and public panics that would trouble the United States for decades to come. Financial-pioneer-turned-confidence-man Andrew Dexter, Jr., writes James Kamensky, "challenged the notions of his Puritan ancestors by embarking on a wild career in real estate speculation, all financed by the string of banks he commandeered and the millions of dollars they freely printed. Upon this paper pyramid he built the tallest building in the United States, the Exchange Coffee House, a seven-story colossus in downtown Boston. But in early 1809, just as the exchange was ready for unveiling, the scheme collapsed. In Boston, the exchange stood as an opulent but largely vacant building, a symbol of monumental ambition and failure."[13]

A democratic society and a free market economy cannot exist without both great ambition and equally great failure. However, in the American experience, financial fraud and the tendency of politicians to use debt and paper money, rather than taxes raised with the active knowledge and consent of the voters, are common elements from colonial times right through to the present day. The collective failure of the Subprime Debt Crisis of 2008 is a larger reprise of the types of mini crises that occurred in the United States centuries before this period, crises that were limited by the relatively primitive state of communication and transportation.

State Debt Defaults

By the mid-1830s, the United States was in the midst of an economic boom characterized by inflation and speculation in public land sales, as well as road and canal projects. Many of these projects were badly needed but were often poorly conceived or entirely money-losing investments. The several American states employed borrowing to finance needed improvements in order to avoid increasing taxes, and they even used sales of public land as a means to reduce debt. States along the Atlantic coast, where the economy was more developed and other sources of revenue such as tariffs were available, generally avoided costly property taxes, while less developed inland states could not sustain their governments with low property taxes and ran into financial trouble. The low or no property tax regimes in many western states are a legacy from the colonial period. This resulting unequal development became even more acute because the areas needing investment and often growing the most rapidly were precisely the western states and territories that were starved for cash, not so much for investment but simply as a means of exchange.[14] In some of these states, the need for money was met in a primitive way by discovering and extracting gold and silver from the ground.

During the 1830s speculation in land also flourished, with state-chartered banks providing the paper to fuel the rising land values. This investment bubble had the effect of making the states look fiscally sound because of rising land prices. Some inland states even suspended property taxes due to supposed "profits" on bank shares, which often comprised a large portion of state investments. But the illusion of wealth and public revenue would fade with the Crisis of 1837, when many of these state banks failed, the equivalent of a nation's central bank failing today. The Crisis of 1837 was the fourth and most stunning depression in the U.S. up to that time and the first financial crisis that was truly national in scope.[15] Between 1841 and 1842, Florida, Mississippi, Arkansas, Michigan, Indiana, Illinois, Maryland, Pennsylvania, and Louisiana ran into serious fiscal problems and defaulted on interest payments. The first four states ultimately repudiated $13 million in debts, while others delayed and rescheduled their debts, in some cases years later. Alabama, Ohio, New York, and Tennessee narrowly avoided default during this period.[16] Because many states used state-chartered banks as vehicles for borrowing, the public naturally became alarmed when the states ran into financial problems and public programs established during prosperous times could no longer be funded.

In the early 1800s, paper money issued by private, state-chartered banks generally traded at a steep discount to the face value when converted into precious metal, especially when it was issued by banks outside of the state or local market where is was presented for payment. The notes used at that time generally promised to pay the bearer of the note a certain amount of physical gold or silver upon demand. The experience of banks failing was all too common for Americans in that period.

There was deep suspicion in the marketplace when a note from a far-away, state chartered bank was presented for payment. This was one reason that payments by and to state and federal agencies were done only in metal coins, not paper, and most contracts of the day likewise specified metal as the consideration. In the 1840s there was no telephone, no internet or even telegraph, and no local clearinghouse for banks to use to validate the authenticity of paper money issued by private banks. No surprise, then, that people in America and around the world preferred the security and certainty of gold and silver coins to paper money, even when the banks issuing the paper were backed by sovereign states.

The suspicion of paper money was part of a broader suspicion of bankers and the economically powerful that flowed through most of American society. Fleeing the religious and economic oppression of European society, Americans came to the New World for a fresh start and also an opportunity to live free of the stratified economic system of Europe, where even in the eighteenth century opportunities for advancement where few. Two centuries later, Western Europe remains a far less dynamic market for new businesses and banks than the far younger U.S. market. Having money that was independent of political authority granted individuals a level of freedom from inflation that was a key part of the American ideal. Thus when the states began to falter financially, the cohesion of the entire nation was threatened. Most Americans still identified themselves with their home state or town rather than as citizens of the United States. The political fact of union among the states had still not quite been settled because of the issue of slavery, but the overall fragility of the state-run financial system contributed to the mounting political pressures on the nation.

As many states fell into default on their obligations during the 1840s, repudiation of debt by state-chartered banks was a hotly debated subject. In Arkansas, for example, Governor Archibald Yell explicitly urged debt repudiation in his 1842 message to the state legislature, which had created various state-chartered banks as vehicles for funding state expenditures via borrowing. Such was the political uproar against banks and debt generally that the Arkansas state legislature passed a constitutional amendment in 1846 to liquidate all state-chartered banks and prohibit the creation of any new banks in that state.[17]

In Pennsylvania, starting in the mid-1830s the Commonwealth had chartered the United States Bank of Pennsylvania to cover fiscal short-falls with debt. By 1839, the bank had defaulted on its obligations several times, but the response from the state legislature was to authorize more borrowing—a charming reminder that the present-day problems of federal deficits are not a new phenomenon. Despite rising deficits, the Commonwealth of Pennsylvania delayed making any meaningful fiscal reforms until the mid-1840s, by which time it was in default on its debt. In payment on the Commonweath's $40 million in debt, its citizens were forced to take scrip bearing 6 percent interest because the state was broke.[18] In essence, Pennsylvania began to issue its own currency when it could not borrow or would not tax in sufficient amounts, a phenomenon that has reappeared in the United States in the twenty-first century. As the states, most notably California, New York, and Illinois, struggle today under mountains of debt, unfunded pension obligations, and other expenses, issuing scrip has again become a popular alternative to tax increases.

By 1840 many American states had gained a well-deserved reputation in Europe for not repaying loans, although the U.S. government managed to service the federal debt in good order. From $75 million in debt in 1791 to a peak of $100 million after the War of 1812, the Treasury paid down the federal debt to a mere $63 million in 1849. The U.S. government only paid down its debt once in the 1830s and then only by the accident of having a fiscal hawk named Andrew Jackson as President. In general fiscal restraint at the federal level was the rule in the first century of the nation's existence. Since the Federal government was not really involved in financing the economic growth of the nation, the remarkable stability of the federal debt contrasts with the spendthrift behavior of the states, counties and cities.

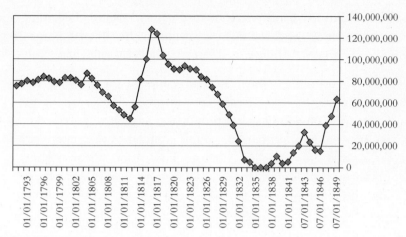

Figure 1.1 U.S. Federal Debt/Annual 1791–1849 ($)
Source: U.S. Treasury

Figure 1.1 shows the total federal debt of the United States from 1781 through 1849.

States such as Louisiana defaulted on loans, evaded their debts and delayed settlement with creditors until the twentieth century. Many foreign investors had believed, incorrectly, that the success of New York and other Atlantic states in building profitable canals and other commercial infrastructure would be repeated in the western and southern states and territories. The states themselves, especially in the south and west, seemed genuinely to have believed in the growth story. But in fact, looking at both the federal and state debts, the United States was a heavily indebted, rapidly developing country with neither organized financial markets nor even a common currency, and with a seriously dysfunctional central government.

When the overheated economy and related financial crisis first started to boil over in the late-1830s, many European banks refused to lend further to the U.S. government or the various states, putting intense pressure on the small nation's liquidity and political unity. This stress was relieved by the issuance of various types of fiat currency and debt securities. In states such as Michigan and Indiana, the number of banks dwindled as first private institutions and eventually

the state-chartered banks were wound up and closed. Regarding the
financial situation in the Midwest, Willis Dunbar and George May
noted in their book, *Michigan: A History of the Wolverine State*:

> The speculation in Michigan land values of the early thirties,
> for example, was fantastic. The enormous note issues of the
> banks were obviously out of proportion to their resources. And
> the internal improvement programs adopted by the states were
> far beyond their ability to finance. The nation was importing,
> primarily from Great Britain, much more than it was export-
> ing, and piling up a steadily mounting debt to British exporters
> and manufacturers. A day of reckoning was inevitable.[19]

Washington had not played a direct role in encouraging the accumulation of debt by the states. The national Congress refused to
support any needed infrastructure improvements such as roads, canals,
and port facilities, and the failure to make progress on the more basic
issue of a national currency made the situation in the American financial markets inherently unstable. When added to this structural defi-
ciency the renewed political ascendancy of Andrew Jackson and the
proponents of the Jeffersonian, anti-federalist view of banks and currency, set the stage for not merely a crisis at the end of the 1830s—but
for a catastrophe. When the crisis finally occurred, it turned out to be
one of the worst economic and financial meltdowns seen in Western
society up to that time and was compounded by unresolved political
issues in Washington.

By the middle of 1837, unemployment was widespread and thousands of companies and banks had failed as the money supply contracted.
This was due in part to events in Washington and, more important, to
a growing antipathy toward banks and paper money among the public. Bad paper money was literally shunned by the mass population, and
the issuance of bonds likewise dried up. By the start of the 1840s, only
official U.S.-minted coins and other types of specie were in broad circulation as Americans avoided privately issued paper notes and debt.[20]
In effect, all of the float or credit in the economy was gone. Americans
were forced to operate on cash or barter terms. Imagine leaving one's
house every morning needing to generate cash or goods via sales, services, or barter every day in order to survive. Most Americans in the

1840s lived with no access to cash or credit, except as provided by commercial exchanges with other people.

The Age of Andrew Jackson

Much of the terrible suffering experienced by the country in the late 1830s owed itself to one factor more than others: the rise a decade before of Andrew Jackson, the Tennessee war hero and political outsider. The arrival in Washington of this former Indian fighter and hero of the War of 1812, known as Old Hickory, signaled the end of the political dominance of Virginia in American politics. Jackson had lost his first bid for the presidency to John Quincy Adams of Massachusetts in the election of 1824, even though the Tennessee native won a larger proportion of the popular vote and also the plurality of votes in the Electoral College. But Jackson still lost the election.

In the so-called "Corrupt Bargain," Senator Henry Clay, a Whig from Kentucky and long-time enemy of Jackson, threw his support to Adams in the vote in the U.S. House of Representatives, ensuring the election of Adams but also making the election of Jackson in 1828 a virtual certainty. Clay was appointed Secretary of State by President Adams as the quid pro quo for his support in the House. Clay himself sought the presidency on four occasions, but he repeatedly underestimated the popular support for the man who had defeated the British Army at New Orleans in spectacular fashion—albeit several weeks after the United States and Britain had agreed to peace. News traveled slowly in those days.

Jackson's succession to the presidency in 1828 followed an unremarkable political career, but was notable as the first time that a southerner swept into power in Washington on a wave of popular support. In a sense, Jackson was the first modern president because his victory marked the earliest instance where an American presidential candidate was actually chosen by the popular vote rather than as the result of the internal selection process dominated by the nation's founders and their descendants. In fact, to complete the picture of upset, Jackson's running mate, John C. Calhoun of South Carolina, had served as Vice President under the incumbent President John Quincy Adams.

The 1828 presidential campaign was a vicious affair, as might be expected when an established order is ended. Jackson was opposed by most of the nation's newspapers, bankers, businessmen, and manufacturers, especially in the Northeast, but still won 56 percent of the popular vote in 1828. Thus began the Jacksonian Age.[21]

The period of Andrew Jackson's presidency was in political terms one of the most difficult in American history, with northern and southern interests competing with new western states for political advantage, even to the point of secession from the Union. Against this contentious political backdrop, Jackson and Congress fought bitterly over many issues, but none of more consequence for the economy and the U.S. financial system than the renewal of the Second Bank of the United States.

With its charter set to expire in 1836, Jackson began in 1830 to attack the Second Bank and proposed instead that a new government bank be set up as an arm of the Treasury. The Whigs led by Clay decided to re-authorize the Second Bank early and were able to get the measure passed by both houses of Congress during the summer of 1832, but the legislation was vetoed by President Jackson on July 10, 1832. He objected to the bank as being unconstitutional, aristocratic, and, most important, because it failed to establish a sound and uniform national currency. The lengthy written discussion of President Jackson's objections to the Second Bank is one of the great libertarian statements against big government and the power of moneyed interests in American history. It also predicted many of the problems caused by the creation of the Federal Reserve System 80 years later. The final paragraph of the Jackson veto message reads:

> Experience should teach us wisdom. Most of the difficulties our Government now encounters and most of the dangers which impend over our Union have sprung from an abandonment of the legitimate objects of Government by our national legislation, and the adoption of such principles as are embodied in this act. Many of our rich men have not been content with equal protection and equal benefits, but have besought us to make them richer by act of Congress. By attempting to gratify their desires we have in the results of our legislation arrayed

section against section, interest against interest, and man against man, in a fearful commotion which threatens to shake the foundations of our Union. It is time to pause in our career to review our principles, and if possible revive that devoted patriotism and spirit of compromise which distinguished the sages of the Revolution and the fathers of our Union. If we cannot at once, in justice to interests vested under improvident legislation, make our Government what it ought to be, we can at least take a stand against all new grants of monopolies and exclusive privileges, against any prostitution of our Government to the advancement of the few at the expense of the many, and in favor of compromise and gradual reform in our code of laws and system of political economy.[22]

Even then, the supporters of a central bank were numerous and outspoken. Ralph C. H. Catterall, the great historian of the Second Bank, said of Jackson's veto:

Jackson and his supporters committed an offense against the nation when they destroyed the bank. The magnitude and enormity of that offense can only be faintly realized, but one is certainly justified in saying that few greater enormities are chargeable to politicians than the destruction of the Bank of the United States.[23]

But Claude G. Bowers, a historian sympathetic to Jackson, defended his action:

Even among the ultra-conservatives of business, the feeling was germinating that Jackson was not far wrong in the conclusion that a moneyed institution possessing the power to precipitate panics to influence governmental action, was dangerous to the peace, prosperity, and liberty of the people.[24]

The veto of the reauthorization of the Second Bank was not the end of the matter, however. The debate over the bank and the nature of money played a significant role in the 1832 landslide re-election victory of Jackson against the party formerly known as the Whigs, and now called the National Republican Party under Henry Clay.

That debate would continue for years as the Senate censured Jackson for his efforts to remove the government's funds on deposit with the Second Bank. But Jackson was adamant that the bank had to go and he was willing to let his political fate be governed by that one issue. In September 1831, President Jackson told Treasury Secretary Louis McLane that he did not intend to pull down the bank merely to set up a new one.[25]

Despite Jackson's strong view on the matter, he could not disregard many voices, even in his own cabinet, who supported renewing the charter of the Second Bank. Yet Jackson remained strong in his conviction that the central bank was a monster that was unconstitutional and concentrated power "in the hands of so few persons irresponsible to the electorate," wrote Marquis James. The great biographer of Jackson continued: "Nor was this all. With deep and moving conviction, the message gave expression to a social philosophy calculated to achieve a better way of life for the common man."[26]

In one of the examples of how personal political battles contributed to the economic problems of the nation, Nicholas Biddle, the head of the Second Bank and a foe of Jackson, fought the President to the last in defense of the Second Bank. When Jackson gave notice that the Treasury would no longer deposit its cash in the Second Bank, Biddle started to withdraw funds deposited with state banks around the country in an effort to discredit Jackson. Specifically, Biddle would present notes drawn upon state banks and demand payment in gold, a move that had the effect of draining liquidity from those communities and generating enormous anger at Biddle and the Treasury. So great was the antagonism generated by Biddle's attempt to hurt the U.S. economy (and thereby wound President Jackson politically) that almost a century later, when the U.S. Congress debated the creation of the Federal Reserve System, the state bankers still referred to the predations of Nicholas Biddle and the Second Bank as a reason for opposing the legislation.

Biddle was one of the great financial minds of the early days of the United States, but he was also a formidable political operator who was not afraid to use the media and lobbying on Capitol Hill to defend his institution. Together with Clay and other supporters of the Second Bank, they mounted a vigorous but ultimately futile defense.

The economy eventually slowed and the financial markets began to weaken as the Second Bank withdrew hard currency from the economy, but President Jackson struck back. In the fall of 1833, he directed that the Treasury withdraw its deposits from the Second Bank, a move which began his famous confrontation with Henry Clay and the Senate, and doomed the Second Bank of the United States to extinction.

Both Clay and Biddle, it seems, believed that hard economic times would help their battle with Jackson and the Democrats, who used the fight over the bank to win the 1832 election. Both men miscalculated badly and Jackson won re-election with 76 percent of the vote, the largest margin since George Washington and James Madison. The pro-Jackson forces likewise prevailed in the 1834 mid-term contest—even as Biddle did his best to "bring the country to its knees and with it Andrew Jackson."[27] The political battle over the Second Bank of the United States between Clay and Jackson distracted the country at a very crucial juncture of American history. The United States would go nearly three quarters of a century without a central bank of issue for its currency until Congress established the Federal Reserve System in 1913, but the immediate impact was the most severe economic crisis the nation had seen since its beginnings.

When the Second Bank closed its doors in March of 1836, the United States was left with no common currency and what credit the bank had provided to the economy was withdrawn. There was no central provider of liquidity for banks, nor any deposit insurance. Only the private shareholders of state-chartered banks were available to support the liquidity and soundness of private depositories. This lack of a currency system and of a mechanism for managing the liquidity needs of banks had been felt earlier in the century, when the Second Bank of the United States called in its loans in 1819 and triggered the Panic of that same year in the ensuing scramble for liquidity. But as with most public issues, the national Congress was largely indifferent to the needs of the nation, preferring instead to defend regional and states' rights from threats, real and imagined.

The defeat of the Second Bank of the United States was not the end of Jackson's reactionary agenda. President Jackson refused to allow the resources of the federal government to be used for financing the construction of roads and canals, and instead retired the national debt and distributed the surplus accumulated in the Treasury. By attacking the Second Bank and at the same time pursuing a very conservative fiscal policy, Jackson created the circumstances for the Great Panic of 1837. Since there was no central bank, the withdrawal of public debt by the Treasury amounted to a deflationary reduction in the nation's money supply. In addition, the retirement of the federal government's debt encouraged states and their banks to issue paper currency in large amounts, which fueled land purchases and speculation. Done in the midst of a growing speculative bubble based on land purchases, the Jacksonian fiscal measures helped to reduce liquidity in banks and worsen the lack of credit in an already cash strapped society. Yet even with what amounted to a tight money policy from Washington over eight years of Jackson's presidency, the speculation that gripped the nation during the early part of the 1830s was just coming to a boil when Jackson left office in the early part of 1837.

As one of his last official acts, Jackson issued the Specie Circular, another hard money and anti-debt initiative, which required that purchases of government land be paid for in coin or *specie* rather than bank paper. By requiring that payments for taxes, duties, and/or the purchase of federal land be made in gold coins, the Treasury was in practical terms draining reserves from the banking system and causing it to shrink. This compounded the fact that the Second Bank of the United States under Biddle had been calling in its loans. This third fiscal action by Jackson, following the closure of the Second Bank and the retirement of the government's debt, was implemented by his successor, President Martin Van Buren, and further exacerbated the liquidity crisis in the United States.

The Panic of 1837

As Jackson travelled home to Nashville in the spring of 1837, he observed that bank notes were trading at a steep discount to face value and farmers were paying 30 percent for credit—all the results of his earlier executive orders. Some bankers, traders, and particularly land speculators clamored for President Van Buren to "strike down the iniquitous Specie Circular" requiring that hard money be used in the purchase of federal land or payment of federal taxes. But Jackson wrote to Van Buren:

> My dear sir, the Treasury order is popular with the people everywhere I have passed. But all the speculators, and those largely indebted, want more paper. The more it depreciates the easier they can pay their debts . . . Check the paper mania and the republic is safe and your administration must end in triumph.[28]

Unfortunately for President Van Buren, Jackson's devotion to hard money was at odds with the needs of a growing nation. With the drain of currency caused by Jackson's Treasury order, as he called the Specie Circular, and the resultant increased stress on the economy, a lack of confidence in the state banks was widespread around the United States. The resulting financial crisis in 1837 caused many banks to fail over a period of several years. This panic was followed by a sharp economic contraction around the world that would last until 1841. To no surprise, President Van Buren was defeated in the next general election.

One of the more significant and mischievous contributions that President Van Buren made to the country's financial development was the creation of an independent Department of the Treasury. In 1837, in a special message to Congress, President Van Buren proposed that the finances of the federal government be formally "divorced" from those of the state chartered banks. This proposal caused considerable political controversy. The Congress passed The Independent Treasury Act of 1840 and then repealed it in 1841. In 1846 Congress adopted the same proposal again. The official goal of the legislation was twofold: to ensure the independence of the banks in the country and also to support the value of the currency. Neither of these goals were met.

In practical terms, the Treasury became a "bank of issue" and a de facto central bank, refusing to accept notes issued by private banks and issuing its own notes in competition with the state banks. The creation of the Independent Treasury had a negative impact on the U.S. economy by draining reserves from the banking system and effectively reducing the supply of money available to Americans for commerce.

By segregating the gold reserves of the government in the Treasury's own vaults and not keeping these funds on deposit with private banks, the Independent Treasury served to exacerbate the structural deficiencies in the U.S. economy for decades afterward. In the years up through the Civil War and thereafter, the fiscal operations of the Treasury were an important factor in the ebb and flow of the supply of money available to support the American economy.

By the 1840s, hundreds of banks existed in America and all of them were printing private bank notes and making loans based solely on their own resources, mostly gold and foreign currency held as reserves. With the demise of the Second Bank of the United States in 1836, only state-chartered banks existed and the United States remained dependent upon limited minting of specie, foreign currency, and barter as means of exchange. During this period, known as the Free Banking Era, state bank chartering standards were not very stringent, and many new banks were formed and failed, but the free banking era was also one of great expansion in the U.S. economy. The Federal Reserve Bank of San Francisco described the period:

> State Bank notes of various sizes, shapes, and designs were in circulation. Some of them were relatively safe and exchanged for par value and others were relatively worthless as speculators and counterfeiters flourished. By 1860, an estimated 8,000 different state banks were circulating "wildcat" or "broken" bank notes in denominations from ½ cent to $20,000. The nickname "wildcat" referred to banks in mountainous and other remote regions that were said to be more accessible to wildcats than customers, making it difficult for people to redeem these notes. The "broken" bank notes took their name from the frequency with which some of the banks failed, or went broke.[29]

In reaction to the collapse of the Second Bank of the United States, New York became the first state to adopt an insurance plan for bank obligations. Between 1829 and 1866, five other states adopted similar deposit insurance schemes in an attempt to stabilize their banking systems. But these modest early attempts at enhancing bank safety and soundness were not effective in controlling the emission of paper currency and forestalling liquidity crises such as the great Panic of 1837.

The Congress authorized a Third Bank of the United States in 1841, but President John Tyler vetoed the measure, leading to rioting outside the White House by members of his own Whig Party.[30] The idea of a central bank issuing paper money was sufficiently popular in Washington and among the business circles that exerted influence in the lobbies of the Capitol. But Tyler, who succeeded to the presidency upon the death of William Henry Harrison, who died after just a month in office, vetoed the legislation creating a Third Bank of the United States twice during his term on states' rights grounds.

The defeat of the Third Bank of the United States also marked yet another political defeat for the Republican leader Henry Clay. As before, Clay had personally championed the idea of a central bank, and as before, he had lost. With the death of Harrison, a retired general and respected member of the Whig Party, Clay believed that a new central bank was assured. But the populist opposition to the idea of a central bank, or even any banks at all, was too strong. President Tyler instead used the bank issue to assert his political independence from Clay and the Whig leaders in Congress.

When Tyler's Whig cabinet resigned over the veto of the bank legislation, Tyler was left with only the venerable Daniel Webster as Secretary of State. Webster knew the political and economic issues in the debate over a central bank as well as any member of the Senate. He had opposed the First Bank in 1814, but then helped John C. Calhoun fashion a compromise that eventually passed by the Congress. Years later, acting in his capacity as a lawyer, Webster represented the Second Bank before the Supreme Court in *McCulloch v. Maryland*, when the high court upheld the implied power of Congress to charter a federal bank and rejected the right of states to tax federal agencies. The ruling in *McCulloch v. Maryland* also recognized the implied powers clause of the Constitution, an evil event that greatly expanded the power of the Congress generally and especially regarding money and debt.

"A disordered currency is one of the greatest political evils," Webster is reported to have said in one of the great arguments ever made by an American for sound money. He continued:

A sound currency is an essential and indispensible security for the fruits of industry and honest enterprise. Every man of property or industry, every man who desires to preserve what he honestly possesses, or to obtain what he can honestly earn, has a direct interest in maintaining a safe circulating medium; such a medium shall be a real and substantial representative of property, not liable to vibrate with opinions, not subject to be blown up or blown down by the breath of speculation, but made stable and secure by its immediate relation to that which the whole world regards as permanent value.[31]

Tyler and Webster appointed a new cabinet comprised of southerners and without any supporters of Clay, whose political era essentially ended with this last battle in the nineteenth century over a central bank.

As discussed in the next chapter, Washington remained largely oblivious to the financial problems facing the nation's economy until the Civil War. Tyler's advocacy for states' rights also meant a strong resistance against using federal revenue to bail out the states from their debts. Clay was particularly keen on giving the new, heavily indebted western states the right to revenue from public land sales, a measure Tyler refused to support. Even though Martin van Buren was defeated in 1840, the influence of Jackson and the public's strong distrust of banks generally gave President Tyler the will to oppose a measure strongly supported by his Whig Party. The Whigs subsequently expelled Tyler. When he left office in 1845, the government received taxes and paid interest in specie, but the rest of the economy was fueled by the rapid growth in paper currency that was, to one degree or another, convertible into gold or silver.

The Gold Rush

The debt crises in the various states of the mid-1840s would quickly be forgotten in 1848 when gold was discovered in California. Within months of the discovery, tens of thousands of people were headed west, overland across the Great American desert, by sea around Cape Horn, or through the jungles of Panama and Nicaragua. The tiny Spanish port of San Francisco was turned almost overnight into a boom town of some 25,000 inhabitants and continued to grow to bursting and beyond with the vast influx of humanity from all corners of the globe.

By 1870, the population of San Francisco had reached nearly 150,000, but this statistic only begins to describe the huge movement of people and resources from the Eastern United States to the other side of the continent. So great was the influx of humanity into California that the territory was organized into a state, held a constitutional convention, and petitioned Congress for statehood in less than two years. California was admitted to the Union as a free state via the Compromise of 1850, the fastest process of accession to statehood of any U.S. state.

The production of gold from the mines of California served to stimulate economic activity in the United States and around the world, resulting in increased imports from Great Britain and other nations, and a steady increase in prices. The influx of new supplies of gold increased the money supply of the United States which, by definition, was still governed by the amount of gold in circulation. But a great deal of gold would eventually leave the United States for destinations such as Britain and other countries to pay for imported goods. More important, the Gold Rush pushed wages and prices higher, even after the initial surge of migration from 1848 to 1852 slowed. Long after the allure of the Gold Rush had faded, wages and prices in distant California remained higher than in the rest of the United States.[32]

But despite the idealized view of the Gold Rush, the fact was that most of the 49ers who made the trip to California did not become rich. Making the trip to California to pan for gold was akin to playing the lottery, which meant that the vast majority of participants were losers in financial and human terms. A significant portion of the participants in the Gold Rush died attempting to reach California or due to violence in the gold fields. Those who ventured north to the Yukon in pursuit of gold faced even steeper odds, as described so beautifully by Jack London in books such as *Call of the Wild* and *White Fang*.

The more enduring, long-term impact of the Gold Rush was to create an alternative to the Puritan, conservative notion of hard work and saving that characterized the early days of the United States with the "American dream" of instant wealth achieved quickly via opportunism and speculation. More than simply a description of the social and economic changes that occurred in California as a result of the discovery of gold, the Gold Rush and eventually the American dream became synonymous with the ability to get a fresh start in life and, with hard work and most important, luck, earn enormous wealth. From the 49ers in the 1850s to oil prospectors half a century later to movie producers and technology start-up companies in the twentieth century, the get-rich-quick image of the American dream became an important fixture in the nation's psyche that would color public attitudes toward money, debt, and the role of government. The American dream was not merely about helping all Americans meet their wants and needs, but to meet them immediately. As H.W. Brands wrote in his classic work, *The Age of Gold*:

> "We are on the brink of the age of gold," Horace Greeley had said in 1848. The reforming editor wrote better than he knew. The discovery [of gold] at Coloma commenced a revolution that rumbled across the oceans and continents to the ends of the earth, and echoed down the decades to the dawn of the third millennium. The revolution manifested itself demographically, in drawing hundreds of thousands of people to California; politically, in propelling America along the path to the Civil War; economically, in spurring the construction of the transcontinental railroad. But beyond everything else, the Gold Rush established a new template for the American dream. America had always been the land of promise, but never had the promise been so decidedly—so gloriously—material. The new dream held out the hope that anyone could have what everyone wants: respite from toil, security in old age, a better life for one's children.[33]

The Rise of Bank Clearinghouses

Another significant development in the history of the American monetary system prior to the Civil War that deserves attention is the creation of private clearinghouses around the country to help banks manage their payments and liquidity. In 1853, when the Clearing House Association began operations in New York, it was located in a single room in the basement of 14 Wall Street. Created even before the National Banking Act was enacted by the Congress a decade later, the

New York Clearing House was a mechanism designed to reduce the cost of clearing claims between banks in the same city.

Twice a day, the banks would total their debits and credits with each member of the clearinghouse, and then settle the difference in cash—or special notes drawn on the clearing member. This basic, non-specie extension of credit between the members of the association was another response to the demise of the Second Bank of the United States and effectively made the clearinghouse a quasi central bank to its members.[34]

The advent of clearinghouse models in many cities around the United States during the mid-1840s and 1850s was an important development, a uniquely American model of mutual risk taking and liquidity sharing that provided an important degree of efficiency to the financial markets without government support. But the credit that could be provided to members was limited by the willingness of the other party to take the special currency, created for members of the association, known as "loan certificates." The clearinghouse in one city did not yet interconnect with its counterpart in another city. This left the movement of credit from one market to another, one city to another, to the limited channels of correspondence between individual banks. But the fact of the private bank clearinghouses provided an important source of liquidity for banks that was not available from other sources.

JP Morgan, it must be said, was not a member of the New York Clearing House until well into the twentieth century and instead cleared all of its transactions with other banks "over its own counters," in the market vernacular of the day. This essentially meant that the House of Morgan wanted the other banks in the New York market to stand in line like everyone else in the lobby of JP Morgan. It also meant that the most prominent and creditworthy bank in the United States was not part of the collective clearing mechanism in the most important city in the country and thus only extended credit to other banks on its own terms.

While the clearinghouse model served to provide liquidity to member banks during the crises of the nineteenth and early twentieth centuries, it was not nearly a sufficient solution to the problems of liquidity that dogged the U.S. markets during economic downturns. There was always a competitive aspect to the relationship among clearinghouse members, to paraphrase Charles Goodhart, a chief economic adviser to the Bank of England. The case of the Building & Loan Society in the Frank Capra film *It's a Wonderful Life* featuring James Stewart epitomizes the example. When a solvent bank required short-term liquidity support, the other members of the clearinghouse might be tempted to withhold their aid and thereby kill a competitor. Goodhart notes, however, that the politically controlled central bank is not the solution to this problem of competitive conflict, since the prejudices and conflicts of the political world are far worse than even those found in the banking sector.

The political corruption and incompetence displayed by the Fed and Treasury during the financial crisis of 2008 seemingly supports Goodhart's judgment. It is, after all, the legal and regulatory limitations imposed by government that created the problems of liquidity and risk with which private banks must contend, argues Richard Timberlake of CATO Institute:

> Governmental dispensation of monopoly powers over note issue, governmental imposition of legal reserve requirements, governmental prohibition of post notes and option clauses, governmental prohibitions of interstate and (often) intrastate branching—in sum, governmental interference with all of the machinery of banking that would have allowed banking to function as free enterprise, was what made the problem that the clearinghouse institution successfully abated.[35]

The clearinghouse model in the United States was an attempt by private industry to address the problems of liquidity and payments that burdened the young country in the mid-1800s. Unfortunately, the already fragile U.S. financial system would next be thrown into the stress and uncertainty of the Civil War, a terrible period that altered the nation's financial system forever.

Chapter 2

Lincoln Saves a Nation by Printing Money

President Abraham Lincoln is viewed as the moral savior of the United States for ending slavery, but his administration also made enormous changes in the basic relationship between the federal government and money, changes which greatly diminished individual property rights and increased the power of Washington over the American economy. The financial needs of the federal government during the Civil War forced change upon the United States as Lincoln relied on the issuance of non-convertible fiat paper currency to support the military effort. In his book, *The Second American Revolution and Other Essays: 1976–1982* Gore Vidal describes Lincoln "at heart . . . a fatalist, a materialist" who "knew when to wait; when to act."[1]

Lincoln's use of fiat paper dollars or "greenbacks" to finance the Civil War and, more significant the passage of laws mandating the acceptance of paper currency as "legal tender" for all debts marked a dramatic change in the system of money and banks in the United States, a change that inspires debate to this day. Prior to Lincoln, most Americans expected to be able to exchange paper money for gold or silver coins upon demand.

However, with the Civil War and the extraordinary measures taken by
Lincoln to finance and direct the military conflict, the role of money
in the United States came under federal government control. Whereas
before the Civil War, many Americans identified more with their home
state than with the United States as a nation, that terrible conflict forged
a nation and with it a national currency, but at the expense of individual
economic rights. The author Kevin Phillips observed:

> The loose, possibly unraveling U.S. Confederation of early 1861
> and the emerging nation-state of 1865 were almost different
> countries. Memoirs of the postwar period describe a sea change.
> And the massive transformation that would last through the
> 1890s was beginning.[2]

When the Civil War began in 1861, the federal government lacked
the funds or taxing power to finance the conflict. The American money
supply consisted of all the physical gold and silver money then in
circulation, domestic and foreign coin, and the paper notes issued by
state-chartered banks. Lincoln's approach to financing the war, which
was carried out by Secretary of Treasury Salmon Chase, represented a
radical departure from past American practice and custom. Timothy
Canova wrote in an essay published by the *Chapman Law Review*:

> Academic interest in Lincoln has mostly focused on the darker
> side of wartime presidential powers, such as the suspension of
> civil liberties and overstepping lines of constitutional authority.
> Far less attention has been given to Lincoln as the activist exec-
> utive who set a new standard for mobilizing public finance in
> a crisis, pursuant to express Congressional authority under the
> Legal Tender Acts, presidential authority at its zenith . . . Lincoln
> is remembered for overcoming enormous political and mili-
> tary challenges. Often overlooked, however, is the economic
> and financial chaos he confronted upon taking office. In the
> weeks prior to Lincoln's inauguration, the nation was swept by
> fear, the hoarding of gold, and a panic perhaps more danger-
> ous than other classic Keynesian liquidity traps in March 1933
> and September 2008, since there was no central bank in 1861

with the authority to issue currency and inject liquidity into the financial system to try to break a downward spiral by restraining the psychology of hoarding.[3]

Americans chose to keep hard money in the form of gold and silver coins and shunned paper money issued by the state-chartered banks around the country. Even in the mid-1800s much of American economic life was still conducted via barter and exchange. Paper notes issued by banks and even the U.S. government were always suspect compared to tangible, tradable commodities and precious metals. When Lincoln took office, about one-third of the U.S. money supply was specie and about two-thirds was comprised of paper notes and checks redeemable for specie at the bank of issue. In the 1800s, any type of paper was seen as a form of debt, a promise to pay the bearer the amount of gold or silver coinage called for by the terms of the note. Notes issued by foreign banks and governments often held higher esteem among Americans than the paper money issued by local banks and state governments.

The traditional prejudice against debt caused the average American and members of both political parties to have grave misgivings about treating paper money as being equivalent to precious metals or other commodities, even if the idea was favored by the Whigs and their descendants in what is now the Republican Party. Despite their pretensions of conservative beliefs and claims to the anti-Federalist heritage of Jefferson and Madison, Republicans since the Civil War have always been at least as friendly to inflation, debt, and central banks as their Democratic rivals. The latter are in theory, at least, the more explicitly socialist of the two political tendencies.

The author William Greider, for example, likes to style himself as a "greenbacker" because of his view that a little inflation is good for the common man. But Greider agrees that sound money is ultimately the best protection for working people. "I'm not against having a functioning central bank," Greider said in a May 2010 interview. "[W]hat I'm against is setting it outside our democratic accountability and the usual principles of whom government must answer to. It's supposed to answer to the people."[4]

The Lincoln Legacy

The transformation in the distinction between the real world of precious metals and other tangible commodities, and paper money and debt, is perhaps the most important aspect of Lincoln's presidency. Lincoln freed millions of Americans from physical slavery and indentured servitude with the Emancipation Proclamation, but ironically he also set the United States down the road to political control over the nature of money via the Legal Tender Act of 1862 and subsequent legislation. Lincoln took the nation to war in 1861 without seeking the financial or political assent of Congress and instead used the argument of government fiat and expediency to justify his actions. More important, even after Lincoln's death, both Republicans and Democrats championed the use of paper money as the political possibilities created by debt and inflation proved irresistible.

Lincoln preserved the Union and ended the evil institution of slavery, but recall that the former was his chief motive. Many historians portray Lincoln's actions as examples of bold and visionary leadership, of unconstrained vision that saw the salvation of a nation from slavery and secession as the worthy ends justifying a crusade, not merely a national mobilization. Economic historian Eliot Janeway argued that Lincoln "never organized the Union for victory—he was too practical to try. Instead, he inspired and provoked it to mobilize the momentum for victory. The result was inefficient but irresistible. A victory small enough to be organized is too small to be decisive."[5] Janeway also notes that Lincoln had to go through half a dozen generals before finding one, Ulysses Grant, who possessed the "brute force" required to drive the Union military effort to victory. The Union Army's supreme commander, Grant eventually would become President and preside over one of the worst periods of public corruption and maladministration in American history.

The cost of the Civil War was measured not just in the blood of the fallen, but also in the growth of the power of the Executive Branch of the federal government into areas where the Constitution is deliberately silent. The political battle over the constitutionality of President Lincoln's greenback laws and the more general issue of the government's issuance of debt marked the defeat of the strict-constructionist, anti-federalist tendency in American politics. The locally focused, agrarian movement associated in American history with Thomas Jefferson and Andrew Jackson was overwhelmed by the rise of the nationalist and entirely commercial Republican tendency centered in New England and Pennsylvania The debate over the nature of money and the power of Washington to issue debt would dominate the American political scene well after the end of the Civil War, into the 1890s and beyond. The modern day arguments against central banks made by figures such as Texas Libertarian, physician, and member of Congress Ron Paul have their roots in the debate going back to the Civil War. "Everybody thinks about money and almost everyone wants more," Paul wrote in his book *End the Fed*. "We use money without thinking about its nature and function. Few of us ask where it comes from, who controls it, why it has value, or why it loses value from time to time."[6]

In the 1860s, Americans were well aware of the ill effects of inflation and bad money. The former colonists were not too far removed from the time when the Articles of Confederation were in effect and the Continental Congress resorted to inflation and legal tender laws to finance public spending by forcing Americans to use the government's fiat money. The Constitution expressly prohibited the states from issuing paper money and allowed the federal government power only to tax and borrow, but not to issue paper money itself. The distinction between the government borrowing and actually controlling the issuance of money is important to our narrative of the American dream. Once the two functions, controlling the amount of currency in circulation, and second the government's fiscal operations, are housed under the same roof, inflation and a decrease in the value of money are the inevitable result. It is always easier to borrow than to raise taxes. Politicians who have access to the printing press will invariably use it.

The economic and political impact of the period under the Articles of Confederation strongly influenced the framers of the Constitution to limit the ability of the U.S. government to issue debt. The occasion of the Civil War and the character of Abraham Lincoln, however, combined to provide the authoritarian formulation necessary to disregard the deliberate silence of the Constitution on this point and to circumvent Congress and the Supreme Court with respect to government finance. Lincoln not only disregarded established custom and tradition regarding money, he also established a precedent for Congress to use debt and the emission of paper currency to finance government and thereby avoid raising taxes. This important political dimension of Lincoln's actions is vastly under-appreciated in the main-stream histories of the period and, when compared to the responses of the heavily indebted states in the 1840s, illustrates how the politi-cal pressure to spend led to radical change. The uncontrolled spending of Congress today is a direct legacy of Abraham Lincoln and one that must be weighed against his undeniable political achievements.

Lincoln's enactment of the legal tender laws would provide the legal and political foundation for the creation of the Federal Reserve System and the gradual nationalization of money and private banking in the United States. One cannot diminish the moral righteousness of Lincoln with respect to slavery, but his refusal to seek explicit support from the electorate for the Civil War was a bold and authoritarian strat-egy. More significantly, the shameful way in which Lincoln and later U.S. Grant imposed legal tender laws on Americans via the subversion of the Supreme Court set a pattern of duplicity by the Executive Branch that remains strongly embedded in American jurisprudence today.

By giving the federal government control over the issuance of "money," which was now defined as a piece of paper, an expedient war leader doomed future generations of Americans to live with inflation and falling real living standards, the bitter legacy of all legal tender laws going back centuries before the founding of the United States. When émigrés from Europe came to the United States seeking freedom, it was not just religious liberty or freedom from physical bondage, but also freedom from the tendency of monarchs to compel their subjects to use the king's money, which was frequently light in terms of metal content. By embracing legal tender laws, Lincoln was adopting one of the most economically oppressive aspects of European society and one millions of his fellow citizens had sought to escape through immigra-tion to the New World. For Lincoln and many future American presi-dents, the end justified such means.[7]

Historian Murray Rothbard wrote in *A History of Money and Banking in the United States before the Twentieth Century*:

> The Civil War, in short, ended the separation of the federal government from banking, and brought the two institutions together in an increasingly close and permanent symbiosis.

In that way, the Republican Party, which inherited the Whig admiration for paper money and governmental control and sponsorship of inflationary banking, was able to implant the soft-money tradition permanently in the American System.[8]

The Civil War led to a vast increase in federal spending, from just $66 million in total federal outlays in 1861 to $1.3 billion four years later, at a time when federal tax revenues were falling. Tariffs had been the primary source of revenue for the federal government since its inception, leading voters to call for "tariffs for revenue only" and not for the unreasonable protection of domestic industries. But with the Civil War, Washington no longer had access to tariffs on southern exports like cotton, yet another reason for the north to resist southern attempts to leave the Union. Northern states had insisted on the right to leave the Union and confirmed the same at the Hartford Convention in 1815, but Lincoln had the abolition of slavery as his ultimate justification for the war.

By the time Lincoln took office, the United States was one of the last nations in the world not to have already outlawed slavery, including Brazil and the Spanish Empire.[9] Although the importation of slaves had been outlawed in the United States by act of Congress in March 1807, the laws were not enforced with any great energy. American participation in the slave trade slackened between 1825 and 1830, but activity revived thereafter and reached a peak around 1860. Lincoln was the first American president actively to insist on enforcement of the existing laws against slave importation, even before the Emancipation Proclamation. As soon as the southerners in Congress withdrew from Washington, Lincoln obtained authorization for the Secretary of Interior to begin suppressing the slave trade.[10]

Financing the War

Since the public was already aware that war was coming and was likewise suspicious of paper issued by private banks, hoarding of hard money was rampant. Credit was also tight because many banks and companies in the North were ambivalent about the war and would have been willing to see the secession of the Southern states so long as commercial and financial ties were not disturbed. The Cotton Whigs of Boston and the Republican bankers of New York all held substantial stakes in southern industry and in the continuance of southern slavery. Many northern Republicans did not support Lincoln's election. New York banks held substantial debt issued by Southern states and one third of all shipping traffic originating from New York was with Southern ports. For many in New York and surrounding states, following Lincoln's election the wish was for the Confederate states to be allowed to depart in peace.[11]

Upon winning the presidency in 1860, Lincoln faced a desperate situation in military and financial terms. The federal government was out of money and literally surrounded by unfriendly troops and states on all sides of the City of Washington. In fact, so great was Lincoln's concern for his personal security that he entered Washington in secret prior to the March 1861 inauguration ceremony. As he took office, there was great uncertainty whether states to the north of Washington such as Maryland and Ohio would remain in the Union. Lincoln was increasingly worried that Great Britain might recognize the Confederacy and provide military support to the South. The Confederate attack on Fort Sumter in Charleston harbor in April 1861 forced the issue of war and gave Lincoln the political momentum he needed to build an army of conscripts and win approval from Congress for financing the conflict. But while the City of Washington was filled with Union troops by the middle of 1861, these conscripts were ill-trained and responsible only for a short-term commitment, leaving open the question of the defense of the capital later that year.

Lincoln called Congress into session in July of 1861 after he issued an emergency message regarding the war in which he provided the justification for the conflict: "Must a Government, of necessity, be too strong for the liberties of its own people, or too weak to maintain its own existence?" With this question, Lincoln began the last major civil war in the English-speaking world and set the template for the next century of American history with respect to the politics of money. Congress authorized an army of 400,000 men and an expenditure of $400 million. The summer of 1861 was also when Congress enacted the first income tax: three percent of all annual incomes over $800.

New import tariffs were imposed, as were taxes on spirits, beer and wine, and tobacco.[12] But these levies did not begin to cover the cost of the war, and Congress did not specify how the Treasury would finance this expenditure.

Because Lincoln dared not raise taxes as the Civil War began, he first tried to borrow the money from the New York banks and, ironically, depended upon a political rival, Treasury Secretary Salmon Chase, to get the job done. A Senator from Ohio and political climber of the first rank, Chase was an "archetypal Republican, pious Abolitionist, hero of bankers, endless plotter to seize power from Lincoln, and forever ungrateful to the president for his appointments as secretary of the treasury and chief justice."[13]

The tenure of Secretary Chase as Treasury Secretary was a decidedly mixed bag, in part because the Independent Treasury law enacted by the Congress in the 1840s strictly limited the interaction between private banks and the federal government. He first attempted to float a government bond issue for $150 million, but when the banks refused to pay for the debt in specie the project was modified. In those days, the sum of $150 million represented virtually all of the hard currency reserves of the New York banks in gold and silver coin, especially when one considers that a good portion of all money in use in the United States in 1860 was in foreign coins. The situation was made more problematic because Chase felt that he must keep in the Treasury's vaults an amount of gold coin equal to the loans made to the government by the private banks.[14]

When a smaller amount of government bonds was purchased by some banks, the specie paid was spent by the government and quickly disappeared from circulation, thwarting attempts to increase the stock of money available to the economy. This would be the first in a series of failed attempts by Secretary Chase to manipulate the financial markets by issuing Treasury bonds in exchange for hard money, one of the earliest examples in modern financial history of the utter failure of market intervention to achieve any tangible result—except increased inflation.

By the end of 1861, hoarding of gold coins was a nationwide problem. First the private banks and eventually the Treasury suspended specie payments on debts in general, an event that many students of

American monetary history consider one of the blackest periods
of the Lincoln Administration.[15] The government quickly enacted
the first legal tender laws in February 1862 and printed $150 million
in new "United States Notes," which were made legal tender for all
debts public and private. "Greenbacks," as the notes were also known,
were convertible into Treasury debt. This conversion feature was little
used and was repealed by the Congress a year later, but the fact that
Congress included it at all illustrates the common understanding that all
paper "notes" were a form of interest-free debt.

The Treasury under Salmon Chase continued its obligation to
pay interest and principal on public debt in gold for a time after private banks had suspended redemptions, but by the end of 1861 specie
payments were suspended by all private banks and the Treasury alike,
sending panic throughout the country. Hoarding of hard money grew
even more acute. The suspension of redemption of notes, like most
debt defaults, caused the value of greenbacks to plummet and inflation to rise. A second $150 million in greenbacks were issued in July
1862 and another $150 million in the early part of 1863, reaching a
peak of just over $400 million by 1864. The reaction to this emis-
sion of unconvertible paper money was to drive down the free-market
value of greenbacks to below half of their face value. Secretary Chase
attempted to blame the drop in the value of the greenback on "gold
speculators," but the true reason was the lack of convertibility and thus
public support for fiat dollars. By June 1864 the value of the greenback
in gold was below 50 cents despite various schemes by Chase to arrest
the decline, including prohibition on gold trading, and open-market
intervention.[16]

Though the North was prevailing on the battle field, the Republic
was taking a beating in financial terms. Creditors in foreign countries
were clamoring for payment in specie, while inside the United States
most coins had disappeared from circulation, including even copper
pennies! The greenback was held in such low regard by the public that
any sort of metal money or even notes issued by foreign countries were
seen as preferable to paper dollars. In many history books, the passage
of the Legal Tender Act of 1862 is portrayed as an advance, a modernizing step to give the nation a stable currency. But in fact the assertion
of a legal tender monopoly by the federal government via legislative

"fiat" was a bold and aggressive expansion of Washington's power over states, and individuals as well; over all aspects of life, from the means of exchange to the store of value for wealth and savings. "Under the exigencies of war, the nation gained a uniform currency to meet the demands of an expanding economy," Senator Robert Byrd wrote.[17]

The Free Banking era officially ended with the passage of the National Currency Act in 1863 and the National Bank Act in 1865, but only after three decades of currency crises, securities fraud, and bank failures. The online history of the period prepared by the Office of the Comptroller of the Currency notes that "[b]y 1860 more than 10,000 different bank notes circulated throughout the country. Commerce suffered as a result. Counterfeiting was epidemic. Hundreds of banks failed. Throughout the country there was an insistent demand for a uniform national currency acceptable anywhere without risk."

With the adoption of a single national currency and the creation of a two-tiered, state and federal chartering system for banks, the die was cast for the evolution of these two separate types of banking business models well into the twentieth century and beyond. State-chartered banks could no longer issue their own currency, but they could gather deposits and issue debt, a fact that would continue to be the source of great instability in the U.S. financial system. Yet this very early model for a national currency did not solve the basic issues when it came to liquidity for banks, whether they were national or state-chartered. Because the national currency remained based on a private banking system with no effective rules for soundness or liquidity, the U.S. economy would swing from boom to bust for decades after 1865. In a national political and economic framework where Washington was still, as the framers intended, lacking in financial resources and the political will to cause great trouble, the shortcomings of the banking system were overlooked.

The creation of national banks was the project of Secretary Chase, who used them not only as vehicles for distributing greenbacks but also and more importantly as a means of financing the war effort. National banks were required to purchase a certain amount of government bonds to back their issuance of greenbacks. When Chase was able to push the National Bank Act through both houses of Congress by narrow margins, he had effectively solved the immediate problem of financing the war effort. And Secretary Chase had also created the engine for future inflation.

It is important to note that since the government had already created a national currency with the passage of the Currency Act of 1863, the United States had no real need for national banks other than to act as vehicles for financing the Civil War. This arrangement was very congenial to the bankers since it allowed them not only to make loans based upon the reserves of government debt held in their vaults, but also to gather interest on the government bonds. Thus if a new national bank had $300,000 in capital, $100,000 would be invested in government debt and the remaining $200,000 could be deployed in loans. But the National Bank Act also allowed the bank to issue $90,000 in greenbacks, which could also be loaned. Thus national banks could essentially earn double interest on their $100,000 in government bonds and generate double-digit returns at a time when the average yield on loans was six percent.[18] Chase thus created a bankers' lobby for inflation.

Salmon Chase and Jay Cooke

By building a system of new national banks, Chase was creating a new way to finance the federal government and possibly finance his way into the White House. A political competitor of Lincoln who served as governor of Ohio and lost the Republican nomination in 1860, Chase gained the post of Treasury Secretary via the support of financial operator Jay Cooke, a fellow Ohioan and like Chase a strong advocate of paper money. Chase's considerable political ambition would eventually take him to the Supreme Court, but not before he made a shambles of the finances of the U.S. Treasury.

Cooke is remembered in history books as fueling some of the more ambitious financial frauds in an era that was fraught with such schemes. He had a knowledge of the "true worth and character" of money that was unusual for his time. Cooke bragged of the ability to tell genuine notes from counterfeits for all the money issued by U.S. banks in the 1840s. He speculated with great success on the Mexican War and the annexation of Texas in 1845, in part because he already knew how

Washington would dispose of the state's debts. "Large sums were realized," Cooke admitted, "by those who were directly and indirectly interested in obtaining the legislation for the final settlement" of the bondholder claims against the Republic of Texas.[19]

Cooke's early knowledge of and appreciation for the tactics used to speculate on the value of debt and paper currency gave him the confidence to execute strategies that would allow him to amass vast wealth in a relatively short period of time. Indeed, whereas most Americans still thought of work as involving some form of honest physical or mental labor, Cooke took the art of enlightened speculation and financial fraud to new levels, but none as grand and sweeping as his main focus after 1862, namely selling U.S. government bonds. Whereas prior to the Lincoln Administration Cooke was involved with selling all manner of canal and railroad promotion schemes, the victory by Lincoln and some vigorous lobbying by the Cooke family landed Chase in the Treasury and thereby opened new vistas of accumulation and gain. It took only slightly more effort for Jay Cooke to be appointed exclusive agent for the sale of government debt, a position that would enable the financier to collect commissions on the sale of some $2 billion in government bonds between 1862 and 1864.[20]

In the pamphlet "How Our National Debt May Be A National Blessing"[21] published by his firm, Cooke described the many reasons why debt is not a problem, first and foremost because it was the interest on the debt, and not the principal amount, that was the burden. Cooke described himself on the cover as "General Subscription Agent for the Government Loans," making clear his official status. In the subtitle of the booklet, Cooke summarized nicely the arguments used by the proponents of paper money and debt to win public support:

> The Debt is Public Wealth, Political Union,
> Protection of Industry, Secure Basis for
> National Currency, The Orphans' and
> Widows' Savings Fund

Of interest, while the pamphlet made a number of familiar excuses as to why the debt was not a problem, it also made an explicit reference to tariffs and the protectionist benefits of debt. In the 1860s, there was a political tendency among the pro-greenback population to see debt

and a declining dollar as an effective barrier to unfair foreign competition, one of the legacies of the oppressive trade ties with Great Britain.
Americans were very sensitive to being put at a disadvantage by foreign
trade. Thus mixing protectionism with easy money was a popular for-
mula in some parts of the United States. In a very real sense, the tone
and content of Cooke's 16-page pamphlet nicely summarizes the popular opinion toward public debt in the 1860s and thereafter, and even by
public officials today.

Despite his reputation as a leader in the anti-slavery movement
and as a U.S. Senator, Chase would eventually be forced out of the
Treasury because of the complete failure of his attempts to maintain
parity in the value of the greenbacks with gold, but the damage was
done. Inflation in terms of an index of wholesale prices during the
Civil War went from 100 in 1861 to 210 in 1865, or a 22 percent
annual rate of increase. States, including California and Oregon, had
refused even to accept greenbacks during the war for payment of taxes.
However, Chase was far from finished with politics. In 1864, after
Chase resigned from the Treasury, President Lincoln appointed the
popular Republican as Chief Justice of the Supreme Court. Cooke continued to sell government bonds for Chase's successor at the Treasury,
Secretary William P. Fessenden, and managed to place hundreds
of millions worth of "short-term loans bearing exceptional interest
rates that were well subscribed to by the American people."[22]

And yet even the inflation brought about by the massive issuance of
greenbacks under Chase would be short lived. At the end of the Civil
War it took $28 in greenbacks to buy a $10 gold piece but by 1879
the $10 greenback had slowly risen back to parity with gold coins.
William Hixson notes in his book *Triumph of the Bankers*: "The decline
and recovery in value of the paper money created by sound banks was
the same as the decline and recovery in value of the paper money created by government."[23] Thus the war was financed and U.S. expansion
accelerated by inflation. A cheap, short-term expedient and much less
divisive alternative than taxes.

At the end of the Civil War, the general assumption was that
Washington would contract the supply of paper money allowed during the conflict and resume the use of specie for all payments. The
total supply of currency in circulation had doubled from 1860 to 1867,

mostly by printing greenbacks and withdrawing gold coins from circulation. But the advocates of cheap money, many of whom had benefitted from the stiff inflation during the Civil War, "opposed any action that would reduce the amount of currency in order to bring the greenbacks back to the level of gold."[24] Both the federal government and the railroads came out of the war years with large debts, so the attraction of keeping the greenbacks in circulation and retaining the "legal tender" status of paper money was enormous for these groups. Wealthy financial moguls such as Jay Cooke and the owners of banks and railroads worked hard to promote the use of paper money and debt to maintain and expand their own fund raising activities.

As much as many Americans opposed paper money as the means of exchange, the ebb and flow in the sheer demand for money and other factors, such as the Gold Rush in the West and the rapid pace of economic growth, increased the need for all forms of money, paper and specie. The increased demand was sufficient to bring the value of paper money back strongly enough that the government eventually was able to restore gold convertibility for the paper dollar in 1879. Many Americans felt that the abandonment of convertibility was immoral and that the greenbacks should be redeemed, but the free convertibility of paper for specie was not restored until forces in the market made the resumption of convertibility convenient for the political class in Washington and their sponsors in business. Salmon Chase reportedly disapproved of the legal tender notes in principle; with no requirement for specie backing they could be printed in unlimited quantities and were therefore inflationary. Chase was also said to have recognized the necessity of issuing paper money in a time of emergency. Later, however, sitting as Chief Justice of the Supreme Court, he would declare the notes unconstitutional.[25]

During and after the Civil War, the political and legal battle raged regarding the legality of the federal government issuing greenbacks and whether such emergency currency could be used, for example, for the payment of state taxes. Murray Rothbard notes that in a large number of state court decisions on the issue of whether paper money was legal tender and thus sufficient to pay all debts, the Republican justices upheld the constitutionality of the greenbacks, but Democrats generally held that fiat money was unconstitutional. The question eventually reached the Supreme Court in *Hepburn v. Griswold*, where the court voted by a 5 to 3 margin to strike down the use of greenbacks.

This decision angered the Administration of President Ulysses Grant, as well as the banks, the railroads and other heavily indebted corporations, who naturally preferred to settle their obligations in paper rather than gold. When a pair or vacancies came up on the Supreme Court, President Grant nominated two railroad lawyers, William Strong of Pennsylvania and Joseph P. Bradley of New Jersey. In May 1871, a 5–4 majority reversed the Court's position and in *Knox v. Lee* upheld the legality of fiat money and the legal tender laws. Largely at the behest of a heavily indebted government and its equally beholden allies among the owners and managers of the railroads, the issue of greenbacks was essentially settled in American law.[26]

Fisk and Gould Profit by Inflation

After the Civil War, politics prevailed and resumption of free exchange of gold for paper dollars was delayed for two decades, providing plentiful monetary fuel for one of the greatest periods of economic growth, speculation, and financial larceny in U.S. history. Led by characters such as Daniel Drew, Jim Fisk, and Jay Gould, the expansion of the American railroads and the related speculation on Wall Street as to the financing for these endeavors created huge opportunities for gain and loss by investors, both in the United States and in Europe.

Jim Fisk, for example, made his first fortune as a Civil War profiteer and then in fraud. He swindled no less than Commodore Cornelius Vanderbilt to the tune of $8 million and in the process also stole control of the Erie Railroad via a partnership with another Civil War-era profiteer named Jay Gould. Fisk went on to create a vast operation in New York City involving Wall Street speculation, real estate, saloons and opera houses, and many other businesses that served as fronts for his criminal activities. Fisk's financial fame and outrageous personal behavior eclipsed that of many contemporary politicians. These predecessors of today's financial buccaneers on Wall Street built their fortunes upon foundations of debt and paper currency.

At some point around 1869 the already wealthy speculator Gould, who was a partner of Fisk in the Erie Railroad but conducted other speculations and business affairs as well, took notice of the fluctuation between the price of gold and greenbacks. The period of the Civil War and Reconstruction was one of opportunity, particularly for the new class of speculators and criminals who began to appreciate the possibilities created by the federal government and Washington politicians on the one hand, and government debt and paper currency on the other. Much like today, the change or lack thereof in terms of government policy could bring wealth or ruin to the politically oriented speculator.

Under the administration of Lincoln and his third Treasury Secretary, Hugh McCullough, Washington adopted an active policy against speculators and responded with market sales of specie if any speculators attempted to "corner" the market in gold. However, upon the assumption of the presidency by Ulysses Grant and the appointment of George Boutwell to the Treasury, the policy changed. Boutwell let it be known that he had a distaste for interfering with the functioning of the markets. A career bureaucrat and former Member of Congress, Boutwell ran the Internal Revenue Service, established the first organized means of manufacturing paper currency, and enabled one of the financial great market corners in the history of the United States.

The modern-day fraud conducted via unregulated securities and derivatives in the first decade of the twenty-first century pales in comparison to the boldness of the individuals who operated in the financial markets of the 1860s. Treasury Secretary Boutwell's antagonism for his predecessor's propensity for interfering with the laws of supply and demand was correct in classical terms, but the government—via the legal tender laws and the creation of the greenback, as well as the massive issuance of debt and related expenditures—had also created a powerful new market relationship between paper dollars and gold. This relationship provided an opportunity that held greater political implications in that day than do modern market indexes such as the Dow Jones Industrial Average. The opportunity created by Boutwell to manipulate the price of gold and literally "corner" this vital market naturally appealed to Jay Gould.

Gould was born Jason Gould in 1836 in Roxbury, New York, the son of John Burr Gould and Mary Moore Gould. According to

W.A. Swanberg, Gould was named after "the fabled prince who won the Golden Fleece."[27] Historians agree that Gould was a repulsive character who had little appreciation for public opinion or public relations and who eventually came to symbolize the excesses of the time. He did know how to make money and acted through bold and often brazen speculations, and not infrequently with the credit of others, to build one of the great empires of the Reconstruction period. Part of his early fortune was amassed in the late 1850s by using the credit of a partner in Pennsylvania, who was in the tannery business, to support his financial operations in New York. His partner eventually took his own life out of shame for the speculative debts amassed by Gould in his firm's name. The business failed and left the small community around the factory in complete desolation, but Gould profited. He was a crook and a cheat of the type that makes average people distrust financial types, plain and simple. The creation of the greenback and the general atmosphere of anything goes that prevailed after the Civil War provided the perfect stage upon which Gould and his contemporaries on Wall Street would operate.[28]

For example, in the spring of 1869, Gould purchased $7 million in gold using greenbacks. Fisk, seeing great risk of government intervention, was not as yet willing to participate in the operation. At the exchange ratio between greenbacks and gold of 1.3 to 1, his purchase of $7 million worth of gold cost about $9.1 million in paper money. From that point on, Gould obviously had an interest in the price of gold rising versus the value of paper money. In a display of extraordinary public-mindedness, he began to express worry about the plight of working people and farmers who did not have access to sufficient currency. Soon a theme that said *a rise in the price of gold would benefit the whole nation* was read and heard widely in various media organs controlled by Gould and his political ally and protector, Boss Tweed, the political kingpin of New York's Tammany Hall organization.[29]

Fisk and Gould together were already among the most influential and feared financial operators of their time. The duo, operating in alliance with Boss Tweed, was seen as "a combination more powerful than any that has been controlled by mere private citizens in America," according to Henry Adams. Though Gould was known for his audacity, particularly when it came to "open market operations," his gold speculation was another notch bolder and more problematic because of the political risk. There was only about $15 million in gold in circulation in the New York market at that time, and Gould was intent upon cornering the market and forcing prices up by literally taking gold out of circulation. Because the federal government had a reserve of nearly $100 million, Gould needed to make certain that the Treasury would not sell gold to relieve stress on the market as had been the practice under Lincoln. Gould had bought his way to power and wealth with little concern for the law, but in this case he proposed nothing less than to dictate government policy on gold via a direct understanding with President Grant.

At first Fisk was suspicious of Gould's plan and refused to participate, even though the previous year the two men had managed a magnificent operation with the Erie Railroad that brought them international notoriety and millions in profit. Gould worked relentlessly to win President Grant, Jim Fisk, and anyone else to the cause of higher prices for gold and a weaker value for greenbacks. Through the summer and into the fall of 1869, Gould—and eventually Fisk—purchased more and more gold, believing that their machinations in Washington, including winning the complicity of Grant's family into the market manipulation, would support their plan effectively to corner the entire market in physical gold in the eastern United States. Gould and Fisk even lured President Grant to take a ferryboat ride up the Hudson River for the express purpose of lobbying him on the issue of the price of gold, but the cautious Grant refused to cooperate.

In early September, Grant's wife wrote to her sister in law Jenny Corbin, whose husband was used by Gould disastrously as the fixer to attempt to influence Grant's views on gold price appreciation. The Corbins had bought gold for themselves and even tried to buy gold on behalf of President Grant, who spurned the attempt and complained to his wife about the behavior of her sister's husband. Upon learning of her husband's unhappiness with Corbin's activities, Mrs. Grant wrote to her sister warning that "the President is very much distressed by your speculations and you must close them as quickly as you can."[30] This revelation made both Fisk and Gould understand that their political stratagems were a failure, but nonetheless the duo persisted in their plan to corner the gold market.

Even though Gould and Fisk understood by the last week in September 1869 that their political scheme was doomed to failure, Fisk made one last attempt to ramp the market higher by using funds he obtained from the Tenth National Bank, which he and Gould had come to control. As the posted price of gold displayed in the Gold Room in lower Manhattan rose past $150 greenbacks for $100 worth of gold, Fisk and his confederates in the gold market bid prices up even higher. This sent a panic through the market and caused financial ruin for many gold bears, who were short the metal at lower prices. On September 22, 1869, Fisk and his surrogates in the gold market made it clear via public statements that President Grant himself supported their cause and would not sell gold from the Treasury's stock.

To no one's surprise, Gould was secretly selling his gold at a profit during this last stage of the market corner. While his friend Fisk bore the financial burden of supporting the market and the brunt of the public attention as a result, Gould quietly disposed of his gold horde to other brokers even as Fisk was buying. Talk that Grant was involved with Fisk and Gould was picked up by the media, creating a national scandal for President Grant, perhaps the most damaging of his already soiled presidency. The following day, Friday September 23, 1869, Gould continued his selling even as Fisk's brokers attempted to keep gold prices up. The entire nation began to focus its attention on President Grant and a couple of market speculators who were threatening the economy. Markets around the United States fell as uncertainty and fear froze investors in place—even as gold prices crept steadily higher. The price of gold in greenbacks peaked at $160 per $100 worth of gold coins just before noon that day. Then came word from Washington that the Treasury would sell $4 million in gold on the following Monday. Prices for gold, stocks, and pretty much everything else collapsed. And Jay Gould sold all the way down, taking full advantage of the crisis that became known as Black Friday.

While Gould was the mastermind of the gold market operation, the flamboyant and effusive Fisk took most of the blame and was forced to go into hiding to escape angry investors. Fisk and Gould defaulted on many contracts to buy gold and used corrupt connections with Boss Tweed and others to avoid collection in the New York courts. It was said that Gould made over $11 million buying and selling the metal, largely the result of his flexible strategy. Even when his original plan was wrecked by the Treasury's sales of gold, he made money. The Gold Room was closed as the nation's economy reeled from this bold market speculation. But both Gould and Fisk reckoned their profits in greenbacks.[31]

The Panic of 1873

The gold market crisis of 1869 orchestrated by Gould and Fisk illustrated that paper money had become a powerful new market for speculation in gold, essentially another form of debt leveraged against the national banks, which in turn supported the state banks and the real economy's need for liquidity. Gold remained the unit of account and store of value, but greenbacks were now accepted as a means of exchange by a growing portion of the population. With the passage of the National Bank Act in 1865, the connection between specie and paper money had in theory been stabilized. Yet as the gold market operation of Fisk and Gould four years later illustrates, speculating on changes in the paper value of gold had become a means to wager on the basic unit of account and therefore on the value of the U.S. economy.

The year 1869 also marked the completion of the transcontinental railroad, a project championed by the railroad lawyer Lincoln, and with it a long period of capital expenditure. Some observers believe that the crisis in the gold markets was the precursor to the financial and economic crisis four years later known as the Panic of 1873, which put the United States and much of the world into years of political and economic turmoil. An important component of the crisis of 1869 and subsequent crises was debt made available by banks to finance purchases of gold and securities. Leverage in the form of bank loans was increasingly available, especially if, like Fisk and Gould, one controlled his own bank. More important was the pyramidal structure created by the national banks, which allowed reserve city banks and, in turn, community banks to expand their balance sheets dramatically, providing finance for the real economy and speculative activities alike.

Rothbard notes in his *History of Money and Banking in the United States* that the whole nation was able to leverage the resources of a few

New York City banks, which provided funding to the larger reserve city banks around the country. These larger banks in turn provided liquidity to community banks.[32] However, this seemingly virtuous arrangement was very fragile. The continued fear of inflation and the vast amount of fraud associated with bank deposits, stocks, bonds, and various other paper financial instruments, left the U.S. economy and financial system extremely vulnerable to sudden shifts in public mood.

Even after the gold market crisis, Gould continued to operate with impunity, manipulating stocks such as the Pacific Mail Steamship Company to great profit. Memorialized as "The Mephistopheles of Wall Street," Gould reportedly took $5 million out of his speculations in Pacific Steamship in the early 1870s, a return that in modern terms ranks with that of corporate raiders such as Carl Icahn and Kirk Kerkorian.[33] Gould was hardly alone among the great investment operators of the age, including Jay Cooke and his Northern Pacific Railroad. Gould's next operation, taking over the Union Pacific Railroad, allowed him to manipulate upward the prices on railroad freight rates in the West and begin a long period of accumulating equity positions in several major rail lines. By 1881, at the peak of his wealth, Gould controlled tens of millions of dollars worth of stocks and bonds, mostly in the railroads. Thus ended the Gilded Age and began the age of the banker and particularly of the House of Morgan. Upon his death in 1892, Jay Gould left an estate worth more than $150 million, divided among his family with the same care and precision that had characterized his financial dealings.[34]

The end of the dominance of the railroads as speculative vehicles in the U.S. economy was partly a function of the completion of the transcontinental rail link, but also due to the volatility and crisis that gripped the financial markets for debt issued by the rail lines. In 1873, not quite four years after the gold market crisis of 1869, the inherent instability of a fiat money system based upon national banks again resurfaced with the Great Panic of that year. Ironically, the crisis was caused by the collapse of Jay Cooke's financial empire, which by that time included a bank in New York and investment sales offices around the United States that had been focused on the finance of the construction of the railroads. The insolvency of Cooke's Northern Pacific Railroad venture set the stage for a financial crisis that began in the Northeast and spread to the rest of the United States and around the world.

After starting his career selling bonds and raising money for the U.S. government during the Mexican War, Cooke had become wealthy enough to capitalize on his connections in Washington, which extended back to before the Civil War. Cooke had formed a banking company in 1861, Jay Cooke & Co., and used this as the primary vehicle for the role as bond sales agent for the U.S. Treasury. In a very real sense, Cooke helped to present the bonds issued by the Treasury and the American states as prudent and reasonable investments, both in the United States and overseas. Given that there were still some U.S. states in default on debts going back to the 1840s, this was no small feat. But Cooke's boldness and bravado in promoting bonds as secure and patriotic investments helped to finance the operations of the U.S. government.

By 1873 Cooke's luck had run out along with his ability to sell debt, exposing the inherent insolvency of his Northern Pacific scheme. Cooke's particular excesses, though, were part of a broader problem. The U.S. economy had been growing at a very rapid pace, and financial and human fatigue were ingredients in the economic reversal that soon developed. Whatever specific factors drove the economic correction that began in September of 1873, the result was the failure of a quarter of all the railroads in the country, the bankruptcy of thousands of private businesses, and double-digit unemployment in the United States and Europe. The virtuous circle of the big New York banks providing liquidity to smaller reserve city and community banks was reversed, with horrible consequences. Banks were drained of gold reserves and the public was left without access to cash or credit of any description. Banks, stock brokers, and businesses failed in large numbers, stock prices collapsed, consumer and commodity prices declined, and unemployment increased nationwide in a deflationary wave of economic instability that lasted for more than two decades.

But Cooke, an intimate friend of President Ulysses Grant, was able to tap bailouts from the Treasury to save part of his far-flung enterprise from eventual ruin. Cooke had other businesses, including Jay Cooke, McCullough & Co. in London, which acted as agent for the Treasury in the United Kingdom and was actually owed money by both Cooke & Co and the U.S. government when the crisis began. By no coincidence, in 1871, Cooke's firm had been appointed fiscal agent for the Treasury regarding all naval expenditures. Navy Secretary George Robeson moved the navy's accounts from Baring Brothers to Jay Cooke, McCullough & Co. "to receive and pay money for the use of the naval service on foreign stations." Over the next few months, the Treasury advanced hundreds of thousands of dollars to Jay Cooke, McCullough & Co. and thereby helped the speculators and his compatriots avoid the worst of the economic depression.[35]

The bailout of Jay Cooke, McCullough & Co. was a historical precursor for many bailouts, large and small, by Washington for private financial companies. At a primitive level, the rescue of Jay Cooke's financial situation was not so different from the political bailouts of Citicorp in the 1980s as the result of foreign lending or Goldman Sachs and other dealers with the collapse of American International Group in 2008. But 1873 marked the first and in many ways the worst general economic crisis in modern U.S. history and one that persisted for many years thereafter. When it came to September 17, 1873, Matthew Josephson wrote in *The Robber Barons*, "[t]he seven years of plenty after the war must now make way for the seven years of dearth in a land literally 'flowing with milk and honey.'"[36]

Despite, and to some extent because of, the existence of national banks and a common fiat paper currency, major banking panics would occur in the United States in 1873, 1884, 1890, 1893, and 1907. Whereas even Canadian banks of that time had the flexibility to issue additional banknotes when currency demand increased, in the United States no such facility existed for national banks and, indeed, was forbidden by law. The ethic of hard money among the American public was still too strong to allow the flexibility permitted to banks in Canada. When U.S. bank deposits grew out of favor with the public and, more important, with the nation's foreign creditors, bank balance sheets shrank along with the money supply of the entire nation.

Gold Convertibility Restored

This period of great growth and excess from the Civil War to the creation of the Federal Reserve System in 1913 was arguably as "pure" a private national banking model as ever existed in the United States, with equal measures of exuberance and loathing found in financial markets as the ebb and flow of human action confronted the limited legal and practical boundaries placed upon commerce and finance. The academic community seems to fall into two camps in describing these ancient financial tumults, "those who see these panics as essentially a problem of illiquidity and those who base their explanations on insolvency."[37] The more general observation to make about the period between the Civil War and 1900, though, is that this is normal behavior for a free market economy with limited government intervention.

One of the ironies of the period following the Panic of 1873 was that the United States would eventually restore the convertibility of the greenback in gold. America had gone off the gold standard during the Civil War and non-convertibility would remain until 1879. The decision to return to convertibility was actually made by President Grant in 1875, who ordered that the convertibility of the dollar would resume on the first day of 1879. At the time, the greenback was trading at about a 20 percent discount to gold, meaning that it took $120 in greenbacks to purchase $100 worth of gold.[38]

The period following the restoration of gold convertibility in 1879 was remarkable for a number of reasons. First, the nation's economy grew strongly, but with remarkably little inflation. Although producer prices fell from the conclusion of the Civil War through the end of the 1880s, wages actually rose in real terms and capital investment flows into the U.S. economy also were strong. There were many factors driving the economic growth of the United States during this period, yet the fact remains that inflation was low and, as a result, the value of wages and savings grew in real terms. Interest rates continued to fall through the 1870s and 1880s, resulting in strong incentives for saving and investment. So while there would continue to be periodic financial crises involving banks and the financial markets in the United States, the real economy actually enjoyed a boom period that increased the value of savings and wealth for the average American.[39]

The low level of inflation during this period was reflected by the fact that prices for gold and silver remained relatively stable, although the latter would soon suffer from increased supply and decreased demand. After the end of the Civil War, in anticipation of the resumption of gold convertibility of paper dollars, Congress actually dropped

silver from the list of monetary metals for use by the Treasury in minting coins. There was great public outcry against the Act of 1873, not
only because it dropped the use of silver for coins, but also because
many people felt that the move contracted the nation's money supply and worsened the economic crisis of that year. However, the law
merely reflected the fact that silver coins had dropped out of favor as a
medium of exchange. Although a ratio of 16 to 1 had existed between
the price of silver and gold going back nearly a century, increased supply in the United States and a drop in demand around the world in
nations such as India and the United Kingdom caused the ratio to slip
to almost 30 to 1 in the free market by the 1870s.[40]

With silver prices falling, the metal was not seen as a particularly
robust store of value, but the attraction of free silver coinage for some
proponents remained very powerful. There were large deposits of
the metal in the western United States and the farmers and ranchers
of those states often owed money for purchases of land. Some silverites,
as the pro-silver advocates were known, sought to provide a more plentiful means of exchange to stimulate the economy. Other proponents of
silver saw a resumption in government use of the metal for making coins
as a natural solution to the decline in market demand, especially since
prices for the silver continued to be under pressure. But three years
later, silver coins were stripped of their status as legal tender, a move
that again caused an uproar from people with stakes in the silver mines
of the West. The proponents of free coinage of silver in the Senate, who
were known at the time as the "Bonanza Kings," sought to have the
Treasury resume purchases of the metal at the old price ratio of 16 to 1
versus gold, even though the market price for silver was half that level.

The Battle Over Silver Money

As Congress slowly came around to the restoration of gold convertibility of dollars, a great political debate developed about the restoration or
"remonetization" of silver coins as legal tender. Those closely aligned
with the Western silver interests made a straightforward argument for
government intervention to stop the slide in the price of silver relative to
gold. But the silver interests found common cause with the "inflationist"

tendency in American politics, people who neither wanted gold convertibility restored nor the retirement of the greenbacks. The idea of returning silver coins to the money supply also appealed to farmers who had enjoyed high prices during the Civil War and believed that increasing the money supply would boost economic activity and thus prices for their goods, while reducing the real cost of servicing their debts.

The public clamor for an increase in the money supply was fierce. Dozens of proposals were floated in the Congress in the next several years either to require government purchases of silver, increase the money supply, or both. Senator John Sherman (R-OH), who was the brother of General William Tecumseh Sherman of Civil War fame and a strong supporter of a return to the gold standard, introduced a bill in the Congress in January 1874 to increase the money supply.

Sherman's proposal to purchase silver had the effect of increasing the money supply via the issuance of greenbacks, which were used to make the purchases. The resulting expansion in the supply of paper dollars was less than was demanded by the inflationist, free silver proponents, but a larger amount than was acceptable to those in favor of resuming the gold standard. Known as the "Inflation Bill," the Sherman legislation was debated for nearly four months. So fierce was the public support for the idea of inflation that the measure eventually passed the Republican-controlled Congress. But on April 22, 1874, President Grant vetoed the legislation, a move that would "make the stand of the Republican Party official" when it came to aligning itself with business interests rather than the working class, according to the Pulitzer Prize-winning Grant biographer William McFeely.[41]

The veto of the Inflation Bill was costly for Grant and the Republicans, however. In November of that year the Democrats won control of the House of Representatives for the first time since before the Civil War and increased their seats in the Senate, which narrowly remained in Republican hands. Between 1879 and 1883, the Democrats effectively controlled the Senate, but the Republicans held the White House, compounding the political stalemate between the pro-silver and hard money forces. But from the time of the Grant veto of the Inflation Bill forward, the Republicans would generally be known as the party of sound money and business interests, and the Democrats as advocates of inflation and the working man. So passionate was the national debate over silver and the broader issue of economic growth that the Republicans would be divided over the question for years to come up to the present time. The debate over the free coinage of silver and the national money supply eventually would be a factor in the undoing of the Republican party's control over Washington.

Although the agitation for free silver coinage did not win acceptance in Washington in 1874, Congress did respond with two compromises in the years that followed. The House and Senate considered measures restoring free coinage of silver and delaying resumption of gold convertibility several times, including a measure sponsored by Missouri Democrat Richard Bland. Each time, however, the Republican majority in the Senate defeated these bills. At the request of Senator Sherman, Senator William Allison of Iowa, the influential Chairman of the Senate Finance Committee, crafted a compromise between Eastern business interests who supported sound money and the rising power of the inflationist tendency of the Western states and their allies in Congress such as Bland, who would be offered the Democratic nomination for President in 1986.

The result of Allison's labor was the Bland–Allison Act of 1878, which authorized the Treasury to purchase a certain amount of silver each year and to mint silver dollar coins, which were made legal tender. Significantly, as had been intended with the Inflation Bill sponsored years before by Senator Sherman, the Treasury paid for the silver purchases with paper money and thereby effectively increased the money supply. President Hayes followed his Republican instincts and vetoed the measure, but both houses of Congress overrode his veto within hours, the House by 196–73 and the almost evenly divided but still Democrat-controlled Senate by a vote of 46–19. Though the legislation was not popular with Republican voters, it made for good politics overall and provided the Republicans with the appearance of both helping the cause of silver and not caving in to demands for aggressive currency inflation. The Bland–Allison Act helped to blunt the political advance and growth of the Greenback party, which nonetheless won 14 seats in the House two years later in 1880.[42]

Under the Bland–Allison law, about 25 million silver coins were minted each year, but relatively few of the coins were actually circulated. Instead the Treasury issued "silver certificates" similar to greenbacks that were legal tender and could be redeemed at the Treasury for the large and unwieldy coins. This compromise measure did not help the price of silver to recover or even stabilize because of the large amount of the metal that was being produced and the continuing changes in the demand for the metal around the world. Neither did the Bland-Allison Act quell the political debate over the role of silver and gold in the money supply or regarding money more generally.

After the 1880 election, the silverites made common cause with a broad coalition of farmers, progressives, and others who felt displaced by the growing industrialization of America. This coalition included members of both parties and formed a powerful bloc in Congress. While they did not have sufficient votes to push their free silver agenda through the national legislature, they could effectively block other business and hold the nation hostage while demanding relief from the "gold conspiracy."

The quaint tendency of Americans to see money matters as one type of political conspiracy or another dates from this period and the larger struggle for free coinage of silver. More than a decade would pass before the advocates of silver were able to force the issue to the top of the national agenda in Congress, but their growing political clout helped them to tie up the Senate. Important national issues such as the passage of the McKinley tariff and voting rights legislation for the Southern states were put on hold by the proponents of free silver coinage.

A Changing American Dream

The changes that were occurring in American life in these years drove the intensity of the national debate over money. The end of the conquest of the American frontier, the consolidation of industries such as steel, oil, and railroads, and the rise of the great fortunes of the Robber Barons, caused many Americans growing unease regarding the direction of the country. This was a situation not unlike the one confronting America today. Urban unemployment, hard times on the farm, and a general sense that the endless vistas and opportunities of early America were not so infinite, affected the national mood. The mini economic depression in 1882–1884 also did a great deal of damage to the view held by many Americans as to the limitless possibilities for economic betterment. The role of wealth in American politics, then as today, made many of our citizens wonder whether the promise of the American Dream could or would really be fulfilled for the vast majority of people.

Prior to the Civil War, Americans generally considered poverty and a lack of economic opportunity to be problems experienced only by slaves and indentured servants. Historian Harold Faulkner noted that "the late eighteen eighties had brought hard times to the farmer, the workingman, and to many businessmen as well, and with hard times, doubts and disillusionment; in the nineties came open revolt, a challenge to old beliefs, a repudiation of old shibboleths, a fragmentation of old parties. There was almost everywhere a feeling that somehow the promise of American life was not being fulfilled."[43]

One way that the American political class responded to popular angst regarding the economy was the imposition of tariffs on imported goods. In the nineteenth century, tariffs were one of the chief sources of revenue for the federal government. Republicans were the traditional proponents of tariffs, in large part to protect domestic industries during this period, while the Democrats generally were opposed. The Treasury was already running a considerable surplus because of the protective tariff enacted by Congress during the economic crisis of 1882–1884, so there was little need for additional revenue. Indeed, the Treasury's accumulation of gold may have been a deflationary factor in the decade prior to 1900. The high tariffs of the 1880s is an important point to remember when later we consider the Great Depression and the impact of the enactment of the Smoot-Hawley tariff legislation in 1930.

The Silver Compromise

President Grover Cleveland attempted to use the growing Treasury surplus and a reduction in the tariff as an issue in the election of 1888 to gain reelection, but he underestimated the attraction of protectionism— a theme that modern American politicians may soon rediscover. The incumbent Cleveland won a slim majority in the popular vote, but when the votes were cast in the Electoral College, Cleveland lost by 233 to 168 to Benjamin Harrison from Ohio, an early example of the election-winning power of the Republican political machine. By 1890 the Treasury had amassed a surplus of nearly $150 million in gold, a symbolic affront to farmers and populists who proclaimed the federal government to be "an octopus" that was strangling the real economy. In that same year, a young lawyer from Nebraska, William Jennings Bryan, won his first term in the House of Representatives.

With the Republicans again in control of both houses of Congress and with President Harrison in the White House, one of the more important items on the political agenda was raising the tariff. Known as the McKinley tariff after Rep. William McKinley (R-OH), the legislation only raised the national tariff slightly, but the political debate around the most important revenue measure quickly slowed the process to a crawl. The Democrats initially opposed the bill, but eventually decided to allow the measure to pass and go to the Senate in the hope of using the tariff issue in the 1892 election.

The election of 1888 was the first election fought primarily over tariffs. The winner, Benjamin Harrison, passed the McKinley tariff, raising the average duty on imported goods to 50 percent. The significance for this discussion is that tariffs on imports were already very high in the United States, four decades before the start of the Great Depression. The tariff was said by its Republican proponents to be necessary to maintain the high standard of living of the American workingman, "but as the employers were fighting (hard) against the trade unions, and were willing to import the new immigrant labor to reduce wages, this could not be taken quite seriously," wrote James Truslow Adams in *Epic of America*.[44] Republicans also presented higher tariffs as a way to protect farmers and the new states in the Western United States from foreign competition—and found a ready audience for that viewpoint. The McKinley bill was signed into law in October of 1890.

The political price extracted by the silverites for supporting the passage of the McKinley tariff was that the Republicans would back legislation to increase purchases of silver and a resumption of free coinage of the metal. In addition to the tariff legislation, the Republicans, led by Henry Cabot Lodge in the House, were pushing for new voting rights laws to protect black voters and Republican candidates in the South. Southern Democrats opposed the measures to protect black voting rights and dubbed the legislation the "Force Bill" because, they claimed, the Republicans were prepared to use federal troops to enforce the political franchise of freed slaves in the South.

When Republicans brought the Force Bill to the floor of the Senate in December 1890, the leader of the silverites, Senator William Stewart of Nevada, seized his opportunity. In January of 1891, Stewart used a procedural motion on the floor of the Senate to substitute legislation for the free coinage of silver for the Lodge voting rights legislation, and the pro-silver forces in both parties sustained his maneuver.

The fact was that free coinage of silver and, more importantly, inflation of the currency, was more popular politically than protecting voting rights in the South. The American economy was again sinking into depression in the winter of 1891, with unemployment and business failures spreading around the country. A solution via increased issuance of paper currency was seen by politicians in both parties as the answer. Even Senator Sherman, who long guarded against allowing the silverites to push their inflationist agenda through the Senate, was forced to concede that the political pressure to allow free coinage of silver was irresistible. A majority of Republicans believed that the combination of the new tariff legislation and a pro-silver bill would protect them at the polls in 1890.[45]

The compromise legislation crafted by Sherman in July of 1890 repealed the Bland-Allison act and called for the Treasury to purchase four million ounces of silver per month, essentially the amount of silver produced in the United States during that time. The Treasury paid for these purchases with paper dollars and this had the effect of rapidly increasing the money supply. The increase in the supply of paper currency caused by the Sherman Silver Purchase Act placed a considerable drain on the government's gold reserves. Many Americans immediately exchanged the paper money for their silver in order to buy gold coins. Even though demand for paper currency continued to rise, the preference for either gold or paper money over silver was pronounced and silver prices continued to fall. Imports of gold into the United States surged as the demand for the metal increased with the supply of greenbacks as the Treasury continued its legally required purchases of silver.

The sad fact was the demand for silver coins was very small and the public had a strong preference for greenbacks instead of silver.

Even though Treasury purchases of silver rose to 50 million troy ounces annually, world production of silver rose from 63 million ounces per year in 1873 to over 150 million ounces in 1892 and thus the market price continued to fall despite the Treasury's purchases, but the silverites were unrelenting in their clamor for further government support. Representative Edwin A. Conger of Iowa, who was Chairman of the House Committee on Coinage, Weights and Measures and supported limited coinage of silver, called the lobbying effort by the silverite forces prior to the passage of the Sherman Silver Purchase Act "the most persistent, courageous and audacious lobby upon this question I have ever seen since my term of service began here."[46]

Despite the passage of the National Bank Act several decades before, the fact of political meddling by Washington in the structure and composition of the U.S. money supply had resulted in nine different types of money being placed into circulation by the 1890s. The legal mandates placed upon the Treasury to redeem paper money with gold or silver, and to purchase and/or coin silver, had become completely unmanageable and were depleting the once-large official reserves of gold. So great was the drain of gold from the Treasury and the increase in the money supply that within three years of the passage of the Sherman Silver Purchase Act, the law was repealed.

While the money supply of the United States had grown dramatically, the impact on the economy was negligible and, more importantly, public confidence in banks, financial markets, the U.S. currency, and the economy was at a new low. The debate over the nature of money and the nature of American society more generally was becoming increasingly intense and divisive as the nineteenth century drew to a close. Over the next decade, America would see more political discord and economic upheaval than at any time since the Civil War and most of it caused by the debate over the nature of money.

Chapter 3

Robber Barons and the Gilded Age

With the collapse of the Free Banking Model prior to the Civil War and the creation of a monetary system based upon national banks, the assumption was that the U.S. economy would become more stable, but in fact the opposite was the case. The tendency of Americans to prefer gold over paper money was unchanged from pre-Civil War days. If anything, the continuing instability of U.S. banks, whether national or state-chartered, and the unreliability of paper money and investments, made Americans more cautious and also encouraged speculation between paper and metal. The example of speculators such as Jay Gould, Jim Fiske, and Jay Cooke was widely emulated by the inhabitants of Wall Street, who earned and lost great fortunes by using paper assets of various types to manipulate the markets and thereby deprive credulous members of the public of their cash.

The rise of the investment trust also occurred during the 1890s and was a very important development in the history of American finance, especially when it comes to the story of money and debt. The investment trust was a way of allowing the Robber Barons to mask their corporate manipulations in stocks and bonds, the leverage used to support these speculations, and to hide obvious violations of anti-trust laws through hidden control stakes in many companies. For the individual, the investment trust was a way for individuals to emulate the investment strategy of the Robber Barons, at least in theory. These trusts of the 1890s were controlled by individuals and were the first derivatives, the precursors of hedge funds and the complex structured financial instruments of the twenty-first century. Trusts would be used a century later to fuel bubbles in technology stocks and real estate based on funding provided by individual investors.

The assets of choice for the Robber Barons of the Gilded Age were railroads, coal, and oil companies, but any industry could and would be the target of an enterprising investment trust operator. The similarity between the trusts in the early nineteenth century and today's world of structured finance lies in the use of debt and other instruments to finance the vehicles and a near-total lack of disclosure. By the 1920s, when these vehicles were distributed to the individual investor, there were literally hundreds of such trusts.

The speculative character of the U.S. markets was made more extreme due to the near-total absence of private commercial rules imposed by the federal government in matters of finance. The Treasury simply operated as another participant in a completely private marketplace where "anything goes" and "*caveat emptor*" were the operative norms. The state and local courts were left to provide legal regulation of banking and finance. Stocks and bonds were sold from private banks, parlors, saloons, and the backs of wagons— much like Wall Street today. Such activities were reckoned to be speculative and thus socially suspect.

The biblical, pejorative view of the "money changers," to borrow the title of the 1926 book by Upton Sinclair, still held sway with many Americans, especially those who supported silver as the means for national salvation. There was as yet little thought given in Washington to restraining the worst tendencies of the markets, let alone setting standards for the regulation of commercial behavior that are the basic requirements of any civil society. The pro-business tendency of the Republican party, which dominated the politics of the nation during much of this period, encouraged and enabled a level of licentiousness and greed that would result in several serious financial crises and economic depressions and eventually led to the Great Depression. Only after a string of economic collapses from the 1880s through to October of 1929 would the United States see the rise of legal interventions emanating from Washington as a counterbalance to unrestrained competition and personal avarice in the American marketplace.

The Age of Speculation

The final decades of the nineteenth century following the Civil War were described aptly by Mark Twain and Charles Dudley Warner in their sardonic book *The Gilded Age: A Tale of Today*, which told the tale of politicians, soiled doves, and other characters who were caught up in the speculative, get-rich-quick environment of the period. Twain used the comparison between Washington and the hinterland to great effect in his classic tale, which like many commentaries of the period employed near-fiction as a foil with which to comment on the political currents of the day. The comparison of Twain's Gilded Age and the technology and real estate bubbles seen in the United States a century or more later seems to confirm the repetitive nature of man's behavior when it comes to money. In the preface, Twain described his work in his typically facetious style:

> This book was not written for private circulation among friends; it was not written to cheer or instruct a diseased relative of the author's; it was not thrown off during intervals of wearing labor to amuse the idle hour. It was not written for any of these reasons, and therefore is submitted without the usual apologies. It will be seen that it deals entirely with a state of society; the chief embarrassment of the writers in this realm of the imagination has been the want of illustrative examples. In a State where there is no fever of speculation, no inflamed desire for sudden wealth, where the poor are all simple-minded and contented, and the rich are all honest and generous, where society is in a condition of primitive purity and politics is the occupation of only the capable and the patriotic, there are necessarily no materials for such a history as we have constructed out of an ideal commonwealth.[1]

Twain's description of American political life and especially Washington in *The Gilded Age* summarized a period of great economic growth and equally great political corruption; a period of enormous political partisanship and also great political reform. Steven Mintz of the University of Houston observed:

> Mark Twain called the late nineteenth century the "Gilded Age." By this, he meant that the period was glittering on the surface but corrupt underneath. In the popular view, the late nineteenth century was a period of greed and guile: of rapacious Robber Barons, unscrupulous speculators, and corporate buccaneers, of shady business practices, scandal-plagued politics, and vulgar display. It is easy to caricature the Gilded Age as an era of corruption, conspicuous consumption, and unfettered capitalism. But it is more useful to think of this as modern America's formative period, when an agrarian society of small producers was transformed into an urban society dominated by industrial corporations.[2]

When it came to matters of money and finance, private banks not only issued the majority of the nation's currency but also operated with almost complete impunity, with little or no interference from Washington or the states. The New York banks sat at the apex of the financial and political world of nineteenth century America, and they had a direct relationship with the Treasury and foreign banks. Institutions controlled by J.P. Morgan and other Robber Barons grew in political influence and power, in part because there was no national bank or federal regulatory structure to counterbalance their economic ascendance. The major banks of New York were the national counterparties for foreign commerce. They helped to finance trade and collect taxes and duties on behalf of the government. The cash balances of the "independent" U.S. Treasury were deposited with these same large banks.

J.P. Morgan, who as Matthew Josephson wrote, "won respect by force of arms as well as business acumen," assumed the role of statesman and *de facto* central banker along with the likes of John D. Rockefeller, who was to the oil industry what Morgan was to banking. Together with William Rockefeller and partners, John Rockefeller created Standard Oil. It was the largest oil refining business in the world and the first great American trust. The founding partners of Standard Oil financed the initial capital for their oil trust through the large New York banks. In 1877, however, John Rockefeller founded his own bank, the Chase National Bank, whose successor operates today as JPMorgan Chase Bank.

The market dynamic among and between paper money, gold, and silver remained one of the most important economic and political issues facing the country. The nature of money was seen as a far more important issue than a discussion of banks or anything else that people today might associate with finance. Sound money was scarce—at least in the public mind, and this made money a hot political issue. During a period after the Civil War when the nation's economy and population grew rapidly, the government actually followed a conscious policy of fiscal restraint and monetary contraction. This was a popular policy with many Americans, who were horrified by the government's fiscal operations during and after the war and wished to see a return to full gold convertibility. After the massive wartime stimulus provided by large increases in federal spending, increases funded via borrowing and inflation, the government was actually shrinking the money supply even as the nation's economy grew rapidly.

Milton Friedman and Anna Schwartz, in their classic work, *A Monetary History of the United States*, found that between 1892 and 1897, the nation's money supply was stable to down slightly, but that the final years of the decade saw "a dramatic reversal of economic conditions."[3] The practical reality felt by Americans as a result of Washington's thrift between 1892 and 1897 was a scarcity of any type of money to use as a means of exchange in daily life, as well as gold for holding value against inflation. This is why many progressives believed that the issue of money, and especially the end of using silver in coins, was connected to falling prices for farm products and a general economic malaise during much of this period.

The irony of the position of the proponents of silver and currency inflation is that as early as 1900, some 90 percent of all commercial transactions in the country were effected via the transfer of credits from one bank to the next; thus the key issue for reforming the U.S. financial system seemingly was to provide adequate reserves for banks, not to facilitate the issuance of greenbacks or metal coins for physical transactions. However, the political popularity of the silver move-ment and the impact of silver purchases authorized by Congress on the Treasury's gold stocks and the supply of specie available to the pub-lic, overwhelmed such practical considerations. The more silver the Treasury bought, the less gold remained in circulation.

Republicans Embrace Inflation

The passage of the Sherman Silver Purchase Act in the summer of 1890 not only failed to stabilize the price of silver, but also drained the Treasury of gold at a more rapid pace as Americans sought to exchange their paper currency for specie. The law roughly doubled the Treasury's purchases of silver. Payment was made for the silver through a new issue of greenback currency, which was redeemable in either gold or silver at the discretion of the Treasury. This not only placed the United States on the road to a dual gold–silver monetary standard, but also confirmed the new position of the Republican party for *soft money* and high tariffs.

Now both major political parties were advocates of inflation, implicitly or explicitly. Whatever enduring commitment the Repub-lican party had made to sound money when President Grant vetoed the Inflation Bill a little over a decade before was swept away in the name of political expediency. The economic times in the 1890s were increasingly volatile and so were the politics, benefiting challengers and making elections very risky for incumbents. Politicians of that day were voted in or out of office with greater frequency, so focusing on the rising public support for inflation was good politics for members of either major party. The inflationary tendencies of the U.S. government were further confirmed in that same year, when the New York branch of the Treasury changed its long standing practice of requiring specie for payment of import duties. Greenbacks largely replaced gold coins in the payment of customs receipts in New York from that time forward.[4]

The increasing popularity of inflation among the American people and the growing tendency of the federal government in Washington to accommodate it did not go unnoticed around the world. Like America's citizens, foreigners reacted with alarm to the shift from gold to silver as a monetary standard in the United States, especially since the fall in demand for the metal had been driven partly by nations in Europe and Asia deciding not to use silver for coins. As it became more obvious that Americans intended to embrace inflation via the monetization of silver, foreign capital inflows to the United States declined and exports of gold grew as foreign banks and individuals sought to exchange their paper dollars for gold.

So great was the outflow of gold from U.S. reserves that in March of 1891 the Treasury suddenly imposed a fee on the export of gold bars from the United States. From this point forward, the export of gold from the United States moved to coins rather than gold bars, but the drain continued nonetheless. When the Treasury began effectively to default on convertibility by forcing U.S. banks to take paper rather than gold, the stage was set for a financial crisis. The final act of political idiocy came from the Republican-controlled Senate, which in July of 1892 passed legislation to take all remaining restrictions off the coinage of silver.[5]

The action by the Republican Congress to placate the advocates of free coinage of silver and inflation was a response to internal political pressures and the approaching election, but the results were felt around the world. The overtly pro-silver forces led by the Progressive Party polled over a million votes in 1892 based on a platform that embraced the free coinage of silver at the old, 16-to-1 ratio with the price of gold; this even though the market price ratio between gold and silver was now closer to 40 to 1.

President Grover Cleveland led the Democrats to an electoral triumph in the fall of 1892, winning control over both houses of the Congress and the White House for the first time in more than a third of a century. The conservative Cleveland regained power just as the U.S. economy was collapsing. Foreign creditors and the country's citizens were fleeing paper assets and demanding payment in gold. Even as the Democrats were savoring their victory in the five-month interregnum between the election and the inauguration of the new president, the global financial markets began to unravel.

In February of 1893, ten days before the end of the term of President Benjamin Harrison, the Reading Railroad declared bankruptcy. The Reading was heavily in debt and was in the process of borrowing more to finance the lease of coal producing lands in northeastern Pennsylvania. At the time of the Reading collapse, all of the producers of coal in that part of the United States were controlled by one or more railroad trusts, which were engaged in cutthroat competition that forced them to sell coal at or below the cost of production. And most of these trusts were using debt to subsidize this uneconomic activity. At the time of its collapse, the Reading Railroad controlled the Philadelphia, New Jersey Central, and Lehigh Valley lines, but all of these acquisitions were financed with debt.[6]

In many ways the collapse of the Reading Trust typified the way the use of private debt to finance business expansion and even interest payments had become a more and more acceptable form of behavior in the financial markets. William Janeway, the former Vice Chairman of the private investment firm Warburg Pincus, in a November 2008 interview, said that the first phase in finance is fully secured lending. One makes a loan and gets repaid. The second phase in finance is making loans where only interest expense is covered, echoing the marketing pitch of Jay Cooke. The second phase relies on refinancing to repay principal.[7]

The owners of the Reading Railroad were already in the third phase, where even the interest on existing debt had not been "earned" in any economic sense and had to be borrowed to keep the enterprise afloat. The ultimate cause of the corporate instability that culminated in bankruptcy of the Reading Trust was the fact that prices for coal had fallen dramatically, below the cost of production in some cases, following the discovery of oil in Titusville, Pennsylvania, in 1859.

When the rail line collapsed, the principals of the Reading were in Europe seeking new money loans in order to pay interest on the company's existing debt, which as mentioned above had been "unearned." Instead of using the proceeds of the company's prodigious borrowing to maintain the rail operations so that the company could earn a profit, the operators used debt to buy more rail lines and lease coal-producing properties in an effort to corner the coal market a la Jay Gould's market operations in gold decades before. Coal was the chief means of heating homes and powering industry; thus the owners of the Reading Railroad, taking the monopolistic example of Gould and other master speculators before them, believed that they could control coal prices if only they could secure control over a sufficient portion of the coal producing properties in the East. The means of gaining control over these physical, coal-producing properties was debt and more debt.

But Gould's influence over the ways and means of high finance was not limited to the use of debt to fuel speculation, an artifice that many Americans were employing. The other notable aspect of the collapse of the Reading Railroad and many other rail lines of its day was the way bankruptcy and receivership had been transformed from a way to liquidate insolvent companies to a mere stratagem, a political maneuver used to advance the private agenda of the speculative class in a given industry. The magazine *The Nation* described the evolution of the art of using bankruptcy for speculative gain in the same year that the Reading Railroad collapsed:

> The old idea of a receivership still lingers in the public mind— that an action for that end should be begun before a court only in case of total failure to meet obligations, and then only as a means of liquidating the affairs or a corporation. Hence, it used to be thought that a receivership was to be entered only as a last resort and only as the beginning of liquidation or complete reorganization. Within the last decade or so we have passed beyond this original theory. It was the late Mr. Jay Gould, we believe, who first developed the idea of a railway receivership until it became merely one of a series of strategic moves for the control of a great corporation or for some special financial result.[8]

The railroads of the nineteenth century were, in this respect, similar to the "too big to fail" banks and commercial companies of the later part of the twentieth century. In the same way that Gould and his contemporaries used the guise of bankruptcy at the end of the nineteenth century to hide their true strategic agendas, a century later the government-led bailouts of Penn Central, Chrysler, Continental Illinois, Citicorp, General Motors, Chrysler (again), GMAC, and American International Group would all be used to avoid liquidation and to pursue a political agenda, namely to conceal the prevalence of incompetence and outright fraud in the financial world. In a sense, the ways and means of Gould and his nineteenth century contemporaries would become the everyday tools of the American political class a century later. In both cases the objectives were criminal in nature but with different goals, the former mere profit and the latter the achievement and maintenance of political power.

The Panic of 1893

By the time Grover Cleveland came to power in March of 1893, the Treasury was already limiting the outflow of gold. Banks began to call in their loans and more businesses failed in what was to become the worst financial crisis in the modern age. More railroads and scores of other businesses and banks would fail in a terrible year that began a decade of privation and economic depression lasting until the turn of the century and beyond. By May of 1893 banks were failing in droves and notes drawn upon depositories in the South and West could no longer be discounted at the large New York institutions, which had cut correspondent ties with banks around the country. Two months later, the silverites held a convention in Denver and, as might be expected, blamed the crisis on an international conspiracy to "demonetize" silver by not using it in coins. But the sad fact was that the only conspiracy, and one that was not well hidden, was on the part of the populist mob of inflation-happy silverites, who saw their salvation, both in economic and religious terms, in restoring the price of silver to the old, 16-to-1 ratio with gold.

So acute was the government's fiscal situation that J.P. Morgan and other leading bankers put together a rescue for the Treasury, agreeing to subscribe to a $50 million bond issue and to stand ready to do so again if necessary. "We all have large interests dependent upon the maintenance of a sound currency of the United States," Morgan cabled to his London office. "If this negotiation can be made, it will be most creditable to all parties and pay a good profit."[9] Morgan and the other participants in the Treasury rescue did profit by their investment. But the image of the U.S. government being rescued by the House of Morgan was galling to many Americans, who recoiled at the ostentatious power represented by the great New York banks. Robber Barons such as J.P. Morgan were American royalty, men who engendered both admiration and contempt; the latter would soon become a central fact in American politics as the economic depression that followed the Crisis of 1893 stretched on for years and would ultimately lead to the creation of the Federal Reserve System.

Senator Robert Byrd wrote in *The Senate* that no one could agree on the causes of the great depression that began in 1893. The various political parties blamed one another, while the orthodox Cleveland and his colleagues blamed the purchases of silver and the perceived decline in the Treasury's credit standing. This seems like the obvious explanation, but the political and social factors that first pushed the government to purchase vast amounts of silver and, in the process, inflate the currency, are complex. The rise of William Jennings Bryan of Nebraska as the leader of the pro-silver movement is memorialized in the pages of the history books, but the vast social movement behind Bryan may not have been motivated chiefly, or even at all, by economic theories about the nature of money.

The great libertarian economist and author Murray Rothbard argued that the conventional view of the economics profession, led by giants such as Milton Friedman and Anna Schwartz, is that the price deflation after the Civil War, especially in agriculture, drove a political conflict between inflationist and pro-gold tendencies in American society. "This conventional analysis has two problems," Rothbard argues. "If Bryan represented 'the people' versus the 'interests,' why did Bryan lose and lose soundly, not once but three times?" The second problem, raised by Rothbard, is the way the economics profession tends to deemphasize the dynamic political situation in the United States at that time. This was a period when the major political parties would go from extremes and great distinctions to increasingly similar centrist platforms of only modestly different colorations, an alignment that remains in force today.

The historian Paul Kleppner observed that the pro-silver forces, despite their political alliance with farm interests, were not "agrarian" parties so much as religious extremists whose purpose was to cleanse the nation of personal and political sin. Biblical references to Bryan illustrate the evangelical tenor of the pro-silver movement. The silverite tendency was more a religious crusade than a coherent economic or political faction focused on money. Kleppner wrote: "The Greenback Party was less an amalgamation of economic pressure groups than an ad hoc coalition of 'True Believers,' 'ideologues,' who launched their party as a quasi religious movement that bore the indelible hallmark of 'a transfiguring faith.'" In addition to embracing a gospel of inflationism and easy money, the silverites were invariably in favor of prohibition, public schools and against parochial education, Catholics, Lutherans, and other non–Pentecostal faiths.[10]

The Cross of Silver

Not surprisingly, none of the proponents of a bimetallic standard for money seemed able to grasp, much less to accept, that the falling demand for silver had robbed the metal of its role as a store of value or a unit of account. Nations around the world were ending their use of silver for monetary purposes, and demand from industry and for jewelry was likewise depressed. Since a majority of their fellow citizens clearly preferred paper money or gold to silver as a means of exchange, the position of the silverites was truly hopeless in economic terms, even though politically it remained very powerful.

No matter how many objective lessons were visible in the marketplace to refute their adoration for the increasingly common metal, millions of Americans were convinced of the righteousness of the cause of silver. The proponents of silver were indeed "true believers" in the power of silver to reverse the economic and social pressures that were building throughout the United States. No amount of evidence to the contrary would dissuade them of the righteousness of their position. The support for silver would continue to grow even as the economy weakened and the U.S. banking system fell into the worst crisis since before the Civil War. William Jennings Bryan, the "Moses" of the silverite movement, declared a holy war in the name of silver money and more currency inflation. At the Chicago convention of 1896, Bryan delivered what many consider to be one of the most important political speeches in American history:

> We do not come as aggressors. Our war is not a war of conquest; we are fighting in the defense of our homes, our families, and posterity. We have petitioned, and our petitions have been scorned; we have entreated, and our entreaties have been disregarded; we have begged, and they have mocked when our

calamity came. We beg them no longer; we entreat no more; we petition them no more. We defy them! . . . Thou shalt not crucify America on a Cross of Gold![11]

In August of 1893, following the collapse of the Erie Railroad in July and the Northern Pacific a month later, President Cleveland called a special session of the Congress and demanded the repeal of the Sherman Silver Purchase Act. To compel quick action by the House, Cleveland used the considerable threat of keeping Congress in session through the dog days of summer in Washington, DC. This charming French-designed city built upon a strip of malarial river sediment and swamp land along the Potomac River was generally evacuated in summer months. Washington has since been raised and filled in by the U.S. Army Corps of Engineers, a wonderful allegory for the history of money and debt in America that concerns this book.

President Cleveland's public call for the repeal of the Sherman Silver Purchase Act was a significant move given that his Vice President, Adlai Stevenson, represented the populist tendency in favor of bimetallism and free coinage of silver that was gaining the ascendancy in the Democratic Party. Stevenson was elected to the House from Illinois twice, running on the Democratic and Greenbacker tickets, but was also defeated twice in the volatile politics of the 1870s, when large portions of the House were swept from office every two years. When Stevenson won his second term in the House in 1878, nearly a third of the members of that body were defeated or retired.[12]

President Cleveland himself was conservative, almost Republican in his views on money and fiscal restraint, and was troubled by what might happen to the financial markets and the economy if his Vice President were to assume power. A heavy cigar smoker, Cleveland had mouth cancer when he took the oath of office in March 1893 and later underwent surgery to remove part of the roof of his mouth and entire upper jaw, a fact that was kept secret for nearly a quarter century afterward. Following the remarkable medical procedure, which left no outward scar on his face, President Cleveland functioned with an artificial jaw made of vulcanized rubber. Cleveland kept the extent of his illness even from Vice President Stevenson, who never knew how close he came to assuming the office of the presidency in that tumultuous summer.

It is interesting to speculate how the financial markets in the United States and Europe would have reacted had a silverite such as Stevenson become president. Rothbard described the scene facing Cleveland in that terrible year:

> Poor Grover Cleveland, a hard money Democrat, assumed the presidency in the middle of this monetary crisis. Two months later, the stock market collapsed, and a month afterward, in June 1893, distrust of the fraction reserve banks led to massive bank runs and failures throughout the country. Once again, however, many banks, national and state, especially in the West and South, were allowed to suspend specie payments. The panic of 1893 was on.[13]

Despite long speeches by Bryan and other pro-silver members of the House, on August 28, 1893, the lower chamber voted 239–108 to repeal the Sherman Act. This was a tremendous victory for Cleveland, but not the end of the battle over silver in Congress. The Senate Finance Committee approved the legislation to end silver purchases to the full Senate for consideration by just a one-vote margin. Then commenced three months of debate in the Senate, during which the pro-silver forces tried to talk the legislation to death via a filibuster. By early October 1893, the White House was growing desperate and, after meeting with key silver supporters, managed to gain their agreement to end the filibuster. On Friday, October 30, 1893, the Senate voted 43–32 to repeal the Sherman Silver Purchase Act.

The Evangelical Silverites

Though the debate in the Congress lasted only three months, the discussion about the issue of silver and, indirectly, the embrace of a policy of steady currency inflation would go on for years, dominate the next several national elections, and tear the Democratic and Republican parties asunder along regional and sectarian lines. One of the shortcomings of the earlier economic interpretations of this period was to look at the evolution of the national debate over silver and assume that the motivations driving the debate were also national in scope. Social researchers such as Paul Kleppner, who focus on local, religious, and social factors in their analyses, attribute much of what occurred in this period to heartfelt differences in the local and regional perspectives of people who still just barely accepted the idea of political Union and were sometimes deeply suspicions of other regions of the country. He characterized Protestant silverites as using the power of the state to stamp out sin and create "a new Jerusalem on earth."[14] Bryan himself explained the struggle by the populists in the 1890s as beginning with the economic crisis in 1854–1856 which destroyed the decrepit Whig Party and saw the birth of the Republican Party. A decade later, those events would lead the nation to a civil war against slavery. "Then began the struggle," said Bryan in his cross of gold speech. "With a zeal approaching the zeal which inspired the Crusaders, who followed Peter the Hermit, our silver Democrats went forth from victory to victory."

The split in each party caused by the rise of the progressive movement provided ready opportunities to William Jennings Bryan and other members of the silverite cause and what would become the progressive movement of the early twentieth century. In 1893, however, these changes were still far in the distance. The mid-term elections in 1894 went solidly for the Republicans, who now included a number of "silver republicans" such as Nevada's Senator William Stewart, the editor of a pro-silver pamphlet entitled *Silver Knight*. The Democrats even more were literally torn apart over the silver issue, so much so that the mine owners and other pro-silver forces began to host scores of "conferences" under the auspices of the People's Party to recruit Democratic operatives to the populist cause. The rise of this third party and its inroads into Democratic ranks after the 1894 Republican landslide set in motion changes that would reshape the political map of America in the early twentieth century.[15]

The repeal of the silver purchase law stabilized the Treasury's stocks of gold and eventually calmed the fears of people in the United States and around the world regarding America's financial stability. There still was not really a coherent monetary standard, with various hard and fiat monies floating in the marketplace. This was a marketplace, it must be remembered, where barter and non-monetary exchanges of goods and services still accounted for a large fraction of total commerce.

Banks and the financial markets were a tiny fraction of the overall economy. In the late 1880s, there were about 1,015 state banks and 2,689 national banks, according to the FDIC. The fact of the existence of these banks and the government-issued greenbacks, however, did not ensure a stable supply of money for the U.S. economy. Due to this fact, the Progressive movement was constantly pressing for an expansion in the amount of silver coinage and consequently an increase in the overall supply of money.

"Greenback doctrines were no longer confined to a narrow tier of frontier counties in the West," wrote Lawrence Goodwyn in *The Triumph of the Corporate State*. "Now they permeated a great mass movement which in turn had created a national third party. The party had deep and still spreading roots, all the way from the tenth district of Georgia on the Atlantic coast to the working class precincts of San Francisco. The crucial political reality lay in the fact that the national Democratic Party had been fatally undermined by the politics of Populism."[16]

Between 1894 and the elections in 1896, Bryan traveled the country on the beginning of a much longer journey in which he commanded the national spotlight for more than two decades. He carried out an active campaign for the forces of free silver, supported by sponsorship from the American Bimetallic League, which was in turn supported by Anaconda Mines, J. Augustus Heinze, and William Randolph Hearst. Bryan received a salary for his column in the *Omaha World-Herald*, which was likewise supported by Western mine owners. "By the time the Democratic convention was held in Chicago in 1896, the silver movement had become so strong that the nomination of Bryan for president was inevitable," wrote Margaret Myers, professor emeritus of economics at Vassar College.[17]

The Turning Point: 1896

William McKinley, Jr. was the Republican candidate for President in 1896. He was supported by much of the Eastern media and political establishment, which in turn supported sound money, the gold standard, and protective tariffs. It was more than a debate over the nature of money, however, and McKinley would eventually win because of a reviving economy and a sense on the part of at least some Americans that silver was not the solution to their economic problems. While fear of the imposition of silver did motivate many Eastern business interests to support McKinley, it was not the only motivator. The White House history profile for McKinley sets the scene:

> At the 1896 Republican Convention, in time of depression, the wealthy Cleveland businessman Marcus Alonzo Hanna ensured the nomination of his friend William McKinley as "the advance agent of prosperity." The Democrats, advocating the "free and unlimited coinage of both silver and gold"—which would have mildly inflated the currency—nominated William Jennings Bryan. While Hanna received large contributions from eastern Republicans frightened by Bryan's views on silver, McKinley met delegations on his front porch in Canton, Ohio. He won by the largest majority of popular votes since 1872.[18]

Myers concludes that the election of McKinley and the Republican sweep of the House and Senate in 1896 did not equate to a plebiscite on the currency. The fact that Western and Eastern interests now saw the necessity of settling the question of the currency of the United States was enormously significant. However, the process of finally reaching agreement and adopting legislation in the Congress was still more than a decade away. A key intellectual influence over the work done during this period regarding the currency and the U.S. monetary system was a paper commissioned by the boards of trade in dozens of cities around the United States to look at the issue of a central bank. Entitled "Report of the Monetary Commission of the Indianapolis Convention," the paper was the work of Lawrence Laughlin of the University of Chicago and his assistants, the economists Carroll Root and Parker Willis. The Report of the Indianapolis Convention is a compendium on the history of money in the United States and the various issues that faced Americans in 1900.[19]

What is remarkable about the report is that it provided a very detailed discussion of some of the issues that were agitating Americans when it came to money. Whether or not they were for or against the use of silver as money, most Americans wanted a more sound and stable money supply to use for the three basic roles that money plays in any economy. The report outlines the three "Functions of Money":

1. A Standard, or Common Denominator of Value
2. A Medium of Exchange
3. A Standard of Deferred Payments.

Regarding the first function, the Report stated that "a common denominator is as necessary in comparing the value of commodities as is a common language among many persons in any city to enable them to readily compare ideas."[20] The needs and frustrations of Americans when it came to the nature of money were pretty basic and more related to economic and personal security rather than to an intellectual debate over the nature of money. As noted, the public had plenty of reason to be suspicious of banks and other issuers of debt. In fact the agitation for free silver and the related instability in the U.S. economy during the 1890s did not help to support the solidity of American banks, whether state-chartered or national banks. Even with the restoration of dollar convertibility into gold in 1879, the U.S. economy and financial system were rocked by a series of market panics.

During the period between 1886 and continuing until 1933, Congress considered 150 proposals to create deposit insurance plans for the country's banks to address the issue of bank safety and soundness, but none was adopted and little progress was made in dealing with the basic issue of a stable and liquid money supply to support the economy. It took an additional 30 years, from the restoration of gold convertibility in 1879 to the creation of the Federal Reserve System in 1913, for Congress to exert federal authority over the issuance of paper currency, ending the private, free market system of national banks issuing currency for Americans.

Following two decades of strong economic growth after the Civil War, when the West was conquered, many Americans in the 1890s began to fear for their prospects. A severe and prolonged economic weakness began to appear in the United States. The reaction of the public was first bewilderment and surprise, followed by anger. Financial panics led to the collapse of railroads and banks, widespread unemployment, and depressed farm prices, and fueled the rise of the Populist movement, but these events also increased the power of the great "money trusts." These agglomerations of companies were created by the leading banks and industrialists of the day to limit competition and control prices.

The rise of the great trusts confirmed the fears of John Adams and Thomas Jefferson regarding the evil tendencies of private banks, and caused fear and consternation among the public. The political reaction against the Robber Barons and the trusts in the late 1890s and early 1900s helped fuel the rise of the Progressive movement. This included figures from both the Democrat and Republican parties. However, it would take a strange twist of history to bring to the presidency a man who was sufficiently radical and independent to take on the money trusts.

When McKinley ran for President in 1896, he had served in the Congress and as governor of Ohio, and ran on a platform of supporting the gold standard and high tariffs to protect American industries and jobs. He had no strong position on silver per se and easily defeated efforts to add a pro-silver plank to the Republican platform. McKinley chose as his running mate Garret Augustus Hobart, a New Jersey legislator and state court judge. Hobart was selected by Marcus A. Hanna, the Cleveland industrialist and political strategist who, along with Charles G. Dawes of Illinois, masterminded McKinley's presidential nomination.

The Gilded Age ushered in the age of the machine political bosses such as Hanna of Ohio, Platt of New York, and Quay of Pennsylvania. While generally seen as being in favor of public versus private interests, McKinley's administration was entirely friendly to the large corporations of the day, which flourished in the final years of the nineteenth century and grew even more in financial and political power. However, the rise of the great trusts, and a more general feeling that the promise of American life was not being fulfilled, served to inflame the electorate and especially the Progressive movement led by Bryan. He called the 1896 election "the first battle." McKinley was the last in a long line of Republican Presidents—including Grant, Hayes, Garfield, Arthur, and Harrison—who had followed a generally *laissez faire* approach to government oversight of business, a program that was now heading for a loud but largely irrelevant collision with reform populism.

The victory of McKinley and the Republicans over the Progressives in 1896 was based on a sweep of the Northern states and a modest showing in the Midwest and South, where Cleveland had won for the Democrats and Bryan did well, as expected. The popular vote garnered by the two candidates was within half a million votes, with McKinley taking a bit over 7 million to 6.5 million for Bryan with the Democrat a distant third. But the election ended the regional balance between the two pre-Civil War parties and vastly changed the nature of national politics for years to come.

The Progressives were thrashed in the North and the supporters of McKinley and the gold cause said that this was a defeat for the idea of "the people" as a political force. Bryanism was popular, but it was not effective in defeating the "patriotic" Republicans and the big city political machines behind them. The party of business was almost exclusively white, Protestant, Yankee, and more than a little xenophobic. Democrats and Progressives were regularly attacked for being too friendly toward foreigners and immigrants, this even though many old silverites were enthusiastically in favor of social exclusiveness as well.[21]

The financial and organizational help of business interests such as Hanna, Platt, and other bosses in orchestrating Republican poll activities seems to have made the difference in this key election. The same powerful political interests behind the Republican Party expected to control the economic destiny of the United States indefinitely. They did not reckon, however, on the strange fate and destiny that would bring a man named Theodore Roosevelt to the White House. The resounding victory by the Republicans in 1896 brought many new operatives like Roosevelt to Washington. With the crucial support of Henry Cabot Lodge, Roosevelt went to work as Undersecretary of the Navy in the first term of McKinley's presidency. He was soon actively engaged in guiding the expansion of the U.S. territory to include the future state of Hawaii.

Theodore Roosevelt was precisely the sort of figure that most Republicans and the machine bosses feared: a man of independent mind and means who was willing to consider new ideas and risk failure in pursuit of great national and personal goals. Roosevelt presented his case directly in a speech entitled "Citizenship in a Republic," delivered at the Sorbonne, Paris, on April 23, 1910:

> It is not the critic who counts: not the man who points out how
> the strong man stumbles or where the doer of deeds could have

done better. The credit belongs to the man who is actually in the arena, whose face is marred by dust and sweat and blood, who strives valiantly, who errs and comes up short again and again, because there is no effort without error or shortcoming, but who knows the great enthusiasms, the great devotions, who spends himself for a worthy cause; who, at the best, knows, in the end, the triumph of high achievement, and who, at the worst, if he fails, at least he fails while daring greatly, so that his place shall never be with those cold and timid souls who knew neither victory nor defeat.[22]

Roosevelt's presidency would begin the era of Progressive change in America and would come about, as is often the case in this narrative, in an unexpected and unanticipated way. The Romanian-born playwright Eugene Ionesco, one of the foremost members of the Theater of the Absurd, said that "you can only predict things that have happened." The remarkable events leading to the political rise of Theodore Roosevelt and the circumstances of his succession to the presidency that will be discussed in the next chapter confirm that judgment.

With the Republicans in control of Congress and the White House, the stage was set for one of the most conservative pieces of monetary legislation in modern U.S. history, the Gold Standard Act of 1900. This law passed by Congress in March of that year established gold as the only standard for redeeming paper money, and prohibited the exchange of silver for gold. This, at least for the moment, reassured the public as to the value of paper money issued by private national banks. The first two paragraphs of the legislation read:

An Act To define and fix the standard of value, to maintain the parity of all forms of money issued or coined by the United States, to refund the public debt, and for other purposes. Be it enacted . . . That the dollar consisting of twenty-five and eight-tenths grains of gold nine-tenths fine, as established by section thirty-five hundred and eleven of the Revised Statutes of the United States, shall be the standard unit of value, and all forms of money issued or coined by the United States shall be maintained at a parity of value with this standard, and it shall be the duty of the Secretary of the Treasury to maintain such parity.

The Gold Standard Act officially placed the United States on the gold standard and marked the political high-tide for sound money in the United States. But the legislation did not preclude the use of silver as money or "bimetallism" as and when international conditions and the "concurrence of leading commercial nations of the world" made a fixed ratio between the price of gold and silver practical.

Myers records that three members of the Indianapolis Monetary Commission who traveled to Europe early in 1901 found that none of their counterparts in Europe would "even discuss the matter seriously," referring to the use of silver as money. And the steady increase in the use and also the production of gold around the world seemed more than adequate to meet international needs. "The United States thus became a member in good standing of the international financial community," wrote Myers, something that would have been impossible under a bimetallic standard incorporating silver as advocated by Bryan and the silverites.[23]

The pressure exerted by other countries due to trends away from silver appears to have played a role in the U.S. position on silver. It is interesting to note, however, that the formal adoption of the gold standard did not help to prevent the Panic of 1901 nor avoid subsequent swings in public confidence in individual banks or in the currency that they issued. The United States was experiencing success regarding diplomacy and war, including the impending annexation of Cuba and the Philippines. Yet the U.S. financial markets remained fragile and prone to sudden crises, events that were often focused on the harvest time, when demands for liquidity strained banks large and small.

Even though the vast majority of Americans were aware of the nation's shortcomings when it came to the currency, the business community and the bankers were not yet willing to support change. Indeed, with the landslide victory over William Jennings Bryan by the Republicans in 1900, the business community loudly rejected Progressive reform. To the contrary, the Money Trusts believed that the way was clear for even more bold acts to expand their power and limit competition, particularly in industries such as steel and oil. However the members of the Grand Old Party, as Republicans became known during and after the Civil War, did not anticipate Theodore Roosevelt.

Chapter 4

The Rise of the Central Bank

P resident William McKinley was the sort of Republican that the business community could rely upon to support the consolidation of industries and the rise of the Money Trusts. Just a month before President McKinley began his second term in office, the U.S. Steel Corporation was formed under the laws of the State of New Jersey. The purpose of the U.S. Steel Corporation was to purchase the stock of numerous steel producers and thereby avoid competition among them. J.P. Morgan bought out Andrew Carnegie as the controlling interest in U.S. Steel. He put Charles M. Schwab, a Carnegie man, in the presidency, and Judge Elbert H. Gary, a Morgan man, in the chief executive chair of the first billion-dollar trust.

Steel prices were weak in 1900 and many of the producers, which were controlled by Andrew Carnegie or the House of Morgan, were preparing to expand the amount and range of steel production, a move that would have certainly caused steel prices to fall further. Instead, by forming U.S. Steel, Carnegie and Morgan were able to pool their far-flung investments in numerous different steel producers and limit competition, which had an immediate and positive impact on steel prices.[1] Charles Schwab told Clarence Barron that the merger of the Carnegie and Morgan steel interests came about after J.P. Morgan, at the suggestion of Schwab, called on Andrew Carnegie on the occasion of the latter's birthday. The two men soon reached an accord to combine their steel interests. When Schwab later left U.S. Steel and purchased Bethlehem Steel, Morgan bought him out and held the company as a personal investment, again to avoid competition.[2] Schwab's counterpart, Judge Gary, who served in the Civil War as an Illinois volunteer, would steer the giant U.S. Steel conglomerate through WWI right up through his death in 1927.

The formation of U.S. Steel was just one example of the way in which the trust operators manipulated prices and limited competition, and all with the blessings of the Republican Party's candidate in the White House and a majority in the Congress. McKinley's Vice President, Garret Hobart, typified the views of the Republican mainstream with respect to the Money Trusts when he said at the time of his election in 1896 that "corporations and aggregations of capital do not make it impossible for a poor man to climb up. The rich man of today is the poor man of to-morrow."[3] Unfortunately, the key operational strategy of the Money Trusts was to limit competition.

The death of Vice President Hobart at the end of McKinley's first term illustrates just how conservative was the government of the United States in 1900. In the first century of the nation's existence, the occupants of the White House had been selected from a small group of the country's founders and their children. In the second century, however, a succession of Republicans from the Northeast had dominated the political stage. Hobart was a New Jersey native and an able man. He frequently presided over the Senate due to the close balance between the parties in the upper chamber after the 1896 election. Like many Republican politicians of his day, Hobart was a man of business before all else. "I am a business man," Hobart was reported to have said. "I engage in politics for recreation."[4]

Hobart was a leading business owner in New Jersey who declined involvement in politics on several occasions. But when he finally was induced to enter public life, he did so with distinction. Hobart helped to negotiate the end of the Spanish-American War and his efforts ensured the acquisition of the Philippines. The former Vice President was immensely popular in his day and might well have run for the presidency had his life not been shortened by fate. Hobart is one of those very significant figures in U.S. history who has faded from our collective memory as the American narrative is distilled and refined over and over again. The Senate biography of Hobart recalling his role as President Pro Tempore paid him tribute and also notes that he died at the very end of his first term in 1900:

> The vice president's speech concluding the second session of the Fifty-fifth Congress was in fact his valedictory, for he would die before the next Congress convened. In addressing the senators for the last time, he noted that "the Senate of the United States is a peculiar body . . . made up, as you know of many elements, and in its membership you will find not only straight and stalwart Republicans, to whose active efforts the country is now looking for relief, but Bimetallists, Populists, Silverites—both Republican and Democratic—and a few gold Democrats."[5]

The election of 1900 was mostly about foreign affairs, particularly the war with Spain and the resulting territorial gains. Bryan again ran against McKinley, who had a kindly personal demeanor and in terms of policy had managed to please just about everyone in the country except for the silver evangelists. He chose as his new running mate Theodore Roosevelt, a former Governor of New York and war hero in the conflict with Spain. "Boss Tom Platt, needing a hero to draw attention away from scandals in New York State, accepted Roosevelt as the Republican candidate for Governor in 1898," notes the White House profile of Theodore Roosevelt. "Roosevelt won and served with distinction." In fact, Roosevelt was too high profile for the taste of Boss Platt, who volunteered the services of the former governor at the Navy Department and then to become Vice President under McKinley in order to get him out of New York.

The McKinley–Roosevelt ticket focused on the successful war against Spain and an improving economy, and won easily over Bryan, who had begun to talk less and less about silver and more about imperialism and the Money Trusts. Whatever talent he had for speaking,

Bryan was an unsuccessful national politician and really the perfect, ineffectual left wing foil for his Republican opponents. McKinley won a great victory in 1900 polling 51 percent of the vote, yet fate struck a year later when on September 6, 1901 he was shot at the Pan American Exhibition in Buffalo, New York. His assailant, Leon Czolgosz, an anarchist from Detroit, justified the killing because he felt McKinley had been in office too long.

Teddy Roosevelt was on a hiking trip in the Adirondacks with his family at the time of the shooting. He was sworn into office about a week later on September 14, 1901, at the Ansley Wilcox Mansion, Buffalo, New York. Roosevelt said at the time: "The course I followed, of regarding the Executive as subject only to the people, and, under the Constitution, bound to serve the people affirmatively in cases where the Constitution does not explicitly forbid him to render the service, was substantially the course followed by both Andrew Jackson and Abraham Lincoln."[6]

The Progressive: Theodore Roosevelt

Teddy Roosevelt was arguably one of the most radical and brilliant Americans to ever hold the highest office in the land. The child of a wealthy Eastern family and educated at Harvard, Roosevelt had all of the tools to be a great president. But he added to this a thorough commitment to democracy and reform that made him the giant of the progressive age. It was one thing for a progressive or a democrat to attack the Money Trusts or big business, but to have a libertarian republican, a Tammany Hall man and former New York governor, become the leader of the progressive movement was remarkable. Years later, J.P. Morgan would remark to Clarence Barron, owner of Dow, Jones & Co: "Who did more than Teddy Roosevelt to smash business?" Morgan also commented to Clarence Barron that public sentiment in America had been against business since the passage of the Sherman Antitrust Act in 1890.[7]

Some members of the left criticized Roosevelt as a lapdog of the big business Republican interests behind McKinley, but Roosevelt actually became more radical as time went on and was certainly more activist and outspoken than many of his Republican and Democratic predecessors. The bankers and political bosses of the age urged the young president to "go slow" and do nothing that might disturb "confidence," but Roosevelt ignored these pleas and eventually put himself at the head of the Progressive movement. Like all politicians, he understood that there was power in the roar of the crowd, a fact that made Roosevelt even more eager to rail at oppressive business practices. His natural tendency was not to be a Progressive, but his response to the popular clamor for social justice in the face of the extremes of wealth and power that had become visible in American society could be quite extreme. The rise of Roosevelt to become the champion of the individual in the age of large corporation dominance is one of those rare moments in modern American politics when the random factor of chance dramatically altered history in favor of the individual.

Despite his reputation as a reformer, Teddy Roosevelt was an often-contradictory figure. Early in his career he fought against Jay Gould's corrupt inroads into the finances of New York City when the elevated trains were being built in that city. Teddy Roosevelt frequently referred to Gould and other moneyed interests of the day in the most colorful terms, playing on the public's growing unease at the role of wealth in American society. Yet he was a personal friend and social peer of J.P. Morgan. Roosevelt never did anything that truly inconvenienced the large banks and corporations of that era—unless he believed them to be malevolent.

Like many politicians of his day, Roosevelt played on the popular suspicion of concentrations of economic power, but he was not against big business or even the trusts themselves. Like many Republicans too, he saw the formation of big business as the natural evolution of a growing economy and a necessary step for America to compete in the world. This belief in policies to support American business also extended to trade. Roosevelt was a strong supporter of tariffs and other trade barriers to protect American industries and jobs from the predatory trade practices of the mercantilist states of Europe. Roosevelt was not in favor of isolationism but rather in a form of selective isolation of America from the evils of the rest of the world.

The major difference between Roosevelt and conservative Republicans such as McKinley was his support for the Progressive approach of balancing big business with an equally muscular government in order to meet the popular anxiety regarding power. As did many Americans of his day, Roosevelt was affronted by the belief on the part of the great industrialists of the age that their power was greater than that of the federal government. As a gifted and often inspired politician, Roosevelt also responded to the widely held fear on the part of many Americans that their stake in the collective patrimony, the "American dream" was being stolen. "The ominous sense of a shrinking margin of practical liberties pervaded men," wrote Matthew Josephson in *The Robber Barons*, "as each successive step in the nation wide consolidation of the country's resources and means of production brought no tangible gains to the population at large."[8]

President Roosevelt did not make money or currency issues a central part of his administration. Yet he did have a significant impact on capital finance for all manner of corporations by starting to address issues of competition and restraint of trade inside the United States. Roosevelt was not against the idea of large companies due to their size, but he was intolerant of companies that restricted trade or used their size to limit personal freedom, "kinder masters" in the socially charged language of the Progressive era. Roosevelt believed not only in legalistic control and break-up of wayward companies, but also in the use of publicity and disclosure to modify the behavior of the speculators and trusts who operated free of limit in the marketplace of the early 1900s. Using the Sherman Antitrust Act and the Hepburn Act, Roosevelt was able to strengthen the enforcement powers of the Interstate Commerce Commission and attack some of the most powerful trusts of the day.

The first anti-trust case was brought just five months after he took office, in February 1902. It was against Northern Securities Company, a trust that held the railroad interests of J.P. Morgan in the Northern Pacific and James Hill in the Great Northern railroads. Northern Securities was buying up the stock of other railroads in competition with E.H. Harriman, the great railroad baron and banker who was second only to J.P. Morgan himself in terms of influence during the era of the Money Trusts. Roosevelt sought to dissolve the Northern Securities Company and eventually won the case by a five-to-four margin before the Supreme Court. President Roosevelt would bring 45 other suits against other trusts under the Sherman Act.[9]

The attack on the Northern Securities Company, however, while politically a very astute move by Theodore Roosevelt, was little more than a nuisance for the House of Morgan.

Other antitrust and restraint of trade cases were brought against trusts set up for a variety of purposes, but all of the trusts targeted by Roosevelt were designed to control trade and thereby limit prices. The irony, however, is that despite the rhetoric, the Roosevelt era saw the continued growth of the trusts overall. Eschewing confrontation, Roosevelt preferred to persuade company management to effect changes rather than use the blunt club of litigation under the Sherman Act to enforce remedies to anti-competitive measures. Sometimes Roosevelt was also overtly friendly to big business, as in the case of the acquisition in 1907 of the Tennessee Iron & Coal Company by U.S. Steel, one of the key Rockefeller Trust Holdings.

The discretion of the White House in deciding whether to sue or not to stop anti-competitive behavior was illustrated by the way Roosevelt pursued selectively his campaign against the Money Trusts. Clarence Barron records a conversation with Judge Gary, the great Chairman of U.S. Steel Corporation, where the latter travelled to Washington, along with the steel magnate Henry Frick, to meet with Teddy Roosevelt. The purpose of the trip was to gain permission for the merger between Tennessee Iron & Coal and U.S. Steel, which had been announced before the 1900 election and the subsequent death of President McKinley. Gary relates that Roosevelt told the delegation led by Judge Gary which represented J.P. Morgan that "while he was President we would not be troubled."[10]

The Tennessee Iron & Coal case was perhaps the most prominent transaction by a trust during the Roosevelt era and, in fact, became so contentious politically that Democrats and Republicans in the Congress demanded an inquiry. The call for hearings embarrassed President Roosevelt, and he was forced to endure an investigation into the decision to allow the merger to go through.[11]

While most Americans and centrist Progressives loved and supported Roosevelt, on the left he was seen as another Republican President and a tool of business interests, albeit one with a taste for imperial expansion. Teddy was, after all, a child of wealth. His Progressive tendencies did seemingly have limits. His support for the territorial expansion of

the United States through the conquest of Cuba and the annexation
of the Philippines, which entailed a six-month war, evidenced an
unconstrained vision that seemed more consistent with an authoritarian world view than a libertarian philosophy. Yet neither Andrew
Jackson nor Abraham Lincoln, Roosevelt's heroes among the American
presidents, were unfriendly to the use of military force when it came
to achieving political objectives.

In the United States a new age of imperialism was dawning under
Teddy Roosevelt, even as an increasingly unsettled American nation
drifted to the political left. But given the possible alternatives presented
by the growing Progressive leanings of American voters, Roosevelt
was a relatively moderate choice. In 1904 when President Roosevelt
ran for reelection, some of the most prominent Robber Barons were
among the largest contributors to his campaign—banker Morgan,
steel and coal magnate Henry Frick, banker James Stillman of National
City Bank, financier George J. Gould, the son of Jay Gould, and H.H.
Rogers, director of Standard Oil, to name but a few.

Despite his strong public advocacy of reform, Roosevelt at the end
of the day was less of a threat to the industrialists and bankers than
might have been feared. The Reverend W.S. Rainsford, minister of St.
George's Church, the spiritual haven where J.P. Morgan sought spiritual
solace, is reported to have said: "The time will come when you will get
down on your knees and bless Providence for having given us Theodore
Roosevelt as our President." When Roosevelt spoke at a dinner at the
Gridiron Club in Washington where Morgan was in attendance, the
President at one point strode toward the banker and, shaking his fist in
the face of the financial colossus, shouted theatrically: "If you don't let
us do this," referring to reform, "those who will come after us will rise
and bring you to ruin." But unlike many other bankers and industrial
captains, Morgan was never persuaded by Roosevelt's protestations.[12]

The early years of Roosevelt's presidency were relatively idyllic
years for Americans, especially compared to events transpiring across
the Atlantic Ocean. The expansion of the supply of gold was greatly
aided by enhanced production in Australia and Alaska. The adoption of
the cyanide process for refining the yellow metal helped the U.S. economy rebound on an expanding monetary base. In the United States,
the period after the Crisis of 1897 was relatively calm and would continue through to the 1907 Panic. But the same could not be said for

Europe, where political and financial crises were nearing the boiling point. In 1901, Rosa Luxemburg published her essay "The Socialist Crisis in France," inspired by the massacre of striking workers on the island of Martinique and the political rot that was destroying France's Third Republic. Europe again was on the road to war.

In the United States, by contrast, a new empire was being born under "the big stick" of Teddy Roosevelt and just in time to take up the colonial standard from faltering imperialist nations such as France and Great Britain. In 1900, the United States forced independent Cuba to give up Guantanamo for the purpose of a naval base. Cuba also was forced to accept the right of the United States to *intervene* in the country's internal affairs, a striking achievement that most Americans supported as their "manifest destiny." But not everyone thought that the annexation of other countries outside the continental United States was a positive development. Under Roosevelt, "the land of the free and home of the brave had become the land of the imperialist bully," wrote labor activist Ralph Faris, "the home of the Wall Street vampire, the land which helped to guarantee underdevelopment and dictatorship in the developing countries."[13]

In addition to political challenges at home and abroad, the young president also had to contend with a financial crisis. In May of 1901, the U.S. stock market suffered a significant decline, but was unlike the panics of 1893 and 1873. In the earlier crises, the use of foreign debt to fuel speculative excess made the overall situation far worse. The crisis in 1901, by comparison, was limited to the stock markets in New York and those firms and investors that could absorb the losses without failing. The fact remained, however, that the U.S. economy was hamstrung by a currency system that was perceived to be inflexible and did seemed prone to swings in the liquidity available based on changes in the public mood, both in the United States and around the world.

The Civil War era practice of issuing currency through the national banks still did not address the dominance of the largest New York banks in the American financial system and the perennial shortage of currency in the Western states. Even though prominent banking institutions such as Bank of America would be established in San Francisco in 1904, the banks in New York and the East generally remained dominant. Bank of America would eventually be acquired by NCNB and its headquarters moved to Charlotte, North Carolina, leaving the

City of San Francisco today with few local banks and financial services companies of any significant size. It is interesting to wonder what
Roosevelt would think about the highly concentrated banking system
of today, with more than half of the assets of the U.S. banking industry
controlled by half a dozen large names—most of those located in the
Eastern United States and concentrated in New York.

While Roosevelt was aggressive when it came to attacking the
Money Trusts and monopoly power, he was far more circumspect
when it came to tariffs and currency reform. Roosevelt stood with the
Old Guard of the Republican Party and ignored Progressive calls for
lower tariffs and currency reform through the Panic of 1901 and the
far larger financial Crisis of 1907. So powerful was the political influence of large business over the Congress that even with Roosevelt's
popularity he might not have been able to make headway regarding
tariffs or currency reform.

By the end of Roosevelt's second term in office, however, a
national consensus had formed regarding the need for lower tariffs and
other reforms. Yet the great Republican leaders of the Senate—Orville
Platt, John Spooner, William Allison, and Nelson Aldrich—kept the
pace of reform at slow to none. Their control over the Senate and thus
national policy was an important practical check on Roosevelt's actions,
particularly regarding domestic economic and fiscal policy. Robert
Byrd put the political situation facing Roosevelt into perspective:

> How much of Roosevelt's reform program shaped by his deal-
> ings and compromises with the conservative leaders of the
> Senate; how far was he willing to go; and how soon was he
> willing to retreat on an issue. Roosevelt saw himself as a man
> of the political center, fending off, on one side, the plutocrats
> who controlled the great wealth and power of American indus-
> try and, on the other side, the masses with their radical and
> destabilizing demands . . . We think of Roosevelt as a reform
> president, but he was really a consensus president, cautiously
> waiting to act until he had public opinion and support in his
> corner, willing to accept half a loaf rather than none. When
> Roosevelt and his program are seen in this light, we can more
> readily perceive the influence that Congress—particularly

the struggle between conservative and progressive forces in Congress—had on his programs.[14]

Both Theodore Roosevelt's achievements and long-term legacy among American presidents seem to confirm Byrd's assessment. Roosevelt wrote in his autobiography:

> Nobody can tell, and least of all the machine itself, whether the machine intends to renominate me next fall or not . . . The big corporations undoubtedly want to beat me. They prefer the chance of being blackmailed to the certainty that they will not be allowed any more than their due. Of course they will try to beat me on some entirely different issue, and, as they are very able and very unscrupulous, nobody can tell they won't succeed . . . I have been trying to stay with the organization. I did not do it with the idea that they would renominate me. I did it with the idea of getting things done, and in that I have been absolutely successful. Whether Senator Platt or Mr. Odell endeavor to beat me, or do beat me, for renomination this fall, is of very small importance compared to the fact that for my two years I have been able to make a Republican majority in the Legislature do good and decent work and have prevented any split within the party. The task was one of great difficulty, because on the one hand, I had to keep clear before me the fact that it was better to have a split than to permit bad work to be done, and, on the other hand, the fact that to have a split would absolutely prevent all good work. The result has been that I have avoided a split and that as a net result of my two years and the two sessions of the Legislature, there has been an enormous improvement in the administration of Government, and there has also been a great advance in legislation.[15]

A Flexible Currency

The uncertain political dynamic of the time, coupled with the power of the Senate chieftains and the great political bosses who were aligned with the status quo of high tariffs and an arcane currency system, may explain why Roosevelt did not focus more attention on the question of monetary reform. The question of the "inflexibility" of the banking system was very much in the public mind and the country remained highly vulnerable to changes in sentiment in foreign capitals, but the Republican program of fiscal sobriety, high tariffs, and trade protectionism still managed to poll a majority in the Congress and win the White House. This did not mean, however, that President Roosevelt failed to address the question of money and the national currency.

In 1903 in Quincy, Illinois, Teddy Roosevelt said:

> It is well-nigh universally admitted, certainly in any business community such as this, that our currency system is wanting in elasticity; that is, the volume does not respond to the varying needs of the country as a whole, nor of the varying needs of the different localities and the different times. Our people scarcely need to be reminded that grain-raising communities require a larger volume of currency at harvest time than in the summer months; and the same principle in greater or less extent applies to every community. Our currency laws need such modification as will ensure definitely the parity of every dollar coined or issued by the government, and such expansion and contraction of the currency as will promptly and automatically respond to the varying needs of commerce. Permanent increase would be dangerous, permanent contraction ruinous, but the needed elasticity must be brought about by provisions which will permit the contraction and expansion as the varying needs of the several communities and business interests at different times and in different localities require.[16]

The comments by President Roosevelt on the monetary system reflected the basic view of Americans of his day, namely avoiding "dangerous" permanent increases or "ruinous" decreases in the supply of money—specifically the means of exchange, yet providing supply of currency to be "flexible." Roosevelt called it "elastic." While there remained among Americans a very powerful constituency for a stable inflation rate and a relatively slow growing trend in the amount of currency available, the fact remains that for the public the "flexibility" of the money supply was a visceral political issue. In 1907, call money rates for credit had fluctuated from 2 to 30 percent, driven by demand from the major New York banks, which in turn "attracted money from the interior banks into that speculative field."[17] Many of the purchases of stocks in this period were financed with credit; thus fluctuations in interest rates due to factors such as the seasonal harvest or changes in the perceived credit standing of the United States could have a significant impact on domestic financial markets. The fact that money is "fungible" and moves for value in terms of investment opportunities also meant that credit the Treasury put into the markets with the intention of helping the farm sector, for example, could just as easily end up deployed in the New York financial markets.

In his message to the Congress in December 1907, Roosevelt noted that the currency in circulation had increased more than 50 percent over a period of 10 years, from $21 to $33 per capita, yet the increased demand for currency visible to all in the fall of each year, and the resulting financial disturbances throughout the economy, showed that the nation still needed basic currency and banking reform. The image of people standing in long lines outside of banks waiting to withdraw their money had become an icon of the American economic experience. The fact of unsafe and unsound conditions in many American banks and the fragility of the system as a whole, as much as the economic definition of money or its uses, would eventually force the Congress to act. It is hard for a politician to sell citizens on the American dream of opportunity and hard work when they cannot depend on the money or the banks that issue it.

In the age of Hamilton, the political class in Washington wanted to force the use of a national currency and thereby bind the people of the various states to the new country. This was the functional equivalent of the Spanish conquistador Hernan Cortes burning his ships and bidding his men to follow him into the jungle of Mexico several centuries earlier. But in the intervening century, from the nation's founding to the return to the gold standard after the Civil War, the dysfunction of the American financial system became a national political as well as economic issue. Many of the motivations and flows within the political dialog over the nature of money still welled up from local and particular regional influences. Yet the U.S. monetary system was an unresolved national question in large measure because the nation remained so dependent upon foreign capital flows. More, the ebb and flow of financial markets was slowly becoming a daily political referendum on the job done by Washington regarding the economy in general, an influence that would be made acute with the invention of radio, television, and eventually the internet over the next century.

The public's concern regarding the adequacy of the money supply in the first decade of the twentieth century is all the more ironic since it was growing at a pretty brisk pace compared with the nation's population, which was at about 76 million at the turn of the century and reached 97 million by 1913. This increase represented between 1.5 and 2 percent growth annually. The increase in money growth can be attributed to the government's reaction to the demand for currency, but this growth came within the context of a government that was loath to use debt or raise taxes for federal spending. Federal revenues and debt were remarkably stable during this period, the former being comprised mostly of the proceeds from tariffs.

Between the end of silver purchases by the Treasury in 1897 and the start of WWI in 1914, the money supply of the United States grew at a reasonably steady rate, begging the question as to whether the supply of money in the U.S. financial system or the ebb and flow of a growing, free market society was the more important factor, which drove the nation into successive financial crises. Indeed, the growth in the supply of gold coins and greenbacks was in excess of 100 percent over the 15 years leading up to the first great world war, yet the United States would see years of instability in the banking sector leading up to the Crisis of 1907.[18]

It appears that the Progressives may have been right; namely that it was where the money was held, not the aggregate amount or supply of currency in circulation, that mattered most to consumers and business. The banks in the South and West did not have the same deep commercial and public sector relationships from which to draw their liquidity, not to mention a close relationship with the U.S. Treasury. The major banks in New York were the customs agents for the United States and held much of the government's cash balances. All of the larger banks in Boston and New York had a natural advantage in good times and bad. But when bad times came, banks east of the Mississippi River and, even better, east of the Hudson tended to have superior chances of survival. It did not matter whether one believed in silver as a form of money or not, the experience of Americans when it came to dealing with money and banks was a source of anxiety.

The flaw in the U.S. banking and currency system, according to Milton Friedman and Anna Schwartz, was the fact that bank deposits were effectively treated as money. A visualization of this issue is again provided by Frank Capra's film, *It's a Wonderful Life*. When liquidity needs in the system taxed banks to maintain liquidity, the public quickly began to get the scent of trouble in the air—thus the crowd of panicked customers besieging George Bailey's Building and Loan for cash. The increased demand for cash would quickly exhaust the reserves of the banks of the 1890s, which had only their shareholders and correspondent banks upon which to depend for liquidity. This is why in the period before the Great Depression, the shareholders of banks often were required to be prepared to inject capital into a bank equal to their investment, effectively double-liability shares. Even today, many markets and nations impose tough standards on bank directors to put their own wealth at risk should the bank encounter problems. The names at Lloyds of London or the clearing members of multilateral exchanges are still at risk for their full capital to support these markets.

"The contemporary and still standard interpretation of this episode is that an apparently rather mild contraction was converted into a severe contraction by the banking panic and associated restrictions of payments by the banking system," write Friedman and Schwartz. "It was this interpretation of the episode that provided the prime impetus for the monetary reform movement that culminated in the Federal Reserve Act."[19]

The Crisis of 1907

One of the key events that drove the mounting public demand for monetary reform was the Crisis of 1907, an event that was a century in the making but was also the result of a growing economy that had far outgrown its financial system. Unlike previous panics, the troubles started in March, not during the autumn farm harvest season, and would last the entire year and beyond. The New York Stock Exchange went into a drastic decline, leading to public panic and depositor runs on banks. These bank runs, in turn, led to large-scale liquidations of "call loans," short-term loans used to finance stock market purchases, causing further declines in stock prices and widespread insolvency for businesses and individuals. Because the reaction to crisis by banks and the entire financial system was to limit the availability of deposits when a liquidity run occurred, the flow of payments through the U.S. economy slowed, causing personal and commercial insolvencies to soar. By November of 1907, the New York stock market averages were almost 40 percent below the levels seen before the crisis began.

A number of historians and commentators of this period believe that J.P. Morgan and the other members of the Money Trust actually precipitated the Panic of 1907 in order to depress stock and bond prices for certain companies they coveted. Morgan disliked the public stock market. He was even less sanguine about the individual speculators in these markets and the smaller trusts that had proliferated by the hundreds and employed bank loans to fund purchases of stocks and bonds. Conveniently enough, the crisis forced the heavily indebted Tennessee Iron & Coal company, a competitor of the great Pennsylvania Steel Trust controlled by the Morgan and Rockefeller groups, to sell itself to Morgan for $30 million, less than 5 percent of its actual worth.[20]

In the fictional work *The Money Changers*, published in 1908 by Upton Sinclair, "a plutocrat very much resembling Morgan provoked a financial panic and turned the people's misery to his own sordid gain," wrote James Grant in *Money on the Mind*.[21] It should also be that the government of President Roosevelt did not attempt to block the purchase of Tennessee Iron & Coal by U.S. Steel even though it was clearly a violation of the Sherman Antitrust Act. Whether or not J.P. Morgan deliberately caused the Panic of 1907 and then arrived as the savior of the nation to counter its terrible effects, many people believed that version of events.

One of the key events in the Crisis of 1907 was when depositors began to "run" on the Knickerbocker Trust Company in New York. During the Roosevelt years, trust companies had proliferated, in part because U.S. national and state banks generally were not allowed to do a trust business. The trusts of the Gilded Age were near-banks, but were not members of the New York Clearing House and did not have the ability to borrow directly from other banks as peers. Trusts historically handled estates and trusts in a fiduciary capacity, thus the client assets did not appear on the balance sheet of the bank.

Soon, however, financial trusts became investment vehicles for the public. Trusts were put forward to the public as banks, but these entities more often than not were just lightly capitalized, speculative vehicles for issuing debt and investing in stocks or commodities. In modern terms, the trusts were more akin to institutional customers of large banks, like a broker-dealer, or hedge fund that clears and finances its business through a large bank. The previous discussion of the railroad trusts were but one example of the hundreds of industrial trusts from sugar to commodes which were formed in order to gain partial or total pricing power over a given market. The legacy of Fisk, Gould, and the other Robber Barons it seems was not that of hard work but rather the pursuit of financial corners.

As with the administration of Grover Cleveland during the Panic of 1897, in the Crisis of 1907, once again there was no agency in Washington to act when calamity affected the markets. And once again, the colossus, J.P. Morgan, was called upon to save the nation. When the emergency began, Morgan was 70 years old. He would retire after this effort. The Knickerbocker Trust was only rescued after many other trusts had failed. Morgan and James Stillman of First National City Bank, acting as a *de facto* "central bank" and specifically as a lender of last resort, ensured that the bank was able to meet its obligations. Chartered in 1884 by Frederick G. Eldridge, a friend and classmate of financier Morgan, the Knickerbocker Trust came to be one of the largest trust banks of its day.

The Panic of 1907, which began with a selloff in the stock market, eventually caused a fatal deposit run on the banks. This run was not unlike the run on institutional sources of funding that would destroy Bear, Stearns & Co. and Lehman Brothers a century later. Terrence Checki, executive vice president of the Federal Reserve Bank of New York, observed about the 2008 financial crisis in a December 2009 speech: "Our system evolved from one funded by intermediaries, to one largely financed by markets. The traditional ties between borrower and creditor were weakened as credit risk became just another commodity to be traded and distributed."[22] And this was precisely the same situation that existed in March of 1907, albeit on a far smaller scale.

More important than the mere issue of market risk, the failure of
Knickerbocker and other banks featured the role of J.P. Morgan as the
de facto central bank and receiver of failed banks. President Roosevelt
effectively made Morgan the agent of the U.S. Treasury and provided
$25 million in government funds deposited in the New York banks
to visibly address the panic. Morgan, acting in the same type of role
played today by the Federal Deposit Insurance Corporation, returned
to New York and assembled a team of financiers to address the crisis. The group included John Rockefeller, James Stillman of National
City Bank, George F. Baker of First National Bank, Edward Harriman
the railroad titan, and an assortment of other bankers and lawyers. As
head of the largest bank in the country and the operational head of
the New York Clearing House, Morgan was omnipotent and decided
which banks were to fail and which would survive.

By putting a great deal of cash on the street, in some cases literally piled up in teller cages to make the point to the public that money
was plentiful, Morgan organized a rescue of banks and trusts, avert-
ing a shutdown of the New York Stock Exchange, and thereby engineered a financial bailout of New York City. First Morgan orchestrated
an orderly closure of Knickerbocker Trust in October 1907 and then
extended loans to Trust Company of America to prevent another large
bank collapse, perhaps one of the earliest examples of the moral dilemma
of "systemic risk." In a stark example of the reality of collective interest
when it comes to matters of finance, Morgan bailed out the larger insolvent trust companies that he loathed and despised in order to keep the
entire financial system from crumbling.[23]

Only days after rescuing the trust banks, the head of the New York
Stock Exchange went to Morgan and told him that the market could
not remain open. Morgan appreciated that the failure of the exchange
would be a catastrophic blow to public confidence, the banks, and
Washington equally. He organized a bailout by members of the New
York Clearing House to support the exchange, again in a very visible
and direct way so as to maximize the positive impact on public perception. At the end of that terrible week in October 1907, Morgan
and civic leaders, including members of the clergy, exhorted the public
to keep their money in the bank. Yet there were still lines of people

standing outside banks on the rainy Monday that followed, waiting to withdraw their cash.

The Crisis of 1907 illustrated the fact that the government was powerless to address the very real problems with the national system of currency and banks, even with the aggressive but limited actions taken by the U.S. Treasury to supply cash to the banking system. The dislike among Americans for a strong central government and especially a central bank was too resilient. Thus through inaction the Congress left the financial sector of the U.S. economy in chaos. The author John Steele Gordon summarizes the situation:

> We paid a heavy price for the Jeffersonian aversion to central banking. Without a central bank there was no way to inject liquidity into the banking system to stem a panic. As a result, the panics of the 19th century were far worse here than in Europe and precipitated longer and deeper depressions. In 1907, J.P. Morgan, probably the most powerful private banker who ever lived, acted as the central bank to end the panic that year.[24]

Between 1907 and 1917, eight states adopted insurance schemes for bank deposits, but such moves did not address the more basic public unease with private banks. The Panic of 1907 was one of the sharpest economic contractions in U.S. history. The crisis finally would prompt the national Congress to start to take action and eventually lead to the enactment of the Federal Reserve Act in 1913. Yet the path to the creation of the central bank was hardly smooth, with the financial system visibly straining under the weight of a growing nation and continuing price deflation in the farm sector, except during the Great War.

The National Monetary Commission

In a precursor to the Federal Reserve Act, the Congress enacted the Aldrich–Vreeland Act of 1908. The law was an immediate response to the horrible social and economic effects of the Panic of 1907 and provided for emergency currency issues during economic crises. At the request of President Theodore Roosevelt, the legislation also established the National Monetary Commission to propose a banking reform plan. Chaired by Senator Nelson W. Aldrich (R–RI), the Commission examined both the financial and political issues that caused the various crises of the previous decades—but from a decidedly Republican, big city bank perspective.

Under the leadership of Aldrich, the commission developed a plan that was largely favorable to the Northeastern banks, but William Jennings Bryan and Progressives in all three parties fiercely counterattacked the proposal. Bryan and other Progressives wanted a central bank under public, not private banker, control—echoing a debate that continues to this day. Aldrich's leadership meant that the Progressives' hopes would be dashed. He was the leading critic of the Progressive movement and a stalwart champion of American conservatism. The fact that Aldrich's daughter was married to John D. Rockefeller, Jr. convinced Progressives and many Americans that Aldrich was the friend of the rich and powerful. Lincoln Steffens and other muckraking writers of the day referred to Senator Aldrich as "the boss of the United States" and "the power behind the power behind the throne," and for good reason. He was one of the most visible and unapologetic advocates of the prerogatives of big business in modern American history.[25]

The disappointment of the Progressives in the period leading to the creation of the Fed was so fierce that it lingers even today. The Progressive complaints of a century ago echo in the issues raised by the Fed's bailout of Wall Street starting in 2008, most notably with the rescue of Bear, Stearns & Co. and American International Group, but including all of the largest banks. No surprise then that the support from the banking industry for currency "reform" in the 1900s was focused on the needs of bankers, not farmers. The Republicans were smart enough to pay lip service to the needs of the agrarians, but the agenda was already set by the politicians allied with the interests of Morgan and Rockefeller.

Laurence Laughlin of the University of Chicago, the author of the earlier Indianapolis Commission report on the U.S. financial system that was produced in 1896, was again pressed into service by the banks, this time as the advocate of "banking reform." Laughlin was a friend of Woodrow Wilson and the obvious champion for the effort—at least from the perspective of the banking industry. Early in 1913, before Wilson's inauguration, he began to draft a banking reform bill that was derived from the work of Senator Aldrich and the National Monetary Commission.

Laughlin helped to marshal business people and bankers to testify before Congress and persistently disputed the idea of the existence of a "Money Trust," a convenient argument for the House of Morgan and other large banks and industrial groups. Then there were groups such as the National Citizens League, organized by Laughlin and funded by some of the largest banks, to provide public support for reform legislation. One of the proposals at that time was to impose limits on the ability of banks to use deposits to finance securities underwriting and speculation, especially the formation of trusts and other types of syndicates that borrowed money from banks "to keep afloat mere stock selling enterprises until the stock is bought by the general public itself," said Laughlin. This story illustrates that in the early part of the 1900s the proponents of the business interests of banks could also still be effective critics of speculation and financial dissipation, unlike the situation on Wall Street today.[26]

The blue-ribbon report produced by the National Monetary Commission recommended new legislation that proposed a National Reserve Association that would issue legal tender notes as required by the financial system. These notes would be backed by a reserve in gold or legal reserve currencies equal to 50 percent of the notes issued. The National Reserve Association essentially would have been a collective owned and controlled by the banks themselves and not subject to direct governmental control. This aspect of private banker control over the new central bank was strongly opposed by the Progressives. While the proposal from the National Monetary Commission offered the promise that the new central bank would provide additional finance to farmers, in fact the Federal Reserve Act eventually drafted by Laughlin *et al.* did not deliver on any of the Progressive demands, including the availability of farm credit. None of the National Monetary Commission's proposals ever made it to the floor of the Congress. With the facts gathered and shaped by the National Monetary Commission, and the more important drafting work of Laughlin done in cooperation with the White House, the stage was set for the emergence of a decentralized central bank under at least the nominal control of Washington but in fact controlled by the largest banks in New York City.

Paul M. Warburg recalled in his book, *The Federal Reserve System: Its Origin and Growth*, that in 1910 most Americans were in favor of a central bank, but only if "not controlled by 'Wall Street' or any other monopolistic interest."[27] The concerns of the turn of the twentieth century echo the concerns of 2010 regarding the tendency of the politically powerful large banks to undermine the independence of a central bank of issue and even the Congress itself. Just as today, in the 1900s members of Congress jumped through virtual hoops of fire like trained dogs at the command of J.P. Morgan and the captains of the other large banks. Then as today, there was no question as to who was boss in Washington regardless of which party controlled the White House or the Congress—it was the executives of the biggest banks. And then as now, most Americans were not expert in finance, but they understood that the financial power of the New York banks threatened both the value of money and the political independence of the national government.

The investigation by the Pujo Committee in 1912 in the run-up to the election also focused attention on the power of the large banks, in this case through the underwriting of corporate bonds, but the proceedings were less than revealing thanks to adroit machinations by the large banks. The FRASER database maintained by the St. Louis Federal Reserve Bank reveals:

> In 1912, a special subcommittee was convened by the Chairman of the House Banking and Currency Committee, Arsene P. Pujo (D-LA). Its purpose was to investigate the "money trust," a small group of Wall Street bankers that exerted powerful control over the nation's finances. The committee's majority report concluded that a group of financial leaders had abused the public trust to consolidate control over many industries. The Pujo Committee report created a climate of public opinion that lead to the passage of the Federal Reserve Act of 1913 and the Clayton Antitrust Act of 1914.[28]

The political context of the Pujo investigation is important to understanding the final form and adoption of the Federal Reserve Act, both with respect to the accepted history and the detail behind it. The

Louisiana Democrat Pujo was actually a supporter of the Republican-sponsored Aldrich plan for financial reform. He attempted to push the plan through the Congress in 1912, but was opposed by Carter Glass and other Democrats, who wanted to wait for Woodrow Wilson's inauguration in March of 1913. Glass also wanted to limit the scope of the legislation to currency reform only, while the Louisiana Democrat had a broader agenda. Pujo did not seek reelection in 1912 and thus cleared the way for Glass to become Chairman of the House Committee on Banking and Currency, a key political inflection point that arguably ensured the Fed's eventual creation—albeit in a different form. Glass, for his part, opposed the work of Senator Aldrich and instead proposed a more decentralized plan for the central bank. Significantly Glass did not introduce a bill himself but instead waited for President Wilson to transmit his legislation to the Congress in June 1913.

The Pujo Committee report published earlier in that year detailed the collusive practices among banks and the ownership ties via trusts that connected many banks to one another. Interlocking boards of directors and secret share ownership essentially tied many of the largest banks together under the control of a single "Money Trust." Under pressure from the committee, in January of 1913 the great Robber Baron George F. Baker was forced to sell his stake in the Chase National Bank, breaking one of the key ties that comprised the Money Trust that the Pujo Committee investigated. Chairman Pujo and members of the Committee, as they were about to interrogate Baker and his colleagues under oath regarding their hidden control over several banks, declared the share sale by Baker as "a great victory."[29]

Yet despite the public hearings and reformist rhetoric, the Pujo Committee ended its work and did not really do more than inconvenience the leaders of the largest banks. After the inauguration of President Wilson, several influential members of Congress attempted to re-open the investigation of the Pujo Committee into the "Money Trust" and the concentration of power vested in the New York banks. Reps. Robert Henry Lee of Texas, the Democratic Chairman of the House Rules Committee, and Charles A. Lindbergh of Minnesota, wanted to resume the Pujo hearings in May of 1913. Lindbergh was elected as a Republican, but almost immediately began to caucus with the members of the Progressive Party in the Congress. Seen from this perspective,

Carter Glass and other members of the Congressional Democratic leadership in 1913 were the moderates in the equation, protecting the large New York banks from attacks by the Progressive, pro-reform elements in the Congress and around the nation.[30]

Given the fierce public debate regarding banking and currency reform, it was remarkable that following the election of Woodrow Wilson in 1913, the Congress actually passed three key pieces of legislation: the Underwood Tariff, the Federal Trade Act, and the Federal Reserve Act. Of all three pieces of legislation, however, the central bank was at the top of the agenda because of the clear need for banking and currency reorganization—especially from the perspective of a growing number of bankers. Most Americans agreed that change was needed, but still there was far from any agreement on the nature of the change that should occur. Bankers and business interests were generally opposed to the legislation proposed by Wilson and sponsored by Democrats like Carter Glass of Virginia. They envisioned a decentralized system of Federal Reserve Banks under government control to provide liquidity to the banking system and serve as the banks of issue for currency.

Southern agrarians and small business interests in the Democratic Party such as Representatives Lindbergh and Lee, however, wanted more radical change. They feared a central bank controlled by the New York banks and the political interests behind them, interests which had controlled the Congress for decades. Ultimately, Chairman Glass, Senator Robert Owen of Oklahoma, and Treasury Secretary McAdoo prepared draft legislation for President Wilson to submit to the Congress that seemed to address the issue of banker control, but only superficially. And ultimately the result feared by the Progressives of private bank control over the central bank was precisely what occurred.

During the work of the National Monetary Commission, the banking industry had met with key members of the Aldrich group to consider the issue of a central bank. In 1910, Paul Warburg and a small group representing the chiefs of the largest banks and corporations in the United States travelled by rail to Jekyll Island, Georgia, to discuss privately the proposal for creating some type of central bank. The Jekyll Island meeting was kept secret because any public hint that Aldrich was consulting the large banks would have doomed his efforts and also would have badly damaged Wilson's own political interests.

Murray Newton Rothbard described the scene in his classic book, *The Case Against the Fed*:

> The conferees worked for a solid week at the plush Jekyll Island retreat, and hammered out the draft of the bill for the Federal Reserve System. Only six people attended this super-secret week-long meeting, and these six reflected the power structure within the bankers' alliance within the central banking movement. The conferees were, in addition to Aldrich (Rockefeller kinsman): Henry P. Davidson, Morgan Partner; Paul Warburg, Kuhn Loeb partner; Frank A. Vanderlip, vice-president of Rockefeller's National City Bank of New York; Charles D. Norton, president of Morgan's First National Bank of New York; and Professor A. Piatt Andrew, head of the NMC staff, who had recently been made an Assistant Secretary of the Treasury under Taft, and who was a technician with a foot in both the Rockefeller and Morgan camps.[31]

But of course the conceptual framework for the central bank already was in place long before the Jekyll Island meeting. The architect of that design, Lawrence Laughlin, became the most visible and credible national advocate of the Federal Reserve proposal. Laughlin testified before the Congress and made statements in favor of the proposal put forward by the National Monetary Commission. His brainchild not only centralized and rationalized the nation's currency system, but Laughlin's creation had the additional benefit of removing the machinations of the private bankers from public view. The Fed would come to shield the banking industry from scrutiny by the public and Congress.

The chosen candidate of the large banks, Woodrow Wilson, who was elected two years later and was considered the leading light of the now centrist Progressive movement, made monetary reform one of his top priorities. The public issue was whether it was even possible to create a central bank that would not fall under the influence and control of the large New York Banks. Just as the negotiations in the early days of the republic over the location of the capital eventually led to the creation of Washington DC, the construction of the Fed also stimulated these same points of debate between the commercial interests in

New York and the other parts of the country. The practical obstacle to moving forward with monetary reform was how to clothe the process in sufficiently populist attire to generate support in the Congress.

The Passage of the Federal Reserve Act

Following his inauguration in March of 1913, Wilson's administration worked through the summer of that year to win passage of what would become the Federal Reserve Act. Each time they reached agreement with either the banks or the Progressive agrarian interests, the other side would bolt, seeking even more concessions in a grand example of Washington political theater. The proposal sponsored by Rep. Carter Glass and Senator Owen, the Progressive Democrat from Oklahoma, contained a regional system of 12 banks and was the only legislation that has a reasonable chance of passage through Congress.

Of note, during the debate Senator Owen pushed for the creation of a banking committee in the Senate and used the occasion of the consideration of the Federal Reserve Act to win approval. Until that time, all banking measures in the Senate were referred to the Senate Finance Committee. Because his first year in the Senate was during the Panic of 1907, Owen was keenly interested in banking issues and currency reform. At the age of 35 he became one of the first Senators from Oklahoma and one of the first Native American members of the upper chamber in the Congress. Owen was also the first Chairman of the Senate Banking Committee, a post he earned by serving as the counterpart to Chairman Glass in the House in pushing for approval of the Federal Reserve Act.

Despite the best efforts by the banking lobby to amend the legislation and impose a central bank explicitly controlled by the New York financial community, the superficially more Progressive plan supported by Glass was the clear choice of a majority of the legislature. The New York banks then set about a campaign to delay and thereby kill the legislation. This strategy would ultimately fail—and do so visibly enough to support the appearance of Progressive support for the legislation. The Progressives rightly viewed the bank-supported central bank as providing big political risk but no solution to the lack of credit available for farmers and their communities. The political truth was that the primary impact of the annual surge in demand for funds by Western banks to finance the Fall harvest was to suppress agricultural prices, something to which bankers and their political allies in Washington raised no objection.

But while the large banks fought the legislation, a growing majority of Americans knew that the recurring financial crises in the United States and the lack of a central bank to supply credit to the financial system generally was a serious disadvantage for the U.S. economy, as well as for individual businesses and consumers. In the early 1900s, for example, when American companies purchased goods from overseas, they often paid for the imports using a letter of credit drawn on a London bank. Because the credit of U.S. banks was considered to be so inferior and because British banks were set up to do business throughout the British empire, London held a tight grip over the financing of American commerce more than a century after the Declaration of Independence. Indeed, while there were many reasons for the Anglocentric view of the House of Morgan and its strong ties to the London banking market, sheer necessity was one of the most important. Morgan was seen as a giant in New York, but in some circles in the City of London, it was still viewed as a colonial upstart right up until WWI. Then the tables of global finance would turn in favor of New York.

The practical shortcomings in the U.S. financial system had been obvious for decades, but with the crisis of 1907 many bankers became convinced of the need for change in the flexibility of the currency, even if their political tendencies had not changed appreciably when it came to the question of sound money and the power of the Eastern banks. The basic political division in terms of populist versus business interests in the United States was illustrated by the debate over the central bank and would become an enduring feature of the popular perception of the American dream. No longer was the economic sky the limit nor the possibilities endless. Unemployment, financial panics, and insecurity were also features of the new American society. As a result, many small town bankers were fearful that the system would break without a change and that even more draconian regulation from Washington would ensue. The key shift in the political equation that made the Federal Reserve Act's passage possible was not a populist rebellion in the farm community but the fact that a greater number of the Main Street banking and business community was willing to revisit the idea of a central bank. This was a notion that had not been seriously considered by the Congress since the days of President Andrew Jackson and was now being advanced by the Democrat Wilson.

After several months of furious delay engineered by the large New York banks, the Senate passed the Federal Reserve Act on December 19, 1913. The committee of bankers formed to attempt to block the passage of the legislation included the Morgan banker Henry Davidson, who had worked closely with Senator Aldrich; Frank A. Vanderlip, head of the National City Bank (the predecessor of Citibank); and Benjamin Strong, head of the Bankers Trust Company, a satellite of JPMorgan & Co. Strong, who is lionized in many histories of the period as the first great Fed governor, was the most active member of the bankers committee and "the generalissimo" of all the Morgan-sponsored and -financed groups that opposed the legislation.[32]

The Federal Reserve Act passed the Senate just as the Congress was ending its session. President Wilson signed it into law on Christmas Eve, yet another irony in the history of the American central bank. The following year, the Federal Trade Commission would be created and the Sixteenth Amendment to the Constitution opened the way for a federal income tax. The age of reform and regulation—and big government—was in full swing. Senator Robert Byrd (D-WV) summed up the generally accepted version of the event in his history of the Senate:

> The creation of the Federal Reserve System was the crown-ing achievement of the Sixty-third Congress and, indeed, of the first Wilson administration. Despite the conservative attack in the Senate, its basic structure—the twelve Federal Reserve Banks, privately controlled, regulated and supervised by the Federal Reserve Board—still remains. It proved to be a signif-icant reform of the very heart of the American economy. It destroyed the control of money and credit by a few banks on Wall Street, created a more flexible and sound currency, and permitted a planned supervision of banking reserves to meet the country's needs.[33]

Given the debate in Washington during 2010 about modernizing the bank regulatory system, it must be noted that Byrd's quotation is somewhat misleading and reflects a modern-day, sanitized view of the central bank. The Fed's Board of Governors in Washington was not part of the original Federal Reserve Act. The number and geographic location of the Federal Reserve Banks was actually determined by the National Monetary Commission led by Senator Aldrich. Indeed, Glass and the other exponents of a decentralized "central bank" deliberately avoided a Washington presence for the Federal Reserve System because of the populist opposition to such visible centralized structures. The official version of events said that the decentralized design of the Fed would prevent the New York banks from exercising excessive control, but in fact that is precisely what happened in practice. Lawrence Goodwyn commented on just that point in his landmark 1976 work, *Democratic Promise: The Populist Moment in America*:

> In a gesture that was symbolic of the business-endorsed reforms of the Progressive era, William Jennings Bryan hailed the passage of the Federal Reserve Act in 1913 as a 'triumph for the people.' His response provided a measure of the intellectual achievements of reformers in the Progressive period. Of longer cultural significance, it also illustrated how completely the idea of 'reform' had become incorporated within the new political boundaries established in Bryan's own lifetime. The reformers of the Progressive era fit snugly within these boundaries—in Bryan's case, without his even knowing it. Meanwhile, the idea of substantial democratic influence over the structure of the nation's financial system, a principle that had been the operative objective of the greenbackers, quietly passed out of American political dialogue. It has remained there ever since.[34]

Virginia Democrat Carter Glass would become Secretary of the Treasury during President Wilson's second term. Even though a small man in physical stature, Glass was a giant in his day and the authority on financial matters in the Congress. Senator Kenneth McKellar of Tennessee called Glass "one of the finest and noblest characters" with whom he had been associated. "I never knew him to do a small thing; he had a big heart and a great mind."[35] Yet it can be argued that, at the end of the day, Glass's devotion to core American principles about the need for checks and balances was thwarted by the power of Morgan and the other large banks to influence Congress and then shape the outcome of the legislative process. A century later nothing has changed.

Glass is credited as the intellectual author of the Federal Reserve Act, but he was hardly the champion of the legislation in that tumultuous year, especially on the floor of the Senate. In fact, all three pieces of Wilson's key legislative reforms were guided through the Congress and to final enactment by Senator John Worth Kern (D-IN), the first member of the Senate to be referred to as the "leader" of the majority and a key ally of Woodrow Wilson. Kern had been the unsuccessful Democratic candidate for governor of Indiana in 1900 and was on the ticket as Vice President under William Jennings Bryan in 1908. He would be defeated in 1917 after only one term in the Senate, but it was Senator Kern, and not Carter Glass, who made the Federal Reserve Act a reality. Glass himself gave credit to Woodrow Wilson for the passage of the Fed legislation. This was understandable since Glass, as noted previously, served as Treasury Secretary in Wilson's second term.

When the Federal Reserve Act finally was passed by the Congress, it contained a number of superficially populist, decentralized features that provided substantial autonomy from Washington and also provided the banking industry with the ability to influence the central bank. Indeed, some of the revisionist accounts of the era suggest that far from losing the battle with the forces of populism, the New York bankers led by J.P. Morgan & Co. actually won the day and did so by design.

Benjamin Strong would leave the Bankers Trust Company in 1914 to preside as the first Governor of the Federal Reserve Bank of New York. Like all of the Morgan Men, Strong was an Anglophile who "wanted to endow the New York Fed with the dignity and prestige of the Bank of England," wrote Ron Chernow in *The House of Morgan*. "Through Strong's influence, the Federal Reserve System would prove far more of a boon than a threat to the Morgan Bank. The New York Fed and the House of Morgan would share a sense of purpose to such an extent that the latter would be known on Wall Street as the Fed bank. So, contrary to expectations, frustrated reformers only watched Morgan power grow after 1913."[36]

Roosevelt, Wilson, and the Politics of Reform

It is important to note that the fight to break the Money Trusts and the debate over the creation of a central bank occurred during the same period of time. The political context of the debate over the creation of the Fed, particularly the rise of the Progressive movement and the generally anti-business environment that developed, is an important point that is often overlooked by traditional economists. Specifically, the use of bank funds to finance these great trusts as well as speculative securities generated enormous opposition from many parts of society.

As today, the public believed that banks should only use depositor funds to finance real commerce and economic activity. This was the key focus of the Pujo Committee as well as many political leaders and communities around the country who felt, for reasons real or imagined, threatened by the large banks. The fact that banks preferred to finance speculation on Wall Street as opposed to financing the activity in the real economy angered many Americans of all political persuasions.

Wilson is portrayed in the history books as the "progressive" president, but the former Governor of New Jersey was still a decidedly conservative candidate compared with Teddy Roosevelt. Chernow in *The House of Morgan* notes that President Wilson lectured "Pierpont" Morgan on his moral duty, but Wilson was very much part of the establishment. As in the case of Teddy Roosevelt, Wilson found it to be good politics to attack the "Money Trust," which was a code word for J.P. Morgan. But Wilson was always measured in his statements compared with the fiery Bryan or Roosevelt. Wilson did, however, have a former New York prosecutor and trust buster named Louis Brandeis as his adviser and thus did embrace financial reform. Wilson made attacking the trusts a key part of his first term in the White House.[37]

In the four-way 1912 election, the incumbent President Taft was perhaps the most conservative and superficially the man of the Republican establishment. Given a choice, the large New York banks would have chosen Taft over Wilson, but the Progressive tide was still rising and the incumbent President Taft was not likely to win, even in a two-way race with Wilson. In fact, Taft ran third behind Roosevelt and ahead of Socialist Eugene Debs, who only polled support in single digits. But another problem with Taft from the perspective of the House of

Morgan was his alignment with the Rockefeller family. While Morgan was often critical of Wilson because of his refusal to finance the belligerents during WWI and his reluctance to enter the war on the side of Britain, when it came to the creation of the Fed the House of Morgan wanted to ensure that Wilson would win the White House.

The story goes that Morgan and the other banks brought Teddy Roosevelt out of retirement and financed the creation of the Bull Moose party to lead the Progressive wing of the GOP. With Roosevelt on the left and Taft heading the conservatives, both men polled in the 25 percent range and Wilson won the election. This split of the Republican vote only served to demonstrate that alone neither wing of the Republican Party could win the White House, a fact that each faction resisted acknowledging for decades.

Teddy Roosevelt was arguably a more authentic voice of Progressive change than Wilson, even if the big banks made the Bull Moose party a reality. Roosevelt advocated lower tariffs and reform planks such as the election of judges, proposals that neither the Rockefeller nor Morgan camp could endorse. He made this comment about Wilson during the election:

> Mr. Wilson says "the trusts are our masters now, but I for one do not care to live in a country called free even under kind masters." Good! The Progressives are opposed to having masters, kind or unkind and they do not believe that a 'new freedom' which in practice would mean leaving four Fuel and Iron Companies free to do what they like in every industry would be much of a benefit to the country. The Progressives have a clear and definite programme by which the people would be the masters of the trusts instead of the trusts being their masters, as Mr. Wilson says they are. With practical unanimity the trusts supported the opponents of this programme, Mr. Taft and Mr. Wilson, and they evidently dreaded our programme infinitely more than anything that Mr. Wilson threatened.[38]

Notice that in the statement above Teddy Roosevelt focuses on the evil fuel and iron companies, which were controlled by the Rockefellers, but has nothing bad to say about large banks. Just as

President McKinley was dependent upon the support of big city machine politicians in his day, both the Democrats and Republicans in the early 1900s had support from the great Robber Barons. In the case of Taft, his support came from the Rockefellers, while with Roosevelt and Wilson the money came from the House of Morgan. Thus when it came time to create the central bank, the House of Morgan had already determined the outcome by first placing Woodrow Wilson in the White House. Whereas the Progressives wanted the determination of interest rates and the supply of currency to be under government control, the final result was an "independent" federal agency controlled by the banking industry.

President Wilson and other politicians of the day spoke at length about the "cooperative" structure of the central bank and the way the Fed specifically would meet the credit needs of rural farm communities. But the only parties that gained easier access to credit were the banks themselves, who were warming to the idea of a central bank after the Crisis of 1907. It is telling that the depression-like conditions and lack of credit affecting the U.S. agricultural sector persisted through the decade after the creation of the Federal Reserve and without relief from private lenders, the central bank, or from Washington. During the Great Depression and WWII, Washington would ladle ample subsidies on large and medium size farms, but the community of smaller family farms and rural laborers were never addressed by the creation of the central bank nor by any of the myriad of farm credit programs emanating from Washington over the subsequent decades.

The way the Progressive movement was marginalized during the debate regarding the central bank is also telling with regard to the way a more corporate political discourse emerged in America after this period. Economics and history textbooks are filled with descriptions of the Federal Reserve Act as a compromise among various political interests, but in fact the large banks and their political allies in the Congress had their way in most aspects of the creation of the central bank. In the process, the agency that became the Federal Reserve System adopted some of the Progressive, silverite world view, particularly the European, corporate perspective on private business, economic management, and the role of government. Seen from that viewpoint, the

Aldrich plan for a banker-controlled central bank was more consistent with traditional American values regarding on individual freedom and money championed by Thomas Jefferson and Andrew Jackson than was the final product, even with the populist façade championed by Carter Glass.

The creation of the Federal Reserve, in fact, confirms the cautionary views of Jefferson and Jackson regarding the anti-democratic, authoritarian nature of central banks. Whether located in the United States, London, or the other nations of the world, almost by definition there seems to be something in the character of any central bank that is antithetical to democracy and individual rights, and promotes the expansion of a corporate state. The support for a strong unitary government and central bank by Alexander Hamilton and other federalist exponents supported the growth of the nation, but at a price. The act of embracing a unified monetary policy implies an acceptance of central planning and corporate direction that seems to color all of the operations of a central bank, no matter how well intentioned.

"The Progressive movement that preceded American entry into World War I also drew largely from classic corporatist theories for its industrial relations policies," said Walker Todd, a former Fed official and researcher. "The main unifying principle of classic corporatism was the idea that Marxist or Dickensian visions of class struggle could be avoided if, somehow, corporate owners and managers, agricultural interests, and urban laborers could be brought together cooperatively under the benign auspices of government."[39]

The explicitly banker-controlled National Reserve Association proposed by Senator Aldrich was to be governed by bankers and other financial experts, but the Federal Reserve Act as proposed by Rep. Glass and Senator Owen created a system that was altogether political. While the National Reserve Association strictly limited the amount of currency issued and required its retirement after a liquidity crisis was ended, the Federal Reserve Act provided for the issuance of currency without any effective limit and all controlled by political appointees who were already under the sway of the largest banks. Thus the pro-inflation tendency of the banks that had been observed after the Civil

War and creation of fiat money had grown to the point that popular caution regarding the central bank was pushed aside.

The American central bank was from its earliest days entirely friendly to big government and big banks, the two chief clients of the Federal Reserve System. Whereas in the past the operations of J.P. Morgan or the other large banks were a matter of legitimate national policy concern, with the advent of the Federal Reserve the large New York banks gained a political foil behind which to hide and also use as a powerful legal protector. This was a considerable boon for the largest banks, especially following the period of the Pujo Committee and related public inquiries. Under the monopoly of first the Federal Reserve Act and three decades later the Bank Holding Company Act of 1956, companies that own banks have enjoyed extraordinary protection by virtue of having the Federal Reserve as the banking industry's regulator.

In the decades since its creation, the U.S. central bank has evolved into a lobbying and advocacy organ for the banking industry, with Federal Reserve governors and senior officials toeing the large bank party line as they testify before Congress and interact with other agencies. "Popular attention thenceforth was to focus upon 'the Fed,' not upon the actions of the New York commercial bankers," wrote Lawrence Goodwyn in 1976. "The creation and subsequent development of the Federal Reserve System represented the culminating political triumph of the 'sound money' crusade of the 1890s."[40] The highly visible role of regulator and liquidity provider played by the House of Morgan in the 1800s and as late as 1907 devolved to the new Federal Reserve. The Fed became the focus for all types of public anger and suspicion in matters of money and finance—right up until the present day.

In his classic 1933 book *The Mirrors of Wall Street*, Clinton Gilbert described the scene as the Congress passed the Federal Reserve Act and the subsequent two decades:

> It is now almost twenty years since J.P. Morgan and Company, its associates and its satellites attempted to induce Congress to create a central bank of issue instead of the Federal Reserve System. They were determined that control of the national

purse should remain in New York. The theory underlying the proposed system that the several sections of the country should control their own finances was preposterous. To them it was anathema. Ten short years later the same group, represented by the same agent who had led their lost cause in Washington, took charge of the Federal Reserve System. For practical purposes the system was transformed into a central bank, and was manipulated to the very ends that its authors had sought to guard against.[41]

Gilbert found that while the first Board of Governors of the Fed was comprised of people "distinguished by ability and character," by the time that President Warren Harding succeeded Woodrow Wilson in the White House, the New York bankers, led by the House of Morgan, largely captured the Federal Reserve Board, which was comprised of the governors of the Reserve Banks. The slogan "Return to Normalcy" replaced the cries of war and the nation was, once again, more interested in ways to "turn the wheels of commerce and accelerate the movements of trade."[42]

The Federal Reserve Act gave the nation's third central bank a 20-year charter, but as noted above, without the Washington bureaucracy that today is known as the Board of Governors. The 12 Federal Reserve Banks were reasonably autonomous entities that set interest rate policy within their geographic territory, albeit with a large degree of communication and cooperation. Over a decade would elapse before the Congress passed the McFadden Act of 1927, creating the Fed Board as an agency of the federal government to supervise the regional reserve banks. By the 1930s, the newly created Board of Governors would be firmly in charge of the reserve banks and any pretension at a progressive, decentralized governance model for the American central bank would be at an end.

The rise of the Board of Governors as an independent agency in Washington not only influenced the evolution of the banking system and the currency, but also played an important role in the trend toward centralized planning and authoritarian political structures in Washington during and after the 1930s. The agency that was supposed to be concerned with the soundness of the nation's currency would over the decades become a source of instability and even systemic risk, within the American political economy, both by explicitly financing irresponsible fiscal and trade policies in Washington with easy money in terms of the currency and also by condoning, even encouraging unsafe and unsound practices by the largest banks. The creation of the Fed may have seemed a political victory for the forces of sound money, as Goodwyn and other scholars of the progressive era argue. In fact the central bank would become an influence supporting inflation, debt, and the rise of even more powerful and largely unaccountable governmental structures in the United States in the 1930s. As Walker Todd noted in "The Federal Reserve Board and the Rise of the Corporate State," the Fed reflected the views of the time, but also remained supportive of statist, anti-democratic governance structures in Washington long after WWI and the Great Depression:

In the history of political economy theory, it generally is believed that a taste for centralization of authority, cooperation and information-sharing to reduce competition, restraint of production to maintain prices and profits, and the coercion of labor by the state into conformance with this design, all die hard once they become embedded in the administrative apparatus of the state. The occasional reappearance and even persistence of some mildly corporatist ideas at the Board since the 1930s might be explained by the hypothesis that such ideas, once having gained sway there in 1931–34, simply have reappeared whenever the economic and political conditions were right.[43]

Chapter 5

War, Boom, and Bust

In the period under Theodore Roosevelt and prior to the administration of President William Howard Taft, the U.S. government's debt hovered around $2 billion, though it began to steadily grow by a couple of hundred million per year to reach almost $3 billion in 1912. With the start of the First World War in Europe and with American assistance, both public and private, however, the debt of the United States began to grow rapidly. This was a significant change compared with the past fiscal behavior of Washington, at least in peacetime. By 1918 the total amount of federal debt outstanding was almost $15 billion, nearly five times the prewar levels.[1]

The change in Washington's spending habits during the period before and during WWI is significant. It marks the start of a steady increase in federal indebtedness and a tolerance for maintaining these levels of debt, both in terms of direct obligations and indirect contingent obligations, that has been mostly unbroken ever since. While in some years the amount of debt did decline slightly, overall the growth in the total obligations of the federal government has been steady and has accelerated in recent decades. The American approach to debt repayment after WWI stands in sharp contrast to that of the UK, which imposed a draconian regime of taxes and fiscal austerity during and following WWI to repay the domestic war debt. Unfortunately the United Kingdom and other European Allies did not repay their war debts to the United States.

With the outbreak of the WWI, most of the nations of the world left the gold standard, either explicitly or as a matter of practice. None of the nations involved could really afford in economic terms to go to war, so debt and inflation were used to finance the conflict. As with the Civil War, the huge cost of WWI doomed the gold standard and launched investors into a new world of financial uncertainty. At the start of the conflict, many American investors feared that the war would drain financial reserves out of New York and into London; in fact the opposite occurred. As raw materials, food, and manufactured goods flowed to Europe, gold and loans came to Wall Street's banks, but this process whereby America became involved in the war on the side of France and Britain was gradual.

At first the Wilson Administration did not wish to provide any loans to the British and French governments, a position that infuriated the bankers of the House of Morgan and the other New York houses. The New York financial community was mostly focused on London, so supporting the British and French against Germany was natural enough and good business besides. The New York banks also had grown very comfortable with the "Dollar Diplomacy" of President William Howard Taft, which was essentially Roosevelt-style "big stick" diplomacy with a dollar wrapped around it. Like most Republicans who preceded him, President Taft was a conservative, limited or no-government politician who believed that business people could essentially govern themselves.

The non-interventionism of the Wilson White House, and in particular the rhetoric of Secretary of State William Jennings Bryan, made many bankers wish for a return of the good old days of Taft, but the Progressive political surge in 1912 made that impossible. Bryan was no better at being Secretary of State than he was as a presidential candidate, but he flattered the non-intervention views of Wilson. President Wilson made staying out of the war in Europe a key part of his reelection campaign in 1916. Having run on the slogan "He Kept Us Out of War," he would change his position immediately following the election.

"What a mess, Oh what an awful mess Wilson is making," President Taft wrote to P.C. Knox in April of 1914. "What an opportunist he has shown himself to be, and how entirely he is giving himself up to the political game in his most reckless use of power to involve the country in war in order to take himself out of a political hole!"[2]

Bryan believed correctly that allowing American banks and investors to underwrite loans for the belligerent powers in Europe would undermine the country's policy of neutrality. The Wilson Administration also discouraged American banks from participating in a loan for China during the same period. When bankers in France and the United Kingdom asked directly for loans from Morgan and the other major banks in New York, the Wilson Administration refused, but the Morgan bankers made no secret of the fact that they were not neutral in the war and were against Germany.

By the middle of 1914, however, other bankers began to press the case for making loans to the governments of France and Britain. Frank Vaderlip, president of the National City Bank, told the French government that he could raise $10 million for them privately. He then went to Washington to challenge Secretary Bryan regarding the matter and specifically contested any authority Washington might claim to have over foreign loans. On August 15th, Bryan retreated and issued a statement that the U.S. government had no legal authority to prevent banks from lending to any belligerent nation, but he added that doing so was "inconsistent with the true spirit of neutrality." By October of 1914, the Wilson Administration had completely reversed itself and was telling U.S. banks that it would not oppose investment in bonds issued by the foreign combatants—a position endorsed by the bankers and exporters alike.[3]

The sharp increase in U.S. exports to the governments allied against Germany had a positive impact on the American economy, which had been in a considerable slump since before the creation of the Federal Reserve System a year before. For many years, the United States had run a trade deficit with the European nations during the first half of the year, and then saw the trade balance reverse when agricultural crops such as corn, tobacco, cotton, and wheat moved from the United States to Europe. The brief prosperity in the United States caused by the WWI pushed prices for everything from iron ore to farm land up dramatically, but also caused a major shift in the financial balance of power in favor of the United States. In terms of national wealth, the United States went from being an agrarian debtor nation to being a rising industrial power and a net creditor of the European nation states.

One of the reasons that Wilson may have been persuaded not to restrict the flow of goods and credit to the Allied countries was that America had a high degree of dependence upon credit from Europe. Just as the cities and states in the Western United States were dependent upon credit from the New York banks to meet their seasonal needs for currency, the entire country remained very dependent upon European markets for seasonal loans to finance American agricultural and industrial production. In that sense, the political ideal of neutrality and nonintervention ran smack into the reality of finance and debt, and the latter prevailed. Johns Hopkins University researcher Charles Callan Tansill noted in his classic book, *America Goes to War*, that in the fall of 1914, the American debt to Europe stood at almost $250 million, "which had to be liquidated either by the export of American goods or by payment in gold."[4] But the debtor position of the United States would quickly be transformed into that of a creditor nation once Britain and France began to demand more and more goods from the United States to support the war effort.

News media around the United States were generally supportive of the cause of the Allies, even if most citizens still felt, like Teddy Roosevelt, that the business of America was America; and that it should be pursued without dependence on foreign nations or interference from them. But echoing the Big Stick of Teddy Roosevelt, the growing internationalist, interventionist tendency in American society had powerful allies. Among them was Clarence Barron, founder of *Barron's* magazine and owner of Dow, Jones & Co. He published a book, *The Audacious War*, in support of the fight against the Central Powers led by Germany. Barron described the cause of wars in Europe with one word: tariffs. By implication, Barron expected Germany to impose economic hegemony over the world in the same way that Britain tyrannized the American colonies, through tariffs. He explained:

> German "Kultur" means German progress, commercially and financially. German progress is by tariffs and commercial treaties. Her armies, her arms, and her armaments, are to support this Kultur and this progress.[5]

Barron was not at all shy about using the pages of the *Wall Street Journal* to attack Germany and proselytize on behalf of the European Allies, but the truth was that the economic pull of the war was too powerful for the United States to resist in any event. The idyllic, nine-teenth century world view of an American republic safely isolated from the world by the two great oceans was shown to be impractical in the world of the telegraph, airplanes, and oil-fired warships.

By January of 1915, some $500 million worth of munitions and war supplies had already been shipped to the Allies in Europe and the vol-umes would only continue to grow. In fact, by that time, it was apparent to the House of Morgan that the available market for the debt of the European governments in the United States would soon be exhausted and other means of financing war exports had to be found. The Federal Reserve Act limited the ability of the central bank to buy only "warrants issued by the States and municipalities of the United States," but a way was soon found for the Fed to provide financing for the war. The firms shipping war materials to Europe would simply present trade acceptances to the Fed for financing, rather than have the importers in Europe do so.

Not satisfied with this solution of having the U.S. central bank endorse letters of credit for war shipments, J.P. Morgan pressed Washington explicitly to allow the Federal Reserve Banks to accept drafts drawn directly on London banks that had been accepted by a New York bank. By April 1915, the Fed complied with Morgan's request and once again proved that the central bank was always ready to do the bidding of the House of Morgan. The decision by the Fed was an active violation of U.S. neutrality, as many German language publications pointed out at the time. Even with this concession, how-ever, the volume of war materials and other goods demanded by the Allies overwhelmed the available financing in the United States. On May 7, 1915 when the steamer *Lusitania* was sunk by a German sub-marine, sentiment in the United States went more sharply against Germany, and J.P. Morgan and the Allies took full advantage of the fact. Later evidence would show that the ship may have been carrying munitions in violation of the declared U.S. policy of neutrality.

During this juncture the press, with the encouragement of Morgan and the other banks, began to carry opinions to the effect that the Allies did not need to pay for purchases of war materials with gold—but instead that the United States should accept payment in paper, that is, debt backed by the future promise of payment in gold. In a May 15, 1915 editorial, the *New York Times* advocated the use of "paper instead of gold for domestic trade" and "the reservation of gold for international use." The *Times* noted that the United Kingdom could no longer maintain the standard of "a pound of gold for every pound of paper" and that hundreds of thousands of dollars worth of gold "will support almost unlimited millions of purchases from a country that has goods and does not want gold."[6]

In June of 1915, J.P. Morgan, First National Bank, and National City Bank boldly floated a $30 million loan for France and created a facility that eventually totaled over $40 million and was secured by U.S. railroad bonds. "With American sentiment towards Germany becoming sharply hostile, the time seemed propitious for the Allied Powers to secure financial concessions formerly denied them" wrote Professor Tansill in 1938. "The financial ties that closely bound America to the Allied governments were forged in 1915, and they were the result of the unwearied efforts of the House of Morgan to provide some satisfactory method of financing the swiftly growing volume of American exports to Europe."[7]

Whatever Americans thought about the war on moral grounds, the surge in demand for all types of finished goods and raw materials was a welcome and positive development. The U.S. economy had been laboring to emerge from a contraction for almost a decade. By the middle of 1915, France alone was purchasing $150 million per month in U.S. goods, frequently using loans from English banks to fund the transactions. In that same time period, H.P. Davidson of J.P. Morgan, writing from London, informed his colleagues in New York that the financing requirement for European imports would reach $400 million by January of 1916. This vast flow of goods provided proportionately huge profits for the banks, but even more for the brokers and producers who provided the goods, sometimes under government contracts. The vast majority of the economic benefit realized by the United States during WWI went to a relatively small group of people and companies and was not widely distributed. After the banks, those best situated to take advantage of the war were the industrialists and the transportation interests, followed by the large agricultural firms, and lastly the small farmer.

The House of Morgan was well aware of the funding needs of the Allies. The bank for months after the start of hostilities effectively supported the value of the British currency at about $5.40 per pound. It is some measure of the commitment to the London market by the House of Morgan that the bank was willing to deploy its own capital for months effectively to subsidize U.S. trade with Britain, especially when it was clear that the Bank of England could not finance its wartime needs. In the middle of August of 1915, Morgan ended its support for the pound, causing the currency to fall almost a full $1 to $4.51 per pound sterling and thereby precipitating a political emergency for the British government. The timing of the crisis, coming just as the flow of commercial orders from French and British buyers was starting to overwhelm the U.S. banks, was a brilliant gambit on the part of Morgan. It forced the U.S. government to become directly involved in underwriting the finances for the European war effort.

In a July 1915 meeting between Fed Governor Benjamin Strong, Frederic Delano, Vice Chairman of the Fed and Colonel Edward House, the confidant of President Wilson and a self-appointed expert on all matters of finance, it was decided that the Fed would have to provide additional financing for war exports or the entirety of commerce between the United States and Europe might be threatened. After weeks of discussions among the Fed, the House of Morgan, and the White House, a consensus was formed that the Fed should be allowed to accept bank paper used to finance exports to Europe, which were expected to total $2.5 billion in 1915.

Opposition on the Federal Reserve Board to the proposal continued for months, however, particularly from German-born Governor Paul Warburg. He objected to the changes proposed by Strong to the Fed's rediscounting regulations because it would "open the way to undertaking of business with foreign governments." In the end, the attraction of the vast commercial opportunity to support the Allied war effort was too strong to resist, especially with the House of Morgan and other large banks lobbying in favor. The Fed approved the changes at the meeting of the Board on September 3, 1915. Acceptances by U.S. banks that were members of the Fed increased more than fivefold during the next year.[8]

Because the Fed had been created just two years before, the central bank was barely operational when WWI began and remained a work in progress for years, some might argue decades or a even a century, thereafter. Treasury Secretary William McAdoo, Secretary of Agriculture David Houston, and Comptroller of the Currency John Skelton Williams took on the task of organizing the 12 Federal Reserve Banks based on the locations chosen by the National Monetary Commission. Because of the emergency authority to issue currency under the Aldrich-Vreeland Act of 1908 and the more important power to buy or "discount" bankers' acceptances conferred by the Federal Reserve Act, the new central bank was able to provide liquidity to the nation's economy. It helped to finance the Allied war effort against Germany until the United States officially entered the conflict in 1917.

The efforts by the House of Morgan and Governor Strong, however, helped the process of moving the United States toward involvement in the war long before the White House was willing or prepared to do so. In this sense, the overt actions taken by the New York banks—led by Morgan—and the new Federal Reserve Bank of New York led the United States into war. The Morgan bankers and Strong also had a great impact on changing the mind of President Wilson toward the conflict in one of the most dramatic political turnabouts in U.S. history.

The period from Wilson's reelection in November 1916 to the decision to enter the European conflict was one of the strangest and most significant ones in American history. Wilson ran on a platform of staying out of the war, in part because of growing public opposition to the conflict, to the uneven economy, and to Wilson himself. Wilson said that "there will be no war." He told his confidant Colonel House: "This country does not intend to become involved in this war. We are the only one of the great white nations that is free from war to-day, and it would be a crime against civilization for us to go in." But House noted that "the President may change his view, for as I have said before, he changes his views often."[9] House was part of the pro-Morgan tendency inside the Wilson Administration that also was overtly supportive of war with Germany. He often commented in his letters of the need to prepare the nation for the conflict. House is blamed by some historians for unilaterally committing the United States to war without the consent of President Wilson or Congress during his visits to Europe, when he often travelled in the company of Morgan bankers.

There are many reasons advanced for Wilson's change of heart about the war between his election and taking the oath of office for a second time. House argues that the prospect of Germany resuming unrestricted submarine operations against shipping in the Atlantic in 1917 was the proximate cause of the U.S. decision to enter the fighting. Wilson himself, after spending much of his first term avoiding the conflict, made a resumption by Germany of unrestricted submarine attacks on U.S. shipping a pretext for entering the war.

The sheer economic and commercial reality was that America's economic resurgence was based upon the flow of goods to Europe. The economic malaise before the war that had stretched as far back as 1907 was gone, and the country was running at or near full capacity in many sectors. Both maintaining the flow of goods and ensuring that the Allied debts were good were clearly priorities for the Wilson government. It is reasonable to ask, though, whether Wilson and the other senior people in the U.S. government believed that the latter was possible and that the Allies would ever pay their war debts.

By the end of the conflict the global balance of financial power had shifted from London to New York. America was rapidly becoming a rich creditor nation and the influence of America's banks was also growing. No longer were American banks treated with contempt in the City of London. The fact that all of this plenty was the result of a truly horrible slaughter on the fields of France mattered little and, indeed, was turned into a virtue, a crusade against evil in the shape of the menacing German horde often referred to as "the Hun." Authors such as Clarence Barron, who personally covered part of the war as a correspondent for Dow, Jones & Co., painted the conflict in epic proportions and thereby made the tough economic situation and the debt incurred to fund the war seem entirely reasonable.

What is notable about WWI from the perspective of money, debt, and the American dream was the easy, almost painless way in which the country accepted the idea of prosperity via borrowing and also a good deal of monetary expansion. The hard money Jacksonian notions of gold coinage and antipathy to paper issued by banks of any description still lingered in many parts of the country. Yet for a growing portion of Americans and the mass of the large business and banking interests, the idea of an aggressive government presence in the credit and commercial markets was entirely acceptable if the end result was prosperity. The war in Europe had drawn the House of Morgan and the entire New York banking community closer. All of the banks collectively were also drawn closer to the U.S. Treasury and the government in general as first the banks, and later the entire nation, lent money to support the Allied war effort.

In 1917 and 1918, the Treasury issued $17 billion in Liberty bonds to help defray part of the cost of the war, some $30 billion in total expenditures for the conflict. This figure must be compared to the federal budget in 1913, which was less than $1 billion. The massive effort to sell Liberty bonds to the public increased awareness of the world of securities and investing. Not only was the war a huge shot in the arm for the U.S. economy, but the war effort also provided a rallying point for all Americans. A population that only a few years earlier had been voting an increasingly Progressive political line based in part upon bleak economic prospects and rising class tensions was united behind the cause of global peace.

Thanks to billions of dollars in foreign loans and Liberty bonds, the American economy was surging. The Allies had the munitions and other supplies necessary to support the offensive planned for 1916. As hundreds of thousands of European soldiers went to their deaths, America was rising on a sudden and unprecedented wave of prosperity and wealth. Exports of munitions, steel, cotton, and wheat surged to several times the levels seen in 1913 and sent expectations soaring regarding America's future prospects. Unfortunately the expectations of global peace and prosperity after WWI were soon dashed, a bitter disappointment for a young nation that was only starting to believe in its own possibilities and place in the world.

More realistic Americans in all types of industries took a practical view of the war, namely the opportunity for profit. The prospect of tapping into the vast demand for materials of every description was natural because the role played by America itself, as a whole nation, was widely perceived as that of a war profiteer. Nations around the world criticized the role of the United States as purveyor of materials and sometimes munitions to both sides of the European conflict. Politicians and academic researchers at the time debated whether the quest for excessive gains was not in fact a cause of war, implying that American bankers, munitions merchants, and other business people fomented the war in order to benefit financially.

In the United Kingdom, food prices were subject to government control, and profiteers were subject to imprisonment. In the United States, however, as in most matters, during WWI the markets prevailed without any real restraint. Prices for many necessities soared. Members of Congress and the Executive branch were bought and sold openly, as today, so that business interests seeking to corner a market in a given commodity operated with impunity. Political influence also helped to win lucrative contracts to supply war materials to the American war effort.

By 1917, the public outcry against inflation and war profiteering became overwhelming. President Wilson signed legislation imposing price controls on food and other products and appointed a Republican named Herbert Hoover as Food Administrator to oversee price controls and punish war profiteers. The great Wall Street financier Bernard M. Baruch, chairman of the War Industries Board during the first World War, demanded government restrictions to eliminate all large profits for industry in wartime. In the event that another war should come, Baruch supported complete federal control over all industries and their workers.

Earlier that year, Baruch was accused of being a war profiteer himself by state Senator William Youngman (R-MA). Youngman, the same Massachusetts attorney who gave evidence against the Supreme Court nomination of Louis Brandeis several years before, was not successful in attacking Baruch, who would be the target of anti-Semitic attacks for most of his public life. Youngman directly vilified Baruch for "making his money on the bodies of the young boys who fought for this country in the war," but Baruch rebuked him publicly and demanded a retraction.[10] The issue of wartime corruption and profiteering in general would remain contentious in the United States for many years to come.

The New York and London banks made good money on the business of war as well. Morgan and other lenders, for example pocketed nearly $22 million on a $500 million loan for Britain and France led by J.P. Morgan and closed in the last week in December of 1915.

That amounted to a 4.5 percent commission for placing government bonds for two of the most creditworthy nations on earth, a nice piece of business for any dealer on Wall Street. Russia also floated bonds in the United States during 1916 and used the proceeds to buy American products. Not surprisingly, J.P. Morgan became the purchasing agent for the British government, negotiated London's acquisition of goods in the United States, and also acted as advisor regarding the United Kingdom government's financing.

Profits to the U.S. farm sector from exports of various types of foodstuffs rose nearly tenfold during WWI, peaking in 1916, a huge turnabout from the previous two decades. Steel exports rose fivefold over the term of the war and the value of farmland likewise soared. Thousands of new millionaires were coined during the period and several companies earned in profits many times their capitalizations. For the vast majority of farmers and industrial workers, however, the opportunity was not shared.

Additional loans were made to France and Britain during 1916 to pay for the vast amounts of exports from the United States. Between November of 1916 and February 1917 nearly $1 billion was borrowed directly by the British government to finance war purchases. Based upon unofficial information provided to the Congress by the Treasury in August of 1914, the Allies borrowed $2.5 billion during the war years, loans underwritten by Morgan and the other New York banks. This included $160 million for Russia, $120 million for Canada for work purposes, $45 million for Germany, and even $5 million for China. America had become banker to the world and was in the midst of an economic boom not unlike that seen at the end of the Civil War—only bigger and fueled by even more plentiful credit from public and private sources.

"World War I marked a great divide in American credit," wrote author and historian James Grant in his book *Money of the Mind*. "Lending and borrowing entered the social mainstream."[11] Grant notes that WWI marked a period when governments, corporations, and individuals gained access to credit on a heretofore unthinkable scale, and even in 1918 it was clear that some of them could not repay these borrowings. Wilson, like fellow Democrat Grover Cleveland, was no apologist for debt, nor was he in favor of debt-fueled speculation of the type that increasingly was found on Wall Street. Wilson had fretted over the idea of loans to the Allied nations and his reservations were well founded. Yet the Allies needed aid and American workers and factories needed the business. The fact that the Allies were effectively broke by the time the first year of the war had ended did not prevent America from eventually entering the war, first as a lender and supplier, and later as an active belligerent. But ultimately the U.S. government would underwrite the largest part of the war effort.

The Fed During WWI

During the early years of WWI, both the White House and the Federal Reserve Board were less than enthusiastic about supporting and financing the war effort. The initial intention of Britain and France had been to issue short-term government bonds to finance the imports needed by these nations, which wanted to rely upon long-term loans to help to fund the effort over the longer term. While the House of Morgan and other banks were vigorous in promoting the debt of the Allied powers, the Fed resisted through much of the process. Even the White House and President Wilson were equivocal at best and embraced the official position of neutrality. As in past financial crises, the House of Morgan and other large New York banks and trusts operated independently of the U.S. government and were often in the position of encouraging change in public policies to support the private business objectives of the banks, their customers, and clients. The goal sought and achieved by the House of Morgan from the outset was to finance the Allied war effort and eventually see the United States enter the war.

With the creation of the Federal Reserve System in 1913, the foundation for a national monetary system was established and with it a mechanism for expanding the role of the federal government in the nation's financial and monetary life. Though not enunciated in the Federal Reserve Act, the initial goal of the central bank was to provide liquidity at times of heightened demand for credit in the economy— the long sought "flexibility" intended by Congress. The idea was to smooth the seasonal variation in interest rates that had been observed annually, generally in the months of October and November, and thus make the currency more "elastic." The stated purpose of increasing the flexibility of the money supply was to avoid financial panics and bank failures and thereby preclude the economic down-turns and asset price deflations that these events precipitated. This issue of bank runs and market panics had become more acute as means of communication improved, and also as the credit and commercial rela-tionships between different parts of the country and the world grew.

Though the job of the Fed may have been to smooth interest rates and thereby prevent the type of periodic economic crises that plagued the country for the better part of a century, in fact the level of real eco-nomic activity in the period *after* the creation of the Fed was more vol-atile than before the creation of the central bank. Even excluding the Great Depression and the huge swings in income and asset values that occurred after the October 1929 market crash, real levels of economic activity were more unpredictable and displayed greater variation after than before the creation of the Fed. This variability occurred in part because of the Fed's willingness to accommodate the huge increase in exports resulting from WWI. The increase in the volatility of economic output and employment was all the more remarkable because the sea-sonal swings in interest rates, which most people associated with the credit demands of the agrarian sector generally observed peaking around the autumnal equinox, actually declined following the creation of the Federal Reserve System.[12]

The decline in economic output following the establishment of the Fed suggests that while the central bank's role in discounting commer-cial paper had the intended effect of making the currency more elas-tic, at least as measured by the visible interest rates charged for loans and other forms of credit by banks, the other operations of the cen-tral bank may have added to the overall volatility in the performance of the U.S. economy during this period. This is not to suggest that the U.S. central bank was the *only* factor affecting the level of production and employment in the United States during the period following 1914, far from it, but the beneficial impact upon the economy that propo-nents of the central bank promised did not materialize. Since the incep-tion of the central bank, the Fed has at best been a neutral factor and at worst a destabilizing and negative factor in the overall performance of the United States in terms of employment and output, the safety and soundness of financial markets, and the evolution of the United States as a political economy.

When one then considers the changing attitudes toward work, investing, and financial speculation that occurred in the United States during the century following the creation of the central bank—all attributes of the American dream broadly defined—the role of the Fed as a positive factor in the evolution of the U.S. economy arguably diminishes even further. The perception of Americans of what activities constituted work changed between the Gold Rush of the 1840s and the Civil War. The growing acceptance of various forms of speculation as substitutes for the traditional forms of economic endeavor and related social trends may have been encouraged and enhanced by the central bank after 1913 and especially after the Great Depression and WWII. This negative influence came primarily through the willingness of the Fed to provide sufficient liquidity to stabilize the price of financial assets under the rubric of protecting the real economy. As with the Fed today, the central bank in its first decade in reality provided a sufficiently "elastic" leadership culture to get the job done for whatever political party happened to hold the White House.

In the 1920s, the assets of greatest concern were bank deposits and the stocks of depository institutions themselves, but starting from the Fed's inception the emphasis on supporting Wall Street, and the speculative portion of the investment equation has only grown in the meantime. It is very clear from the provisions of the Federal Reserve Act that the primary role of the Fed was to be the purchaser of commercial paper from banks to support the legitimate needs of commerce. This role of financing commerce was greatly expanded during WWI to include foreign trade with belligerent nations. The method employed to finance bank credits to the trade was the purchase or "rediscount" of bankers acceptances and other types of commercial paper through the 12 Federal Reserve banks by commercial banks that were members of the system. The Fed was also empowered to buy and sell government securities in the open market, thus the term "open market operations," to either add or drain cash from the financial system, again to meet the needs of commerce. "The rediscount operations of the banks were fundamental," Gilbert wrote in *The Mirrors of Wall Street*. "The open market operations were supposed to be incidental."[13]

Almost from its inception, the Fed began rapidly to increase the supply of money available to the economy, delivering the "flexibility" in terms of liquidity available to banks that the Progressives had demanded and more. The irony was that the demands for liquidity were no longer coming from the Progressives as much as from the banks, especially those larger, foreign-oriented banks intent upon doing business with Europe during the first World War. In this sense, the Fed did accede to the demands of the Progressive proponents of silver, effectively substituting the Treasury's purchase of silver prior to the repeal of the Sherman Silver Purchase Act in 1890 with a steady, at times torrid, rate of increase in the supply of paper money. Prior to the creation of the Fed "high powered money" had consisted of gold, national bank notes, and various other Treasury notes issued over the previous half century. Now deposits at the Federal Reserve, or the actual notes themselves were high powered money. By 1920, almost three quarters of the high powered or "Federal Reserve Money" consisted of Federal Reserve notes and deposits.[14]

Before the creation of the Fed, the movement of gold and the overall trade balance were the chief determinants of the amount of credit available in the U.S. economy. With the creation of a central bank, the Fed became the primary factor behind the price and availability of credit for banks and, indirectly, the U.S. economy, at least during peacetime. The Fed gave the country and its political class "choices," the respected Washington polymath Timothy Dickinson observed in April of 2010. He went on to compare the creation of the Fed with the unanticipated increase in the supply of gold produced in the 1880s and 1890s, necessarily increasing the supply of money and also the means for politicians to buy votes.

The United States had not had a central bank since before the Civil War and thus depended upon the issuance of currency by the Treasury, the supply of gold into the markets, and foreign trade and credit, to fuel the American economy. The creation of the Fed brought with it a far greater range of alternatives for the national political and business leaders, and thus made possible dramatic changes in how the economy could and would be managed. These were by and large negative changes that neither Congress nor the public at large thoroughly considered, but which the ancient opponents of a central bank going back to Jefferson and Jackson had long predicted.

Milton Friedman and Anna Schwartz compared the period immediately after the creation of the Federal Reserve System in 1913 to the greenback period under Abraham Lincoln, a very apt comparison.

These two events in American history signified a huge change in the "flexibility" of the money supply but also shifted control over this flexibility from the private markets to the political class. For example, they note that when the Fed was created, no guidance was given by Congress to the central bank as to the money supply or how to handle the ebb and flow of foreign capital. The key powers of the Fed were to discount commercial paper and provide currency, while requiring banks to maintain part of their reserves with the Fed. Initially the Fed was required to keep a gold reserve equal to 40 percent of the money supply and to also keep commercial paper as collateral for the currency.[15]

During the First World War, as a byproduct of the war finance effort, the financial center of the world gradually shifted from London to New York, in large part because of the end of the gold standard internationally. As the conflict in Europe grew, the flow of gold into the New York markets in partial payment for war materials as well as for safety greatly enhanced the influence of the largest U.S. banks. These flows of gold, Friedman and Schwartz wrote, were independent of Fed policy moves during the war, which in any event were constrained by U.S. government policy to support the Allies with loans. The massive borrowing program by the United States via the issuance of Liberty bonds also provided important financial support for the war. As noted earlier, Liberty bonds also introduced millions of Americans to the idea of investing—something other than keeping the money in the bank.

The possibility of an increased money supply care of the central bank added a dimension to policy that was not anticipated by Congress in 1913 nor was the idea of the entry into a European war the highest priority in America. Nonetheless, the U.S. banking industry and the central bank financed much of the European war effort with debt and American trade benefitted accordingly, but at the cost of sharply higher prices during the war and thereafter. As with the Civil War, half a century earlier, WWI was paid for by American workers via inflation. In a 1917 editorial, the *New York Times* reminded readers that the increase in prices was not necessarily due to profiteering as much as the sheer weight of expenditure, recalling the words on Bonar Law: "The remedy is to be found in the control of that expenditure." Unfortunately the end of the surge of war borrowing and purchases by the Allied nations would very quickly correct prices downward.

As discussed in the next section, most of the foreign debt from WWI would never be repaid, highlighting the fact that an equal measure of the wartime prosperity in the U.S. had no real economic basis and was the product of federal fiscal stimulus via borrowing. But perhaps more important was the idea held by American political leaders that expecting the Europeans to repay the debt was a reasonable policy in the first place. Americans really believed that the nations to Europe would repay their debts from the war, even as the United States hoarded global gold supplies and erected ever-higher tariff protection for domestic industries. In that sense, at least, America still clung somewhat to pre-WWI isolation from the world and thought to enjoy the benefits of war without the costs. But the more profound change in the American attitude toward money and debt was the new knowledge that government, operating via the Federal Reserve or by borrowing, could create economic prosperity out of thin air. Over the ensuing decades, this new "flexibility" empowered the American political class and gave it an entirely new role in society. The power to print money and issue debt and other obligations was a vast new political franchise.

No less than Alexander Hamilton, the great advocate of public debt as a mechanism for national unity, pointed out that government debt was a pretty close, one-to-one substitute for money. "He who has government debt has tradable capital," remarked central banker and scholar Walker Todd.[16] The realization that government debt could purchase goods and services and even drive the nation to prosperity was one of the results of WWI. This proves yet again that wars are not only about change but usually change of a decidedly negative cast. In historical terms, this revelation about the borrowing power of the fiat state begins with the legal tender laws of Abraham Lincoln and the Civil War, but blossoms into full awareness in the United States during WWI. Though many Americans would be violently opposed to such a policy were it clearly articulated and presented for a vote, the voters were never consulted. And once Americans appreciated that the Europeans either could not or would not repay their war debts, the disillusionment with international cooperation became even more intense, but it had little effect on policy.

Almost immediately from the end of the war, the Allied nations attempted to escape from their obligations to repay war debts to the United States, but Wilson spurned requests from Britain and France for debt cancelation and left the problem for his successor. Over the next decade or more, the Allies would borrow yet more money from the United States to drive economic growth on both sides of the ocean. The United States restructured and reduced the Allied loans during the 1920s, but by 1931, the major Allied nations had all defaulted on their war debts. Only Cuba, Liberia, and Finland repaid their WWI loans to the United States.[17]

After the war, the U.S. government would actually pay down the total federal debt, from $27 billion in 1919 to a low of $16 billion in 1931. From there the total federal debt would climb through the Depression and WWII to reach $250 billion by 1949. But the boom that occurred after WWI was fueled by private debt and changes to the financial system that allowed banks to provide far greater leverage for the financial markets and also to real estate than ever before. Although the federal government generally returned to a conservative, even restrictive stance in terms of spending and debt, the period of the 1920s would see a vast expansion of private debt and financial activity.

By the end of 1920, the Republican Congress was facing a revenue shortfall of $3 billion for the next year and cost cutting was the order of the day. The presidential election of 1920 was decided largely on the perceived inability of the Democrats to control spending, an ironic twist given the huge economic benefit that had come from the foreign borrowing and deficit spending by the Congress during WWI. But the fact was that Wilson's popularity and that of the reform program in general was wearing thin long before the end of his second term. The primary cause of Wilson's slip from popularity was the lengthy process of negotiating an end to the war and the failure of the process to achieve an all-encompassing framework to avoid such conflicts in the future.

Observers of the period identified the concept of "justice" as embodying both Wilson's position regarding the resolution of the war and the desire of the parties in negotiating an outcome. But once his idealistic and vague position regarding the war was reduced to dealing with concrete issues, Wilson's popularity deteriorated. The delays that marked the opening of the Paris peace conference in 1918 and the natural competition from the leaders of the belligerent nations all worked to undermine the position of Wilson, who had largely managed to stay away from the political fray until the very end of the conflict. When

President Wilson entered the peace negotiations and had to begin making tough choices to support or oppose the demands of the French,
Italians, and other victors, Wilson's popularity vanished.[18]

But Wilson was also subject to criticism in the United States for a
number of other reasons, among them financing a larger portion of the
war effort via taxes on excess profits than any other nation had managed to raise through similar levies. While Wilson and his Treasury
Secretary McAdoo did finance a great deal of the war effort via bonds
and paid the political price for the resulting inflation, the price controls
and taxes imposed during the war also took a toll on Wilson's political
popularity. By the time that the fourth Liberty bond was floated in
the United States in 1918, some 21 million Americans participated
in the issue and most of these had committed to a personal regime
of savings and economy to maximize their support for the war effort.
War Savings societies were instituted in cities around the United States
and children gathered pennies to buy 25 cent "thrift stamps" which
could be accumulated to earn a savings bond. The entire nation had a
personal and financial stake in the successful outcome of the war and,
when it did not materialize as hoped and promised by Wilson, the disappointment felt by many Americans was equally great.[19]

A Return to Republican Normalcy

With the conflict in Europe over and the U.S. economy in a slump,
control over the federal government swung back into Republican
hands under President Warren Harding in 1921. The political shift
had actually begun two years earlier in 1918, when Congress moved
back under Republican control. The nadir of the Wilson Presidency
was perhaps reached when he presented the Treaty of Versailles to the
Senate for ratification and it failed by seven votes. The promises of
global peace and prosperity advanced so confidently by Wilson were
seen to be a lie by many Americans, a reality that was already being
felt in a contracting global economy. Bruce Minton and John Stewart
described the feelings of Americans at the end of WWI:

> Men felt themselves the victims of a shabby hoax. The strug-
> gle to preserve the democracy of the world had brought not

liberty but the vengeful Treaty of Versailles. President Wilson has crassly violated his oaths of fealty to the people; his assurance of a just peace had proved as illusory as the New Freedom. Once the Armistice had ended the four-year slaughter in Europe, Woodrow Wilson's brave moralisms—moralisms that had sunk deep into the consciousness of America—were discarded, and in their place arose the determination of the victorious to plunder the vanquished.[20]

With the alluring promise of global peace and harmony dashed, Americans wanted to return to the relative simplicity of the pre-WWI republic, almost harkening back to the confident days of Teddy Roosevelt and the "Square Deal." But even this familiar and reassuring figure was soon lost. President Roosevelt died in January 1919 in his sleep at his beloved home of Sagamore Hill of a coronary embolism (arterial blood clot) at the very young age of 60. Had the former President not suffered an untimely death, there is little doubt that Roosevelt could have been the Republican presidential candidate in 1920. Americans wanted to return to the confidence and certainty that President Roosevelt represented, but the same remarkable twist of fate that put Theodore Roosevelt in the White House took him away. In 1917, President Roosevelt said of WWI: "Peace is not the end. Righteousness is the end . . . If I must choose between righteousness and peace I choose righteousness."[21]

The age of Progressive reform under Wilson and the Democrats was over and the "return to normalcy" promised by Warren Harding in his 1920 campaign was well underway. In September of 1920, just prior to the election, labor leader Samuel Gompers declared that normalcy under Warren Harding meant going backward, and he was right. The Democratic candidate, Ohio Governor James Cox, was a choice for "progress," Gompers reflected, and this was also correct from a left-of-center perspective. But the American voter would have none of Gompers' advice that year. Harding assailed the Democrats for "extravagance and autocracy" and for being unprepared for war or peace.[22] Cox and his running mate, Franklin Delano Roosevelt, were handily defeated by the Harding–Coolidge ticket and by the largest popular vote margin in modern history, 60.3 percent. The Democrats carried only 11 states, including neither Cox's home state of Ohio nor Roosevelt's home state of New York.

Harding was the first sitting member of the Senate to be elected president and, as might be expected, he soon proved to be one of the more incompetent if likable chief executives. With a seemingly strong Cabinet comprised of Andrew Mellon at Treasury, Herbert Hoover at the Commerce Department, and Charles Evan Hughes at State, President Harding was well served in these areas at least, but he would lead an administration best known for corruption and ineptness. The infamous "Teapot Dome" oil scandal erupted during Harding's first term and would feature some remarkable accomplishments, including the first Cabinet official sent to prison (Veterans Bureau chief Charles Forbes) and a number of suicides and related events. In July of 1924, Representative Cordell Hull (D-TN) attacked the "wholesale corruption" and "public immorality" of the Harding-Coolidge Administration, but the Republican hold on power was unaffected by such fusillades.

Later scholars of Harding have suggested that his abilities were underestimated and the scandal of his presidency exaggerated by at least equal measure. Harding would die of a heart attack after just 27 months in office and his Vice President, Calvin Coolidge, would succeed to the presidency. Coolidge was "distinguished for character more than for heroic achievement," wrote a Democratic admirer, Alfred E. Smith. "His great task was to restore the dignity and prestige of the Presidency when it had reached the lowest ebb in our history . . . in a time of extravagance and waste. . . ."[23] Even more laudatory was the view of Dow, Jones & Co. President Clarence Barron, who was said to have considered Coolidge to be the "ideal statesman . . . because he never rocked the Ship of State and gave business the go-ahead signal."

Whereas Woodrow Wilson had reflected nineteenth century attitudes toward money and debt, under Harding and Coolidge the cautious attitudes toward monetary expansion and the increase of speculation in the financial markets were discarded in favor of a return to the laissez faire role for the federal government and renewed economic growth, at least internally. Coolidge coined the term "the business of America is business" and proceeded to make that a reality. Members of the Republican Old Guard, such as Senator Henry Cabot Lodge, were openly contemptuous of Coolidge, who they considered a neophyte. But the new president would eventually marginalize detractors and install a new regime of business people and public relations flaks to help him steer the ship of state.

In terms of relations with the outside world, after WWI many Americans and most Republicans in Washington expected to return to the time-honored methods of trade protectionism and collecting war debts from the European allies—thus the attraction of Teddy Roosevelt, at least among Republican ranks, immediately after the war. Even though most of the industries in Western Europe were in disarray and the United States had built a mighty industrial base during the years of supplying the war effort, Americans seriously thought that they could protect these same industries, which had no equal in the world, and compel the foreign debtor nations to slowly repay their war obligations. This was precisely the economic position that Great Britain had taken toward the original American colonies, albeit on a far larger scale. The Federal Reserve System added further to the deflationary tone of the period immediately following WWI by restricting credit to deal with the inflation that had existed during much of the war. Inflation quickly disappeared when demand for all manner of goods and services dried up even before the Armistice.

Coolidge was the last conservative Republican president and advocate of limited markets. With his first message to Congress in December 1923, Coolidge announced his intention to cut taxes on income and also to abolish the nuisance and inheritance taxes. Coolidge made positive statements about collecting the war debts from Europe. But the key part of the "Coolidge Plan" was tax cuts, which drove a final stake through the heart of the Republican Old Guard and gave Coolidge a direct connection with the business community. Treasury Secretary Andrew Mellon led the charge on Capitol Hill and the financial markets surged, but the optimism was premature. Senator James Couzens (R-MI), the former business partner of Henry Ford and one of the wealthiest men in the country, objected to tax cuts for the rich. The Democrats and Progressives in Congress cut back the Mellon proposal to a reduction in the top tax rate, from 50 to 40 percent, and added insult to injury by not abolishing the inheritance tax and making tax files open for public inspection. Congress also passed legislation for a bonus for war veterans over a Coolidge veto. The president was able to beat back an effort by farm interests to subsidize food prices.

With the re-election in 1924 of Calvin Coolidge with 54 percent of the vote, the Republican control over Washington was strengthened—this despite the raucous scandals of the preceding years. Coolidge was a close friend of the great Morgan banker Dwight Morrow and during his administration the financial markets began truly to roar, fed by the greatest speculative fever since the Great Gold Rush and ample credit from the Federal Reserve. The native of Vermont was an isolationist who believed in limited government and would take full credit for the credit-fueled "Coolidge prosperity" of that time. Protective tariffs were back in vogue, regulation of business was out, and tax cuts were enacted. Unfortunately, Coolidge was no more inclined to limit the excesses of the banking industry than was his predecessor Warren Harding, although he continued to follow a tough fiscal line and paid down the outstanding federal debt.

The political power of business and the banks grew with the speculative frenzy that gripped the U.S. population after 1924 and became more visible and overt than in many decades. Ron Chernow wrote in *The House of Morgan*: "By 1924, the House of Morgan was so influential in American politics that conspiracy buffs could not tell which presidential candidate was more beholden to the bank . . . The bank's peerless renown in the Roaring Twenties was such that the Democratic candidate was the chief Morgan lawyer, John W. Davis."[24]

The Roaring Twenties

The economic boom experienced by the United States during and after WWI was a striking and welcome reversal of fortune for the nation that had been through seven grinding years of economic depression following the Panic of 1907. In that earlier economic slump, production dropped nearly 11 percent in the first year and would remain depressed well into the twentieth century. Restrictions on bank payments were lifted in 1908 and the economy slowly began to recover, but by the start of WWI America had still not fully rebounded to the level of activity seen prior to 1907. The renewed prosperity felt by some Americans during WWI created a desire to maintain that level of consumption and opportunity, but equally strong was the feeling by many Americans that they had missed the proverbial party. With millions of people living in poverty in post-war Europe and millions more in America who had not felt the benefit of the war years, the division between rich and poor in America was increased by WWI. When the economic benefit of the war began to wane in 1917, many of the old issues of social justice and the distribution of wealth that drove the Progressive movement came back into focus. How much more stratified and more volatile would this still very young American society have become had the war in Europe continued beyond 1918? Authors such as Kevin Phillips say that it occurred in any event.

The end of the war allowed the country to refocus on domestic issues and on that increasingly American pastime—namely consumption—but the road to prosperity was uneven to put it mildly. The sharp economic slump immediately after WWI is one of those details in the historical narrative of the American dream that has been edited out of modern-day treatments of the period. Social tensions that resulted from the slowdown after the war were a function not only of the fall in output and employment all over the Western world, but also of the upheaval across Europe that resulted from the May 1917 Russian revolution.

The apparent wealth of Americans in comparison to their counterparts in Europe was illustrated by the remarks of H. Perry Robinson of the London *Times* at a May 1920 meeting of the Council on Foreign Relations. Saying that Americans were so "beastly rich," Robinson related how an American cab driver had complained at paying $3 for a new pair of socks, but said they were really worth $1.50. "If a London taxi-driver said he had paid 15 shillings for his socks, we would say that was preposterous." Robinson's comments illustrated how much the product price inflation during the war years, which had seen prices rise by hundreds of percent in some cases, had made Americans seem more wealthy than the people of Europe.[25] In reality the wealth felt by many Americans was an illusion resting upon tens of billions of dollars in debt incurred during the war and an inflation rate that had seen prices double in less than a decade.

Immediately following the end of WWI, the U.S. economy experienced a downward correction in economic activity and employment that would last almost four years. By the time the United States entered the war in April 1917, the allies were in a state of military collapse and the French Army was on the brink of mutiny. The United States scrambled to send what Army and Marine units it could to the European front. The resulting frenzy of activity was an enormous distraction to the country and affected the economy in a significant and negative way. Congress enacted legislation mandating military conscription and within a year over 23 million males between the age of 21 and 30 had registered for possible service in the war. Nearly three quarters of a million men would be selected in the first draft alone, leaving jobs and families to fight in Europe. The effort to mobilize and arm the military, and to sell war bonds and save money to purchase war bonds, sent the domestic economy into a stall.

By 1919, the borrowing binge by France and Britain was over and both nations sharply curtailed their spending for U.S. imports. Cities, counties, and states around the United States followed suit as the boom years of WWI ended, provoking an instinctive, conservative reaction to stop spending money. So sudden and swift was the change in U.S. economic activity that government and civic officials, who had spent the previous several years urging thrift and the purchase of government war bonds, began instead to push for consumers to slow their savings efforts and spend! In April of 1917, Howard E. Coffin, a member of the Advisory Commission of the Council of National Defense, publicly called for consumers to spend more money and to "keep the home fires burning" because the thrift on the part of individuals and even local governments was causing domestic output to fall sharply. So powerful was the marketing push behind the war mobilization effort, compounded by the deflationary effect of the purchase of billions of dollars in war bonds, that domestic economic output dropped dramatically in 1917 and through the end of WWI. As before WWI, austerity once again gripped the nation.

Both in Washington and around the nation, governments responded to the decline in private demand from consumers by cutting spending and attacking deficits, which had the effect of making the overall economic situation even more difficult. The United States refused to make more loans to the Allies by the end of 1919, which caused an abrupt decline in all manner of exports. The momentary feeling of security that many farmers, large and small, had felt during the war years suddenly was replaced with a double-digit decline in demand for their products.

During the conflict, farm acreage in the United States had grown almost 10 percent, thus the cutoff by Washington of credit to the Allies and the related efforts by the government to dampen inflation by reducing credit produced a terrible economic contraction. So brutal was the adjustment process for American farm communities that in 1924 the Progressive Party reappeared and fielded a candidate, Robert LaFollette, who helped ensure the victory of Republican Calvin Coolidge and his running mate Charles Dawes in that year. The desire of European consumers to buy necessities and replace goods following the war's end did help to support prices through 1920, but by 1921 the American farm sector was in the worst crisis since the Civil War and remained in depression through the decade of the Roaring Twenties.

Concerns about the rise of radical political groups and even the threat of revolutionary uprisings in Europe made Americans turn inward and unite against perceived domestic threats. The so-called "Red Scare" of 1919–1920, caused by the collapse of many industries due to the economic slump after the war, was comprised mostly of ineffectual strikes by workers seeking to regain buying power lost during years of stiff inflation and austerity at home. Fears of anarchists, communists, and immigrants of all persuasions were rife in the country as the election of 1920 approached. The police strike in Boston in the fall of 1919, when then-governor Calvin Coolidge used state militia to break the labor action and restore order to the city, illustrated the frustration and despair felt by many Americans at the war's end. Coolidge fired the striking officers and broke the union by hiring returning soldiers from the war as replacements. Overnight this tough action made Coolidge a national figure.

A New Era of Debt and Investing

The Roaring Twenties is presented as a time of innovation and rising expectations in America, a time that witnessed an increase in production and productivity that lessened the need for skilled labor to produce goods. The age was symbolized by industrialists such as Henry Ford, who was widely seen as a revolutionary figure who cared for the common man, even though the truth is far less clear cut.[26] In the same way that the story of Ford is more complex than the distilled, officially endorsed versions of the Henry Ford narrative suggest today, the 1920s was a period of extremes. Equal to the changes observed in technology and industry during this period was the evolution of public mores regarding the use of money and debt.

Also significant was the growing willingness of government agencies to manipulate markets in order purportedly to manage the outcome— and all to no effect, interestingly enough. Friedman and Schwartz called the 1920s the "High Tide" for the Federal Reserve System and note that the new central bank immediately embarked upon an exercise in central planning via monetary policy. While the inhabitants of the Federal Reserve System may have believed that they were the "guiding hand" of the American economy, during this crucial decade in American history, the central bank seemed to have little or no effect compared with the massive changes underway in society. Factors such as the electrification of the United States, the growth in the use of consumer credit and the growing acceptance of the use of debt to finance all manner of economic activity, seem to be far more significant factors than the actions taken or not taken by the central bank.

In many respects, it was WWI and the period immediately following the conflict, and not the Great Depression of the 1930s, that was the most significant inflection point for the United States in both economic and political terms. The creation of the central bank and the new feeling of freedom in Washington with respect to the use of public debt was one of the key changes in the WWI era, but the national outlook also changed in important social and political dimensions. Though there remained a basic fiscal conservatism in society as a whole, the willingness to use government debt to fund "necessary" expenditures was a new development. The sale of stocks and bonds, rather than bank loans, to fuel business and speculative operations also grew enormously. The portion of bank balance sheets devoted to investments as opposed to cash and loans also grew, coincident with the sale of government securities to the public. Whereas in the nineteenth century the Treasury sold bonds directly to the banks, by WWI the Treasury was selling most of its debt to individuals. But banks also supported public purchase of all manner of securities with collateral loans on margin, one of the key developments of what was known as the New Era in investing, the phenomenon James Grant would years later dub the "democratization of credit."

One example of the change in thinking on the part of Americans about money and debt came with a change in how they viewed investments. The 1920s marked a change in focus for analysts and investors from the actual performance of a company or public entity to looking at what might occur with respect to an investment in the future. This alteration in the attitude of the investing public was most pronounced with respect to stocks and was summed up beautifully in *Securities Analysis*, the classic 1934 book by Benjamin Graham and David Dodd. Though the book is best known as a text on fundamental analysis of companies, there are significant passages in the volume which reflect on the advent of "New Era Investing" and on the social changes that were occurring in America which drove these changes in investment preference. Primary among these was the pace of change seen in the economy, in industries, and markets.

Just as the shift from the nation's founders to the proceeding generations of Americans heralded a shift away from the cautious work and save ethic of the country's earliest days, the period after WWI was marked by enormous change in many aspects of life. The mighty railroads that had dominated nineteenth century finance were swept aside by the automobile. Similar upheaval was seen in other industries as once-mighty names fell and new marquees were created. "The new-era concepts had their root, first of all, in the obsolescence of the old-established standards," wrote Graham and Dodd. "During the last generation the tempo of economic change has been speeded up to such a degree that the fact of being *long established* has ceased to be, as once it was, a warranty of *stability*." Dodd went on to describe how "the new theory or principle may be summed up in the sentence: 'The value of a common stock depends entirely upon what it will earn in the future.'"[27] Graham and Dodd then go on to list three corollaries that follow from the "New Era" theory of stock investing:

1. That the dividend rate should have slight bearing upon the value.
2. That since no relationship apparently existed between assets and earning power, the asset value was entirely devoid of importance.
3. That past earnings were significant only to the extent that they indicate what *changes* in the earnings were likely to take place in the future.

The shift in the financial mindset of Americans from the actual performance of a company to what it might do *in the future* had far more significance than merely changing the theory of investing to a culture of speculation. Bernard Baruch defined a speculator as "a man who observes the future and acts before it occurs," a very close analog for the gold rush, risk-taking image of opportunistic entrepreneurship that has become the ideal for generations of Americans. As with the changes in the nation from the agrarian, work hard, and save your money model of Adams and Jefferson to the opportunism of the industrial baron or gold rush speculator, the shift away from looking at the historical earnings of a company to speculating about its future performance said a great deal about the permanence and stability of the American economy. Today, even among auditors and federal regulators, the use of speculative estimates and "forward looking" indicators is widely accepted as a reasonable means to conduct oversight and surveillance of the internal workings of companies and banks.[28]

Instead of gradually sharing in the additive growth of a company through dividends, the prevailing "investment" model became to buy a stock at one price and sell it at a higher price to another market participant—in part because the rate of change in a given company or industry was so rapid that the traditional buy and hold investment strategy could not keep up. This transient view of the value offered by a company stock or government bond is typified today by television programs such as *Mad Money*, the CNBC program hosted by former Goldman Sachs trader Jim Cramer. Cramer derides buy and hold or "value" investing of the type advocated by Graham and Dodd, and instead instructs his viewers to jump from one stock to the next in a speculative fashion. This view of money and investing as an essentially speculative activity says a great deal for the way in which modern day Americans view their world. The roots of this perceived instability in the U.S. economy, companies, and even government institutions go back to the turn of the last century.

Uncertainty or doubt about the solidity of the economy seemed to push Americans into a more tactical, more short-term, and speculative mode of existence. And the rise of the model of speculation as a means to achieve the American dream did not always bring with it positive developments in society as a whole. Minton and Stewart commented in *The Fat Years and the Lean*:

> The machine brought the Golden Age, making life more complicated but not more significant. The new abundance of material wealth failed to stir the creative energies of the people. The monopolists set the cultural standards of America just as they controlled the political life of the nation. The businessmen were enthroned, the arbiters of taste, the prelates of a civilization that had salesmanship as its art.[29]

The imagery raised about the growing role of the machine and of mass production of all types of goods in American life is an important part of understanding why the WWI period was such a powerful inflection point for the country. Whereas the English model of industry placed the primary focus on building complex and exquisite tools used by craftsmen to manufacture goods by hand, the American model of industry focused instead on adding speed and productivity to the procedure of transformation from raw material to finished products. The growing use of standardization and interchangeable parts in American industry in the later part of the nineteenth century allowed the country to increase production rapidly to meet the needs of WWI—something that never would have been possible in the United Kingdom or in Europe. The "American System" of mass production provided a source of inexpensive consumer goods, from clothes to automobiles to aircraft, the like of which the world had never seen.[30]

Henry Ford is held up as the great icon of mass production during this early period of American industrialization, but his company actually began its operations assembling kits manufactured to Ford's design by the Dodge Brothers. When Ford Motor Company did begin to build its own cars, it was James Couzens and the Ford managers who made Ford into a standardized and replicable manufacturing wonder—often despite the best efforts of the great inventor. From the early years of the twentieth century, American industry was already sufficiently advanced for an infant company such as Ford to outsource the manufacturing of its first product and then begin to make its own parts based upon suppliers all over the country.

Henry Ford was in his heart a designer and visionary, an authentic American entrepreneur but certainly not an "operator" in the sense that we today associate with corporate managers.[31] But the managers and operators who did make Ford a vast enterprise managed to push down the cost of the Model T over the more than two decades it was produced. Ford and other U.S. automakers such as Dodge and General Motors excelled in terms of economy and flexibility in standardized industrial production, production that could be replicated and scaled up without practical limit. This production capability not only enabled the Allies to fight the war against Germany, but made the victory in the war itself possible. The same flexible aspect of American industrial organization, combined with the entrepreneurial spirit of the American people, also made possible the victory against Germany and Japan in WWII. The willingness of Americans to use debt to finance this flexible industrial expansion was the final ingredient of success for the Western Allies in fighting and winning two world wars. Once these two conflicts were won, however, the industries that were created to support and supply the war effort needed to find a way to maintain output and profits.

The Rise of Consumer Finance

In his 1999 book, *Financing the American Dream: A Cultural History of Consumer Credit*, Lendol Calder of Augustana College presents a detailed history of the "culture of consumption" in the United States and how the gradual acceptance of the use of debt to purchase consumer goods represented an evolution in attitudes toward debt that developed over a period of centuries. Calder details the slow but steady growth of consumer credit, from its roots in the late nineteenth century, a period he describes as "growth and stigmatization" from 1880 to 1915, to "growth and legitimization," from 1915 through 1930. Of particular note is Calder's characterization of the tipping point in terms of the broader acceptance of consumer debt as occurring in 1915, the middle of WWI. "It is now generally recognized that just as it would

be ridiculous to write a history of a medieval European town without its attention to its cathedral," Calder writes, "so twentieth century
America cannot be understood apart from its department stores and
shopping malls."[32]

The use of consumer debt to finance immediate purchases based
on future income was one of the more important developments of the
1920s. Professor Calder, relying on the work of the noted economist
Raymond Goldsmith, notes that the use of consumer debt during the
1920s soared by over 130 percent and that the number of borrow-
ers increased dramatically. A large portion of the increase had to do
with one consumer product in particular, the automobile, but installment credit was also used to buy many other types of goods. "Credit
financing made the automobile the quintessential commodity of the
American consumer culture," notes Calder. "Credit plans also figured
prominently in the selling of radios, refrigerators, vacuum cleaners,
fine jewelry, and other expensive consumer durable goods."[33]

Perhaps the most prominent example of the new age of consumer
finance was the founding of General Motors Acceptance Corporation
(GMAC), a remarkable story that came only after GM had been through
two financial failures. Founded in 1919 as a wholly owned subsidiary
of General Motors Corp., GMAC was established to provide GM dealers with the financing necessary to acquire and maintain vehicle inventories and to provide customers a means to finance vehicle purchases.
The company's products and services expanded through the years to
include insurance, mortgages, online banking, and commercial finance.[34]
GMAC, which was the brainchild of Alfred P. Sloan, the great business
executive who led GM's operation from 1920 as a vice president until
he stepped down as chairman in 1956, was one of the first "captive"
financing vehicles established by a consumer products company.

GM was the creation of William Durant, the Wall Street speculator
and serial industrialist who combined his first acquisition, Oldsmobile,
with a number of small auto makers and parts suppliers into a new corporation called General Motors in 1908. The fact that Durant chose
to organize GM—known at the time as "Durant's Folly"—during
the grim economic depression after the Panic of 1907 exposed him
to ridicule and derision, even more so when he set a capitalization of
$10 million for the new company. Many observers laughed at Durant,

especially when the former carriage manufacturer predicted in 1907 that Americans would require 1 million new automobiles per year a decade later, a prophecy that proved to be more than prescient. A year later, when the new GM reported $34 million in sales and net profits exceeded the firm's capitalization, the laughter ceased. Bankers flocked to provide funding to GM and helped Durant finance a breathtaking expansion of brands and models that was meant to help him overtake Henry Ford, then by far the volume leader in the auto business.

When the U.S. economy again began to look uncertain in 1910, however, the bankers pulled the plug and GM collapsed into the unkind arms of its creditors. Were it not for the change of heart by his lenders, Durant might have acquired Ford as well, but instead he was ousted from the company he had built over almost a decade of astute acquisitions and audacious borrowing. Undaunted, Durant immediately started a new car making enterprise known as Chevrolet. By 1915 the tiny automaker was profitable and Durant, always the shrewd speculator, used stock in Chevrolet and the growing support from his loyal bankers to regain control of GM. This remarkable comeback by Durant was aided by two of the largest industrialist of the day, John J. Raskob and Pierre S. du Pont, and the E.I. du Pont de Nemours Powder Company as it was known in those days because of its manufacture of gunpowder and ammunition. By 1920, the du Pont corporation had invested nearly $50 million of wartime profits into GM, but once again the use of debt to finance the endeavor proved the weak point in the Durant empire.

Against Durant's advice, the GM board mounted an aggressive expansion during WWI funded with debt. The torrid growth in vehicles produced during the conflict drove the company's profits up sharply. Investors talked openly about GM reaching $1,000 per share versus $24 in 1915 when the great speculator began his campaign to regain control. Having lost GM once before due to overexpansion, Durant knew that the wartime boom would eventually end and again he was proven prescient. With the end of the war, credit became tight, prices for stocks and bonds plummeted, and an economic depression caused consumers to limit purchases to all but the necessities of life and, in particular, stopped buying cars. With the economic downturn in 1920, the company again collapsed into the arms of the banks led by J.P. Morgan. The end came only after Durant spent most of his fortune, estimated at some $90 million, to support GM's stock and make many of his investors whole. The banks, led by the House of Morgan would later buy out Durant's stake in GM for a mere $40 million, a fraction of what the shares would be worth only a few years later.

Although GM was just seven years old in 1920, the company had collapsed under the weight of debt twice and was now placed under the control of the du Pont family. Alfred Sloan was then an executive at the company and would eventually be made President by Pierre du Pont, who was Chairman of the Board of GM from 1915 until 1929. Sloan's genius for operations and sales was enormous, but there were several aspects of his tenure at GM that helped the company take the lead in the auto industry away from Ford.

First, Sloan wanted to have a new product every year, "a product for every purse," whereas Ford manufactured the same car, the Model T, for almost two decades from 1908 to 1927. Second, Sloan realized that the lack of financing for new car purchases after WWI was pushing consumers to buy used cars instead of new models. Even a two-year old Chevy, Sloan realized, was more attractive than the cranky and increasingly obsolete Model T. And third and finally, Sloan understood that GM's "AAA" credit rating, a function of the support of du Pont and the rational management system that company established within GM, enabled the company essentially to finance manufacturing, distribution, and sales at a very low cost.

GMAC provided credit to both the dealer and the end customer. When GM manufactured the car, it was "sold" to the dealer, who was required to pay for the vehicle when it arrived. But GM provided financing to the dealers via GMAC, which issued bonds to investors to finance the unsold inventories. Because the cost of the credit for dealers was below the rates charged by banks, the dealers were able to earn more profits for every car sold. And by providing credit for consumers at likewise rock bottom rates, GM was able to increase new car sales and grow far faster than Ford. In essence, by managing its accounts payable to its suppliers and providing financing for dealer inventories and final sales, GM was able to gain up to five months of free float and was therefore able to invest in new manufacturing capacity and other expansion in a way that Ford could not.

Henry Ford was an extremely conservative man who ran his entire company on a cash basis until the end of WWII. Suppliers bringing raw materials and parts to the Ford factory were paid in cash. Ford distrusted bankers and hated debt. By 1929 Ford was one of the largest cash depositors in the U.S. banking system. Never thinking of using credit to encourage sales, Ford believed that pushing down the cost of his beloved Model T and making incremental improvements to the perfect car was all the incentive needed to spur sales. And Ford's inability to grasp the significance of consumer credit to expanding demand for his products would allow GM to capture leadership in the auto industry by the mid-1920s, a position of dominance that GM holds to this day—even after a bankruptcy reorganization in 2009. In fact, through much of the twentieth century Ford would compare its sales not to GM, but to the Chevrolet division of GM, such was the difference in the market share of the two firms after the 1920s.

America Transformed

Only one in ten people who left the farm to fight in WWI actually went home to rural America once the conflict ended. A huge pool of labor was available in American cities, labor that provided a ready market for the rising consumer products giants of corporate America— corporations which still dominate the market today. Industrial enterprises such as Ford and General Motors had arisen or taken modern form to challenge the established business giant money trusts like U.S. Steel and Standard Oil. All of these companies and others had expanded greatly during the war years and in the process had spawned a vast network of suppliers and dealers. While automobiles were the most prominent examples, similar national networks of suppliers and sales outlets were created in many other industries so that companies increasingly took on a national scope, unlike the smaller organizations that had been typical in the nineteenth century.

Following WWI, life in urban America was transformed into a continuous quest for prosperity in an economic sense, with every step in life, from early education to professional training meant to support advancement in a business sense. Acquisition of certain items of consumer apparatus became the measure of personal advancement and success, part of the journey to "make something of yourself." The vast consolidation and concentration that occurred in many industries during and after WWI encouraged this trend as larger and larger companies sought to defend their markets and brands via media outlets that these same conglomerates controlled through sponsorship if not owner-ship. Success in life could be measured by the types of products which individuals owned or consumed and the use of debt to purchase these products became increasingly acceptable. The industrial power that made it possible to meet far greater consumption of consumer goods of all types arguably required that greater use of credit become acceptable to a larger and larger number of Americans.

The changing social attitudes toward saving and debt that occurred after the Civil War, and especially from the 1920s onward, seemingly made Americans focus on more short-term and speculative forward-looking yardsticks for trying to understand the vast social change occurring around them, changes that were very much evident in the financial world. The approach that existed prior to WWI of assess-ing past records and facts in selecting an investment was discarded in favor of assessing the likely *trend* in future earnings. With this change in emphasis, from the present to speculating about the results of a company *in the future*, the distinction between investment and specu-lation disappeared.[35] While Graham and Dodd focus on WWI as the demarcation point in terms of broadly accepted American perceptions of investments, other scholars such as William Janeway of Cambridge University argue that the change began much earlier in the late nine-teenth century, a point supported by Calder and others.

The significance of when the inflection point occurred in America's view of money and debt is less important than the striking departure this attitude represented for the way Americans acted with respect to borrowing and the basic function of saving. The stay home, work hard, and save model advocated by Thomas Jefferson or John Adams was in complete opposition to the opportunistic, short-term model of the gold rush or the twentieth century stock speculator such as William Durant. The traditional rule of prudence defined by Edmund Burke as "the first of all virtues" was a life spent carefully weighing the trade-offs and minding one's own business, Thomas Sowell noted in his book *A Conflict of Visions*.[36] But in the unconstrained world view of writ-ers such as anarchist William Godwin, life was seen as ever expand-ing and man as perfectible beyond the mere rewards of material goods.

The optimistic world view of Godwin and his belief in the unlimited potential of human beings is very much reflected today in American attitudes about economic and personal potential—the guideposts if you will to the American dream that place no finite limit on the advancement of an individual. In that sense, the libertarian political tradition of the United States has found economic expression in a decidedly casual and almost libertine view of money and debt.[37]

One perspective saw the American dream as a thing to be earned over many years of consistent work, saving, or cash investing, while the other depended mostly upon luck and avarice, the availability of new credit, or a greater fool to ensure gain or immediate gratification. The former is the cautious world of cash investing, Graham and Dodd, and deliberate choices made after careful consideration and analysis. The latter an aggressive, imaginative but speculative model of endless vistas and unconstrained vision, the common denominators of any mass movement, religious cult or financial get-rich-quick financial scheme. The war profiteers of the Civil War like Jay Cooke and Jay Gould, the Robber Barons of the nineteenth century, the even more grotesque war profiteers of WWI, and the traders of the 1920s on Wall Street were all using leverage and market power—and luck—to try and make a buck.

The difference between the perspective on money and debt that existed before and after WWI was that by the 1920s, credit had become available to one and all. In the same way that improvements in communication in the latter part of the nineteenth century changed financial panics and bank runs from a local to a national problem, the greater availability of credit enabled more diverse forms of speculation by far larger numbers and groups of players. The purchase of a consumer appliance and the use of margin credit to buy stocks were seen in some quarters as equally virtuous acts. Domestic and overseas companies, and even foreign nations and banks, all issued stocks and bonds to American investors during the Roaring Twenties. Within this time of seemingly endless economic possibility, newly affluent consumers purchased all sorts of products and began to use consumer credit to further enhance their ability to satiate their *immediate* demand for goods. Whether in the form of forced savings programs, buying a home appliance on time, or borrowing to finance a speculative investment, American consumers had access to credit in ways that were not widely known or understood a generation before.

The financial services industry expanded dramatically during this period and banks began to offer mortgages, installment credit, and even margin loans to individuals to fund securities purchases. Consumers began to buy bonds and equity securities, and Wall Street expanded capacity to meet and encourage the new demand. Banks began to offer various types of structured assets to consumers and even participated directly in land speculation, conveying at least the image of wealth to America's earliest real estate entrepreneurs. Much of the financing of this period was provided via trusts, special purpose entities created solely for the purpose of issuing securities. Like the subprime mortgage-backed securities of a century later, these "complex" investments were more often than not a dodge to relieve the credulous investor of his or her investment. And many of the supposedly "sophisticated" investment strategies of the early twenty-first century were in used in the 1920s.

Among the more popular schemes employed by banks and their securities affiliates in the 1920s was to repackage loans to Latin American nations and sell participation to retail investors in the United States. Much like the complex subprime mortgage paper that would cause a crisis in America nearly a century later, these bonds were completely opaque and the buyers of these securities usually had no idea about the credit standing of the obligors. The securities affiliate of First National City Bank, predecessor of Citibank NA, was one of the more notorious offenders during this period. At the high tide of the investment boom of the late 1920s, National City Company—as the brokerage firm was known—had more than 2,000 stock brokers selling securities to retail investors. The reckless actions of National City would serve as a major impetus behind the eventual imposition of a separation between securities dealing and banking via the Glass–Steagall law of the 1930s.

One critical account of the era was a 1937 book by Bernard J. Reis and John Flynn, *False Security: The Betrayal of the American Investor*. The authors chronicle a financial zoological tour of structured financial instruments that could have come out of Wall Street in the late 2000s, but in fact were being sold in the period after WWI, a decade and more before the 1929 market crash. Under the heading of "investments the public believed to be gilt edged," Reis and Flynn take the reader through a dizzying collection of guaranteed mortgages, foreign bonds, investment trusts, and real estate bonds. All manner of debt was in use during the 1920s and much of the apparent prosperity during the period resulted from the issuance of the debt. As had been the case during WWI, borrowing was employed by many Americans to enable all sorts of activity, from consumption to speculation, and the nations of Europe likewise continued to borrow in the United States to fund exports. The authors conveyed the bitterness and anger felt by many Americans in the 1930s in a comment at the end of their book:

> Simply stated, honesty plays little part in American business. Our morality, on the contrary, in a game of cards or in sports is irreproachable. And so it is that we are gentlemen of honor when engaged in life's pastimes, but devoid of it when engaged in serious pursuits. The public has a subconscious awareness of this state of business immorality, but for some reason remains apathetic to it, and even condones it. True, a simple criminal act is condemned (and when simple it is invariably of small dimensions) but where large profits have accrued or an enormous institution erected on no matter how fraudulent a foundation we give it respect and applause.[38]

Part of the appeal of the interpretation of the 1920s by Reis and Flynn is the perspective of the aggrieved consumer. Like the work of Graham and Dodd, their description of the public mania regarding "new" investment vehicles in the 1920s could be applied almost word-for-word to the events in the U.S. markets over the past decade. And the book beautifully illustrates the ancient precursors of modern structured finance with numerous examples of specific transactions and issuers drawn from the time. At first the securities firms sold only participations in mortgages; that is, on a single piece of property to one investor that they guaranteed. But soon the Wall Street firms devised securities based upon pools of mortgages "which were designed to give the investor greater safety by reason of diversification, on the principle that one should never keep all of one's eggs in one basket." The authors found that of the $10 billion or so in mortgage-backed securities issued during the period, some $8 billion of original face amount were in default by the early 1930s when Congress launched various inquiries into the practices of Wall Street.[39]

The important point to take away from this period is that the very same type of mortgage-backed securities that caused the financial crisis of 2007 were actually first conceived and sold to the public a century earlier—and by many of the same banks and financial institutions. Billions more worth of bonds issued by foreign nations, states, cities, and other issuers were likewise sold in the United States during this period. Much of this debt was used to purchase American goods for export and most of it was in default by the mid-1930s. The issuers were not only from Europe, but also included many Latin American nations and their internal jurisdictions, entities that had hitherto been unknown to U.S. investors. In those days, when a bond went into default, the word "shrinkage" was used to describe the reduction in value. With the end of the Roaring Twenties, the U.S. economy not only suffered from the decline in demand due to the inability of these foreign governments to issue more debt, but also from the shrinkage of value to American investors who held the defaulted paper. The resulting financial deflation and economic dislocation would cause the worst economic crisis the American republic had yet experienced.

Prelude to the Depression

In 1927 Congress passed the McFadden Act, which established the Federal Reserve Board as a permanent oversight agency of the central bank and, more importantly, prohibited interstate banking, a limitation that remained in place until 1994. But the McFadden Act also authorized hometown branches for national banks, if allowed by the state, a change that put national banks on a more even footing with state banks. National banks still could not establish branches outside of the city in which they were headquartered, but significantly, the legislation gave national banks authority to buy and sell marketable debt obligations and make loans on real estate. This was a significant change for banks and the investing public and increased the supply of credit for speculation in both stocks and real property. Friedman and Schwartz wrote that when combined with changes to the Federal

Reserve Act in 1916, the McFadden Act increased the amount of credit bank available to the real estate and other sectors.[40]

The author of the McFadden Act was Rep. Louis McFadden (R–PA), who chaired the House Committee on Banking and Currency during the late 1920s and early 1930s. A banker by profession, McFadden became a staunch critic of the Federal Reserve System and many of the financial officials of the U.S. government following the 1929 market crash. What is interesting about the McFadden Act in terms of our narrative of the evolution of money and debt in the United States is that the law was initially proposed several years before as a means of allowing national banks to establish branches.

The Banking Act of 1865 had been silent on the issue of branching by national banks and thus national banks were at a significant disadvantage compared to the far more numerous state-chartered depositories. The Treasury supported the proposal, but the Federal Reserve and the state banks opposed it. Indeed, in 1923 the Federal Reserve Board actually passed a resolution prohibiting member banks from branching outside a bank's home city and geographic area. After several years of debate on the issue, the Congress finally passed a law, which allowed national banks to establish branches to the same extent allowed by state law for other banks. But the McFadden Act also prohibited national banks from expanding outside the state where they operated.[41]

The primary logic behind the McFadden Act was to protect banks from competition, a policy perspective that was in line with the traditional American use of tariffs and a weak currency to protect domestic industries from foreign predation. Despite the boom that was occurring on Wall Street during the 1920s, a boom that was fueled by the expansion of the domestic credit base by the Federal Reserve System via open market operations and the floatation of a large number of foreign and domestic bond issues, the number of bank failures in the United States had risen to alarming proportions during the 1920s.

Part of the reason for the number of bank failures was the large number of state chartered institutions, many more than were really needed to serve the communities in which they were located. Even in rural parts of the United States, there were often more banks in a given state, city, or town than could survive financially in good times; thus when times got tough banks failed in droves. Over 1,000 banks failed in the United States during 1926 alone, but by that time there were almost 18,000 state-chartered banks in the country and another 8,000 national banks. These institutions had a powerful political following in their communities. No surprise then that many members of Congress during that period were motivated by a desire to protect banks in their communities. The solution—prohibit banks from expanding geographically—did not really address the problem and may have arguably made things worse following the financial market break of 1929.

Another issue addressed in the McFadden Act, however, was far more significant to the long-term development of the U.S. political economy and our story of money and debt, namely the creation of the Board of Governors of the Federal Reserve System in Washington. While the 12 regional reserve banks had been chartered by the Congress in 1913, it was only with the creation of the Board of Governors of the Fed in 1927 that the central bank became a permanent fixture in Washington among the other agencies of the federal government. Once the Board was made part of the incestuous political community that is Washington, any notion that the central bank was independent of the Executive Branch of Government was quickly dispelled. And given the significant degree of political influence that the large New York banks have exercised over the political workings of Washington, the Fed Board quickly became entirely politicized. The significance of this development for the central bank and the independence of U.S. monetary policy will be discussed further in Chapter 6.

A final point with respect to the Federal Reserve during this period has to do with the influence of the House of Morgan and its *de facto* agent Benjamin Strong, who served as the first governor of the Federal Reserve and chief executive of the Federal Reserve Bank of New York from 1914 until his death in 1928. In the official history of the New York reserve bank, Strong is described as "a dominant force in U.S. monetary and banking affairs" and indeed he was all of that. But because of his personal links to J.P. Morgan and, through the anglophile tendencies of the Morgan Bank, to the Bank of England, Strong's independence manifested itself in ways that were ultimately at odds with his duties as an officer of the U.S. central bank.

The eminent British economist Lionel Robins, in his classic 1934 book *The Great Depression*,[42] wrote that the credit expansion by the

Federal Reserve after 1925 was a deliberate effort by Strong to help the economic situation in Britain. The United Kingdom had gone back onto the gold standard in 1925 and the results on the British economy were so negative that by 1927 the country was facing economic depression and political strife due to labor unrest. The United Kingdom had gone back onto the gold standard at the prewar rate of $4.86 per pound, in essence ignoring the adjustment that had been forced upon English authorities after J.P. Morgan ended its support operations for the British currency in the early years of WWI.

Most historians now accept that the decision by English authorities was badly misguided and began a period of deflation in the United Kingdom that soon combined with a recession in the United States starting in the middle of 1927. The Fed's use of easy money in the United States to address the economic weakness in the United Kingdom was the start of a symbiotic relationship between the two nations in monetary terms that is an important part of the history of the post-WWII era. In the United States too, the economic boom that had accelerated after 1925 was showing signs of ending; thus Strong and a majority of the Federal Reserve governors supported a policy of easy money starting in 1927 that arguably would make the market break two years later more severe.

Bust: Stocks Fall and Tariffs Rise

In the Summer of 1927, after eight years of blissful inaction and inattention by Washington to the problems developing in the financial markets and the economy, President Coolidge decided to move the executive offices of the nation to Rapid City, South Dakota to prepare for the upcoming Republican convention in Kansas City. The economy apparently was booming and the financial markets were soaring, so the president felt no reason not to give his full attention to politics. And true to his reputation for political acumen, Coolidge soon announced in August of 1927 that he would not seek the presidency for a second full term, leaving the field to the other candidates such as Herbert Hoover, who was then Secretary of Commerce. Of all the possible candidates, Hoover, who unsuccessfully sought the Democratic nomination in 1920, was the only one with the natural talent and who truly sought the job.

Coolidge was a clever man—but too clever in this instance. He hoped that in a field of relatively weak candidates, none would be able to command a majority at the convention and that the party eventually would turn to their popular president to run for another term. With the death of Teddy Roosevelt in 1919, Coolidge was essentially the grand old man of the Grand Old Party, but not nearly the same magnitude of public figure as Theodore Roosevelt. He hoped to be asked to take up the Republican standard yet again in 1928, but he underestimated the ambition and political skills of the great engineer.

Hoover was ever loquacious and had no problem speaking to the press. Coolidge, on the other hand, was a man of few words and even fewer real ideas. With the exception of Hoover, he had surrounded himself with men of similar qualities. Chief among them was Treasury Secretary Andrew Mellon, a loyal Republican partisan of Coolidge but a man, like most Republicans of that age, who had trouble assembling consecutive sentences at the best of times but particularly when in front of the media. By picking Mellon to be his point man at the Republican convention in 1928, Coolidge ensured that he would not run for a third term as president.

The Republican convention of 1928 nominated Hoover on the first ballot, praising Hoover as the great engineer, the great administrator, the great economist, "the greatest humanitarian since Jesus Christ," as Al Smith quipped at the time. The Republicans were in no mood to take any controversial positions in 1928 and hoped that Hoover would merely continue the glorious age of prosperity and economic good times that was visible in urban America. Calls from Progressive elements in the party to focus on the deflation and crisis that existed in the farm sector fell upon deaf ears, as did calls to repeal the prohibition on sales of alcohol that had been enacted in 1920. The GOP had been returned to power in 1920 on the promise of a "return to normalcy" and the goal of the party in 1928 was to continue that successful run.

Herbert Hoover was the first president born west of the Mississippi River, and he represented a change from his Republican predecessors. He ran on a platform that supported a continuation of the policies of Calvin Coolidge and prohibition under the mantra of "a chicken in every pot and a car in every garage." He easily defeated the Democratic ticket led by former New York governor Al Smith, who was a loyal if independent and literate member of the Tammany

Hall political machine. Although Smith was nominated by Franklin Roosevelt, supported repeal of prohibition, and had the active support of corporate titans such as John J. Raskob of General Motors, Hoover defeated him in a landslide that saw a number of Southern states brought into the Republican column for the first time. This result heartened the Republicans even more and convinced them of the correctness of the policies of the previous eight years. Following the election, when the lame duck session of Congress met, President Coolidge told the legislators: "No Congress ever assembled, on surveying the state of the Union, has met with a more pleasing prospect than that which appears at the present time."[43]

Upon taking office in March of 1929, Hoover focused on issues such as relief for farmers and reduction of tariffs. He championed federal export assistance for American farmers via the Agricultural Marketing Act and, after considerable debate, the Congress eventually gave Hoover his way. The Act encouraged the formation of farm cooperatives and also provided some early support by the federal government for farm prices. Hoover's action represented a significant victory for agrarian interests, even if a large portion of the aid ended up going to larger commercial farms rather than the family farmers.

When Congress next turned to the question of tariff reduction to help the farm sector, as President Hoover requested, the temptation instead to *raise* levies further to protect domestic industries was too great. By raising tariffs, it was believed in the late 1920s, the prices for industrial and consumer goods could be pushed even higher with corresponding increases in profits to big business. In this sense, the American business community had the same mindset as the great speculators of the Gilded Age such as Jay Gould—namely limit supply and competition—and thereby capture higher profits for their goods. The mindset of business leaders and politicians of the day was the opposite of that which prevailed in the United States after WWII, when large corporate interests became the active advocates of free trade and open global markets.

Senator Byrd wrote in his history of the Senate that lobbyists for every industry imaginable besieged Congress to press for greater tariff protection, in some cases hiring special trains to bring the lobbyists to Washington to press their demands. Industrial and agrarian interests actually made common cause to seek higher tariff rates. Even as the stock market was collapsing, the Senate debate on increasing tariffs continued and even intensified as, Byrd wrote, "businesses looked to the tariff as its salvation." Congress would not pass new tariff legislation—known as Smoot-Hawley after the bill's authors—until more than six months after the October 1929 market crash in June 1930, but the impact of the increase in the existing tariffs would be quite dramatic. Progressives denounced the legislation, with Senator George Norris (R/I-NE) calling it "one of the most selfish and indefensible tariff measures that has even been considered by the American people."[44]

What is missed by many discussions of the period, however, is the fact that the economic collapse of the 1930s was already a given with or without the new tariff law. The impetus behind the political decision to raise tariffs was a misguided reaction to the collapse of the speculative bubble on Wall Street. It had little to do with the economic depression that occurred as a result of the long-term deflation in the farm sector following WWI and the overproduction in many industries. Support for protectionism was the consistent refrain from the corporate and farm lobbies in Washington in the nineteenth and early twentieth centuries and was provided by members of both political parties. But the real underlying cause of the powerful political push to raise the *existing* tariffs even higher at the end of 1929 may be found in the substantial changes that were occurring in the American economy.

Many historians and economists blame the level of tariffs after WWI and particularly during the Great Depression for making more severe the economic contraction and unemployment following the 1929 market crash. The passage of the Fordney-McCumber Tariff Act in 1922 symbolized the unique Republican penchant for trade protectionism and inflation that stretched decades back in time to the party's inception in the 1850s.

In his book *Making Sense of Smoot Hawley*, Bernard Beaudreau argues that the imposition of tariff protection for U.S. industry in 1930 was simply a continuation of the policies implemented by the Republican party after they returned to power in 1920. Beaudreau cites the rising productivity of U.S. factories, the spread of electrification throughout America, and the continued influx of foreign-produced food and manufactured goods as the cause of the deflation.[45] Imports were still perceived to be a threat by the American manufacturers of that day, despite already high tariff levels. Underemployment was the result of the lack of demand and thus falling product prices that resulted in the 1930s. In simple terms, American industry became too efficient too quickly, resulting in a global surplus of goods and an equally dangerous lack of demand—an imbalance that Congress sought to correct by limiting imports via the Smoot-Hawley tariff. While there is no doubt that higher tariffs made the Great Depression worse, higher levies on imports may not have been the primary factor.

This alternative view of the role of Smoot-Hawley in turning the market crash of 1929 into the Great Depression of the 1930s is important to our narrative. Following the Great Depression and WWII, the U.S. position regarding tariffs changed dramatically, in part because much of the industrial capacity of Europe and Asia was destroyed by the conflict. Under the rubric of rebuilding the post-war world, America embraced a policy of open markets and free trade. This policy created enormous wealth and prosperity in the first several decades after the end of the Second World War, but later it sacrificed American jobs and industrial capacity in the name of rebuilding the global economy. Another way of looking at this issue, however, is that once the large business interests in the United States realized that they could no longer extract above-normal prices for their products by hiding behind the tariff barriers that were widely supported prior to the Great Depression, they instead chose to pursue growth and new business opportunities by embracing a policy of promoting free trade.

During the post-WWII period, the Federal Reserve System would complement the policy of free trade by keeping the dollar artificially strong and importing wage and price deflation via lower wages and low cost goods from abroad. This deliberate policy, followed over successive decades by the Federal Reserve, conveniently allowed the U.S. central bank to pretend that it was controlling inflation even as the United States accommodated growing public and private debt and fiscal deficits. The period from WWI through the Great Depression marks an important inflection point in the way the U.S. economy interacted with the rest of the world in some very fundamental ways.

The threat of regressive actions in Washington in the form of increased tariffs was barely noticed by the citizenry in 1929, who were too busy celebrating the New Era on Wall Street. Breathless accounts of fortunes made overnight in the stock market filled the media of the day, describing the wealth possible by investing in stocks in terms that put even the most optimistic sales literature from the banks and their securities affiliates to shame. But there were signs of trouble in terms of a slowing economy even as Hoover took office.

The Coolidge Administration, as was the practice at the time, had been on a program of austerity, cutting spending in Washington in response to a slowing economy. Hoover would continue that approach, calling for greater economy in Washington even as the nation sank into depression. The federal debt reached a low of $16.1 billion in June of 1930 as the government continued to pay off its debts and follow a program of fiscal austerity to match falling tax revenues, as was the practice in most states, cities, and towns around the country. This already deflationary tendency was only made worse by the belated actions by the Fed to rein in growth in the supply of money.

The interest rate increases by the Fed caused bitter complaints from the speculative class on Wall Street. These protests were led by the likes of Bill Durant, who was now pretty much out of the auto industry and focused instead on his role as one of the great stock operators of his age. Durant would travel secretly to Washington to visit President Hoover in December 1929 and warn the new president that the Fed's actions were making the crisis worse and that catastrophe would follow "unless something is done to limit the Federal Reserve Board to the functions stated in the law that created it." He continued: "Those functions are to stabilize money rates and prevent panic. It did neither. Call money jumped to twenty percent. The country experienced the worst crash in history."[46]

Within the Federal Reserve, a heated debate had been underway for years regarding the use of central bank credit to fund speculative activities. This debate had been ongoing for most of the previous decade, but the surge in stock prices had brought the issue to the forefront as differences among the different parts of the Fed system emerged. In February of 1929, the Board actually wrote a letter to the Reserve Banks stating that "a member bank is not within its reasonable claims for rediscount facilities at its Federal reserve bank when it borrows either for the purpose of making speculative loans or for the purpose of maintaining speculative loans."[47]

For the next several months, officials of the Federal Reserve Banks and the Board in Washington debated how to deal with the issue of speculation and the increase in credit, which had been expanding at better than twice the rate of growth in terms of business output. George L. Harrison, who was appointed governor of the Federal Reserve Bank of New York to replace Benjamin Strong in November of 1928, was an advocate of raising interest rates to cool the expansion of credit, while the Board in Washington wanted to simply prohibit banks from using the discount window at all to finance speculative loans.

The Fed of New York voted on a number of occasions in the first half of 1929 to raise the discount rate, but each time the Board refused to approve the move, albeit by narrowing margins. The Fed Board of Governors continued to hold to the position that "direct action" to keep banks from making or maintaining speculative credits at all was a better course than an increase in the discount rate, in effect preventing the banks from using Fed credit at all instead of simply raising the price. In this period, banks did in fact do business with the Fed on a regular basis and without the stigma that attaches to use of the discount window today; thus the discount rate had real commercial and economic significance. It was not until August of 1929 that the Fed's Board of Governors finally approved an application by the Federal Reserve Bank of New York to increase its discount rate to 6 percent.[48]

While the debate raged inside the Fed during 1929, the equity markets were slowly starting to fall. The driver behind the rise in the markets had not been primarily the Fed's policies regarding interest rates or the discounting of commercial paper by the central bank, but instead the marvelous ingenuity of the American people in the form of private debt creation. Hundreds of different types of investment vehicles were available in the marketplace, created by banks, trusts, and other entities. In the 1920s, title and surety companies also were great issuers of bonds and hybrid securities, instruments that look remarkably like the structured finance vehicles of a century later. Many of these vehicles were listed on the major stock exchanges around the country and sold openly to anyone, adults, widows, and orphans alike. The Wall Street firm Goldman Sachs launched a vehicle called Goldman Sachs Trading in 1928 that was listed on the New York Stock Exchange in 1928, even though the firm remained a separate private partnership. The shares rose as high as $121 in 1929, but would close in December 1935 at less than $5.

Inflation versus Deflation

Although the general level of prosperity in the United States rose during the 1920s, at least as measured by indicia such as the use of consumer goods and electricity, the situation in the farm sector was dire. Prices for farm products were going in almost precisely the opposite direction as the rising value of stocks. Between 1920 and 1929, stock prices in the United States had tripled in value, but deflation and bankruptcy were the predominant experience for American farmers. Banks in many U.S. cities became directly involved in the underwriting and sale of securities, lending against these securities, and also retained portfolios of these same securities for speculative gain. These loans and investments would be the cause of numerous bank failures and, again, would serve as a major impetus for the Congress getting the surviving banks of the 1930s out of the securities business through the Glass-Steagall laws.

Some researchers have argued that U.S. stock valuations were not excessive in 1929 based upon an assessment of the fundamental value of the companies included in the major market indices.[49] Friedman and Schwartz make the point that the lending policies followed by many banks during the 1920s were not necessarily reckless and that the expansion in the availability of credit was part of the growing efficiency and productivity of the economy. They go further, however, and state that "the collapse from 1929 to 1933 was neither foreseeable nor inevitable."[50]

All of these arguments may seem quite reasonable from the perspective of an economist, especially revered economic researchers such as Milton Friedman and Anna Schwartz, but when their conclusions are viewed from the point of view of a credit officer or trader, a different analysis emerges. Economists from the Chicago School such as Friedman have long believed that the market price of a security and the intrinsic value of a security in a long-term sense are equivalent, but this view seems to ignore the transient factors such as the availability of credit, which can greatly affect demand for stocks. The market action in the later part of the 1920s had all of the attributes of a nineteenth century speculative market movement where the only real driver was the irrational exuberance of the participants and particularly their belief that prices would move higher.

Sylvain Raynes of RR Consulting, who teaches at Baruch College in Manhattan, put the issue in perspective in September 2007, just as the subprime financial crisis was unfolding:

> Valuation is not the most important problem in finance; valuation is not the most interesting problem in finance; valuation is the only problem for finance. Once you know value, everything happens. Cash moves for value. More price does not mean more value. If you do not recognize the difference, the fundamental difference between price and value, then you are doomed. Now it didn't really matter in corporate finance because the two were supposed to remain equal forever. Who has been telling us that? These people do not live in New York. They live in Chicago. The Chicago School of Economics has been telling us for a century that price and value are identical, i.e., they are the same number. What this means is that there is no such thing as a good deal, there is not such a thing as a bad deal, there are only fair deals.[51]

As already noted, many "investors" during this period had already dispensed with the old fashioned idea of using fundamental factors such as profits or earnings to assess the relative value of a security. These same investors often used debt to fund their speculative purchases of securities, thus when these same securities defaulted and the prices of these bonds collapsed, the debt accelerated the decline in the markets. The more pertinent observation to make about the equity markets in this period seems to be that much of the market's valuation in the late 1920s was the result of the use of credit to purchase stocks and bonds on margin. While the cost of such margin loans was quite high even by modern standards, comparable to using a credit card today to finance stock purchases, the fact that credit was available at all seems to have been the most significant factor in pushing the U.S. financial markets toward the eventual collapse in October of 1929.

Valuation in an old fashioned sense of fundamental analysis in the tradition of Graham and Dodd does not seem to have been the true driver of the move in stock prices during the Roaring Twenties. Instead, the public euphoria created by new products and technologies, an apparently booming economy, and an ample supply of credit seemingly were the true sources of the financial market surge. This situation was clearly a precursor of the period of the Internet bubble in the 1990s and early 2000s, as well as the subsequent bubble in real estate.

Human nature, rather than economic laws or a carefully considered analysis of value, seems to have been the real impetus behind the remarkable ascent of the markets in the 1920s, but the finite supply of credit and a dwindling pool of market participants certainly drove the markets lower. As with a game of poker, the ability of players to raise the bid is limited to the number of chips on the table—a metaphor for the credit available to investors in a fundamentally speculative market. As the pool of available credit was exhausted and the number of "greater fools" who would buy securities at ever higher prices gradually diminished, the only direction that the markets could go was down. This adjustment was then exacerbated by the actions and inaction of the Fed and the White House under Herbert Hoover, neither of which seemed to understand fully the events that unfolded around them.

Since most economists have never taken risk or traded securities in a hostile market environment, the confusion over the distinction between price and value is understandable. It may be unfair to criticize the economists for failing to understand the true precursors of the Great Depression, namely the ingenuity of the American people and their desire for short-term speculative gain. There seemed no limit to the innovation of the American people or their financial intermediaries when it came to selling stocks and bonds. But among the Washington political class as the 1920s came to a close, there was as yet no hint that an economic crisis lay directly in the path of the nation, a catastrophe that would change permanently the nature of the relationship between private banks and the U.S. government from implicit support to explicit regulation and oversight. John Kenneth Galbraith described the problem beautifully in his book *The Great Crash*:

> No one can doubt that the American people remain susceptible to the speculative mood—to the conviction that enterprise can be attended by unlimited rewards in which they, individually, were meant to share. A rising market can bring the reality of riches. This, in turn, can draw more and more people to participate. The government preventatives and controls are

ready. In the hands of a determined government their efficacy cannot be doubted. There are, however, a hundred reasons why a government will determine not to use them.[52]

Galbraith wrote in *The Great Crash* about how the real economy in the United States had been deteriorating for months before the market break, starting with the collapse of commodity prices in the farm sector and then the wonderful boom in land speculation in Florida. Finally, in the autumn of 1929 as seasonal demand for credit peaked due to the harvest cycle in the farm sector, the financial markets turned down sharply and sent the entire nation into what is now known as the Great Depression. In the space of a week, the Dow Jones Industrial Average dropped 30 percent and the previously exuberant business environment was dashed as both consumer and business confidence plummeted. President Hoover, one of the greatest technocrats ever to hold the highest elective office in the United States, declared after only a week of market upheavals that the worst of the crisis was past. But by July 1932, the Dow closed at 41.22, an 89 percent drop from the pre-crash high and a level that would not be reached again until 1954. By March 1933, about half the banks in many states were closed, the nation's economy was imploding under 25 percent unemployment and a decline of 50 percent in GDP, and barter re-emerged as bank runs and company closings drained cash from the economy. Many banks that failed did so as a result of margin lending on stocks, one of the enduring lessons of the period leading up to the Great Crash.

Hoover has been somewhat demonized by history, but it is often overlooked by popular accounts of the Great Depression that President Hoover, and not FDR, created the Reconstruction Finance Corporation (RFC) and the Federal Home Loan Banks, two of the most significant and interventionist initiatives ever taken by Washington up to that time. The RFC, operating under Jesse Jones, was empowered to make loans to banks, insurers, and industrial companies almost without limit. The RFC was initially set up with the idea of repaying the government and then some on its investment and would serve as an important part of the government's response to the Depression during the 1930s.

The Federal Home Loan Bank Board was authorized by Congress to charter and supervise federal savings and loans. It established the

Federal Home Loan Banks, which were given the authority to lend to savings and loans to finance home mortgages. Whereas the Fed merely provided facilities to discount acceptances and made available short-term liquidity, the FHLBs provided government-subsidized term liquidity to thrifts to support residential mortgage loans. The creation of the FHLBs was the start of federal support for home ownership that would gradually grow by the 1990s into one of the largest governmental programs, including many trillions of dollars of government-backed loans and guarantees support to the latest addition to the American dream.

The Great Crash was a political tragedy for Hoover, who was genuinely different from many of his predecessors in the Republican Party. The GOP had been in power, with exceptions such as Grover Cleveland and Woodrow Wilson, for a long time. They looked down upon the Democrats as unfit to govern and especially despised Franklin Delano Roosevelt, Wilson's Vice President, as a traitor to his class. But America was still a very young country and had not had to live through anything like the crisis that would unfold during the Depression. With the bloody exception of the Civil War, Americans had lived a fairly safe and stable existence in the country's first 150 years. If WWI represented an opening of American vistas, the Depression was a crushing downward adjustment of expectations. Europe had collapsed and the United States was headed into a period of deflation and falling economic activity that would stretch on for many more years and long after FDR took office in March 1933.

Americans had experimented with imperialism, but not in a serious way because they believed that there was more than enough opportunity to be found in the United States. The Great Depression shook that faith. When the financial markets collapsed, it was quickly revealed that Hoover was not the ideal man for the job of dealing with the crisis—nor were the Republicans as a group prepared to lead the nation. Probably none of them grasped the magnitude of the fiscal and credit contraction that was unfolding; thus the Hoover government spent 1930 and 1931 doing relatively little about the collapsing demand for many goods and services.

By 1932, however, discussions about how to inflate the currency were top of the agenda and the prevention of further deflation and unemployment was a national priority. Hoover appointed Eugene

Meyer to head a bipartisan board for the RFC and recruited Charles
Dawes as President and chief administrator, and Harvey Couch and
Jesse Jones as directors. Ogden Mills, who replaced Andrew Mellon as
Secretary of the Treasury, was an *ex officio* member of the RFC board.
Thus the RFC was configured and ready to begin dealing with the lack
of financing in many markets, but this was only done in the fourth
year of Hoover's term. A hesitant Congress actually took away some of
the RFC's powers during this period, but the powers of the RFC were
restored and more. During FDR's presidency and under the guidance of
Jesse Jones, the RFC was given *carte blanche* by the Congress because
of the enormous respect and trust that the self-made Texan possessed
and the support he had from members of Congress such as Carter Glass
as a result.

Hoover's tidy and beautifully organized memoirs are essential reading for students of the period of boom and bust in the first three decades of the twentieth century. Along with Jesse Jones's remembrances
of running the RFC for more than a decade, the chronicle of Herbert
Hoover is an engineer's report on the progress of the country during
and after the financial crisis that began in October 1929. He divides
the Great Depression into five phases, which he sadly also labels "during my administration," taking personal responsibility for the terrible
events of those early years of the 1930s:

- October 1929 to April 1931: Liquidation of Stock-Exchange Loans
- April to August 1931: The Panic in Austria and Germany, Exchange
  and Gold
- August to November 1931: The Effects of the British Collapse
- November 1931 to July 1932: Reconstruction Finance Corporation,
  Expanding the Land Banks, Creating the Home Loan Banks
- September 1932 to March 1933: Attempts to Cooperate with
  Roosevelt After Defeat, Refusal of Roosevelt to Cooperate on
  Economic Conference or War Debts

After his chronicle of the years up to the start of FDRs presidency,
the second half of volume two of President Hoover's memoir is a scath-
ing critique of his successor. It features several times the word "fascism" to describe many of the Roosevelt-era prescriptions for fighting

the Depression, a blunt reminder that much of what FDR did during these dark years was borrowed from the strong men of Europe—Mussolini in Italy, Hitler in Germany, and Stalin in Russia. But the fact is that Hoover handed FDR a country that was on its knees, so history has tended to be kinder and more forgiving to Roosevelt and very critical of his predecessor. FDR himself was critical of Hoover, in one campaign speech in 1928 referring to "the Hoover theory of a God-inspired political thinker at the top."[53] The thoughtful engineer Hoover was an easy target for his sharp-witted political opponent FDR, but the New York governor would soon find himself the owner of the Great Depression.

Ford, Couzens, and the Detroit Banks

One of the less-known threads in the story of how American navigated from the market crash of October 1929 to the start of FDR's Administration in 1933 involves the long-standing quarrel between two former business partners, Henry Ford and James Couzens. Their long-running dispute made the dark days of 1930–1933 even more terrible and more dramatic, and directly set the stage for many of the Roosevelt-era sound bites that decorate contemporary history of the Depression. At the inception of Ford Motor Co., Couzens had been Ford's general manager and represented the provider of capital for the infant company, a local Detroit coal dealer named Malcomson. He was also the driving force who commercialized the Ford car, over the objection of Henry Ford, a perfectionist and inveterate tinkerer who would continuously improve his creation. Eventually Henry Ford bought out his partners and forced Couzens out of the company as well, leaving the Ford family in control and a less than cordial relationship between the two men. The conflict between Ford and Couzens highlights the nineteenth century, hard money view of Henry Ford, who as noted earlier literally ran Ford Motor Co. on a cash basis until he ended his day-to-day control of the operations. It also shows the desperate attempts by Hoover to keep some of the nation's most important banks afloat in the dark days of February and March of 1933, when banks in many states in the country were forced to close.

In his final months in office after the election of FDR, Hoover attempted to enlist the help of Henry Ford to support several insolvent banks in Detroit. These were banks where the Ford family kept much of its wealth, all in cash deposits, and in which Edsel Ford had already invested despite his father's opposition. Edsel Ford was an intelligent, enlightened individual who understood the real and symbolic significance of his family's wealth—and what the failure of the Detroit banks would mean to the larger community. On the Sunday before Lincoln's Birthday in 1933, Treasury Undersecretary Arthur Ballantine attempted to convince Ford to put more financial support behind the Detroit banks. Hoover even telephoned Ford on February 12 and spoke with the auto king for almost an hour. Hoover went to bed believing that he had turned Ford around, but awoke the next day to learn that a banking holiday had been declared by the governor of Michigan.[54]

The day before Ford's meeting with Ballantine, the *Detroit Free Press* had carried an interview with James Couzens, Ford's estranged former business partner who became Senator from Michigan after leaving Ford Motor Co. Couzens stated that the weak banks should be allowed to go under and, after a general moratorium, the stronger banks would be allowed to re-open. When Clifford Longley, the Ford Company's counsel and a director of Guardian Trust Company reported Couzens's remarks, Henry Ford replied: "For once in his life, Jim Couzens is right." Ford would ultimately refuse to help Hoover and the Detroit banks, and even threatened to withdraw his money the following Tuesday, setting the stage for the bank holiday in Michigan that would ripple across the United States in the weeks leading up to FDR's inauguration.[55]

On February 14, 1933, all banks in the state of Michigan were closed for eight days by order of Governor William A. Comstock. This began a domino effect that would lead to the final collapse of the nation's banking and financial system three weeks later. Michigan was forced to default on its bonds and the state government was crippled, an event that rippled through the savings and balance sheets of individuals and companies around the world. The home mortgages of many workers from the automobile factories went unpaid, taxes were not collected, and the local economy began a forced contraction as businesses large and small shriveled without access to cash. Auto traffic on the streets of Detroit dwindled. Horses reappeared in large numbers. The stock prices of the major steel, oil, automobile makers, and other companies tumbled. As the historians of the era have documented, more value was destroyed in the early 1930s than in the 1929 market crash.

On March 4, 1933 President Franklin Roosevelt took office. Most of the nation's banks were closed and panic ruled the streets of American cities and towns. New York, which held out almost a month after the bank crisis began in Michigan, declared a bank holiday on the morning of Inauguration Day. Terrified citizens were lined up outside New York banks as the new president took his oath of office. Ten days after FDR's inauguration, he ordered an extended bank holiday. Even as the stronger banks in the nation gradually were allowed to re-open, the banks in Detroit remained closed. Almost a million individuals and businesses in Michigan were cut off from their funds for over a month and the larger depositors of the banks—including Henry Ford—were compelled to wait for the liquidation of the insolvent banks.

Jesse Jones, the legendary chairman of the Reconstruction Finance Corporation under FDR, laid the blame for exacerbating the Banking Crisis of 1933 at the feet of Ford and Couzens:

> Detroit's banking collapse may have been inevitable, the situation in the sorely stricken automobile industry being what it was, and the laws being what there were at the time; but the circumstances would have been less painful, the personal tragedies fewer, had not insurmountable difficulties been created by personal, industrial, and political hostilities at almost every step of our approach to the problem in February 1933.[56]

Malcolm Bingay, editor of the *Detroit Free Press*, interviewed Couzens several times following the crisis of 1933. He concluded that far from being a matter of hard money principle, Couzens' chief reason for opposing the bank bailout was "pure spite and vindictiveness" directed at Henry Ford and others in the Detroit business community.[57] In fact, Couzens had told President Hoover before the bank holiday was declared in Michigan that he would gladly come up with a further $1 million for the bailout if it would prevent suffering for "800,000 small depositors of the Detroit banks," but subsequently reneged on the commitment. Hoover's memoirs suggest that Couzens ultimately could not bring himself to assist the "old club" of Detroit bankers who had previously shunned him because of his concern for the common man.[58]

Some 4,000 commercial banks and 1,700 savings and loans would ultimately fail during 1933 alone. Some 10,000 banks would fail between 1929 and 1933 with a loss to depositors of $1.3 billion. The Congress and FDR responded to this calamity with some of the most interventionist legislation to date, the "fascism" that Hoover decried in his memoirs, with laws that created the quasi-governmental system of heavily regulated and subsidized "private" banks that survives in the United States to this day. "During Roosevelt's first eight years the guiding phrases of the New Deal were not 'Communism,' 'Socialism,' and 'Fascism,' but 'Planned Economy,'" wrote Hoover. "This expression was an emanation from the cauldrons of all three European collectivist forms."[59]

Chapter 6

New Deal to Cold War

T he Administration of Franklin Roosevelt during the 1930s was a period of great change for the perception and reality of money in America. FDR is lionized in many history books while Hoover and the Republicans are demonized. The truth is that neither governing party really understood nor controlled the path of the economy during the Depression. The Democrats actually controlled Congress during Hoover's presidency, so they cannot escape a fair share of responsibility for not foreseeing the catastrophe. FDR and the Democrats clearly worsened the banking crisis in 1932 by refusing to cooperate with the incumbent Hoover during the long transition period from November to March. The handoff of power between Hoover and FDR in March 1933 was painful, culminating with the oath of office as most of the nation's banks stood closed. The transition in 1933 provided an especially fateful example of why the period of time from the election of a president to inauguration had to be shortened by the Twentieth Amendment to the Constitution that same year.

Hoover believed that FDR deliberately chose not to cooperate openly with his government to contain the banking crisis in 1932 and thereby use the larger emergency as a pretext for imposing authoritarian controls over American business and labor. But even more, the former president laid the blame for the public's panic in March of 1933 at the feet of FDR and particularly the imposition of the New Deal. "It was the most political and the most unnecessary bank panic in our history," Hoover wrote. Echoing the rhetoric of the Wilson and Teddy Roosevelt eras regarding kinder masters, Hoover continued to say that "the breakdown in confidence which sounded the advent of the New Deal is of course a helpful statistical point when they want to show how good they have been to us."[1] The "they" in the previous sentence refers to FDR and his lieutenants, men who the orthodox Hoover described bluntly as "traitors."

The period under FDR was one of the most fateful and significant for the United States over the past century, but due more to the statist legacies left behind by FDR than to his accomplishments at the time. FDR ran against the budget deficits of Hoover's years, but ignored the collapse of federal tax revenue caused by the worsening Depression. Like Wilson, he ran against the war, but would involve the United States in assisting the British from the outset of hostilities. FDR subsequently ran even bigger deficits than Hoover and eventually took American back to war. Ever duplicitous, FDR at first campaigned against tariffs in the months leading up to the 1932 election, promising that trade liberalization would be a key part of his administration. Echoing Democratic leaders such as Bryan and Al Smith, FDR made tariff reduction a centerpiece at the start of his campaign against Hoover. By the end of his campaign, FDR was singing from the protectionist gospel of the Republican Party. His flexibility in regard to these serious issues of economic and financial policy evidenced an agenda that was first and foremost political. The same could be said for FDR's approach to foreign policy and especially developments in and relations with Europe.

Whereas Theodore Roosevelt was a libertarian and an advocate for traditional American values of individualism and self reliance, FDR was an apologist for the unitary state and dependency. FDR believed in a decidedly American version of European style corporate statism very much like that which was then rising in fascist Italy and Nazi Germany. Hoover said of the New Deal that it was "an attempt to cross-breed Socialism, Fascism and Free Enterprise" and this was not far from the truth, even if FDR was less than definite as to his actual beliefs. Supporters of FDR claim that times were desperate and thus experimentation was in order, but FDR's attacks on business were at best politically expedient and evidenced a certain hostility to America's unique commercial culture.

Of course both Teddy Roosevelt and FDR were wealthy men who knew all of the top business leaders and Wall Street bankers of the day. FDR himself came from very old New York money care of the Roosevelt and Delano branches of the family, including estates in the Hudson Valley. The Delanos were the sort of old New Yorkers who lived on Collonade Row in lower Manhattan in the 1830s and considered the Astors *nouveau riche*. Frederic Adrian Delano, FDR's uncle, was a second-generation railroad baron. While he spent much of his life focused on the transportation industry, as noted earlier, Delano served as the first vice chairman of the Federal Reserve Board. Despite their wealthy backgrounds, both presidents knew how to use bankers and business leaders as targets of opportunity when the situation arose. In short, FDR was a politician but one who was in many ways antithetical to the political views of his cousin Theodore Roosevelt.

FDR and the Era of Broken Precedent

Today the image of FDR in the public mind is larger and more intense than that of Teddy Roosevelt, in part because of the powerful experience of WWII. Arguably Teddy Roosevelt was the larger figure in the long run of historical and political events. The proof of the failure of FDR as an ultimately transformative figure was the lack of any enduring popular movement from grass roots America in response to the New Deal. Both the Republican and Democratic parties had become largely institutionalized. As the 1930s began, already there was ferment among the public in favor of a third, independent party, but none materialized. Of the election in 1932, Minton and Stewart wrote in *The Fat Years and the Lean* that "the campaign was never more than a contest between Hoover and Roosevelt, between the representative of the political machine in power and the nominee of the political machine wanting power."[2] But the fact remains that FDR was a machine politician as much as was Teddy Roosevelt and had little appeal to real Progressives. In that sense, as men of the left, FDR and

Wilson both seem to share an establishment respectability garnished
with a veneer of Progressive liberalism.

The members of FDR's "brain trust" were less revolutionary and
more bureaucratic at the end of the day, but many on the left saw him
as a "transmitting instrument of the new world order," according to the
Fabian socialist writer H.G. Wells. A devoted socialist, Wells visited FDR
on several occasions and called the President and Mrs. Roosevelt "unlimited" people in a sense of their willingness to embrace new, revolutionary
ideas.[3] His description of FDR recalls the distinction made by author
Thomas Sowell regarding people with "unconstrained vision" in his
book *Conflict of Visions*.[4]

Whereas Herbert Hoover was seemingly a man with constrained
vision, who saw human nature as comprised of fixed values and charac-
teristics, FDR instead acted like a man of unconstrained visions, a gam-
bler and opportunist, who used the promise of transformation and the
pretense of concern for his fellow man to make seemingly radical changes
in society. These changes were largely comprised of calculated political expediencies rather than deliberately chosen and visionary depar-
tures from past practice. Like most Republicans, Hoover saw the world
as comprised of immutable rules and values that were to be cherished
and defended. FDR seemed to see those very same rules as factors to be
manipulated and, when convenient, violated, to achieve a larger end.

Contemporary observers such as Eliot Janeway differ with the
conservative demonization of FDR. Janeway, who began his writing
career at the age of 24, wrote a series of articles for *The Nation* predicting the 1937–1938 recession. In his first book, *The Struggle for Survival*,
Janeway argued that Roosevelt had no strong view of theoretical political distinctions or economic systems:

> Roosevelt was no more a radical than was Queen Elizabeth.
> Never was a political free-booter more cynical about all the-
> ories . . . Temperamentally, the man could not bring himself
> to believe that good administration ever accomplished or pre-
> vented anything. He simply did not believe in Planning—with
> a capital P—as the answer to the problems of society. And he
> certainly did not believe in the Planners who looked down
> their noses at people for being people and at politicians like

him for catering to them. No doubt, legend will confuse coincidence with cause, and Roosevelt will be credited with having established Government as the dominant entity in American life. What he actually did was to keep pace with a revolution that no man was big enough to have started or stopped.[5]

Loyal apologists for FDR the man and the legend, such as Janeway, tried to make his policy caprices seem more reactive than revolutionary, and in large part they are correct. The events that were moving in the 1930s were too large for any one person or country to affect. FDR was just another American politician from New York, albeit with more than the usual personal flair and affectation due to his inherited wealth. He started his political life as a State Senator in New York, a position he had gained over Tammany Hall boss Charles Murphy because of infighting within the organization. As with Teddy Roosevelt, fate helped to give FDR a chance to succeed politically amidst the chaos of Tammany Hall.

Like his cousin Teddy, FDR was a political accident set in motion by the internal convulsions of New York politics. After serving as Assistant Secretary of the Navy under Woodrow Wilson and Vice Presidential candidate with James Cox in the 1920 election against Warren Harding, Roosevelt went home to New York to resume his life as a Hudson Valley landholder, but fate would strike him down with polio. In 1924, his mentor from Tammany Hall, Al Smith, convinced the still recuperating Roosevelt to come to New York City to place Smith's name into nomination at the Democratic Committee to run against President Coolidge. Four years later in Houston, he again nominated Smith to a second unsuccessful run for the presidency, this time against Herbert Hoover. At the insistence of Tammany Hall, FDR ran for governor of New York in 1928 and won the most populous state in the union by 25,000 votes. Al Smith lost the state by 100,000. FDR then cleaned Tammany Hall out of Albany and installed his own gang. He launched a series of reforms and state development initiatives that were the testing ground for the New Deal. Two years later, FDR managed a nearly unthinkable re-election victory with a plurality of 725,000 votes at a time when few Democrats anywhere could stand against the Golden Age of Republicanism.

Despite his popularity, FDR was not a remarkable governor in terms of actual accomplishments outside politics and showed little appreciation for economics, supporting the contention of Janeway and others that Roosevelt lacked any deep-rooted political or economic convictions. Superficially at least, his main quality seemed to be political adeptness and the ability to please people of all political persuasions. In his early years, FDR was the stereotype of the modern American politician, never daring to do anything too radical or too controversial.

Roosevelt was "a highly impressionable person without a firm grasp of public affairs and without very strong convictions . . . He is an amiable man with many philanthropic impulses, but is not the dangerous enemy of anything," Walter Lippmann concluded. "[FDR] is a pleasant man who, without any important qualifications for the office, would very much like to be President." Lippmann, who was one of the most influential and powerful journalists of his age, would soon completely change his view of FDR.[6] As one observer remarked, FDR entered the White House in 1933 as the best liked man in America. Even after a none-too-successful year in office, he was still more popular than when he was elected—but the nation was desperate.

In 1930, when Hoover and the Republicans lost control over Congress to the Democrats and Progressive party, then-New York governor Roosevelt saw his opportunity. Assisted by long-time supporters such as Louis McHenry Howe and James Farley, FDR began to plan his ascension to the White House. By the time the Democratic party met to nominate a presidential candidate, FDR had almost sufficient votes to win the prize, but still had to work hard for days to clinch the nomination. In the 1932 Democratic platform, the party promised economy in government, a sound currency—and "a competitive tariff for revenue" with other nations. The Democrats called for the repeal of prohibition, self-determination for the Philippines—and the collection of war debts from the European nations.

After losing twice before, Al Smith hoped to be picked for a third time to lead the Democratic ticket, but his protégé and former subordinate in the Tammany Hall organization stole the prize—with help from House Democratic leader Sam Rayburn of Texas, former Treasury Secretary William McAdoo, and publisher William Randolph Hearst. These men provided the key support from California to get FDR the nomination that year. FDR was also helped by the assistance of Joseph

Kennedy, who donated and raised hundreds of thousands of dollars for FDR and travelled with him on the campaign trail. Kennedy was the modern-day embodiment of the gold rush, taking flyers on bootleg booze, Hollywood movies, and even the election of a president.

After the fact, Joe Kennedy claimed to have been the decisive force in winning the active support of Hearst for FDR at the 1932 Democratic convention in Chicago. He was also responsible for suborning significant defections from the pro-Al Smith camp, including Honey Fitz and Jim Curley from Boston. "Roosevelt could not afford to shut the door on anyone with money," Richard Whalen wrote in his 1964 biography of Joe Kennedy. "Alone among the party's contenders, he indicted erring business leadership for the country's misfortunes . . . Such radical sounding talk alarmed John J. Raskob, now chairman of the Democratic National Committee. He dropped all pretense of impartiality and threw his weight behind the party's 1928 standard bearer, Al Smith."[7]

Had the Republicans not been caught completely flat-footed by the Great Crash of 1929 and the ensuing two years of economic contraction, they might have had an opportunity to win the election of 1932 — so powerful was the Republican political machine in those years. But with Hoover predicting that "prosperity is around the corner" nearly every day and without any success to back his claims, the Republicans got slaughtered and rightly so. FDR and his running mate John Garner won against Hoover and Charles Curtis with 57 percent of the vote and carried all but a handful of Northeastern states.

Joe Kennedy would become the first Chairman of the Securities and Exchange Commission and performed remarkably well. This was an era that was the golden age of the federal government and when the SEC staff was considered among the elite in Washington. In an article appraising the first five years of the SEC's existence, *Fortune* reported that Kennedy's primary job was bringing investors and business back together, a job that suited Kennedy "superbly."[8] Today there are not many close analogs for the type of political and market operator that was Joseph Kennedy, a man who combined bootlegging and Hollywood deal-making seamlessly with his operations in the financial markets and national politics. Unlike many Hollywood speculators, Kennedy made money. He knew how to capitalize on a losing situation and succeed.

Putting Joe Kennedy at the SEC would be like today appointing the head of a leading hedge fund or financial firm, like appointing Goldman

Sach's Henry Paulson Secretary of the Treasury. But few of today's leaders of Wall Street have anything like Kennedy's political acumen and
willingness to get their hands dirty—sometimes very dirty. Kennedy was
a pit bull who did the political dirty work, collected money, and made
things happen to help FDR become president and to exercise power.

The first 100 days of the Roosevelt Administration are presented in
most of the FDR hagiographies in dramatic and heroic terms not unlike
newsreel footage from the Soviet Union or Communist China. The
suffering in the country did make the times dramatic. The response of
the federal government was equally serious and substantial, including an
initial, almost Republican effort by FDR to cut federal spending. Later
in his term deficit spending would be the order of the day, first for
fighting the Depression and later to finance a war. But early on, many
of FDR's efforts to repair the economy were quite conventional in the
same way as Hoover.

FDR's first task was to respond to the economic crisis and in
particular the banks. The Emergency Banking Act was introduced on
March 9, 1933, passed the same day, and signed into law. Congressman
Henry B. Steagall reportedly walked into the House chamber with the
text of the legislation newly transmitted from the White House and
waiving it in the air said "Here's the bill. Let's pass it."

After a few minutes of debate and no amendments, it was passed
and the Senate soon followed suit. The first section of the law simply
endorsed all the executive orders given by the President or Secretary of
the Treasury since March 4. The law gave FDR the power to confiscate gold, seize banks, and impose currency controls. It also authorized
the Treasury to issue $2 billion in new greenback paper dollars that
were not convertible and instead were secured by the private assets of
the U.S. banking system.

The Seizure of Gold and Dollar Devaluation

The Banking Act authorized the Fed to make loans to any individual based on Treasury bonds as collateral, very tight requirements that
would be changed decades later eventually to enable the bank bailout of
2008. The law also authorized the Reconstruction Finance Corporation

(RFC) to invest in the preferred stock and capital notes of banks and to make secured loans to individual banks.[9] Walker Todd wrote that Benito Mussolini organized the *Istituto per la Ricostruzione Industriale* (IRI) in January 1933 to accomplish, with respect to large business trusts in Italy, some of the same functions that the RFC performed for insurance companies and banks in the United States. IRI came to own much of Italian industry and continued to operate as a state holding company through WWII and into the end of the twentieth century.

As soon as the Banking Act was passed, the Federal Reserve Board announced that it was preparing lists of people who had withdrawn gold from banks in the previous weeks, a none-too-subtle reminder that hoarding gold now carried criminal penalties. Nearly 15 percent of the currency in circulation in the United States had disappeared in the weeks prior to FDR's taking office and an immediate means of bringing that cash back into the banking system had to be found. Within hours of the Fed's announcement, long lines formed outside banks and Federal Reserve Banks to exchange gold for greenbacks. The Fed then announced that it was widening the hunt for gold hoarders to withdrawals made in the past two years. By the end of the first week of FDR's term, enough gold had been returned to the banking system to support nearly $1 billion in new currency issuance.

That same week, the Bureau of Engraving in Washington began to print money—$2 billion worth of new greenbacks to be precise. So pressing was the emergency and so short the time that the Bureau printed dollars with old plates that bore the legend "Series of 1929" and used old signatures from the 12 Federal Reserve Banks. By Saturday, March 11th, planes filled with newly printed dollars began to leave Washington to deliver badly needed funds to banks around the country. While the emergency was far from over, the closure of the banks and the rapid distribution of new cash around the country enabled FDR to slow the deflationary aspect of the banking crisis and buy some time to formulate the next steps to be taken.

FDR's abandonment of the gold standard and confiscation of gold coins in 1933 was among the most memorable actions taken by FDR when it comes to money and debt. FDR's decision to take the United States off the gold standard and devalue the dollar had a far more profound impact on the country and the world than many of the dozens of other programs that were put in place during the period. FDR put in place assistance for the unemployed, relief for farmers, and many other programs, but his decision to move off of gold and thereby devalue the dollar had great ramifications for the country and the world. Recall that under Hoover, the Fed pursued an aggressive, inflationist policy, especially in the last year of his term. For most of 1932, the Fed aggressively added cash and purchased government securities, yet the bank deposit base and the supply of cash continued to contract even after the election of 1932 and as FDR began his term. This period in history bears a troubling resemblance to the behavior of the markets in 2009–2010, when the Fed likewise is trying to encourage new credit creation and a higher rate of turnover or "velocity" for money.

The Emergency Banking Relief Act renewed the powers granted to the president after WWI to exercise authority over all foreign exchange transactions as well as all payments by banking institutions. FDR signed an Executive Order confiscating all private gold as it became clear that the public was reacting negatively to his presidency by hoarding gold coins and shunning paper dollars, repeating the behavior seen in 1837 and other crises since. There was essentially "a run on FDR" between November 1932 and the inauguration in March 1933. He banned banks from making payments in gold, essentially forcing U.S. citizens to accept legal tender dollars for all payments. FDR later through legislation made greenbacks "legal tender" for all debts.

The Democratic "rubber stamp" Congress did not object to and even ratified the decision by FDR to leave the gold standard with the Gold Reserve Act of 1934. Treasury Secretary Henry Morgenthau, Jr., announced on March 11 that "the provision is aimed at those who continue to retain quantities of gold and thereby hinder the Government's plans for a restoration of public confidence."[10] Keep in mind that FDR made this weighty decision to leave the gold standard and devalue the dollar only weeks after the collapse of the nation's banking system, suggesting that his decision to confiscate all gold had been under consideration for some time.

Farm prices and wages had been falling for months. Many Americans and a majority of the Congress anxiously called for the old palliative of currency inflation to stem the terrible depression that affected the entire country as a result of falling business output and consumption. What they got from Roosevelt, however, was not incremental inflation

based upon the existing gold regime, but a completely different financial order. Anticipating FDR's actions to deliberately inflate the dollar, in
February 1933 the financier Bernard Baruch, who had been an adviser
to President Hoover and also to FDR, told the Senate that only by keeping expenditures within income can the people of the United States
retain confidence in its credit. Inflation is "the road to ruin," Baruch
declared. Without confidence, he continued, money loses value and
sinks beneath the level of commodities that can be consumed. Baruch
recalled that inflation had been going on for years during the Depression
and that the Federal Reserve Banks had been purchasing nearly all of the
debt issued by the Treasury to fund federal deficits since the Great Crash
of 1929. The Treasury itself, Baruch observed, had been producing inflation by "coining a deficit" to pay for greater government expenditures.
Baruch warned: "We have kept that credit above reproach for so long
that people think that it can stand any abuse," he told the Senate. "But
this is an era of broken precedent. We are witnessing the disintegration
of the institutions of an era."[11]

In the early days of 1933, most members of Congress were not
in the mood for lectures about sound money. Senator Tom Connally
(D-TX), who won election to the House in 1917 and to the Senate in
1929, questioned Baruch closely on the issue of inflation. A staunch
advocate for the farm community in Texas and of currency inflation,
Connally hammered Baruch over the question of whether a little
inflation now would not help the American farmer in an immediate
sense. Baruch conceded that in the past inflation had provided temporary relief to farmers as in the period during WWI, but he further
stated that he did not believe that farm prices would necessarily rise
with greater inflation, because of the lack of demand. Senator Robert
La Follette likewise endorsed the powers granted to FDR, illustrating
the strong support in Congress for inflation at that time. But Baruch was
unimpressed by the inflationist tendency in the Democrat-controlled
Congress and rejected their thinking:

> I regard the condition of this country as the most serious in its
> history. It is worse than war. In war there is a definite enemy.
> We know what and where he is and how to fight him. We can
> measure the necessary sacrifices and make them with certainty

of effect. But this enemy wears no uniform and takes no position on any front . . . So far as I am concerned, there is no sac-
rifice I would not be willing to make to fight this terror—no
plan, however revolutionary and bold, that I would not try if
I could see in it an even chance of success. If I did not know
that there was nothing but destruction to be derived from the
project of inflation, I would be the first to advocate its trial.
But I am as certain as that we are sitting here that the path
proposed is the road to ruin.[12]

Regardless of how one feels about the conservative indictment of
FDR, the seizure of gold owned by individuals, companies, and the
private banks that were members of the Federal Reserve System was
an extreme step that was not necessary for helping the nation recover
from the worst aspects of the Depression. As in the case of the financial rescue of 2008, which was financed with trillions of dollars worth
of monetary expansion by the Fed, in the 1930s elected officials were
unwilling to raise taxes to pay the nation's bills. The economic emergency of the Great Depression gave our leaders sufficient political cover
to disregard past precedents and established rules, and to print money
with a level of recklessness that only a few years earlier would have
ensured their political destruction. The seizure of gold by FDR and
the devaluation of the dollar were the type of behavior one expects
from unstable developing nations. That description may be appropriate
given the dire economic circumstances that prevailed in the 1930s and
serves to remind citizens that America is still a very young country.

The FDR move with respect to gold actually hurt public confidence
in the United States and the dollar, which was already badly damaged
by the banking crisis. But FDR's motivation also was ultimately political, to prevent the declining value of the dollar measured in gold and the
related deflation from sinking him politically. Richard Whalen observed
in discussions about this book that FDR's decision to leave the gold
standard "was about keeping the people out of the streets," but it is not
clear that the decision had any positive impact on the economy. Though
the appearance of growth was created by inflating the currency, prices
generally rose with the start of WWII and have risen by an order of
magnitude since the 1920s. To put that in dollar terms, the dollar has lost

90 percent of its purchasing power since the Great Depression, but living standards in the United States have risen dramatically over that same period—largely due to improvement in technology and the expansion of the world economy. And over this same period, the use of debt to finance purchases of homes and consumer services, and to finance public expenditures, also increased. Once the link to gold was removed, the government was free to inflate and borrow without effective limitation and this freedom with respect to the uses of debt has also spread to the private sector.

Ogden Mills, who served as President Herbert Hoover's Treasury Secretary, said that "it was not the maintenance of the gold standard that caused the banking panic of 1933 and the outflow of gold. . . . [I]t was the definite and growing fear that the new administration meant to do what they ultimately did—that is, abandon the gold standard." That quote was used in an article in *The Freeman* by James Bovard, who summarized the FDR actions with respect to gold succinctly:

> Curiously, FDR retained his denigrating tone toward so-called gold-hoarders even after he defaulted on the federal government's gold redemption promise. Even though people who distrusted politicians' promises were vindicated, they were still evil people because they had not obeyed FDR's demand to surrender their gold. In the moral world of the New Deal, justice consisted solely of blind obedience to political commands. FDR had absolutely no sense of embarrassment or shame after he defaulted on the federal government's gold promises—it was simply political business as usual.[13]

The immediate goal of the Roosevelt abandonment of the gold standard was clearly inflation, but this did not occur even though the value of the dollar measured in other major currencies was cut in half. Commodity prices in 1933 were roughly half of the levels in 1926 and there was little relief in sight. Whereas production had risen by almost 50 percent between 1919 and 1927, the advent of electricity and the impact of tariffs to boost corporate investment in certain industries caused producer prices to plummet and with it U.S. factory employment. Throughout the 1930s in fact, the U.S. economy arguably had excess capacity—extra production capability that would conveniently be absorbed by the onset of WWII.

Always astute politically, FDR decorated his administration with a goodly portion of Bryan Democrats, men who were advocates of inflationism and ending the gold standard. In June 1934 FDR even asked Congress to make the dollar convertible into silver at the same time that he sought further legal powers to confiscate private gold. The advocates of the use of silver as money would be disappointed, however, because FDR's seizure of gold and the devaluation of the dollar only increased the price ratio between the two metals. After the Roosevelt era devaluation of the dollar, the price of gold was set at $35 per ounce but silver traded around $0.40 per ounce, a ratio of 80 to 1.

Dollar Devaluation Hurt World Trade

While there was no appreciable recovery in terms of commodity or producer prices, the drop in the value of the dollar cut the cost of debt repayments to the United States for the nations of Europe and also cut the cost of U.S. exports. But American imports from Europe and other nations fell dramatically. This drop in U.S. consumption of imported goods suggests that it was the Roosevelt era currency devaluation, as well as the Smoot-Hawley tariff, which caused the further contraction of the global economy in the 1930s. Gold flowed out of Europe to the United States because our trading partners were still obliged to pay their debts in metal, but the devaluation did not have the desired effect of reflation of prices or employment in the U.S. economy.

Hoover noted that the dollar devaluation by FDR was effectively an increase in the tariff from the perspective of the cost to American buyers: "The Democrats have made a great issue out of the disasters they predicted would flow from the modest increases in the Smoot-Hawley tariff (mostly agricultural products). The fact was that 65 percent of the imported goods under the tariff were free of duty, and that legislation increased tariffs on the 35 percent dutiable goods by somewhere around 10 percent. But the greatest tariff boost in all our history came from Roosevelt's devaluation." Hoover goes on to illustrate that both imports and exports per capita declined in the United States between 1935 and 1938.[14]

In addition to a selection of Bryan Democrats around FDR, there was also a cadre of left-wing operatives that openly took inspiration if not direction from fascist regimes in Rome and Berlin. These New Dealers were true believers and welcomed the permanent debasement of the dollar as part of the road to world revolution.[15] The bankers and communists alike who populated FDR's "brain trust" ultimately agreed on the government's policies regarding gold, even if many of FDR's more conservative advisers were aghast and some even resigned in protest. The bankers who were then in charge of the House of Morgan provided intellectual support for FDR's move against gold, something that would have shocked JP Morgan, who fought to restore the gold standard only decades earlier. But the fact was that the seizure of gold was more than anything else a political move by FDR. He knew that Americans and foreigners were voting with their feet, selling paper dollars and buying gold even as he tried to resuscitate the sagging U.S. economy.

Despite the large gold stocks held by the U.S. government, the metal was flowing out of the country in reaction to FDR's election and the weakening dollar. There was fear that the monetary base would contract further. Morgan banker and New Dealer Russell Leffingwell, along with legendary Morgan banker Thomas Lamont, met with the prominent newspaper writer Walter Lippman in early April 1933 to discuss leaving the gold standard. Lippmann then wrote a column advocating an end to the gold standard that appeared in the *Herald Tribune* on April 18, 1933. FDR, who trusted Leffingwell perhaps more than any other member of his inner circle, announced to his advisors that day that the United States was moving off the gold standard. The President made a statement regarding the negative effects of the hoarding of gold on the following day.[16]

Not surprisingly, the FDR strategy regarding gold was good for stocks and caused an immediate rally on Wall Street. The move to leave gold, however, was much the same as other aspects of the New Deal economic program, namely to create scarcity in order to defeat and ultimately reverse deflation. FDR's Republican and Democratic opponents did not understand, however, that when Roosevelt spoke of maintaining *sound money* he was not promising to restore the pre-Depression gold value of the dollar. Instead, FDR proposed to make money entirely a function of government policy. Part of this change was clearly meant to address the nation's economic crisis, but part was also political, namely to remove the dollar value of gold as a daily barometer of FDR's political standing.

Unfortunately, the lack of understanding by FDR and his economic team as to the true nature of the crisis rendered the change largely ineffectual in economic terms. Members of the New Deal team, as we've noted, wanted to foster inflation and thereby get domestic prices to start to rise. Most of the policies implemented by FDR, however, had the opposite effect. Despite the obvious political motivations and a brief upward rally on Wall Street, FDR's efforts to boost farm and industrial prices by manipulating the price of gold and the value of the dollar during the period 1933–1934 were a failure.

The Rise of the Corporate State

One fascinating aspect of FDR is that apart from his departure from the gold standard, his initial approach to economic problems was not revolutionary at all and was precisely the same as had been used by generations of Americans before him, namely to manage prices and markets via scarcity. He took the process further by borrowing from European fascism with corporatist initiatives such as the National Industrial Recovery Act, which created a nationwide network of industry boards to set wages and prices. These initiatives had dubious value in terms of fighting the Depression, but the times were desperate and new solutions were being sought.

Researcher Walker Todd set the scene in his monograph, "The Federal Reserve Board and the Rise of the Corporate State, 1931–1934":

> Once one understands the degree to which politicians, jurists, businessmen, and economic policymakers of the early 1930s were attracted to any political economy model that held out the promise of relieving the symptoms of what Friedman and Schwartz (1963) called "the Great Contraction, 1929–1933," it becomes easier to understand how quickly and how thoroughly corporativist ideas like the National Recovery Administration became permanent fixtures of the Washington political environment.[17]

Instead of trying to increase consumption and therefore firm prices, the New Dealers actually took a page from WWI, or even from the likes of Jay Gould and Andrew Carnegie, and attempted to firm up wages and prices by squeezing and managing supply. Writer and author Robert Higgs examined this issue in a 1995 article in *The Free Market*:

> In their understanding of the Depression, Roosevelt and his economic advisers had cause and effect reversed. They did not recognize that prices had fallen because of the Depression. They believed that the Depression prevailed because prices had fallen. The obvious remedy, then, was to raise prices, which they decided to do by creating artificial shortages. Hence arose a collection of crackpot policies designed to cure the Depression by cutting back on production. The scheme was so patently self-defeating that it's hard to believe anyone seriously believed it would work.[18]

During this period the British economist John Maynard Keynes was formulating his theory regarding business cycles and the need for countries to leave the gold standard in order to foster growth. In a meeting with Walter Lippmann in June of 1933, Keynes described why nations needed to float away from gold and to run fiscal deficits to spur consumption and investment in order to generate economic expansion. So long as consumer demand remained stagnant, Keynes argued, businesses would not increase investment and employment would not grow, regardless of the level of savings. His arguments ran directly counter to the conventional wisdom of spending cuts and tax increases in times of recession, a tendency that persists within business and government to this day.

What is peculiar about the discussions between Keynes and Lippmann is that his views on restoring growth in the Western economies seemed to be completely at odds with his changing view on free trade. Writing in the *Yale Review* in 1933, Keynes condemned free trade in no uncertain terms. He made clear that the global interconnections between financial markets had worsened the Depression, a view that runs directly counter to the neoliberal view of free trade today.

"I was brought up, like most Englishmen, to respect free trade not only as an economic doctrine which a rational and instructed person could not doubt, but almost as a part of the moral law," he wrote. "Yet the orientation of my mind is changed; and I share this change of mind with many others. . . . I sympathize, therefore, with those who would minimize, rather than with those who would maximize, economic entanglement among nations. Ideas, knowledge, science, hospitality, travel—these are the things which should of their nature be international. But let goods be homespun whenever it is reasonably and conveniently possible, and, above all, let finance be primarily national."[19]

Expanding on his work of a few years earlier in the *Treatise on Money*,[20] Keynes argued that government should use debt to support public works and other types of expenditures during bad times and tax during good times to retire the indebtedness. His very British view of the need to repay the debt immediately upon the end of a war or economic crisis reflected the custom in the United Kingdom. The United Kingdom of course paid down its *domestic debt* from WWI, as noted earlier, but like France defaulted on war loans from the United States. Keynes was not an apologist for debt or inflation, but he did advocate a strong role for government in times of deflation—precisely the prescription that fit the times. Keynes, after all, was a mathematician and speculator first and foremost; a man who understood and played the markets. Grasping the fact that growth, or at least the desire for growth, had outstripped the capacity of the gold-based monetary system was not an arduous process for Keynes.

Three years later, Keynes would elaborate upon his hypothesis regarding the role of government in *The General Theory of Employment, Interest and Money*,[21] a work that radically changed the way that nations and their political leaders looked at money and debt. As with the creation of central banks, the new fiscal mechanics articulated by Keynes created novel alternatives for political leaders such as FDR and at precisely the time when conventional policies were failing. The alternatives of deficit spending and public debt had the notable attribute of not requiring the direct assent of the voters, but would be paid for via future inflation.

The traditional response of imposing greater economy and cuts in expenditures by government during times of depression was clearly making matters worse in the United States and around the world. The wave of global deflation fueled the rise of fascism in Italy and Germany during this same period. The leaders of the major European nations fully expected revolution at home; thus the idea of government spending and even borrowing to offset extremes of economic and social conditions was enthusiastically received. And because Keynes himself was a believer in central planning, his views fit into the rising tide of corporatist thinking that was flowing through many western capitals in the early 1930s—including Washington.

Keynes believed that the nations of the world needed to end their slavish devotion to the gold standard and to allow their currencies to decline in value by as much as one third to revive global growth. Years later, he would argue that the new currency regime was the opposite of the gold standard and the nations of the world were now free to make of it whatever they wished. This thinking impressed Lippmann, who framed the argument for leaving the gold standard in another column in the *Herald Tribune* of June 29, 1933. It also impressed FDR.

In the age of media plentitude in which we live today, it is difficult to appreciate the influence of Lippmann and his internationally syndicated column in the *Herald Tribune*. The connection among FDR, Lippmann, and Keynes gave momentum to the process of responding to the deflation visible in the markets of America and Europe. A few days later, on July 3, 1933, FDR sent a message to the World Economic Conference meeting in Europe denouncing currency stabilization as "a specious fallacy." Through his emissaries, FDR made it clear to the other nations that the United States was not prepared to agree on either tariff reduction or stabilization of the dollar until it was on the way to economic recovery.

FDR's actions with respect to gold and the dollar hurt the reputation of the United States with foreign countries and led many observers, even close allies of FDR, to wonder if the Roosevelt Administration was sound in its thinking. Not all of the leaders of Europe disagreed with FDR's actions with respect to gold, however, including a conservative back bencher in the United Kingdom named Winston Churchill. Keynes subsequently wrote an article supporting FDR's action. More than a few politicians understood that FDR, by following the thinking of Keynes, was essentially creating an alternative, a "middle way" between the *laissez-faire* capitalism of nineteenth century America and the Marxist socialism that was destroying Russia. Many people believed that a communist revolution threatened Europe and America equally.

But for most Americans, FDR's actions with respect to gold and the dollar marked a repudiation of the past. In the wonderfully sarcastic book *The New Dealers*, published anonymously in 1934 by Simon & Schuster, the "Unofficial Observer" described the FDR devaluation and repudiation of gold, and what this meant for the way the U.S. economy performed:

> On the one hand, you have the good old traditional way of doing business, which required the entire population of the country to "walk home" at twenty-year intervals in the name of God and the Gold Standard. On the other hand, you have the new technique of the financial sheik who claims that you can use buttons instead of money. The old school claims that buttons belong in button-holes, the new school asks what is the Gold Standard between friends. The times are on the side of the new school, for the financing of a revolution—even an unconscious one—takes a lot of money, and a lot of buttons.[22]

Under the guise of economic nationalism, FDR took the United States down the path to economic recovery, first by embracing debt and inflation as the primary tools of national policy, then plunging America into a second world war in Europe and Asia. The former was done, at least in part, out of a very real fear that the weak economy would lead the United States down into violence and social revolution. This is the reference to the invisible, "unconscious revolution" above and in many other descriptions of the New Deal. But there was a great deal of deliberate calculation in FDR's domestic decisions during the Depression. The U.S. involvement in WWII was also a deliberate plan on the part of FDR and Winston Churchill, who together worked to draw the United States into the conflict. But a large part of FDR's plan was also political. As he told the Democratic convention in Chicago a year before the currency devaluation:

> I pledge you, I pledge myself, to a new deal for the American people. Let us all here assembled constitute ourselves prophets of a new order of competence and courage. This is more than

a political campaign; it is a call to arms. Give me your help, not to win votes alone, but to win in this crusade to restore America to its own people.

In an October 27, 1933 letter to Will Rogers, Bernard Baruch predicted that using the RFC to buy gold by issuing debt would lead to "a loss of confidence in government credit." Foreign governments around the world criticized the break from the gold standard as a negative development, but FDR cleverly cast his decision as "a constructive move" that would "aid somewhat to raise prices all over the world." Of course FDR's nationalistic repudiation of the gold standard and, by implication, a policy to devalue the dollar, did none of these things and instead convinced our trading partners that America was pursuing currency inflation and protectionism. FDR told his advisers that he hoped that measures to restructure American agriculture via price supports and restrictions on imports would allow for the eventual liberalization of trade and the restoration of a link to gold. But most of FDR's early policy moves were merely a continuation of the protectionism of Hoover and the Republicans "for the present emergency," with a future hope held out for cooperation with other nations.[23]

The summary version of histories of this period makes it seem that the Smoot-Hawley tariff was a prime factor behind the worsening economy, but the currency devaluation by Roosevelt and his refusal to lower tariffs that were already in place after decades of enlightened Republican rule may have been more significant. It may be closer to the mark to say that tariffs did not help, but the devaluation of the dollar seems to have been a major new negative factor for the economy. First and foremost, the devaluation of the dollar made the public recognize the considerable inflation in terms of currency issuance that had occurred since the United States had restored gold convertibility.

FDR stressed on a number of occasions that abandoning the gold standard was necessary because even with the largest gold reserves in the world, by 1932 the United States only had sufficient quantities of the metal to back a tiny fraction of the currency and debt that was then in circulation. The process of currency inflation begun with the Civil War had reached the point of no return, at least in the Roosevelt world view. Abandoning the gold standard was inevitable, he argued, because the nation only had enough gold to redeem four percent of the currency and debt that was then in circulation.[24] But the real force behind the devaluation seemed to be the powerful deflationary forces at work in the real economy, forces that in the middle of 1933 terrified FDR's inner circle and all Americans.

When the new American President attended a World Economic Conference in Europe later in the summer of 1933, the fact of FDR's abandonment of the gold standard and his refusal to cooperate at all with the other nations in terms of stabilizing currencies and tariff reduction did nothing to help the dire international situation. Roosevelt gave general support for removing embargos, import quotas, and other arbitrary restrictions, but he had no intention of agreeing to remove trade protections or making any effort to stabilize the dollar against the major currencies.

The fact that the United Kingdom still had not settled its debts to the United States from WWI added to the delicacy of the situation facing FDR in 1933. With the Europeans led by the French demanding some understanding regarding the dollar and Roosevelt still unsure whether and when the U.S. economy would recover, there was no incentive for compromise by either side. As a result, there was little basis for agreement. Roosevelt returned to Washington empty handed—and happily so.

The Reconstruction Finance Corporation

By the fall of 1933, armed with the new legislative powers granted by Congress, FDR began to devalue the dollar further by purchasing gold using newly minted greenback dollars. Agricultural prices had been falling all year and unemployment was worse than when FDR was inaugurated six months earlier. The Fed had refused to participate in purchases of gold; thus FDR turned to RFC boss Jesse Jones to buy the gold. The RFC issued debt and purchased gold at a price set personally by FDR. Assisted by Treasury Secretary Morgenthau and RFC director Jesse Jones, FDR arbitrarily set the price of gold that day for government purchases.

Jones was one of President Hoover's original appointees to the RFC, a self-made man who was astute in business as well as in politics. A native of Tennessee who moved to Houston to build a fortune in lumber and real estate, Jones was easily the wealthiest man in the New Deal and the most action oriented. By the middle of 1932, Jones put himself in touch with FDR. During the interval between the November 1932 election and the inauguration in March 1933, Jones kept the president-elect abreast of developments in the economy and particularly in the banking sector. Jones and Roosevelt spoke frequently by telephone. In February 1933 Jones met the northbound train carrying the president elect to brief him on the severity of the banking crisis. FDR had been traveling at sea for two weeks on Vincent Astor's yacht, but as one contemporary observer noted, "Hoover had been at sea for four years."[25]

In March 1933, after much of the Hoover-appointed board resigned, Jones elected himself Chairman of the RFC. If Roosevelt had someone else in mind for the RFC job, the President never let on who that might be and Jones never gave him an opportunity to make another selection.[26]

The RFC quickly became a key part of the New Deal because Jones was willing to do jobs that were difficult, even where the legal authority was less than clear. Most people in the Roosevelt Administration thought that using the RFC to purchase gold was illegal, but Jesse Jones sold bonds to raise the necessary cash and purchased the gold as per the President's orders. Jones particularly enjoyed the gold purchase operations because they were executed by the Federal Reserve Bank of New York. Like much of Wall Street, New York Fed governor George Harrison opposed FDR's gold policy but was compelled to execute purchases on behalf of the RFC. The role of the RFC in this early stage and the divergence in views on gold with the Fed illustrates the powerful political role played by Hoover's creation under FDR. The RFC gave both Hoover and FDR choices in 1933 that would not have existed otherwise, choices about how to borrow money and purchases assets to manipulate the economy.

Since the Fed was unwilling to get involved in the decision to devalue the currency, rightly believing that this was a question for the Treasury, the RFC provided a powerful fiscal agency that could implement government policy. In a very real political sense, the RFC provided an alternative to the Fed. This was especially true when the RFC became empowered to purchase stock in and/or lend money to

banks. This reflected the view of President Roosevelt and many of
his inner circle that the government needed to act directly to stem
deflation.

When the Treasury and the Fed moved too slowly to deal with
failed banks, in a snap Jones volunteered the RFC to take over the
problem and within weeks the backlog of failed institutions was being
reduced. Jones was precisely the type of direct, no-nonsense leader who
fit beautifully into the unorthodox world of the New Deal. Such was
the urgency of the times that the appearance of Jones as a forceful and
motivated leader of the RFC must have seemed a godsend to FDR
and certainly was fortuitous for the United States.

In the second volume of his memoirs, *The Public Years*, Bernard
Baruch comments on FDR's compassion and concern for people as
being the motivations for using direct assistance via tools such as the
RFC. He told the story of going for a drive with FDR and General
Hugh Johnson, head of the National Recovery Administration, and
what the President said to Baruch during their trip:

> He took Hugh Johnson and me for a drive in his car, which had
> been specially built so he could drive it himself. We meandered
> around the country roads for a while, and came at last to a high
> ridge, where we could look down on a village nestling in the
> valley below. "There's a bank in that town," the president said,
> "and it holds the mortgages and notes of all those people living
> there. Now what I want to know, Bernie—are we going to get
> recovery by squeezing these people out through the wringer by
> natural processes, or are we going to help them? I don't think
> we can put them through the wringer." I agreed, but warned
> that we must help them to help themselves, and not make them
> dependent on government.[27]

The dollar price of gold was gradually increased between October
1933 through January 1934, Hoover writes in his memoirs, with the
idea being that "if the number of inches in the yardstick were lessened then there would be more cloth in the bolt."[28] Bankers around
the world reacted with horror. Montagu Norman of the Bank of
England said: "This is the most terrible thing that has happened. The

whole world will be put into bankruptcy." The great economist John
Maynard Keynes, who was an early supporter of Roosevelt, characterized the gyrations of the dollar under FDR "more like a gold standard
on the booze" and characterized as "foolish" the idea "that there is a
mathematical relation between the price of gold and the price of other
things."[29]

In January of 1934, Congress ratified all of FDR's executive
actions regarding gold by passing the Gold Reserve Act. The next day,
FDR set the price of gold at $35 per ounce and was to purchase the
metal at that price but sell to foreigners only. Roosevelt abolished
gold coins completely but, in a bow to the silverite tendency in the
Democratic Party, retained silver coins and set about purchasing silver to add to the national hoard. Not all members of Congress were
entirely intimidated by FDR, however, including Senator Carter Glass
of Virginia, who attacked FDR's decision in private and in public
statements.

When FDR called the senior Democrat Glass to the White House
to reveal his plans to "profit" through the revaluation of official gold
stocks, the widely respected Senator and former Treasury Secretary
under Woodrow Wilson ridiculed the notion with open contempt.
FDR believed that by merely changing the dollar price of gold upward,
the government would gain a "profit" of some $2 billion measured in
greenback dollars, but Glass immediately saw through the canard. "That
isn't a 'profit' as you call it—it is nothing more than a bookkeeping
mark-up," Glass told Roosevelt. "Furthermore, the gold you are proposing to confiscate belongs to the Federal Reserve Banks, and the
Treasury of the United States has never invested a penny in it. You are
proposing to appropriate something that does not belong to the government, and something that has never belonged to the government."[30]

Several years later, on April 27, 1937, Glass criticized FDR on the
floor of the Senate regarding the decision to leave the gold standard.
Significantly, he was still the only Democrat to publicly challenge FDR:

> England went off the gold standard because she was compelled
> to do so, not by choice. Why are we going off the gold standard?
> With nearly 40 percent of the entire gold supplies of the world,
> why are we going off the gold standard? To me, the suggestion

that we may devalue the gold dollar 50 percent means national repudiation. To me it means dishonor; in my conception of it, it is immoral.[31]

Despite the elite's disdain for Roosevelt, the voters went for the Democrats big in 1936. FDR won reelection in a lopsided vote that saw Democrats take 76 seats in the Senate with only 16 Republicans and four Progressives to keep the minority party company. In the House, the Democrats were 331 to 89 Republicans, giving FDR a comfortable margin in Congress. With this type of mandate, FDR's approach to managing the economy became even more aggressive in his second term—in part because of the lack of success regarding unemployment and growth generally.

America under FDR was seen by Hoover and the Republicans as an imitation of Mussolini's Italy or even Stalin's command economy in the Soviet Union. George Creel, one of Roosevelt's intimates over two decades, would later denounce American "liberalism" as "anti-American" because the people operating under that label gave "allegiance to a foreign power." This bitter debate over whether members of the New Deal, and the American political and business community, held allegiance to foreign capitals such as Berlin or Moscow went on for decades, through WWII and beyond. But the fact remained that FDR ran up some considerable deficits through the first four years in power. He spent $31 billion on public works and other relief efforts, and had little to show for it. And many liberal observers did not like the authoritarian nature of the New Deal.

Walter Lippmann wrote in *The Good Society*:

A reaction, definite and profound as that which in the late eighteenth century set in against the *Ancien Régime*, which in the nineteenth century set in against the crudities of laissez-faire, has, I believe, already begun. But the popular and influential leaders of contemporary thought are in a quandary . . . They do not like dictatorships, the concentration camps, the censorship, the forced labor, the firing squads or the executioners in their swallow tail coats. But in their modes of thinking, the intellectuals who expound what now passes for "liberalism," "Progressivism," or "radicalism" are almost all collectivists in their conception of the economy, authoritarians in their conception of the state, totalitarians in their conception of society.[32]

Central Planning Arrives in Washington

The various experiments in central planning in the United States in the twentieth century started with WWI, a period when many of the players involved in government during the Depression were in their formative years. Hoover, for example, played a key role in organizing food and other production during the war and coordinating other matters for President Wilson. Later, as President, Hoover organized and encouraged currency support loans to foreign central banks, and organized syndicates of bankers willing to lend funds to troubled banks.[33] Next under Hoover came the creation of the RFC and subsidies to banks and to the states, but not to the degree that would come under FDR and the New Deal. Hoover created the potential of the RFC, but FDR greatly expanded the scope of its operations.

FDR's efforts to implement central planning in the United States were somewhat thwarted by the U.S. Supreme Court during the early Roosevelt years, but later the White House managed to intimidate the Court. While the Supreme Court early on voided 6 of 14 New Deal laws passed by Congress at the behest of FDR, after the 1936 election the President began direct attacks on the Court in the media and threatened to "pack the court" with new appointees. The Court subsequently upheld New Deal laws such as the Railway Labor Act and the Social Security Act, actions that were evidence to Hoover and other conservatives that FDR had successfully forced to Supreme Court to back down in favor of his *revanchist* campaign against big business.

Such was the level of fear and the very real economic crisis in the United States that FDR was able to obtain and exercise huge powers from a frightened Congress. Members of the public were fearful of revolution from abroad, but were also reluctant to criticize FDR as well, a fact evidenced by the large number of anonymous critiques of the New Deal that were produced during this period by mainstream publishers. The growing ranks of the Socialist and Communist parties in America, wrote Robert Byrd in his history of the Senate, "forced Democratic leaders constantly to reassess their programs. While there was a 'New Deal Boom' in 1933, improving economic conditions, the nation was still locked in a terrible depression and millions of people were still out of work."[34]

Roosevelt had openly discussed his plans for price fixing to solve the problems of the farmer, borrowing a page from earlier efforts to institute federal price controls and supports for farmers during WWI. Hoover had created the Federal Home Loan Banks, the RFC, and convened a special session of Congress to seek modest farm support. He had also begun many different types of public works, but FDR was far more aggressive and willing to go outside the norms of the time because of the seriousness of the economic situation. The staid Hoover, it seems, never truly understood the magnitude of the problems facing the country, but FDR certainly did. By 1934, there were more than 17 million unemployed out of a total U.S. population of 130 million.

Under FDR, Congress held hearings on the suspicion first stated by Herbert Hoover that "bear raids" by Wall Street speculators were behind the country's economic woes. Some speculators did, in fact, admit to selling the markets short when President Hoover made positive statements about the economy. Known as the Pecora investigation after Ferdinand Pecora, the chief counsel of the Banking Committee, the inquiry involved all of the major banking figures of the day. Charles Mitchell, head of the National City Bank, was forced to resign after testimony that he evaded income taxes. Morgan partners likewise were shown by Pecora, a former New York prosecutor, to have paid no income taxes in 1931–1932.[35]

The Pecora inquiry was part of a broad attack on business and Wall Street that was both politically calculated and focused with the precision of a Madison Avenue ad campaign. FDR employed a command economy model that demonized business and used a preponderance of penalties to enforce compliance, all the while glorifying FDR and the federal government and its various agencies. One after another, government programs and agencies emerged from Washington to address some part of the economic crisis. This oppressive regime of attacks on business and expansion of the federal government actually encouraged thrift and less production.

The National Recovery Administration was one of the more notable of FDR's attempts at centralization that was eventually voided by
the Supreme Court. It prescribed work rules for most industries and
was almost immediately attacked from all sides. Consumers thought
it unfair and arbitrary. Conservatives complained about higher prices
while liberals warned that the NRA was protecting monopoly. FDR's
prescriptions for the economy and industry implied a degree of regi-
mentation and control that Hoover and many other Americans found
repulsive. During the 1930s numerous schemes were put in place to
use the government's credit to raise capital for housing and for commercial activities, all this while FDR inveighed against "economic
royalists," his reference to financial and business interests. But at the
end of the day, FDR was merely substituting the federal government
and various agencies thereof for the "kinder masters" who directed
the Money Trusts of the nineteenth century, the moneyed interests
inveighed against by Woodrow Wilson and Theodore Roosevelt alike.

FDR Embraces Federal Deposit Insurance

Congress was largely cowed during the first four years under FDR,
passing legislation drafted by the White House almost without question. The Securities Act of 1933, for example, was passed without
specific hearings by Congress on the legislative provisions. Many other
pieces of legislation during that era were enacted in similar fashion
as was the TARP bailout legislation in 2008. The Banking Act of
1933 was a response to the collapse of the U.S. banking system earlier that year. The bill sponsored by Senator Glass and Congressman
Henry Steagall was actually their second effort, the first being legislation passed in 1932 and signed by President Hoover to expand
the Fed's lending authority. The better known 1933 law created the
Federal Deposit Insurance Corporation on a temporary basis, which
immediately examined nearly 8,000 state-chartered banks that were
not members of the Federal Reserve System and allowed only solvent
banks to re-open. Known as "Glass Steagall," the Banking Act sepa-
rated traditional banking from commerce, including securities dealing
and underwriting.

Of interest, neither Senator Glass nor Congressman Henry Steagall envisioned the FDIC becoming a government-supported guarantee agency for bank deposits, but that is precisely what has happened over the years. Here is what the two main sponsors of the Banking Act of 1933 said about their creation:

- Senator Carter Glass: "This is not a government guaranty of deposits." He continued, "The Government is only involved in an initial subscription to the capital of a corporation that we think will pay a dividend to the Government on its investment. It is not a Government guaranty."
- Congressman Henry Steagall: "I do not mean to be understood as favoring the Government guaranty of bank deposits. I do not. I have never favored such a plan."[36]

Despite his other governmental creations, FDR was not a big supporter of government-sponsored bank deposit insurance nor was it supported by the banking industry. The deposit insurance fund put in place during the dark days of 1933 was meant to be temporary and was only made permanent in 1935, above vigorous opposition from the banking industry. The idea for the FDIC was proposed by Rep. Henry Steagall and Senator Arthur Vandenberg (R-MI), who were big supporters of federal deposit insurance because they saw it as a way to stem the decline in the number of banks and the destruction of money due to bank failures. The final model for the FDIC as a liquidating corporation was influenced by the Fed, which advanced its own proposal for the agency during this period.

An average of 600 banks per year had failed in the United States during the 1920s, but these banks were mostly in rural areas. Big city bankers discounted such attrition and bragged that tough standards made the industry stronger, but that song would soon change. The "tough love" policy regarding funding support for banks was also adopted by the Fed, which took the position that bank failures, which were mostly among non-Fed member state banks, were beyond the control of the central bank. The Fed's posture greatly exacerbated the crisis and, ironically, forced the issue with respect to federal deposit insurance for banks. By 1933, with larger banks in urban areas failing in droves and most state insurance funds in shambles, Steagall and Vandenberg finally got their way and federal deposit insurance became a reality.

The eventual legislation to make the FDIC permanent provided for assessments of deposit premiums by the banking industry to cover the cost of deposit insurance. The fact of federal backing for the FDIC has always been secondary to the support of the industry itself. Charles Calomiris of Columbia University contended in his book, *United States Bank Deregulation in Historical Perspective*, that making federal deposit insurance permanent and allowing state-chartered banks to join was a big win for smaller community banks. "In particular, access to federal insurance did not require small banks to pay the high regulatory costs of joining the Fed, and insurance protected virtually all of their deposits."[37] Such legislation was ultimately popular with the electorate even if it was resisted by the banking industries for decades to come. The failure of The Bank of the United States in 1930 and the increase in the type and number of failures thereafter captured the attention of the public and federal officials, and made it easier to get Congress to agree—especially with the Fed quietly pushing for the legislation.

As the rate of bank failures rose into the thousands per year in the early 1930s, the glaring inadequacy of the policy stance taken by the Fed forced Hoover to attempt to fill the gap using loans from the RFC. However, when the Democrat-controlled Congress required that the RFC begin to disclose the names of banks borrowing after August 1932, use of the RFC by banks declined. Echoing the debate today over requiring the Fed to disclose the names of banks and other entities that used emergency credit facilities in 2008 and 2009, the FDIC found in the early 1930s that "the appearance of a bank's name was interpreted as a sign of weakness."

The pressure on the U.S. banking system would intensify through the fall and winter of 1932, when fear of a currency devaluation by FDR was in the streets and this fact effectively helped to drive the nation into the banking crisis of 1933. Most of the banks that failed during the 1930s were not FDIC insured, but the agency was able to help to deal with hundreds of bank resolutions. Over the decades since its creation the FDIC has evolved into a highly successful, industry-funded but federally backed mutual insurance fund that also acts as a regulator and data collection agency, and as the statutory receiver of insolvent banks. Today when an FDIC insured bank is declared insolvent, by process of law the FDIC is automatically appointed receiver of the bank to protect depositors and maximize the recovery on the failed bank's estate.

The Legacy of FDR

The Depression and war years under both Hoover and FDR were one of the most important in terms of the way the federal government participated in the economy and used debt to support these activities. The role of the federal government had been expanding in the United States since the late 1800s and had begun really to increase with WWI—a period dominated by the Republicans. Just as the Republicans after the Civil War saw increased pensions for Union soldiers as good politics, so too the Progressives and Democrats of the 1930s were not afraid to build legislative monuments to their political legacy based upon increased federal spending. Indeed, the percentage increase in government spending under Hoover was larger than during the first two terms under FDR, at least until the start of WWII.[38]

· While Hoover may not have been afraid to expand the role of government, FDR took the focus and tone of the federal government to a new level of interference with and active oversight of business. Taking a direct example from fascist Italy, the American government created and expanded the new players in our tale of money and debt—namely the government sponsored enterprise (GSE). FDR added to the list of GSEs left over from WWI, including the War Finance Corp (WFC), the Federal Land Bank, and the Sugar Equalization Board, and expanded the powers of the RFC. Everything from export finance to financing for farm exports to residential mortgages was provided through new or expanded government agencies. The housing agency Fannie Mae was created in 1938 in the second part of FDR's New Deal economic plan, one of many "temporary" Depression-era GSEs that became permanent fixtures in Washington.

Since FDR was not particularly successful in addressing either unemployment or the overall state of the economy; he was in essence saved by the mobilization for WWII. In 1937, when the economy peaked under FDR, unemployment was still in double digits and the great contraction was still underway. Contrary to the Progressive political agenda, many of the tariffs that were in place under Hoover's administration were left in place or even raised by FDR. In that respect, at least, FDR showed a wonderfully consistent position for a New York politician, albeit a Democrat. FDR also raised taxes dramatically, tripling tax revenues from $1.6 billion in 1933 to $5.4 billion in 1940.[39] Milton Friedman summed it up:

> Admirers of FDR credit his New Deal with restoring the American Economy after the disastrous contraction of 1929– 1933. Truth to tell . . . the New Deal hampered recovery from the contraction, prolonged and added to unemployment and set the stage for ever more intrusive and costly government.[40]

Friedman and his colleague Anna Schwartz basically concluded that the Fed caused the Great Depression by not responding sooner and in particular for not supporting all banks, national and state-chartered, with liquidity. With the creation of the central bank in 1913, many bankers now looked to the Fed instead of to their private clearinghouse for support in times of panic. The private bank clearinghouse system in the United States atrophied after the creation of the government-controlled central bank and is one more negative impacts on the private banking system from the creation of the Fed. No private corporation can compete with a GSE nor could even a cooperative, mutually owned bank clearinghouse compete with the liquidity facilities of the federally backed central bank. The Fed's existence actually weakened the private banking market and made the banks dependent upon the support of the government-sponsored liquidity provider and lender of last resort.

Through the centralization of the power to provide liquidity into a single entity, the Fed created a single point of failure for the entire economy. Instead of buying bonds from the banks and providing them with cash, the Fed watched hundreds of banks fail each year. Had the "risk" in a monetary sense been more distributed via a private clearinghouse system, the result in the mid-1930s might have been very different in terms of the number of bank failures. When the Fed refused to act, as Friedman and Schwartz suggested, through purchases of government bonds from banks to add cash to the system, the central bank doomed many institutions to failure. As banks failed and savings were lost, the overall liquidity in the financial system—the money supply— shrank and Americans in normal fashion reacted by cutting spending.

To put the 1930s into perspective, imagine the entire banking system shrinking by one-third over the course of a year. By comparison, the U.S. banking system has shrunk by about 7 percent between 2007 and the end of 2009, more if one includes the collapse of the "gray market" banking system where much of the subprime real estate debt problem grew through the 2000s. The speed and suddenness of the bank failures of the 1930s and the lack of any response from the government doomed the U.S. economy to a forced contraction in consumer and business spending. Compare that to the crisis of 2007 or even as early as October 1987, when governmental mechanisms were available and did respond with liquidity to slow the impact of a crisis.

By 1935, there were about 10,000 state-chartered banks and 5,000 national banks in the United States, a level that would remain remarkably stable into the 1980s. And through those years the government was regulating and supporting those institutions with a variety of government programs and liquidity mechanisms meant to restore the banking sector, housing, and many other segments of the U.S. economy. The FDIC recorded 26 bank failures in 1935, but by 1938 the number of failures rose to 74 as the recession of 1937–1938 took Americans back into the worst years of the Great Depression. Yet thousands more state-chartered banks that were not FDIC members failed during this period. The damage done to the U.S. economy and the banking industry was profound, so that many of the Depression era–institutions created to support bank lending or to create new channels for home mortgage lending such as the GSEs and FHA, as well as agricultural lending via the Farm Credit Banks, became permanent.

Even after WWII and the resulting surge in economic activity, the GSEs were not dismantled. Their ability to issue debt and incur other obligations on behalf of the American taxpayer became an embedded part of the U.S. economy and also a means of achieving the American dream—albeit by driving an underlying rate of inflation that has steadily sapped the purchasing power of the dollar. These monuments to European fascism and the corporate state were expanded under the successors to Franklin Roosevelt and live on today. As will be discussed in the next chapter, GDP, bank lending, and consumer activity all grew rapidly with government war spending, as did federal deficits. But by then deficits were no longer seen as a bad thing. As the thinking of Keynes and other commentators who favored aggressive fiscal action proliferated, and as Keynes's theories were applied by neo-Keynesian theorists, complaints about deficits and inflation faded from the political foreground. The appeal of using fiscal measures today to increase economic activity, despite the impact on the financial condition of the state in the future, is a very powerful political incentive for deficit spending.

James Galbraith provided a spirited defense of the "deficits are good" camp in a May 2010 interview the *Washington Post:*

> Since the 1790s, how often has the federal government not run a deficit? Six short periods, all leading to recession. Why? Because the government needs to run a deficit, it's the only way to inject financial resources into the economy. If you're not running a deficit, it's draining the pockets of the private sector. I was at a meeting in Cambridge last month where the managing director of the IMF said he was against deficits but in favor of saving, but they're exactly the same thing! A government deficit means more money in private pockets.[41]

The Fed and The RFC

As previously described, with the passage of the McFadden Act in 1927 the Fed acquired a Washington Headquarters that institutionalized the Board of Governors as the supervisor of the 12 regional banks. In practical terms, from the 1930s the central bank became a unitary entity and lost any pretense of federalist representation via the regional federal reserve banks. The reserve banks became sources of local political patronage and in operational terms provided cash and check clearing services to their districts.

Of greater interest than the physical centralization of the Fed into Washington is the intellectual role the Board of Governors played in advancing and supporting the corporativist evolution of the federal government. In fact, researchers have documented that the Fed Board played an aggressive role in terms of managing the economy even during the term of Hebert Hoover.

Walker Todd in his paper, "The Federal Reserve Board and the Rise of the Corporate State, 1931–1934," notes that Hoover's first encounter

with the Fed's Board of Governors was in 1925 when he communi-
cated with Governor Daniel Crissinger, a friend of President Warren
Harding, about the Fed refraining from backing the United Kingdom's
progression back to the gold standard. Yet later in 1927, Todd finds
Hoover again trying to dissuade the Fed from running an easy money
policy to help the United Kingdom preserve the sterling exchange rate
with the dollar. As previously discussed, the hopeless anglophile Ben
Strong at the Fed of New York pushed easy money to help his friends
at the Bank of England. Hoover made the following wonderful appraisal
of the Fed in his memoirs:

> Crissinger was a political appointee from Marion, Ohio, utterly
> devoid of global economic or banking sense. The other mem-
> bers of the Board, except Adolph Miller, were mediocrities, and
> Governor [Benjamin] Strong [of the New York Reserve Bank]
> was a mental annex to Europe. I got nowhere [arguing with
> them]. President Coolidge insisted that the Board had been set
> up by Congress as an agency independent of the administration,
> and that we had no right to interfere.[42]

Hoover apparently had no illusions as to whether the Fed should
take its lead from the Treasury and Executive Branch, especially on
matters affecting foreign relations. Todd illustrates the fact that Hoover,
upon becoming President-elect in November 1928, began to urge the
Fed to jawbone banks against making loans for speculative purposes.
Hoover preferred a method of "credit rationing" to control speculative credit, reflecting his experience in WWI. This view was adopted
by the Fed's Board of Governors in Washington, while the Federal
Reserve Bank of New York advocated a policy of raising the discount
rate and targeting the cost of credit to control speculative loans. Todd
suggests that the Board was acquiescing to the policies of Hoover in the
period leading up to and after the 1929 market crash, suggesting that
the incorporation of the central bank into the Washington equation
was already well-established before FDR.

But perhaps more important to the Fed's evolution as the pre-
mier economic management agency in Washington was when Hoover
selected Eugene Meyer as governor of the Fed Board in September
1930. With the resignation of Roy Young, Hoover made one of the

key appointments to the Board of the central bank during its entire history. In the brief few years he served as governor, Meyer would lay the groundwork for the Fed's role in the New Deal and in supporting the growth of a European-style, Keynesian world view within the Washington bureaucracy that would be capped with the tenure of Mariner Eccles as chairman. Meyer had headed the War Finance Corporation (WFC) in WWI, which made loans to exporters during 1919 and 1920, but lapsed in 1921. Later, when it was re-activated by Congress over the veto of Woodrow Wilson, the WFC was used to bail out banks from bad loans in the farm sector. The WFC was one of the earliest examples of a government-sponsored entity at the federal level in the United States and it expanded into agricultural lending under the encouragement of Meyer and then-Commerce Secretary Hoover. The WFC served as the operational example for one of the government's most significant assistance efforts during the Great Depression, namely the RFC.

Meyer was a respected Wall Street financier of generally Democratic persuasions who not only led the Fed Board, but at the request of President Hoover encouraged the establishment of, and organized the RFC when it was first created in 1932. From the time he joined the Fed Board and even before, Meyer urged President Hoover to create a new government agency to deal directly with the economic crisis. But that said, Meyer was not nearly as radical in his views on what should be done to help the economy as the New Dealers who would follow him. Jesse Jones opined in his classic memoir, *Fifty Billion Dollars: My Thirteen Years at the RFC*, that neither Meyer not Atlee Pomerene, who succeeded Meyer as RFC chairman in 1932 and remained until FDR's inauguration, "was in favor of boldly making credit available on all fronts in an effort to stop the downward trend in our whole economy. Neither of these men can necessarily be censured, for it was only fair to say that the country was in a situation that it had never before experienced. Few members of Congress probably thought that the government could afford to put its credit behind our whole economy, which we later did under Roosevelt."[43]

Jones knew from first-hand experience about the coming banking crisis. In 1931, Jones organized the rescue of two Houston banks. He organized the city's bankers and business leaders and asked each to contribute capital to the rescues. After several days of round-the-clock meetings in the headquarters of his own bank, the National Bank of Commerce, Jones announced the purchase of one failing bank by his institution and the purchase of the other, Houston National, by the family of another prominent member of the Houston business community. In this fashion, Jones acquired some very relevant experience in rescuing insolvent banks, familiarity that would stand him in good stead in the years that followed.[44]

Of note, Meyer was drafted to chair the RFC only after Bernard Baruch turned President Hoover down for the job. Baruch did not accept any formal role during the Great Depression or WWII, but he was an important adviser to FDR and other New Dealers. He had long warned of the need to prepare for war. "Far from being a power behind the scenes," Baruch wrote of the FDR years with the banker's modesty, "my role during the New Deal was largely that of observer and critic. There was much in the New Deal that I applauded. But there was also much that disturbed me, and moved me to protest."[45]

Regarding the RFC, Todd found that Meyer "may initially have been approached on this matter by representatives of J. P. Morgan"[46] regarding the creation of the government's vehicle for providing emergency credit to the U.S. economy. Recalling the role of the House of Morgan in supporting the United Kingdom in WWI, it would have been remarkable for the bank not to have a view on the need to revive government support for commodities and industries. As an organization, JP Morgan had always taken a keen interest in the larger picture and had operatives monitoring most industries where the bank had credit exposure—especially the railroads. While the RFC may have eventually been used to provide credit to the economy under FDR, its creation was a boon to the House of Morgan and other wealthy interests who held debt issued by the railroads during the 1920s—debt that could not be repaid. The classic case in point was the Van Sweringen brothers who borrowed $75 million from the RFC to rescue their ill-advised purchase of the Missouri Pacific Railroad.[47]

The RFC made over $1 billion in loans during its first year in operation, many to politically well-connected banks such as J.P. Morgan and Kuhn, Leob and Company. Governor Meyer supported lending tens of millions in RFC loans to rail companies to be used to repay bank loans and thereby "promote recovery." In fact the loans were a bailout for the banks with loans to insolvent rail companies, such as the Missouri Pacific, which was allowed to slide into bankruptcy after the Van Sweringens repaid their loans to J.P. Morgan. "The extent of Meyer's humanitarianism in this affair may be gauged from the fact that his brother-in-law, George Blumenthal, was a member of J.P. Morgan and Company, and that Meyer had also served as a liaison officer between the Morgan firm and the French government," Murray Rothbard wrote in *America's Great Depression*.[48]

As the Depression worsened and the number of bank failures grew, Meyer and the Board staff encouraged Hoover to declare a bank holiday, an event for which the Fed had prepared since the previous year. Hoover instead wanted simply to guarantee 80 percent of all bank deposits to stem withdrawals and restore confidence, reflecting the cautious world view of a nineteenth-century Republican, albeit an engineer. But the Fed Board felt a stronger measure was needed. Hoover offered to make the bank closing proclamation in the waning days of his presidency, but FDR turned him down. Hoover apparently wanted FDR to agree to temper his New Deal program in return for Hoover issuing the bank closure proclamation. Later Hoover compared the refusal of FDR to cooperate regarding the bank closings as a supreme act of selfishness. "It was the American equivalent of the burning of the Reichstag to create 'an emergency,'" Hoover wrote in his memoirs.[49] But this would not be the last time that FDR was accused of duplicity when it came to a national crisis.

Not surprisingly, Meyer was a frequent target for populists such as the crusading Father Charles Coughlin, who referred in his broadcast sermons to the "Four Horsemen of the Apocalypse" of Wall Street as Morgan, former Treasury Secretaries Andrew Mellon and Ogden Mills, and Eugene Meyer. Meyer was strongly in favor of government action when the markets failed and had publicly called for the restoration of the War Finance Corporation as early as 1920. As the man who organized the RFC, he attracted criticism from Progressives outside the Northeastern United States, who viewed him as another New York banker. Meyer was far, far more than merely a financier from New York. He was a public citizen and a statesman who would end a long and successful career as the owner of the *Washington Post*, succeeded by his daughter and granddaughter.

Echoing the complaints made today about Wall Street influence in and around the Obama Administration in 2008, in the 1930s Huey Long of Louisiana chastised the New Dealers for their tolerance of "the same old clique of bankers who had controlled Hoover." Arthur Schlesinger recounted Long's commentary: "Parker Gilbert from Morgan & Company, Leffingwell, Ballantine, Eugene Meyer, every one of them are here. What is the use of hemming and hawing? We know who is running the thing."[50] Then as today, the large banks paid to have the best people representing their interests in Washington, much to the delight and continuing preoccupation of characters such as Huey Long. The Louisiana populist disliked Wall Street bankers and disparaged FDR for being subservient to them. Long made great political use of these facts in his continuous diatribes. But Meyer, significantly, resigned from the Fed at the start of FDR's presidency, which he saw as unlikely to instill confidence in the country.

In the classic biography of Carter Glass by Rixey Smith and Norman Beasley, *Carter Glass: A Biography*, the encounter between Glass and FDR on the eve of the latter's inauguration shows how doubtful was the legal authority for the President to declare a bank holiday in March 1933. FDR proposed to use the WWI Enemy Trading Act, this even though the general counsel of the Treasury had advised that the law was inadequate and had arguably lapsed at the end of the conflict. But the President-elect had the will to act and, again, he had clearly been considering these issues for many weeks and months.

FDR told Glass that Meyer and the Fed Board asked President Hoover for a declaration of a bank holiday just prior to the inauguration, but neither Hoover nor FDR thought that such a step was necessary. After taking a telephone call from Hoover, Roosevelt turned to Carter Glass, the most respected Democrat in the country and the dean of Congress when it came to financial questions. FDR explained that he would not give Hoover his support to declare a bank holiday despite the fact that the Fed Board had made such as request several times in as many days.

"I see. What are you planning to do?" asked Glass after hearing FDR's report about his telephone conversation a few moments before with Hoover regarding the banks.

"Planning to close them, of course," replied Roosevelt, referring to his plan to do precisely what Hoover had suggested—but only upon taking office himself.

Glass then went on to protest that Roosevelt did not have the authority even close national banks, much less order the closure of banks chartered by the states. But Roosevelt replied that "I will have the authority" and he proceeded to make a series of proclamations on the following day closing the nation's banks without the benefit of authority from Congress.[51] The giant of the Senate on financial matters, Glass knew the law, but FDR acted nonetheless because the times were so desperate that no one questioned his authority.

Once FDR was president, the Fed under Meyer and Eugene Black helped to engineer the seizure of gold and the devaluation of the dollar in an eager and rather shameless fashion, disregarding the fact that the gold belonged to the Fed's member banks. Walker Todd recalls, for example, that when FDR made his first "fireside chat" radio broadcast to the American people after ordering a bank holiday, the text of the comments was published in its entirety in the *Federal Reserve Bulletin*. "A circumstance," writes Todd, "that in light of everything else that transpired then, causes one to wonder who actually drafted that text for Roosevelt." Todd adds that Representative Hamilton Fish of New York, after hearing Roosevelt's first "fireside chat" on March 12, "proudly pronounced the new regime 'an American dictatorship based on the consent of the governed without any violation of individual liberty or human rights.'"[52]

The Fed had been clamoring for months for the Hoover White House to declare a bank holiday, thus finding a willing ear in FDR no doubt came as a relief to Meyer, Black and other members of the Board of Governors.[53] The Fed enthusiastically enforced the Roosevelt decree expropriating public and private gold, sending directives to the reserve banks asking them to compile lists of people not compliant with the edict from Roosevelt. The Board was entirely complicit in the seizure of the gold held by the federal reserve banks, assisting the Treasury even before Congress had gone through the motions of passing enabling legislation. The Gold Reserve Act of 1934 explicitly vested the reserve banks' title to gold in the United States (that is, the reserve banks' title to the gold was transferred to the Treasury) and offered the reserve banks gold certificates in exchange.

The Fed's Washington staff, which included more than a few Hoover holdovers, participated in the evolution of the New Deal, working with the Treasury and the other parts of the Executive branch to help shape some of the most important and most statist FDR initiatives in the New Deal. Much of what was done in the early days of the New Deal was done via Executive Order, and the Fed staff saw many of the initiatives from the Treasury before they were issued. There was fierce competition for ideas underway in Washington during this period, and the existence of the RFC made the political situation for the Fed a challenge.

Leading figures from the Fed staff expressed support for statist, arguably fascist constructions of public policy to compete with the views coming out of other agencies such as the RFC. Leading Fed staffers such as E. A. Goldenweiser, who served at the Fed for almost 30 years and headed the Division of Research for two decades, "was no fascist," writes Todd in "Rise of the Corporate State," yet he found it politically expedient to recommend that the Federal Government provide a system of guarantees for individual citizens' standard of living, together with the economic regulations and controls necessary to achieve such a living standard.[54]

When Eugene Meyer retired from the RFC and the Fed in early 1933, there was no longer any human connection between the leadership of the two agencies. In those days, the RFC was the dominant force in the U.S. money markets, not the Fed. This vast *parastatal* corporation headed by Jesse Jones, one of the most respected business figures in the country, operated informally. Jones reported directly to FDR and to Carter Glass. The RFC also featured ponderous political players such as the great Washington operative Tommy "the Cork" Corcoran as general counsel, and Columbia professor Rexford G. Tugwell and presidential adviser Adolph Berle as governors. All of these men were supported by FDR and wanted to see the RFC expand its operations "to become a permanent agency controlling the flow of capital throughout the entire economy," wrote Todd. Like two brawling siblings, the Fed and the RFC would contend with and compete for the attention of FDR during the Depression and into WWII.[55] Jesse Jones and Eugene Meyer would even get into fisticuffs at a dinner in Washington years later, still apparently arguing over a conflict regarding RFC policies.

In 1934, the Fed operating under Governor Black, J.J. Thomas from Kansas City, and M.S. Szymczak of Chicago, explicitly proposed that the RFC end all lending and instead have the Fed make such loans with the RFC as guarantor. As today, in the 1930s the Fed was very jealous of its bureaucratic turf and rightly saw the RFC as a threat to its unique operational mandate as the Corporation issued debt to fund its own operations. In 1934, responding to a call for more credit for business by the White House and the Congress, the Fed proposed that it be authorized to operate 12 new intermediate credit banks "to discount commercial paper and make direct loans of up to five years to industry." The New Deal planners saw the creation of an intermediate credit facility under the RFC, Treasury, and Fed as a key step toward the full nationalization of the U.S. securities markets. Fortunately the proposal had little support in Congress and in other government agencies and was not seriously pursued. Many Americans forget or never knew how close this country came to a nationalized financial system in the 1930s.[56]

Despite the strong current in favor of central planning and control in Washington in the early 1930s, the RFC never realized the full potential to become an agency of the state for the simple reason that the chairman of the RFC, Jesse Jones, did not allow it. Such was Jones's stature upon taking over at the RFC that when he was given broad powers by Congress to buy and sell commodities, make loans, and take equity stakes in banks and businesses, the personal confidence of Carter Glass was all the endorsement he required. Instead of making the RFC into a vehicle for central planning, Arthur Schlesinger observed, the RFC "took on the character of Jones" and was run like a profitable but flexible merchant bank, lending money and buying and selling assets and businesses. Schlesinger suggested that Mills and the other bankers saw the RFC as a backstop for the *rentier* class—"for people anxious to ensure steady returns for stakes they already had"—while Jesse Jones was more inclined to support the rising class of promoters and entrepreneurs. The difference between Jones and the Wall Street bankers who populated much of the New Deal government, Schlesinger concluded, helped to shift from "the hard money, gold standard, coupon-clipping groups in the East to those who, for better or worse, were prepared to risk monetary inflation because they deeply believed in economic growth."[57]

The lending powers eventually granted to the RFC and the Federal Reserve were somewhat overlapping and led to different results, but the Fed was a less aggressive lender than the RFC. This period is especially significant because it began to condition government officials in Washington to the idea of the use of the GSEs such as the RFC and the Fed as lenders and guarantors of loans, a practice that continued through WWII and into the post-war period. As argued before, the existence of the central bank and its balance sheet created possibilities for politicians that did not heretofore exist—and empowered them to deliver certain results and outcomes to voters in the short run without recourse to new taxes. The RFC too was funded from the markets and did not require taxes to make loans. But neither the loans by the Fed nor from the RFC had a great impact on the economy or employment in the 1930s. Both expanded credit and without great result. American consumers were still not buying enough goods to restore balance to the economy.

In terms of related developments at the Treasury during this period of crisis, among the most notorious was the creation of the Exchange Stabilization Fund by an amendment to the Agricultural Adjustment Act of May 1933 by Senator Elmer Thomas of Oklahoma, the staunch silverite and New Dealer who managed to combine "four major inflation suggestions into one omnibus measure and granted the president permissive powers to use none, one, or any combination of currency inflation techniques. After meeting with Thomas, the president accepted the amendment, and it became part of the 'One Hundred Days' legacy of the Roosevelt administration."[58]

The provisions of the Thomas Amendment essentially created a $3 billion slush fund for the Secretary of the Treasury to use for currency inflation operations in the open market, and was entirely beyond the supervision or oversight of Congress. The provisions included the right to issue billions in new greenback currency to fund operations as necessary. Originally meant to help agricultural exports, the ESF, as it became known decades later, would cause significant mischief as an off-balance-sheet vehicle for subsequent Secretaries of the Treasury to play games in the currency markets and with global politics. But compared with the RFC and the Federal Reserve Board, the Treasury itself was a relatively minor player during the Depression years.

Corporativist Reform at the Fed

When Eugene Meyer resigned from the Fed Board in May of 1933, he was replaced by Eugene Black of Atlanta, who would himself resign just over a year later in August of 1934. Treasury Secretary Henry Morgenthau recommended an official from the Treasury, Mariner Eccles, to replace Black as governor of the Board, as the chairman of the central bank was called in those days. Eccles was a Mormon from Utah whose family had operated banks in that state for many years. Eccles had drunk deeply from the cup that led to the revelation of Keynesian economics. He was quickly recognized by Morgenthau and others as an effective advocate for deficit spending to address the lack of private consumption and capital investment during the Depression.

In 1932, FDR and Morgenthau both contended that the surest path to economic recovery was a balanced budget and cuts in government spending, but Eccles believed just the opposite. When FDR asked him to become governor of the Fed Board in November 1934, Eccles stipulated that he would take the job only if he were given a free hand to reform the Fed. Eccles and his collaborator, Lauchlin Currie, a Canadian-born economist and a member of the "brain trust" at the Treasury, would be the chief architects of the new U.S. central bank. Currie, one of America's foremost Keynesian, socialist economists, prepared a memo for FDR that outlined basic changes in the operations and governance of the Fed.

Part of the cell of communists that included Harry Dexter White, author of the IMF, Eccles and Currie had two main goals: first to centralize control of Open Market Operations under the Board and second, to subject all of the governors of the reserve banks to annual appointment by the Board. His ultimate proposal was less radical that the earlier work of Currie, which envisioned a complete nationalization of the Reserve Banks and a unitary, European style "Federal Monetary Authority." Currie's extensive work on the organization of the Fed informed the debate on the issue. "The stage was set for the Board to become the focus of the economic and legislative drama of the second half of the 1930s," wrote Todd, "featuring the Banking Act of 1935, the doubling of reserve requirements in 1936–1937, the overhaul of discount-window policies, and the regulatory agreement of 1938."[59] But neither Currie nor Eccles recognized even then the political constituency the reserve banks held among the banking industry and the local and national politicians in the immediate vicinity.

More than simply acting as the governor of the Federal Reserve Board, Eccles became a leading advocate of change in government fiscal operations, to make federal spending more counter-cyclical in terms of increased public sector spending when private sector activity failed. Eccles favored a more equitable distribution of wealth, high taxes on the wealthy, and a national planning board to coordinate public and private activities. John Kenneth Galbraith would later describe the Fed under Eccles as "the center of Keynesian evangelism in Washington."[60]

Allan Meltzer recorded in *A History of the Federal Reserve: 1913–1951* that Eccles opposed the FDR wage and price controls and applauded when the Supreme Court struck them down. Meltzer added in the same portion of his landmark book that Eccles was not an apologist for deficits generally, but only to offset deficits in investment spending. He observes that despite the prominence of Keynes's work at the time, Eccles claimed never to have read his books nor to have derived any of his own views on deficit spending from Keynes main work.[61]

Meltzer documents how Eccles came to be associated with the term "pushing on a string" in 1935 during testimony before the House Committee on Banking and Currency. He knew that monetary expansion did not work in the Depression because people were unwilling to spend or borrow. But Eccles went further than many of his contemporaries and attributed the excess of savings to inequitable income distribution. "Eccles differed from his predecessors in his belief that government had to take responsibility for the economy," wrote Meltzer. "He devoted much of his time to advocating fiscal measures, especially increased spending on investment financed by government borrowing to expand demand."[62]

Part of Eccles's fascination with income and consumption came about as a result of his observations of the Depression, where he saw time and again the process of deflation and liquidation destroying lives. His Mormon upbringing and keen business sense enabled him to discern the value to the economy of thrift. Yet he also saw the available wealth of the nation being drawn into a very few hands, including his own. Eccles felt a sense of frustration at the fact that his fellow citizens could not consume the products America produced. The boom and bust of the 1920s was due not to profligacy, Eccles came to believe, but overmuch thrift. "We did not as a nation consume more than we produced," Eccles said. "We were excessively thrifty." Eccles noted what many Americans already knew, namely that economic contractions built upon themselves, deflating the economy until internal and/or external forces reversed the trend and expansion began again.

Eccles saw that external force as the federal government and deficit spending, a conclusion he came to himself and spoke about three years before Keynes published the *General Theory*. "Eccles was an untutored pioneer," wrote author Bill Greider. "An American banker from Utah, a man who had never studied economics or even attended college, who was able to see what the great British economist himself saw, and Eccles had the uncommon courage to articulate this thinking before it became fashionable."[63]

Eccles was a recess appointment by FDR and was not confirmed by the Senate until April of 1935. He was opposed by Carter Glass, who disliked Eccles personally and also did not care for his proposals to centralize the Fed Board in Washington. Eccles proposed to limit the Federal Reserve Bank presidents to a purely advisory role and give the appointed governors full voting control over open market operations. The compromise advanced by Glass and other members of Congress kept a role in monetary policy for the Reserve Bank "presidents," as the governors of the individual banks are now known. Glass made it very clear during the debate that he was not in favor of any of Eccles proposals and at several stages of the process suggested that the portion of the bill dealing with the structural changes sought by Eccles be put aside.

The final provisions of the Banking Act of 1935 completed the centralization of the Fed's Board of Governors. It also expanded the type of loans that the Fed could make, particularly in time of emergency. But in a larger sense, the Banking Act of 1935 completed the transition of the Fed from an institution that at least nominally paid homage to the gold standard and an asset currency, to one that was entirely devoted to a fiat currency that was not convertible into anything. "Currently, the American monetary system is composed of a series of procedures based on statutes and statutes based on procedures, which reflect no integral concept of money but, rather, a series of residual concepts," wrote Jane D'Arista in *The Evolution of U.S. Finance: Federal Reserve Monetary Policy, 1915–1935*, "Since at no point is any concept of money firmly repudiated, the system may be said to accommodate a process of selection among alternatives. It preserves the procedural framework of an asset currency system but in reality is closer to fiat money."[64] D'Arista writes that like the Federal Reserve Act in 1913, the Banking Act of 1935 is silent on monetary policy and gives no guidance as to what metrics the Fed will use to judge the effectiveness of its policy actions. At the end of the day, the legislative changes made to the Fed in 1935 did not entirely resolve the internal contradictions raised by traditional American exponents such as Carter Glass, who wanted the regional reserve banks to retain their autonomy.

The imperfect Fed system is precisely consistent with American ideas of check and balances, with friction between the different players and regions. But it also confirms the long-standing pattern in America of bankers calling the shots in Washington. The fact remains that bankers still control the boards of directors of the Federal Reserve Banks and thereby get a seat at the monetary policy table of the Federal Open Market Committee. While Eccles was successful in bringing the conduct of Fed open market operations into the public domain and under Washington's control, he was not entirely successful in destroying the independence of the 12 regional reserve banks. The most recent example of the bailout of American International Group by then-New York Fed President Timothy Geithner illustrates the fact that the Fed is still unable to control the Federal Reserve Bank of New York.

The irony of the Eccles period at the Fed is that much of the time and attention of the central bank was dominated by dealing with secular deflation, the activities of the RFC and, in WWII, the national priorities of global war. Most measures of the money supply tracked by the Fed in those days stayed remarkably stable from 1933 through 1941, when America threw itself into a two-ocean war and a national mobilization that far exceeded that of WWI. The Fed of New York cut its discount rate from over 3 percent in 1933 to 1.5 percent in 1934 and did not change this rate until 1936, when Eccles increased reserve requirements from 12.5 percent to 25 percent. When interest rates rose and a recession began to materialize, the Fed reversed course in 1937, when it dropped the discount rate down to 1 percent. The discount rate in New York remained at 1 percent from 1937 through 1951 as the central bank adopted what Galbraith described as a passive posture.

Most economists agree that the low private demand for capital funds in the United States and the growing flight of private capital from fascism in Europe combined to make Federal Reserve policy largely irrelevant during this period and through WWII. The irony of the Great Depression is that for much of the period, the solvent commercial banks in the country had record levels of excess reserves. There was simply a lack of demand for loans—which made some of the great minds of the period on all points of the political compass wonder if the democratic, market economies had lost the ability to foster economic growth—at least short of war or inflation. This is the same issue that confronts America in 2010.

The truth about this point, like anything else involving economics, is hard to prove with finality, but the experience under FDR in the 1930s does suggest very strongly that a sustained economic rebound was elusive. Even if one accepts all of the conservative views on the negative financial and political impact of the New Deal on the economy, the fact that the private sector did not heal itself to a larger degree raises troubling questions. A more reasonable view seems to be that much of what FDR and the New Dealers did in the 1930s was made ineffectual due to the effects of technology and the resulting economic changes around the globe, changes that manifested themselves in powerful deflation and unemployment.

America Goes to War

Between 1929 and 1938, the outstanding debt of the federal government more than doubled from $16 billion to $40 billion, but private balance sheets of banks and companies were just barely growing. After the terrible years of Great Contraction, the U.S. economy rebounded modestly, followed by the mini-Depression of 1937–1938. Wages for those workers fortunate enough to be employed had risen in real terms during the FDR era, but unemployment and inflation remained stubbornly high.

Fed Chairman Ben Bernanke allowed, in an essay on the period, that "maybe Herbert Hoover and Henry Ford were right" in terms of understanding that paying workers more increased their ability to consume goods and services. The key insight of Henry Ford and his business partner James Couzens was the reality that a factory worker at Ford Motor Co. in 1914 could not afford to own a Ford car. Bernanke found that "Higher real wages may have paid for themselves in the broader sense that their positive effect on aggregate demand compensated for their tendency to raise costs."[65] The trouble in the Depression was that wages and prices had fallen and the overall flow of economic activity had contracted. The result of the high tariffs left as a legacy from the Republicans and FDR's devaluation of the dollar was lower U.S. exports, including farm exports.

With over 10 million men unemployed or on government makework jobs, the U.S. economy could not be said to be prospering after eight years of FDR. William Manchester wrote in *The Glory and the Dream*[66] that the unskilled workers building the East River Drive in New York were being paid less than $1,000 per year. This would have seemed a reasonable wage only a few generations before, but inflation had eroded the purchasing power of the dollar to such a degree that it was a remarkably small sum in the late 1930s. High unemployment led to high default rates on home mortgage loans. The failure to address the employment issue before WWII is a notable shortcoming. Malnutrition was rampant, so much so that nearly half of all of the men examined for military service in that period were rejected by U.S. authorities. Overall, America was lean and hungry after a decade of deflation and depression, and wanted a break. But there were few prospects for jobs. Nothing done by Congress or FDR had much changed that grim outlook. Harkening back to the period during WWI, the idea of entry into another war was almost an attractive prospect for some Americans in terms of giving the nation purpose and a sense of momentum.

One of the more remarkable statistics from the Depression period is the degree of under-employment faced by many Americans. From the boom years of the late 1920s, hours worked per adult dropped to just 70 percent of the pre-bust levels and did not recover even after the end of the 1937–1938 economic contraction. By 1939, hours worked per adult were still just 80 percent of 1929 levels, again illustrating the degree of deflation and slack in the U.S. economy. Milton Friedman and Anna Schwartz found that an unusually large portion of economic output through 1937 was focused on nondurable goods intended for government purchase, part of a strategy meant to offset the huge decline in private capital investment. By the end of the decade, the United States was still operating at levels of private industrial capacity and investment that were significantly below 1920s levels. The respected economists also determined that government policies to artificially raise wages and regulate business served to push down private capital formation and arguably made the Depression longer and more severe than necessary.

With all of the government stimulus, increased spending, taxes, and debt, the U.S. economy still had not really found its footing—even as Europe once again edged toward war. Deflation in central Europe had been as bad or worse than in the United States, causing the Revolution in Russia in 1917 and the terrible economic situation in Germany due to WWI reparations. The rise of Mussolini, Hitler, and Stalin in Russia all owed their origins to the economic and political collapse in Western Europe following WWI. It can be argued that FDR took the United States to war consciously and even deliberately, and there is ample documentation of both. Supporters of FDR point out that the war mobilization saved the U.S. economy and created jobs. The point to take though, is the degree to which the fact of the war and the mobilization to support it masked underlying structural defects in the U.S. economy—shortcomings that would remain concealed for half a century thereafter.[67]

Not quite a year passed between British Prime Minister Neville Chamberlain's failed attempt to appease Hitler at Munich in 1938 and the resumption of hostilities among allied France, Britain, and Germany a year later with the invasion of Poland. As in the case of WWI, Britain and France were broke at the start of hostilities and did not have the resources to fight a prolonged war. The United States had largely demobilized after WWI and Congress cut appropriations for many different types of war expenditures. General George Patton, who wrote and spoke extensively about the need to rearm during the 1930s, did not receive funding to re-establish the American armored forces within the U.S. Army until 1940, when German tanks and mobile infantry were already rolling across Europe.

In 1939, Albert Einstein and other scientists called upon Roosevelt to begin work on an atomic bomb. As former assistant Secretary of the Navy under Wilson, FDR understood defense issues and relished the task. The wealthy, Harvard-educated Roosevelt lent a great deal of respectability to the Democratic Party and did his job as Assistant Secretary of the Navy with great competence. The U.S. Navy was prepared when war came. FDR launched an effective defense against German submarines when conventional wisdom in the military community said that successful anti-submarine operations were not possible. Unfortunately, FDR's facility with military affairs did not translate well to matters involving the economy.

FDR assumed dictatorial "emergency powers" to set prices and ration all types of goods and materials, and greatly increased spending. Whereas during WWI, the profiteering occurred in the streets, with all manner of vendors and companies vying for government contracts, by WWII under the bureaucratic aegis of the federal government, defense spending and procurement had become an entirely inside-Washington game. The supply and logistical support for the war effort greatly increased the power of the federal government and embedded defense and other types of federal procurement as important elements of the economy of each state. One great accomplishment of the FDR period was to increase the size of the federal government's purchases and to entwine state politics with Washington in pursuit of access to largesse. The debate over federal base closings is just one small example of the financial importance of federal procurement activities to many states.

Just as the United States was beginning to mobilize for the conflict in 1940, Keynes published a pamphlet, *How to Pay for the War*, which set forth the three ways a war can be financed: taxation, inflation, and forced savings. Keynes favored the last and believed that along with taxes and debt, savings by individuals should be the way government not only financed the war but also managed supply and demand. We've noted that Keynes was no apologist for big government. He believed that other than regulating aggregate demand, the government should basically leave the private sector to its own devices.[68]

Yet by making allowance for intervention by the state to remedy the imperfections of the free-market system, whether unemployment or war, Keynes opened the door to the enlargement of the corporate state. Ever a weaver of schemes and political scenarios, perhaps Keynes' advice should be taken lightly, to season his speculative imagination. But he was clearly among the most influential economic thinkers of his age, even though he was very conservative in his social views. Robert Skidelski, in his recent book on "the master" economist, included this comment from 1938 by Keynes discussing his losses in the 1929 Crash:

I find no shame at being found still owning a share when the bottom of the market comes. I do not think it is the business of [a serious] investor to cut and run on a falling market . . . I would go much further than that. I should say that it is from time to time the duty of a serious investor to accept the depreciation of his holdings with equanimity and without reproaching himself. Any other policy is anti-social, destructive of confidence, and incompatible with the working of the economic system. An investor . . . should be aiming primarily at long-period results and should be solely judged by these.[69]

Keynes would spend the rest of his life until his death in 1946 working to help the United Kingdom manage its war finances and the British economy. The British government needed all of the help that it could get given the "nationalist" foreign policy of FDR. When Winston Churchill succeeded Chamberlain in May of 1940, he sent a very specific note to FDR seeking all manner of war support, including the sale of steel and old warships on credit, part of a voluminous correspondence between the two men during the war. FDR governed the country as a dictator to a large degree, but not entirely. For example, he did not have the authority to sell warships or to go to war without the consent of Congress. But in his conduct of foreign policy as the head of government and head of state, FDR certainly played the role of autocrat. "It is obvious that Churchill regarded Roosevelt as an American dictator who had little concern for the opinions of the Congress and the American people," Professor Charles Tansil wrote in *Back Door to War*. "With reference to the matter of war, the Churchill cablegrams reveal that he believed Roosevelt could plunge America into the conflict in Europe any time he desired. The French Cabinet apparently had the same viewpoint."[70]

With the fall of France in June 1940, FDR's willingness to assist Britain with material and warships increased. This was the start of a massive mobilization and transfer of resources to the Allies in Europe. With his election victory in November 1940, Roosevelt could, like Woodrow Wilson before him, put aside his nonintervention rhetoric and more actively helped Britain. Churchill pressed FDR to make his assistance free of immediate requirement for payment because the moment was approaching when the British government would no longer be able to pay cash for non-military imports.

By January 1941, FDR and his lieutenants began drafting Lend Lease legislation and the law was passed by Congress and signed by Roosevelt in March. FDR and many Americans believed the propaganda that the Lend Lease program to provide ships and other armaments to Britain was a form of "peace insurance." The reality was closer to the prediction by Senator Robert Taft that America could conduct an undeclared war "without actually being on the shooting end of the war." By May 1941, Roosevelt had not so secretly ordered the U.S. Navy into the battle of the Atlantic, occupying Iceland and beginning destroyer escort operations for U.S. merchant vessels. WWII had begun.

Wartime Inflation and Debt Finance

Friedman and Schwartz record that between 1939 and 1948, wholesale prices in the United States more than doubled and the money stock had nearly tripled, resulting in stiff inflation at the consumer level.[71] But even though these statistics may seem eye-popping, the degree of inflation experienced during and after WWII was less than either the Civil War or WWI—although the money creation was greater in WWII. Gold poured into the United States during WWII as nations in Europe and around the globe sought a refuge for their monetary assets.

By the time the Japanese attacked Pearl Harbor on December 7, 1941, the United States had created a rationed economy and many consumer goods became unavailable until after the war. The Fed, acting under FDR's authority, imposed controls on consumer credit, but such moves had little effect since consumer goods of all descriptions already were very scarce.[72] In stark terms, from the 1929 market crash through the end of the 1940s, Americans lived with constrained incomes and choices, making the collective image of the American dream one of basic survival.

During the Depression and going into the WWII years, the Fed took a very accommodative policy and explicitly supported prices for Treasury bonds, at the expense of inflation. This policy would end in 1951, essentially amounting to a declaration of independence for the Fed from its wartime subservience to the Treasury. Friedman and Schwartz documented the sensitivity of the New Dealers within the Washington community to the idea that the Fed would no longer subsidize government borrowing. "The Great Contraction and the New Deal," they wrote, "had bequeathed both an increased sensitivity to fluctuations in economic activity and a widespread acceptance of the view that government had direct responsibility for the maintenance of something approximating 'full employment,' a view that found legislative expression in the Employment Act of 1946."[73]

The depressed private sector economy and the large government borrowing during the war pushed the ratio between the federal debt and GDP above 100 percent during and after the war years. As the U.S. economy began to expand and grow after WWII, the ratio of federal debt to GDP would fall to a low of about 30 percent during the presidency of Jimmy Carter. In addition to selling bonds to individuals during WWII, the U.S. government also sold them to commercial banks and to the Federal Reserve Banks, resulting in a substantial growth in reserve bank credit during the conflict. But after the war, in many ways the domestic monetary indicators of demand became less and less relevant because the dollar had become the world's currency.

During the years immediately following WWII, the United States pumped the equivalent of $100 billion in today's dollars into the European economies, half of which was provided on a grant basis and the rest as loans that would mostly not be repaid. Responding to the growing Cold War confrontation with the Soviet bloc nations was not immediately the intention of the Marshall Plan, but American support for Europe would soon become part of a larger American strategy of containment focused toward the Soviet Union and its allies. But an even bigger and more significant result of the American aid effort was the movement toward the Treaty of Rome and European unification itself.[74]

In the United States, the expenditure of billions of dollars per year to help Europe at a time of slack in the economy following the war did not sell easily. Eventually it did gain support, however, when posed as an alternative to a future war. Truman eventually proposed the expenditure of $17 billion in 1947 and after months of lobbying by its namesake, Secretary of State George Marshall, it was adopted in 1948. Marshall later reported that American women were vastly in favor of the plan and "electric" in persuading the Congress to go along with the proposal.[75]

Bretton Woods and Global Inflation

The Marshall Plan to rebuild Europe, followed by the creation of the International Monetary Fund and the World Bank, created the conditions for European recovery and eventually political union in Europe. Under the Bretton Woods accord, the financial and economic discussions that had been ongoing through the war years were brought together in an ambitious effort to impose a multilateral model on the world and particularly on Europe. In keeping with the popularity of central planning among economists, a coordinated policy on trade and financial flows was envisioned. A liquidity facility was provided to stabilize global financial flows and avoid the extreme movement of cash and gold from one nation to the next. Responsibility for maintaining "equilibrium" in the global system fell upon the United States, a reflection of the influence of Keynes and the British side in the negotiations.

With the benefit of the commerce clause of the Constitution and the Civil War, Americans had settled most issues with respect to internal trade and commerce, but Europe at the end of WWII had not. Thus the genius of Marshall and his inner circle was to require joint action by the states of Europe in return for American assistance. The Marshall Plan and Bretton Woods would create a structure for global trade and finance that was measured in and supported by the dollar, a construct that supposed the existence of an international currency based upon the economy of just one large, politically dominant nation.

The Bretton Woods agreement of 1944 also marked the end of Great Britain as a significant global power in financial and strategic terms. With the financial collapse of the United Kingdom after the war, the United States assumed responsibility for much of the colonial possessions of the British Empire and, once again, bailed out London financially. The mechanism for the bailout was a regime of fixed exchange rates pegged to the dollar, with the U.S. currency retaining some residual link to gold.

The guns in Europe had barely fallen silent before the United Kingdom was seeking accommodation with respect to its obligations under the Lend Lease Act of WWII. The British also sought further loans or grants-in-aid and justified these requests as consideration for the suffering of Britain at the hands of the German air force. In September of 1945, Keynes himself led a British delegation to the United States seeking precisely those terms. He received a correct but friendly reception from the new administration of President Harry Truman. Truman was as conventional in his thinking about the economy and foreign affairs as FDR had been willing to be aggressive and experiment.

Opposite Keynes was the equally new Secretary of the Treasury, Fred Vinson, a former member of Congress from Kentucky who would later become Chief Justice of the Supreme Court. In the classic book *Sterling-Dollar Diplomacy in Current Perspective*, Richard Gardner described the interaction between the two men as the United States and Britain negotiated the forgiveness of much of the latter's war debt and another loan. Both Baruch and Hoover spoke strongly against the new loan to Britain, insisting that American needs first be reckoned.[76]

Vinson had not reached Washington by taking risks and in 1947, with Truman down badly in the polls and the American electorate restive, selling Congress on forgiving the Lend Lease loans to Britain, much less make new loans to London, was difficult. Public opinion, led by major media organs like the *New York Times*, condemned Bretton Woods and the idea of trade liberalization—unless the United Kingdom and other nations of Europe followed suit and dropped their tariffs as well.

Eventually, after lengthy negotiations and sometimes difficult exchanges between Keynes and Vinson, the two sides agreed on forgiveness of the lend-lease obligation and low-interest rate loans to finance

Britain's balance of payments deficit. The United States agreed to this formulation in large part to get the United Kingdom to follow up with a multilateral trade agreement removing the prewar tariffs. But the bitter reality for the British was that agreement with the United States was a necessary condition for the country to be in a position to ratify the Bretton Woods agreement by the end of December 1945.

The American side made more than a few concessions to the British during the final talks to ratify Bretton Woods, balancing the increasingly isolationist mood of the American people after WWII with the need to be generous to an ally after a difficult victory. The sad fact was that Britain was broke at the end of WWII and badly needed American help to avoid real economic hardship. While Britain's earnings from foreign trade and investment had fallen during and after the war, the country's military obligations around the world were still massive and included shouldering much of the cost of the occupation of Germany and supporting military installations around the world.

By 1947, British reserves of gold and foreign exchange had fallen to dangerously low levels and the country was headed for a serious fiscal crisis. While the loan agreement between Washington and London signed in 1946 had contained a commitment by the British to maintain the convertibility of sterling, it was increasingly doubtful that a devaluation could be avoided—even with the flow of further loans from the United States. Much of Europe and the United States were headed into an economic recession by the end of 1947 and the prospect of a lengthy standoff with the Soviet Union loomed. The end of WWII was not as cheerful as the residents of the victor nations might have hoped—but things would soon start to improve. Under the powerful push from the Marshall Plan starting in 1948 and the movement toward lower tariffs and multilateralism in terms of trade policy championed by the United States in the years that followed, the global economy would soon start to expand rapidly and bring renewed prosperity to the United States and the nations of Europe. The combination of the imperative of the Cold War and the United States embrace of trade liberalization provided a rising tide that would lift all boats in the Western nations.

Chapter 7

Debt and Inflation

A Rising Tide Lifts All Boats

At the end of March 1945, President Roosevelt travelled to Warm Springs, Georgia, to rest before his appearance at the conference in New York to celebrate the founding of the United Nations. Two weeks later, on April 12, 1945, FDR collapsed while sitting for a portrait. A few hours later, the President was declared dead of a brain hemorrhage. Former Senator Harry Truman, the vice president whom FDR scarcely knew, had become the thirty-third President of the United States. FDR had led his country through 15 terrible years of depression and war.[1] The only leader that a generation of Americans had ever known was gone. The nation was still at war and still struggling to find its way back to economic stability.

Two weeks after Roosevelt's death, the Russian and American armies met on the banks of the Elbe River in the Village of Torgau in Eastern Germany. FDR and Stalin had been at odds for weeks because of the

Soviet leader's refusal to abide by the terms of the Yalta Agreement. The media, and even some American military leaders such as General Dwight Eisenhower, still believed that there could be peace between the Soviets and the Western Allies. "Nothing guides Russian policy so much as desire for friendship with the United States," Ike said after visiting Moscow. To his eternal shame, Ike prevented General Patton from leading the Third Army into Prague and freeing the people of Czechoslovakia, Eastern Germany, and Berlin. Patton's tanks and troops could have liberated these areas before the Soviet Army seized them and plunged millions of people into decades of darkness under communist rule.

Germany surrendered in May 1945 and within weeks it was clear to both sides that the Russian and Allied Forces would not be cooperating as envisioned under the Yalta Agreement. Patton wanted to organize the defeated German forces and attack the Russians immediately, a view that is nicely presented at the conclusion of the 1970 Frank Schaffner film *Patton*. He told General Joseph McCarney, Eisenhower's deputy commander in occupied Germany: "We are going to have to fight them sooner or later. Why not do it while our Army is intact and the damn Russians can have their ass kicked back to Russia in three months?" Patton was soon relieved of his command.

Of course Patton was right. Dealing with the Soviet threat right then and there was the proper course, especially since the United States had perfected the atomic bomb. Instead the civilian leadership of the United States and the other Allied nations clung to the naïve hope that there could be peace with the Russians following the fall of Hitler. Winston Churchill, who was unexpectedly defeated by the Labor Party in May 1945, the month the conflicted ended, had warned Eisenhower to "shake hands with the Russians as far east of the Elbe as possible." Unfortunately Ike did not get the point.

The failure of Eisenhower to understand the true strategy of the Soviets for post-war Europe is remarkable given that he was supreme commander in Europe. Moscow had already started to set up puppet governments in Eastern Europe even as the Red Army moved westward. By 1947, the Allies and the Soviets were in a confrontation over Berlin, which remained encircled with the Soviet occupation zone. Two years later, the North Atlantic Treaty Organization (NATO) was formed to protect Western Europe from the imminent threat of Soviet aggression. The U.S.

would maintain a permanent military presence in Europe—a sharp break with American history and pre-WWII policy. It is no small irony that Eisenhower was NATO's first Supreme Allied Commander in Europe.

The advent of the Cold War, a term originally coined by Bernard Baruch, had some significant economic effects on the United States and Europe. First and foremost, instead of a total demobilization after the conflict as was the case following WWI, the United States and the Western Allies were compelled to maintain a substantial military presence in Europe. In Asia, the United States undertook the occupation of Japan and would be required to continue to make extraordinary expenditures to maintain a large ground, sea, and air presence in the region. In 1945 alone, the United States spent almost $1 trillion on defense, a vast sum compared to the size of the U.S. economy, which only generated $223 billion in gross domestic product (GDP) in that last year of the war effort. The chart in Figure 7.1 shows military spending as a percentage of GDP.

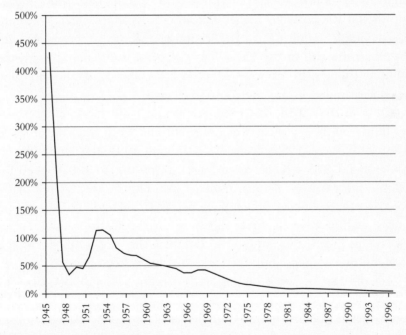

Figure 7.1 U.S. Military Spending as a Percent of GDP (1945–1996)
SOURCE: BEA, DOD/Center for Defense Information.

Figure 7.1 illustrates the fact that for nearly three decades following WWII, military expenditures as a portion of GDP were extremely high and were arguably the single most important portion of the economy. Margaret Myers estimates that the direct expenses of the war were estimated by Treasury Secretary Henry Morgenthau at $325 billion in mid-1945, but added that "the cost of the war to all the countries involved is simply incalculable."[2] The same could be said for all wars.

Later estimates of the overall cost of the war would be much higher, especially when compared to the cost of WWI and including the cost of debt forgiveness for the allies. The cost also included the reintegration of 12 million people into the American civilian economy via such measures as the GI Bill of Rights, which was passed by Congress in June 1944. While the war mobilization had absorbed a large part of the slack in the predominantly male U.S. work force, and even drew in millions of women into the workforce as well, this was not the same as gainful employment in the private sector. The GI Bill provided cash for returning service personnel, unemployment insurance for up to a year, and loans for housing or to purchase a farm or a business. Most important, the GI Bill provided higher education to veterans, many of whom missed completing their formal education in order to go to war. As with Lincoln at the end of the Civil War, Congress was generous with the returning soldiers. In many ways the GI Bill helped to define and fulfill the American dream for generations of citizens.

Only in the 1970s, as the economy grew, did U.S. military outlays drop well below 40 percent of GDP and from then on dropped to single digits by 1980. From 1948 through 1991, the United States would spend $13 trillion on defense, according to the Center for Defense Information. Annual military spending by the United States would average almost $300 billion per year during this period and is only slightly lower if direct spending for the Korean and Vietnam Wars is excluded, illustrating the fact that the vast majority of the expenditure was focused on the Cold War with the Soviets.

Yet the fact of rising output and inflation, accommodated by the Federal Reserve and driven by the demographic surge of the Baby Boom, made military outlays and the level of federal debt shrink in comparison to the overall economy. From a high of 120 percent of GDP at the end of WWII, the federal debt remained stable in nominal terms and fell as a portion of the economy through the 1960s and 1970s, but began to grow again in the 1980s as economic growth slowed.

The other observation to be made about the period of the Cold War is that it illustrates the inflation experienced by Americans since that time—a loss of purchasing power that tracks almost precisely the expansion of public and private sector debt. Using the constant dollar series from the Bureau of Economic Analysis, if one compares the nominal GDP in the United States in 1945 of $223 billion in inflation-adjusted current dollars, that amount of national economic output would total *$2 trillion* measured in today's money. That represents a 90 percent loss in the purchasing power of the dollar today versus the real, inflation-adjusted value of the dollar at the end of WWII. Figure 7.2 shows nominal GDP, total federal debt, and military expenditures over the Cold War period.

Figure 7.2 illustrates several interesting trends during the Cold War period. First, from the end of WWII until almost 1970, federal debt outstanding was relatively stable. This period spans the presidencies of Harry Truman through John F. Kennedy and includes the relative increases in spending during the Korean and Vietnam wars. During the same period, the U.S. economy was relatively free of financial crises until the early 1970s, when the United States finally left the

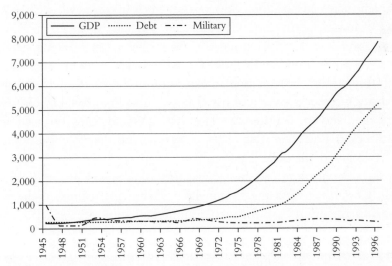

Figure 7.2   GDP, Federal Debt, and Military Spending (Billions of $)
Sources: BEA, DOD, U.S. Treasury.

pegged currency system of Bretton Woods and stopped redeeming dollars for gold upon demand by foreign central banks. The U.S.
government essentially paid its way for two decades after WWII, then
unilaterally defaulted on an agreement with other nations. Unlike
the United Kingdom after WWI, however, the United States did not
increase taxes in order to pay down the war debt. As in earlier conflicts, the Congress was not willing to pass on the cost of the war to
the taxpayer. Instead the Congress funded the wartime outlays with
borrowing and simply rolled the debt over for decades thereafter.

Another striking aspect of the chart in Figure 7.2 is the divergence
of GDP and debt from military spending after the end of the 1960s,
when Washington began to greatly expand non-defense outlays in a
variety of different areas of social spending. Military spending was a
very significant part of the U.S. economic expansion during the first
two decades after WWII, but gradually, as the threat of imminent
major conflict receded, domestic priorities and related spending and
borrowing grew. Again, the taxpayer was not asked to shoulder the
full burden of these outlays and, again, the spending was financed with
public debt.

With the Civil War, WWI and WWII, and the Cold War, Americans
used debt to finance military expenditures rather than carry the burden
through increased taxation. This was not such a great evil after WWII
since in absolute terms the level of military spending remained stable even
as the overall economy expanded. The problem came several decades
later, when non-military discretionary expenditures were likewise funded
with federal debt, necessitating an expansion of the currency by the Fed.
In that sense, not a great deal has changed since President Lincoln saved
the Union and emancipated the slaves with a Grand Army financed with
greenback dollars. The scale of the enterprise and the rate of erosion of
the real value of the dollar has simply increased.

In recognition of the decline in purchasing power of the dollar, in
1946 Congress passed the Employment Act, which directed the federal government to "promote maximum employment, production, and
purchasing power." Taxes were cut to stimulate the economy after the
war concluded, so that the United States did not experience a severe
downturn in economic activity, as was the case following WWI. This
act marked one of the early instances of Congress mandating full

employment as a matter of government policy and giving responsibility for this goal to Washington. Like the promises made by Washington of financial regulation or consumer protection, the promise of full employment is worth no more than Washington's paper money, but none-the-less helps define the American dream.

As with much of the government effort and expenditure in the 1930s, the ostensible goal of Washington was to use a postwar surge in economic prosperity as an antidote to the return of national socialism or anything like it. Consumer prices rose slowly in the late 1940s as wartime shortages were satisfied, but soon abated. Economic busts could be avoided, it was believed, through the use of "compensatory finance" to counter cyclical downturns. With unemployment still stubbornly high even during the war, the political focus on job creation was understandable even from a domestic perspective, but the priority of avoiding a repeat of the downturn after WWI and the needs of the Cold War gave these efforts even more urgency. G.J. Santoni of the staff of the Federal Reserve Bank of St. Louis noted regarding the Employment Act: "The new theory promised the success of centrally directed economic stabilization policy and provided the nucleus around which the proposed legislation was built."[3]

Santoni discovered in his research that when Congress voted on the Employment Act, it had no statistics on employment or the labor market for the period prior to 1942. He also documents that while the original legislation stated that Americans were *entitled to* employment, the final law said it was the policy of the United States to *promote* employment. The economy did promptly recover, independent of the actions of Washington. Unemployment dropped from the double digits seen after WWII back to the 4 to 4.5 percent joblessness that had prevailed in the three decades before the Great Crash of 1929. This return of prosperity and single-digit unemployment prevailed until the early 1970s, when jobs again became a hot political issue.

Federal Revenues Grow

Despite the imposition of the income tax under FDR, tariffs and corporate taxes still generated the majority of U.S. government revenues until 1943, when personal income and other taxes surpassed these two traditional sources of revenue for the federal government. The U.S. government never asked the taxpayer to pay the cost fully of WWII, the Korean War, or the Vietnam War, but there was little immediate need to do so. The strong post-WWII economic recovery that occurred following the war and especially after 1949 increased federal revenues even with a reduction in the tax base. The Revenue Act of 1945 took millions off the tax rolls by increasing the exemption to $500. In 1948, Congress passed further tax reductions over President Truman's veto. The chart in Figure 7.3 shows the current expenditure and receipts from the federal government during the Cold War period, along with the current balance and total federal debt outstanding.

An important point to take away from these three figures is that the United States never made any attempt to reduce or even extinguish the federal debt accumulated during the WWII years in the subsequent decades of rapid economic expansion in the 1950s and 1960s, when federal outlays were still relatively small compared to the size of the U.S. economy. These were also the years when the U.S. external account was in surplus and exports exceeded imports in most years.

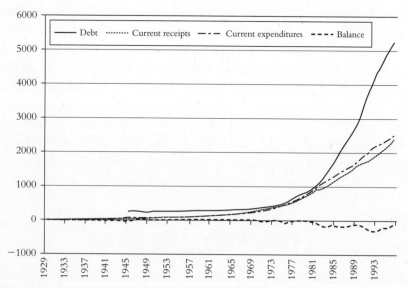

Figure 7.3 Federal Receipts, Outlays, and Total Debt: 1929–1996 (Billions of $)
SOURCE: Office of Management and Budget.

The primary reason for this accumulation and maintenance of federal debt was the Cold War mobilization and the need to maintain a relatively high level of military spending. There was also the traditional argument that a great nation needed to have some debt in order to function in the global financial and commercial markets.

With the domestic political emphasis on employment and the continuous crisis atmosphere surrounding the strategic standoff with Moscow in the international sphere, debt reduction was not at the top of the Washington political agenda during the Cold War. The fear of communism provided a very convenient rationale for many policy decisions in Washington and justified continued military spending at high enough levels to buoy the economy. In the end there was no war with the Soviets but hundreds of billions of dollars were spent on weapons systems that were never used. The end of the largest period of expenditures on the military saw a slowdown in the U.S. economy and a rapid increase in the outflow of gold from the U.S. Treasury.

Author Richard Whalen commented that "the Cold War was in large measure a fiction" that was convenient for the political leaders on both sides:

> The Russians wanted to bring Poland back under their control and have an Eastern European buffer between them and Atlantic Europe, which they had always had. They wanted a big enough piece of Germany so that Germany would not be troublesome for another couple of generations. America was fortunate. We were victors. We did not have to fight a war here at home. We were safe behind our ocean moats. If anything, after the internationalist fever passed, the Cold War confirmed the wisdom of the people that all of that business in Europe has nothing to do with us. This country is inherently isolationist, protectionist and non-interventionist, despite globalist rhetoric and pretensions. Many generations ago, we gave up on the old countries of Europe and left to find a new home. Our future agenda should center on the American economy and generating growth here.[4]

Recalling the earlier political reluctance of state governments during the nineteenth century to impose property taxes and other levies to finance their operations, the unwillingness of Congress to impose the

burden of debt repayment on taxpayers after the war is not that surprising. In the early 1960s, for example, political and opinion leaders
wanted to hear about jobs and increased exports, not higher taxes. In
fact, as the economy accelerated in the late 1950s and early 1960s, policy makers worried that the growing revenues of the federal government would hurt economic growth. This made life more than a little
difficult for a young President John Kennedy, who wanted to increase
spending and expand the scope of government for the same reasons as
FDR—creating a political base and a political legacy. The Democratic
Congress was way ahead of Kennedy in this regard, however, cutting
taxes and increasing federal spending without any encouragement from
the White House.

But even in those days, many observers knew that a large portion of the prosperity of the post-WWII period was built upon federal spending and debt. Two years after President Kennedy defined the
future with his "New Frontier" speech in 1960, the *Richmond Times
Dispatch* ridiculed the young leader. "Yale would have done well to
have created a special degree for J.F.K.—Doctor of Mythology—not
the old, but the New Frontier mythology, based on the illusion that a
nation can spend its way to prosperity." But the *San Francisco Chronicle*
reported that Kennedy put the priorities in plain terms:

> What is important to discuss are the matters of full employment,
> how to generate buying power which can consume what we
> produce, how to build up U.S. exports and staunch the outflow
> of gold, how to provide adequate profits and wages. These,
> Mr. Kennedy said, are the economic problems that political
> parties should be talking about . . .[5]

The partisan ire directed at Kennedy for the relatively modest deficits of the 1960s seems almost ridiculous today, but JFK was elected
just a decade after the U.S. economy really began to recover from the
Great Depression and WWII. Some Americans who had endured
the worst part of the Depression felt that the government should do
more, while affluent Americans looked upon the FDR years as a betrayal
of core values and an act of theft. The reality was that both feelings
were genuine and sincere, but the politics of the 1960s leaned in favor

of more spending and inflation. If you take 1930 as the start of the economic slide, the United States was in an economic contraction, at least in terms of private sector activity, until almost 1948, or some 20 years.

Only with the death of FDR and the assumption of the Presidency by Harry Truman would investors begin to feel comfortable increasing private investment. At the time the political constituency for direct government action still was strong and reinforced by a largely Democratic Congress. Conservatives had begun to win back seats in the Congress in the late 1930s, but the business community was not ready voluntarily to come back to the political bargaining table until it was certain that FDR-style big government was dead and buried.

Robert Higgs, editor of The *Independent Review*, analyzes the post-war boom in his essay, "Regime Uncertainty: Why the Great Depression Lasted So Long and Why Prosperity Resumed after the War." Higgs writes that the information we have about economic output and inflation during WWII is largely useless because of government price controls and rationing under the New Deal and wartime measures such as the Work Projects Administration (WPA), the largest New Deal agency.[6] He reviews the literature from researchers who documented the failure of the New Deal to attract sufficient investment to achieve a sustained private recovery.

Higgs also finds that the negative impact of FDR's New Deal on the American economy delayed the start of the recovery in the U.S. economy to almost 1950 and the Korean War mobilization: "In 1945 the death of Roosevelt and the succession of Harry S Truman and his administration completed the shift from a political regime investors perceived as full of uncertainty to one in which they felt much more confident about the security of their private property rights . . . Only in 1946 and the following years did private investment reach and remain at levels consistent with a prosperous and growing economy," he concludes.[7]

WWII was called truly "the New Dealers War." During the conflict, Washington ran the private economy with a heavy hand. Rationing and shortages were the shared experience of a generation of Americans. Wartime profits were high for businesses and their executives. "Excess profits" were taxed at punitive rates. In California, a new movie star named Ronald Reagan found that the government took 92 percent of his pay.

The Fed Regains Independence

Part of the reason for the reluctance of private investors to invest during the Depression was the government's aggressive manipulation of interest rates through the 1940s. "In April 1942, after the entry of the United States into World War II, the Fed publicly committed itself to maintaining an interest rate of 3/8 percent on Treasury bills," wrote Bob Hetzel and Ralph Leach of the Federal Reserve Bank of Richmond in a 2001 research paper. "In practice, it also established an upper limit to the term structure of interest rates on government debt. The ceiling for long-term government bonds was two and a half percent. In summer 1947, the Fed raised the peg on the Treasury bill rate. However, the Treasury adamantly insisted that the Fed continue to place a floor under the price of government debt by placing a ceiling on its yield."[8]

The Fed chafed under the interest rate regime imposed during the war. When the economy bottomed in 1949 and began a strong rebound, the Federal Open Market Committee under the leadership of New York Federal Reserve Bank President Allan Sproul began to discuss increasing interest rates. Fearing a surge in inflation after years of wartime price controls, discussions began in the middle of 1950 about raising rates. By August, Sproul was openly challenging Treasury Secretary John Snyder over the interest rate issue. Eventually the FOMC allowed rates to rise.

By the end of 1950, the Chinese had entered the Korean War and there was an open confrontation between the Fed and the Truman Administration. The President imposed wage and price controls on non-agricultural sectors of the economy and demanded that the Fed maintain a cap on interest rates for the duration of the conflict to prevent holders of war bonds from seeing their securities trade below par. But Fed Chairman Thomas McCabe, who had replaced Marriner Eccles in 1948 when Truman declined to reappoint Eccles as Fed chairman, refused and thereby won back the independence of the central bank.[9]

The heroic faceoff between Eccles and McCabe against the populist political bullying from Treasury Secretary Snyder and Harry Truman was one of the great standup moments of the American central bank as an independent agency. Eccles in particular bore the full brunt of Truman's populist anger, but refused to resign as a Fed governor.

Though not reappointed as chairman, Eccles remained on the board and fought for the Fed's independence during the remainder of his term as governor until he resigned in 1951. McCabe was pressured repeatedly by President Truman and Snyder to continue supporting artificially low interest rates, publicly and privately. Yet he, Eccles, Sproul, and the other members of the FOMC stood their ground and defended their responsibility for controlling inflation, which was a plausible threat from 1946 to 1950.

With the famous Accord of 1951 between the central bank and the Executive Branch, the Fed and Treasury agreed on a set of rules with respect to their respective operations. The Fed agreed to seek to maintain the Treasury's ability to issue debt while limiting the degree of monetization of federal obligations. McCabe was eventually forced out of the Fed in March of 1951 by President Truman, who nominated Assistant Secretary of the Treasury William McChesney Martin as chairman. Martin had led the negotiations with the Fed for the Treasury when Snyder became ill and Truman assumed that he would take a more cooperative stance than Eccles or McCabe. Robert Hertzel recalls that Truman believed Martin would capture the Fed once McCabe and Eccles were out, but Martin turned out to be a supporter of Fed independence and a strong dollar. Chairman Martin put the case for low inflation in his acceptance speech:

> Unless inflation is controlled, it could prove to be an even more serious threat to the vitality of our country than the more spectacular aggressions of enemies outside our borders. I pledge myself to support all reasonable measures to preserve the purchasing power of the dollar.[10]

Compared to the capitulation by Chairman Bernanke and the FOMC in the 2008–2009 market collapse, when the central bank subordinated itself to the Treasury in order to bail out private banks, the U.S. Treasury, and entire markets, the posture of the Fed in 1950 was heroic and remarkable. Mariner Eccles, Tom McCabe, and Allan Sproul were unsung champions to American consumers in the story of money and debt. And in a telling lesson for today's policymakers, only when the Fed regained control of monetary policy in 1951 were market rates truly reflective of investor sentiment instead of the wartime fiscal priorities of the Treasury. More than pleasing the vanities of economists, an independent central bank that protects the value of money is the ultimate consumer protection agency.

The Post-War Economy Soars

In the early 1950s, when unemployment was still in double digits, only ardent conservatives spoke about budget deficits or debt. But as employment and output did eventually grow with the end of wartime controls, the Keynesian crowd in the economics world looked with satisfaction as GDP grew faster than the federal debt. Their thesis, that government spending would generate consumer demand and thereby increase private investment, was still wrong, but the short-run improvement of the economy was embraced as validation of the master's vision.

Growth accelerated in the 1950s and 1960s, conveniently reducing the ratio between debt and GDP. This served to confirm the Keynesian view of the growth that could be obtained via deficit spending—even if it were only nominal growth. Even in those uncertain days, there was plenty of comment about federal deficits, but soon the policy focus would swing back to inflation. The Fed under Chairman Martin consistently maintained support for price stability. This task was made easier by the election of President Dwight Eisenhower in 1952 and the fact that inflation moderated during his two terms in office. As Hertzel concluded: "Under Chairman Martin, the Fed's overriding goals became price stability and macroeconomic stability."[11]

There were also new calls for greater federal involvement in areas such as housing. In 1950, for example, the Truman Administration explicitly focused on housing as a key area of private investment, but with federal guarantees for the debt used to finance home purchases. The widespread use of government loans and guarantees to fight the Depression and WWII opened the door for a more aggressive role for government generally. And in the early 1950s housing slowly started the booming ascent whereby it soon would supplant the defense sector as the focus of government activity. The GI Bill offered low-cost loans to ex-servicemen. Newly formed families pushed into the exploding suburbs springing up from corn and potato fields around major U.S. cities, fulfilling the

American dream of home ownership. More than a return to normalcy, the victors of WWII set about to making up for lost time and then some.

The Legacy of War

The great unspoken secret in American life is the refusal to maintain anything like fiscal balance in the national government. The refusal of successive governments in Washington to ask taxpayers to truly pay their way is a key thread in the modern part of the story of the American dream. As with the gold rush and the silverites, modern-day Americans want and feel entitled to a certain living standard, but in the twentieth century we have shown a growing unwillingness to pay for it. The relatively new, post-WWI tendency to bail out European allies from their war debts and to use subsidies to boost U.S. employment and exports encouraged even more liberal uses of debt for all purposes in the years beginning in the 1950s and after.

Half a century on, the end result of America's fiscal lack of discipline is growing government debt and an underlying level of inflation far higher than official statistics suggest. The steady erosion in the real value of the dollar has eaten away at the purchasing power of American consumers and reduced real long-term growth and employment opportunities. The tendency to fabricate the appearance of growth via debt and inflationary fiscal policies began with the U.S. aid program for Europe after WWII and became institutionalized in the decades that followed. The power of demographics, innovation, and technology propelled America's growth naturally for several decades. The Cold War and the growing tolerance for public deficits starting in the 1970s accelerated the nominal growth. The overarching logic of the Cold War justified any expenditure or policy prescription that fulfilled the main objectives of containing the military advance of Soviet communism and promoting the economic stability of the Western nations. But soon that extraordinary rationalization would be applied to any and all domestic priorities as well as mere desires became priorities.

Henry Hazlitt mused in a 1947 article that making heavy loans or outright gifts to unstable European nations was not the best way to fight world communism. Entitled "Will Dollars Save the World?"

it argued that "if the overriding emergency seems to demand it, let our government give food, not money to Europe. Demand no government reforms in exchange for it; but stamp an American flag, literally or figuratively, on every package." Hazlitt made the case that the U.S. policy of flooding the world with dollars, via loans, grants and other measures, would not generate wealth in the United States or the recipient nations.[12] That is precisely the policy that Washington followed, however, on again and off again, since 1867; to use the expansion of the paper money supply to drive *nominal* economic growth, even if it meant a reduction in the real value of the currency. In a similar vein, Milton Friedman and Anna Schwartz calculated the growth in the U.S. money supply over the period of their classic study of American money, 1867 to 1960:

The public held 50 times as many dollars of currency at the end of the 93 years spanned by our figures as at the beginning; 243 times as many dollars of commercial bank deposits; and 127 times as many dollars of mutual savings deposits. The total we designate as money multiplied 157-fold in the course of these nine decades, or at the rate of 5.4 per cent. Since the population of the United States nearly quintupled over the same period, the stock of money per capita multiplied some 32 fold, or at the annual rate of 3.7 per cent.[13]

And yet this brisk expansion of the supply of money, described by the two great monetary economists of the twentieth century, stretching over the period from the Civil War to the election of John Kennedy in 1960, was only the start of the great American infatuation with inflation and debt. A large part of that inflation was driven by the expansion of the U.S. government in all aspects, a growth that is best measured by the portion of the annual output of the United States attributable to the public sector. Before 1933, the share of gross domestic product represented by government at all levels of the United States was about 10 percent. Today the national average of the share of GDP accounted for by government, including the Federal Reserve System and the housing agencies such as Fannie Mae, Freddie Mac and the Federal Home Loan Banks is closer to half and rising.

The expansion of the federal government during the Depression and WWII and afterward is understandable given the fact that the U.S. economy was still extremely soft at the end of the war. As stated by Higgs, the period of regulation and attacks on business during FDR's presidency drove private capital into hiding for two decades. Private debt financing essentially collapsed after the 1929 Crash and FDR's 1933 dollar devaluation. In 1929, private debt outstanding in the United States equaled nearly twice the level of GDP, but by the end of WWII the level of private debt capital was just 50 percent of domestic output, a grim illustration of the staggering deflation and de-leveraging that occurred during that 15-year period. The United States won WWII militarily, but the American system of individual capitalism was a casualty, replaced by the corporation and the government-sponsored entity.

While the level of private debt in 1929 was peaking, an outlier that was closely related to the issuance of speculative debt during the 1920s, the post-WWII level of debt was still well below the average for this indicator between the two world wars. In fact it would not be until the late 1990s, or half a century later, when U.S. economic growth levels had begun to slow and financial speculation again grew to significant levels, that the amount of private debt to GDP would again reach 200 percent and then go even higher.[14]

The decline in the rate of private investment during the New Deal and the fact that private debt in the United States did not reach the levels of the Roaring Twenties until 1996 has implications for how to interpret the subsequent decades. Benjamin Friedman found that there were three major trends in the U.S. financial markets in the postwar period: an increase in private borrowing, the rise of the use of financial intermediaries, and the increased reliance upon government guarantees, regulation, and financial intermediation by government agencies.[15] The sustained rise in private debt financing observed following the end of WWII was made more dramatic by the sharp decline in the previous 20 years. Likewise the introduction of government support for housing and other types of domestic infrastructure projects, such as roads, bridges and other improvements, slowly changed the nature of the U.S. economy and made possible the real estate boom of the 1990s and 2000s. We shall discuss both in the next chapter.

By the 1970s, when growth slowed and unemployment began to rise, total federal debt and GDP began to climb even more rapidly. The United States began to run larger and larger deficits each year due to growing domestic spending. By the early 1980s total federal debt began to grow far more rapidly than either spending or federal revenues, boosted by accrued interest and, most importantly, the accumulation of surpluses in the Social Security and other federal trust funds. By 1996, the Social Security Trust fund alone reached $514 billion in assets, all invested in non-marketable U.S. Treasury bonds. The figure grew from there to almost $2.5 trillion at the end of 2000 as these future obligations of the U.S. government to retirees accumulated, but were only part of a larger body of IOUs from the taxpayer to various constituencies. How America reached the early twenty-first century and saw the road open to national insolvency and hyperinflation is closely bound up with the changing reasons behind America's devotion to free trade following the two world wars.

Cold War, Free Trade

In the years immediately following WWII, and especially with the start of the Korean War in 1950, many political leaders in the NATO countries believed that a war with the Soviet Union and its growing group of allied nations was inevitable. The classic example of the public's perception of the imminent threat of war during these years was the 1964 election between Democrat Lyndon Johnson and the Republican from Arizona, Barry Goldwater, who ran with former New York congressman William E. Miller. Democrats sponsored the infamous "Daisy Girl" television ads, which showed a little girl plucking the petals of a flower followed by an ominous countdown to a nuclear explosion. This ad demonized Goldwater as a nuclear war monger. Although the ad was aired only once, it showed the deadly immaturity of Democratic image-makers exploiting the "balance of terror" that threatened world peace.

The Republican candidate made the mistake of suggesting the use of tactical nuclear weapons in Vietnam. The Johnson campaign pounced on the opportunity. But long before that, Americans came to know and understand that their lives were at risk because of the background threat of nuclear war. The buildup of United States and Soviet military forces and strategic systems capable of delivering nuclear warheads was front-page news in the United States and around the world for decades. Events such as the Korean War in the 1950s and the Cuban missile crisis in 1962 brought the reality of war home to the entire world. In American politics, the means of response to the "Soviet threat" was a key point of debate for decades.

For the author, the menacing image of the Soviet Union was a very personal one. When the Whalen family moved from New York to Washington in 1966, my father Richard Whalen was working as a speech writer for presidential candidate Richard Nixon. He had previously worked as a writer for *Fortune* magazine and during that time had written a cover story entitled "The Shifting Equation of Nuclear Defense."[16] This was the first public disclosure of the American multiple-warhead technology for U.S. ballistic missiles. The development gave the Soviets an insolubly complex first-strike problem that was beyond their ability to solve, a move observers thought strengthened "deterrence."

A framed copy of the cover of the magazine hung in his office and depicted an imaginary scenario of incoming nuclear warheads being intercepted by American anti-missile defenses. The Nike Hercules missiles deployed by the U.S. military at that time were designed to shoot down 1950s era strategic bombers and really could not knock down a nuclear warhead re-entering the earth's atmosphere from space.

While the wartime scenario may have been fictional, the reality of the perception of the nearness of nuclear war was not. The Cold War colored the thinking of generations of Americans and especially in Washington. The domestic political contest between the Democrats and Republicans turned on how the Cold War was or was not being won. JFK gained the upper hand in his campaign against Richard Nixon by alleging that a "missile gap" between the United States and the Soviets had developed under Eisenhower. The widely shared view of the likelihood of global conflict was captured in phases such as "mutually assured destruction" and influenced many areas of American policy, including the international role of the dollar and the growth of U.S. trade with nations outside the Soviet bloc. American leaders in politics, business, and the defense community believed that increasing the flow of goods between the United States and the other nations of the free world was an effective bulwark against communism. They believed that free trade was more effective than merely lending nations money—but the United States did plenty of lending as well, directly and indirectly through the IMF and the World Bank. The United States "dollarized" the world to defend it.

The American aid effort after WWII began with a primary focus on the Marshall Plan and helping to rebuild Europe. The effort soon became more global and was focused on expanding trade between the United States and other nations as a means not only to help the U.S. economy but also to fight against the hegemony of the Soviet Union. In simple terms, the United States dropped most of its protectionist import barriers while allowing Germany, Korea and Japan to protect their markets. These nations used very similar trade barriers to those the United States had employed prior to 1945. The United States embraced free trade, at least to a degree, but encouraged its former enemies to rebuild their economies behind a protective wall of tariff and non-tariff barriers and quotas.

The Bretton Woods Agreement of 1944 and the multilateral trade framework created under the auspices of the United States essentially allowed the participating nations to peg their currencies to the dollar and direct their attention and resources to domestic economic recovery. By basing the post-war world on the dollar *and* gold, the Allies sought to avoid competitive currency devaluations between nations and thereby sidestep the sharp swings in growth and reserve balances that had characterized the pre-WWII period.

The Bretton Woods scheme and the related proposal to form an international trade body was entirely statist in conception and utopian in its objectives. It envisioned macroeconomic central planning and management on a global scale, but without an authoritarian political structure to enforce it. Bretton Woods explicitly sought to moderate and control the free flow of capital around the world. In the statist and socialist mindset that governed thinking in many world capitals in 1945, it was the free movement of capital around the world that destabilized national economies and set in motion the competitive devaluation of national currencies.

This decidedly authoritarian evolution of thinking among the post WWII powers is hardly a surprise given the strong political and intellectual current toward central planning and fascist models of political economy that was seen in Europe, the United States, and around the world during this period. To one degree or another, the mobilization for war made the United States and allied nations become like the enemy and more in terms of military might, but there was a political cost along with the financial burden. It is surprising that members of the U.S. political community of all stripes were so willing to discard traditional American values regarding individual liberties and the rule of law to embrace the socialist economic theology that was at the heart of Bretton Woods.

It seems to be in the nature of all people to be fatally attracted to "new ideas," in much the same way that "new era" thinking described by Ben Graham and David Dodd spread through the world of investing at the start of the twentieth century. The kindest interpretation that can be made of the abandonment of core principles regarding money and debt in the United States at the end of WWII is that the horrors of the Great Depression and the two world wars were so great that any expedient was seen as valid. The manifest failure of the *laissez faire* system of Robber Baron capitalism that had prevailed in the United States prior to 1913 seemed to offer no alternative to a larger role for government.

Yet after WWII, the governing elites in U.S. business and political spheres seemingly signed on for a very comfortable codependency, first in defense and later in housing and other areas. This cooperative relationship had its roots in the mobilization effort for the great wars and also perhaps the fear that once the war effort was done, the global economy might slip back into the malaise of the 1930s. Combined with the priority of commerce that underlies the American dream, the union of the two primary political parties with the corporate relations community produced a uniquely American form of statism that endures to this day.

Once business and government became fully aware of the risks and the possibilities for profit created by statism in such formulations as price controls and government allocation schemes, an alliance of convenience was created that was far more extensive than the particular influence of a J.P. Morgan or Standard Oil in the pre-WWI era. The template for this government–private sector cooperation was the defense sector, which Dwight Eisenhower called the "defense military industrial complex" as he left office in January 1961. He warned:

> Until the latest of our world conflicts, the United States had no armaments industry. American makers of plowshares could, with time and as required, make swords as well. But now we can no longer risk emergency improvisation of national defense; we have been compelled to create a permanent armaments industry of vast proportions. Added to this, three and a half million men and women are directly engaged in the defense establishment. We annually spend on military security more than the net income of all United States corporations. This conjunction of an immense military establishment and a large arms industry is new in the American experience. The total influence— economic, political, even spiritual—is felt in every city, every state house, every office of the federal government. We recognize the imperative need for this development. Yet we must not fail to comprehend its grave implications. Our toil, resources and livelihood are all involved; so is the very structure of our society. In the councils of government, we must guard against the acquisition of unwarranted influence, whether sought or unsought, by the military industrial complex. The potential for the disastrous rise of misplaced power exists and will persist. We must never let the weight of this combination endanger our liberties or democratic processes. We should take nothing for granted. Only an alert and knowledgeable citizenry can compel the proper meshing of the huge industrial and military machinery of defense with our peaceful methods and goals, so that security and liberty may prosper together.

Eisenhower's warning was prescient and not limited to the defense sector. Not only had the defense industry become intertwined with the federal government during WWII, but what Eisenhower called the "military industrial complex" was entirely subsumed inside the government. The late William C. Green, formerly of CalState San Bernadino, commented years ago when we both worked at the Heritage Foundation in Washington, DC that during the Cold War the U.S. defense sector became the least competitive part of the U.S. economy, while the Soviet defense sector was the most competitive part of that nation's economy. But to the point of our story of money and debt, the wartime mobilization in WWI and in the 1940s for WWII institutionalized the existence of corporatist structures not only in the defense sector, but also for managing and directing the non-defense sectors of the economy. These structures would become part of a framework for "deficit government," as Iwan Morgan describes it, which in concert with the Treasury made use of the federal budget to manage the economy.[17]

With powerful motives such as fighting communism and preventing economic depression, the rationale of total mobilization for war was gradually expanded to include all areas of government policy and public endeavor. And with the equally powerful enabling theology of Keynesian economics to justify what we today label "counter-cyclical" fiscal policy, the way was made in an intellectual sense for many of the attempts by government to manage employment, currency movements, and even commodity prices during the second half of the twentieth century. Most of these attempts failed miserably, but the fact remains that the policy mindset of government intervention, of management from above, became an acceptable viewpoint—even if it was entirely erroneous. As Thomas Paine observed: "A long habit of not thinking a thing wrong gives it a superficial appearance of being right."

During and after WWII, the notion of managing government from the national or macro level, a "God's Eye View" in classical terms, was received as wisdom and gospel, an embedded part of the narrative of American government. Members of both major political parties in the United States became convinced that deficit spending would employ unused resources correct market failures, and produce optimal economic results. This narrative, this deliberate act of collective delusion, has governed the direction of the U.S. economy ever since. The author Nassim Taleb talks about the importance of narrative in how human beings come to believe that they understand a complex issue:

The narrative fallacy addresses our limited ability to look at sequences of facts without weaving an explanation into them, or, equivalently, forcing a logical link, *an arrow of relationship*, upon them. Explanations bind facts together. They make them all the more easily remembered; they help them *make more sense.* Where this propensity can go wrong is where it increases our *impression* of understanding.[18]

Generations of American politicians became aware of the possibility of spending more money on more different things and thereby building a direct, commercial relationship with the voters as well as with foreign countries. The flow of dollar subsidies from Washington became a flow of political influence that touched every American and the citizens of many of the other nations of the world. Since the fiat paper dollar was the center of the post-WWII financial world, America's ultimate victory in the Cold War was assured. But as with the Civil War, the cost of victory has been extremely high.

The Dollar's Golden Age

The 1950s and 1960s are considered the golden age of modern American culture, albeit one that existed in a highly controlled economy. Today the idea of using price controls or a currency peg to manage an economy may be considered laughable, effectively creating a target of opportunity for George Soros and other global speculators—the modern day heirs of Jay Gould—to attack. But in the restricted financial markets of the 1950s and 1960s, when much of the global economy was still recovering from decades of depression and war, the system of pegging other currencies to the dollar appeared to work, at least initially. A trade expansion initiative under the General Agreement on Tariffs and Trade (GATT) was meant to be the companion to this managed currency arrangement, ultimately culminating in the creation of the International Trade Organization (ITO).

The utopian vision of one world guided by a collective, cooperative political union of nations, managed by a new class of international bureaucrats, was very much in vogue in the period immediately after WWII. But the United States would ultimately refuse to go along with the concept for the ITO. The World Trade Organization, as it came to be known, would not be approved until the end of the Cold War in January 1995, but this did not prevent the United States from pushing for greatly reduced trade restrictions during the 50-year interregnum—albeit for reasons seen through the prism of the East-West conflict with the Soviet Union and China. This change in focus from the internationalist vision of the United States coming out of the 1930s to the Cold War focus of the United States following WWII is a very important turning point in the road for the United States and the global economy.

In the 1930s, mainstream thinking within the Democratic Party had come to the conclusion that trade barriers and shifts in the flow of capital—that is, gold—were a major cause of both world wars. Even before the WWII ended, the Roosevelt Administration drafted a document authorizing the ITO and enabling legislation from Congress for broad powers to reduce tariffs at the discretion of the Executive Branch. The support for trade liberalization was consistent with the traditional Democratic opposition to tariffs, which Progressives saw merely as a means of enhancing the monopoly profits of big business for the benefit of the rich.

Republicans, on the other hand, were the traditional protectionists and built the government's limited finances on tariff revenue. But the most important domestic factor behind the broad and largely bipartisan support for trade liberalization was the fact that while much of the world lay in ruins, U.S. industrial capacity had grown to first in the world. The "hegemonic trade and payments position," to quote Robert Baldwin, of the United States in the world economy required a policy of openness since American industry was the exporter to the world and American banks the lenders.[19]

From the early 1930s through the Tokyo Round of the GATT in 1974–1979, the United States oversaw a process of trade opening that, in theory at least, reduced tariffs around the globe by almost 80 percent compared to pre-WWII levels. This trade opening largely benefitted the U.S. economy, which generated an abnormally large share of manufactured exports and services for decades after the war. Most of the other nations of the world did not liberalize their trade very much, leading some researchers to argue that the economic recovery following WWII was not primarily a function of U.S. trade opening. In Japan and Germany, for example, the size of imports relative to these rapidly growing economies actually fell during the Cold War period. This suggested to some observers that "freer" trade rather than free trade was the more accurate description of the goal of U.S. policy from 1950–1996.[20]

As the Cold War progressed and the cost of the military confrontation with the Soviets and related assistance to allied nations grew, the

United States showed a growing disinclination to continue the policy of pursuing free trade with all nations. Whereas global trade liberalization and the expansion of world trade were regarded as synonymous by U.S. policy makers at the end of the conflict, by the 1950s the focus had been narrowed to rebuilding Europe as a bulwark against Soviet expansion. The need for rearmament to meet the predatory Soviet threat and fight the expansion of communism in Asia during the Korean War conflicted with the original "internationalist" vision of Bretton Woods.

By the time Eisenhower was elected President in 1952, the commitment of U.S. leaders and the public at large to the liberal vision of free trade was increasingly in doubt. Congress had already begun to erect barriers to imports from our NATO allies. The infamous "cheese amendment" to the Defense Production Act of 1951 placed import quotas on foreign dairy products from all nations. But in addition to manifestations of these types of pre-1930s protectionism, the United States also saw legislation to limit trade with the Soviet Union and China, as well as their satellite nations. The fact that commodity prices suffered a series of sharp declines during this period did nothing to quiet the desire among American politicians to lash out at nations unfriendly to the United States. All trade concessions were withdrawn from Soviet bloc nations, including Czechoslovakia, which was a member of GATT, ironically enough. The shift away from the previous American policy of tariff reduction in the early 1950s did a great deal to undermine America's position at the trade bargaining table.[21]

The shift from a global commitment to free trade to a targeted strategy to beggar the communist nations marked a change in strategy that was not easy for the United States to sell around the world. Not only did the United States attempt to embargo trade with the Soviet bloc, but it also threatened to impose sanctions on nations that did not agree to follow the embargo on the Soviets with respect to strategic materials. Sanctions were most harshly imposed on the Soviets and "front line" communist states such as Fidel Castro's Cuba, while Eastern European nations such as Poland and Czechoslovakia were treated with more flexibility.

The period of the 1970s marked a transition point for the United States as it moved from being a net lender to the world to being a net

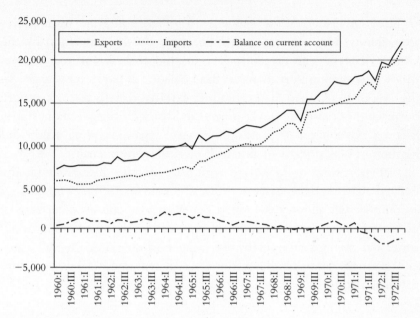

Figure 7.4 U.S. Balance of Trade (1960–1972)
SOURCE: Bureau of Economic Analysis.

borrower, an "importer of capital" in the popular language of economics. America's trade balance also moved into the red as Americans started
to import more than they exported to the world. Figure 7.4 shows the
trend in imports, exports, and the net balance of the overall current
account (commercial and financial flows) from 1960 through 1972.

As the Cold War years progressed, the industrial nations of Europe
and Asia were rebuilt and more, new industrial societies began to
emerge in Asia and Latin America. Much of this industrial development came about not as the result of U.S. aid, but because these societies made industrial policy a priority. The old policy of beggar thy
neighbor was replaced with a more modern version of the mercantilist
model. By the first couple of decades following WWII, when capital
flows and trade policies did not change appreciably, the United States
in the 1970s showed new focus on exports and a renewed interest in
international lending to finance them. Once many of the nations of the
world were rebuilt and their economies had stabilized from the trauma
and stress of war, however, the same global pressures and instabilities
that were in evidence prior to and after WWI again began to emerge.

Two key events in the reemergence of these financial disturbances after almost three decades of stability were the 1971 decision by the United States to end the dollar peg to gold entirely and the reemergence of sovereign borrowing to fund balance of payments deficits. In the case of the United States, funding external deficits did not require borrowing because the government could simply finance these shortfalls via government debt and monetary expansion. The world did business in U.S. dollars—a unique American convenience.

Other nations were not so fortunate. As two researchers at the Federal Reserve Bank of New York observed in 1998: "The current account deficit allows the United States to maintain a higher rate of investment spending than would be possible by relying on domestically generated savings alone. However, the corresponding foreign capital inflow is essentially a loan; therefore, it represents claims on future national income."[22]

Global Imbalances Return

Under the pegged currency arrangement created at Bretton Woods, a global financial institution for countries was created—the International Monetary Fund—which was authorized to make changes in the agreed exchange rates in the event of "fundamental disequilibrium." The idea was for nations to accumulate sufficient foreign currency— that is dollars—to manage their trading relations, and in the event of an imbalance adjust their pegged rate downward rather than resorting to trade barriers. Nations that did not wish to devalue could borrow from the IMF for the purpose of short-term adjustment, with the idea being that the nation would make changes to its economy to eliminate the imbalance and repay the adjustment loan.

In simple terms, the IMF was a bank from which nations could borrow to help balance their short-term imbalances in trade and capital flows. This facility was intended to avoid situations such as those that affected Great Britain before and after WWI, when the country almost ran out of foreign reserves and collapsed. More modest fluctuations in currency values were meant to be managed by the various members of the IMF or by drawing upon "special drawing rights" (SDR)—a form of ersatz global currency that, like the dollar, was and is backed by nothing. This arrangement did not really address the underlying economic problems in the various nations, but merely obscured the reality with a veneer of government intervention.

John H. Barton, Bart S. Fisher, and Michael P. Malloy put the key issue succinctly:

> The obvious question was how currency values were to be maintained at a fixed relationship, even though governments might engage in inconsistent economic policies. The answer was through a duty of exchange market intervention. When its currency fell more than a defined percentage in comparison with others, a state was obliged to buy its currency and sell the foreign currencies in order to maintain the desired relationship. And a state whose currency rose above the margin was to sell that currency and buy others. The practical limiting factor was the state's store of foreign hard currency, a major component of its currency "reserves." A creditor state could always print more of its own currency to sell to maintain the price relationship. But a debtor state had to buy its currency and sell foreign currency.[23]

Essentially participating nations had to accumulate foreign currency sufficient to manage their trade position or borrow from the IMF or international investors. This arrangement worked—or appeared to function—for three decades after WWII, but only because it was underpinned and lubricated by the wonderful stuff of inflation and debt. The United States provided loans and grants to the developing nations of the world and expanded the supply of dollars to accommodate both domestic and international need for liquidity. Much of the assistance provided to Europe under the Marshall Plan, like the loans to Europe in WWI and WWII, were largely forgiven. The Bretton Woods Conference in July 1944 was organized, wrote Henry Hazlitt, because of the widespread existence of inflation. But rather than return to the gold standard or some other fixed discipline for maintaining the real value of global currencies, the Bretton Woods Agreement crafted by John Maynard Keynes and his contemporaries institutionalized global inflation under the aegis of the U.S. dollar. "And in spite of the

mounting monetary chaos since then, the world's political officehold-
ers have never seriously reexamined the inflationist assumptions that
guided the authors of the Bretton Woods agreements," noted Hazlitt.[24]

One of the key measures of the global role of the dollar and inflation in helping to float the world economy after WWII was the growth
of the offshore market in dollar deposits—the so-called "Eurodollars."
From $1 billion in 1950, the offshore market in U.S. dollars grew
to $10 billion at the end of 1965, $100 billion in 1990, over $5 tril-
lion in 2000, and reached more than $10 trillion by the end of 2009.
As U.S. trade and external deficits increased after the 1970s, offshore
holdings of dollars grew along with the global economy. More than the
International Monetary Fund, the Federal Reserve System became
the *de facto* liquidity provider to the world, a role now made explicit
in the wake of the 2008 subprime crisis. While the IMF could act as
a lender of last resort to smaller nations, it does not have the ability to
create money out of thin air as does the Fed.

Paul Blustein notes that "The Fed's duty is to lend as much cash as
the banks need to cover their depositors' demands—and keep lending
until the panic eases, because otherwise the whole system may crash."[25]
But when the Fed's domestic priorities as liquidity provider are
extended to the entire world, the result is the very global inflation and
financial market instability that the classical economists warned against.

The type of crashes that the world has experienced with increasing
frequency since the 1970s seem to be the financial legacy of Richard
Nixon and the other political leaders of that day. It is easy to criticize
the Bretton Woods Agreement from the enviable position of perfect
hindsight, but it was very much a product of the time. From the years
of war and government mobilization, a centralized system of managed
currencies made sense to the leaders of that day. Marshalling industries and entire nations under government authorities was after all the
means of defeating fascist Germany, Italy, and Japan. The organization
of military and logistical resources was a crucial part of the effort, so
naturally government was meant to play a role in the post-war world.
When the military and strategic threat of the Cold War is layered atop
this existing propensity to embrace statist solutions and mechanisms,
the Bretton Woods framework has a certain logic—but only so long
as the United States itself maintains fiscal discipline.

Unfortunately, the United States never embraced fiscal discipline after WWII and instead created a culture of debt and deficits that has only grown with the succeeding decades. Under Bretton Woods, all of the major currencies of the world were defined in dollars, thus when chronic external deficits brought the need to devalue the U.S. dollar, the entire pegged arrangement disintegrated. The beginning of the end of Bretton Woods started in the late 1960s, as the Federal Reserve Board attempted to balance the inflationary impact of the Vietnam War spending with the powerful domestic political imperative for growth. In 1966, the Fed tightened interest rates to slow domestic price increases, almost leading the United States into a serious recession a year later. Mortgage money was tight, consumer prices were rising, and civil rights protests drove many Southern white voters into the arms of the Republican Party. The GOP picked up several governorships including Ronald Reagan in California and Spiro Agnew in Maryland. The Fed subsequently loosened policy and Congress moved to increase domestic spending in 1967. The intense public protests against the Vietnam War and the slack economy eventually caused President Johnson to declare his decision not to seek another term in March 1968.

James R. Jones, who was appointments secretary to President Johnson in 1968, wrote that the most important reason LBJ "decided not to run again was his passionate desire to conclude the Vietnam War honorably."[26] But the political reality was that Johnson was a lame duck following the 1966 election, when the Republicans picked up the seats lost in 1964 and then some. By 1968, Republican partisan politics intersected with the international crisis of the dollar as Richard Nixon, who had rehabilitated himself politically by campaigning vigorously for Republican candidates, gained power.

Richard Nixon's Betrayal

The decision by President Johnson "to walk away from power" had been under consideration for more than a year, Jones writes, and dates back to a meeting between LBJ and Texas Governor John Connally, who urged him to retire and would become Nixon's Treasury Secretary. The eventual determination by President Johnson to leave public life threw the race for the presidency open for both parties. For the Republicans, it set the moderates led by George Romney and Richard Nixon against the left wing of the GOP led by New York Governor Nelson Rockefeller. Ronald Reagan was "an ideal television candidate," wrote Richard Whalen in *Catch the Falling Flag*, "but had never spent a day on duty in Washington."[27] Thus the eventual contest came down to Nixon versus Rockefeller for the Republican nomination, but the dull and serious New York governor was no match for the devious Nixon.

Seeing the way in which LBJ was savaged by the media over the war and the direction of the U.S. economy, Nixon felt vulnerable to Rockefeller on the question of jobs. Nixon eventually embraced a left-wing economic program out of political expediency and because he did not see any politically palatable alternatives. What passed for mainstream economic thinking at the time called for more spending and increased deficits, but this policy was stymied by the failure of increased spending to create jobs. "Watch what we do, not what we say," was the famous advice Nixon's first Attorney General, John Mitchell, gave the press at the onset of the Nixon presidency in 1969. That admonition was essential when it came to the confused economic policy of Nixon.

Nixon's policies quickly alienated conservatives. In his first campaign, Nixon declared his intention to start "getting people off the welfare rolls and onto payrolls," but then initiated an income maintenance program which had the effect of adding 15 million Americans to public assistance. This stroke of genius was engineered by Daniel Patrick Moynihan, one of the cadre of Rockefeller Republicans who turned the Nixon years into the "New Deal III" or what Nixon would eventually call the New Economic Policy. *Time* magazine wrote in 1971: "Welfare reform, cutbacks in defense spending, advocacy of deficit spending, and Keynesian economics were difficult enough for Nixon's conservative supporters to tolerate, but for many, rapprochement with Communist China was the final straw." But Nixon's repudiation of Bretton Woods and devaluation of the dollar had far more significant impact on issues that conservatives hold dear, particularly the value of the dollar and the stability of the U.S. economy.

Under the Bretton Woods arrangement, gold and dollars had been established as the reserve for all of the nations outside the Communist sphere. Since in the 1940s there was not sufficient gold to underpin global trade and financial flows except in a fractional way, Keynes and the other Bretton Woods framers essentially made the dollar equal to gold as a backstop for the global economy. Since the United States had virtually all of the monetary gold in the world at the end of WWII with some $35 billion in gold (valued at $35 per ounce), this arrangement seemed to make sense, and for a while it appeared to work. But as the nations of the world recovered and the United States exported capital and jobs, the gold stocks of the United States dwindled. The United States had just $11 billion in reserves in 1970. Since federal law required that the U.S. Treasury have $25 in gold for every $100 in greenbacks in circulation, the Washington was reaching a tipping point.

The End of the Dollar Peg

By 1970, when inflation was starting to rise and the United States was running its first trade deficit in the twentieth century, the global financial markets essentially began a run on the dollar. U.S. official gold stocks fell precipitously. Like FDR, Nixon was faced with the political fact of the market's lack of confidence in the fiscal integrity of the United States. Increased domestic spending and external deficits caused an outflow of gold from the U.S. Treasury, effectively forcing Nixon to abandon what remained of the gold standard. Even though FDR had taken away the right of Americans to hold gold as money, under Bretton Woods the United States still maintained the legal commitment to honor gold convertibility of the dollar in its dealings with other nations. Only a month after President Nixon announced his trip to China, he went on national television, announced that the United States was in the worst crisis since the Great Depression, and took the dollar off the gold standard. Nixon effectively devalued the U.S. currency for the second time in 40 years.[28]

In 1971 Nixon unilaterally ended the gold convertibility of the dollar, bringing an end to the Bretton Woods system of managed currencies and ushering in a period of floating exchange rates. Taking a page out of the Democratic playbook of Truman and FDR, Nixon also imposed a 90-day freeze on wages and prices and a 10 percent surcharge on imports. Following the Kennedy–Johnson administration in the United States, there was a massive effort to manage the marketplace, in part by controlling wages. In their book *The Commanding Heights*, Daniel Yergin and Joseph Stanislaw described the bizarre fact of Richard M. Nixon, a California Republican and conservative stalwart, taking America once again down the statist road to government wage and price controls:

> This initiative was not the handiwork of left-wing liberals but of the administration of Richard Nixon, a moderately conservative Republican who was a critic of government intervention in the economy. As a young man during World War II, prior to joining the navy, Nixon had worked as a junior attorney in the tire-rationing division of the Office of Price Administration, an experience that left him with a lasting distaste for price controls.[29]

And yet such was the severity of the perceived crisis in 1971 that Richard Nixon, who had been elected in 1968 in a very close contest against Senator Hubert Humphrey of Minnesota, veered to the left in terms of economic policy. Yergin and Stanislaw describe how Nixon declared himself to be a "Keynesian" in 1971, a change that the economist himself might have found troubling. Despite his conservative credentials as vice president to President Eisenhower, Nixon was uncomfortable with economic issues and allowed his administration to essentially be hijacked by the Rockefeller-wing of the GOP—and by his own fears and paranoia. Gary North described Nixon's betrayal of conservative principles after winning the 1968 election:

> In 1968, millions of Republicans voted for Richard Nixon. They voted for him overwhelmingly in 1972, the year after he had unilaterally severed the dollar from gold. He had run back-to-back deficits of $25 billion—a huge annual deficit in that era. It is unlikely that the ineffective gas bag Hubert Humphrey would have had the courage to destroy the last traces of the international gold standard. Yet Humphrey almost won in 1968. Republican die-hards had kept this from happening. In the summer of 1972, Richard Whalen's book, *Catch the Falling Flag: A Republican's Challenge to His Party*, documented the story of the

takeover of the [Nixon] Administration by Rockefeller operatives. Whalen had been a speechwriter for Nixon during the 1968 campaign. He knew firsthand what had occurred. Republicans paid no attention to his book in November. "Nixon is ours." They re-elected him in November.[30]

Nixon represented a milestone in American economic development, where deficit spending was explicitly embraced to maximize employment even though the economy was not in recession or the nation at war. The leadership for this evolution of the culture of deficit spending came from the left wing of the Republican Party, which at the time was led by New York governor Nelson Rockefeller. The irony of Nixon's adoption of the Rockefeller tendency once he won the White House is that he won because of conservative support, but ultimately migrated from pretend Goldwater conservative to Eisenhower moderate to deficit spending socialist by the early 1970s.

The columnist Hugh Sidey observed of Nixon that "he abandons his philosophy, his promises, his speeches, his friends, his counselors. He marches out of one life into a new world without any apologies or glancing back."[31] But Sidey's description of Nixon could have also applied to FDR and to many other modern American politicians. Nixon's actions were a major repudiation of the original vision of Keynes as well as the other framers of Bretton Woods, none of whom were apologists for inflation or borrowing except in times of emergency. Nixon's final repudiation of gold and his explicit embrace of deficit spending to ensure full employment was a radical departure from the stated practice of either political party. While Lyndon Johnson established the Great Society programs to fight poverty and improve education, their impact on the federal budget was modest compared to the level of federal spending authorized under President Nixon as part of the Soviet-style New Economic Policy.

Federal revenues grew strongly during the Johnson years, but growth stagnated under Nixon in the 1970s. The response from Nixon to economic stagnation was more federal spending combined with price controls to mask the resulting inflation. Whereas Hoover had resisted massive federal expenditures in the early 1930s for fear of permanently expanding the size of government, Nixon delighted in a growing federal budget as

he felt, just as Johnson did, that more spending would insulate him politically. Doing so did protect him from defeat in the 1972 election, when
he overpowered George McGovern handily on a platform of economic
growth and national security, but at the expense of higher inflation.
Nixon beat Hubert Humphrey in 1968 because of the public's concern
over the Vietnam War and mounting budget deficits, but by 1972 Nixon
was spending like there was no tomorrow—like a Democrat, in fact.
"To improve his chances of re-election, he would pre-empt any position
that the Democrats might take in the 1972 campaign," wrote Richard
Whalen, "as he had done by adopting their program for the economy."[32]

In July 1971, Fed Chairman Arthur Burns, who had been outspoken about his worries regarding inflation, told the Joint Economic
Committee of Congress that "the rules of economics are not working in quite the way that they used to . . . I wish that I could report
that we are making substantial progress in dampening the inflationary spiral. I cannot do so." Burns had been head of the Council of
Economic Advisors from 1953 to 1956 under Eisenhower and knew
Nixon well, but when he was named Chairman of the Fed in 1970
his relationship with the President began to deteriorate. The fiscal priorities of the White House and the inflation fighting priorities of the
Fed were in direct conflict. Burns was in favor of defending the dollar
and, if necessary, selling all of the U.S. gold if need be. "What the hell
are reserves for?" Burns thundered. The Fed Chairman also believed
that the United States should begin borrowing in other currencies to
manage the dollar's value, but neither of these suggestions were well
received by the White House.

In that same month of July 1971, the Fed hiked interest rates a
quarter of a point and indicated that higher interest rates were likely.
From 1952 to almost the end of the 1960s, the Federal funds rate
had tracked an unremarkable pattern between below 1 percent in the
slack years and as high as 6 percent in years when the economy was
near capacity. Prices began to rise. The cost of short-term funds rose
in the late 1960s close to double digits as the Fed attempted to act
alone to cool inflation. When President Johnson refused to propose
a tax increase in 1966 or thereafter to pay for the Vietnam War, the
result was rising inflation, more than doubling by the 1968 election.
By 1971, inflation was over five percent, but then cooled for several

years due to increased interest rates engineered by Arthur Burns and the Federal Open Market Committee.

In punishment for committing the crime of speaking the truth in public, Burns was subject to an ugly campaign of vitriol and personal attacks by members of the Nixon White House staff. The attacks on the Fed in that summer of 1971 only further weakened confidence in the United States and the dollar, but in the Nixon White House the priority was to keep the old man happy. In October of 1971, Nixon warned Burns that he was worried that the slowing economy would force him "to go out of town fast," a reference to losing the election in a year's time. Nixon also told Burns that his would be "the last Conservative administration in Washington," referring to the political pressure for social programs and more federal spending. The President also opined that the problem of too much liquidity in the financial system was "just bullshit."[33]

Nixon had watched unemployment rise from 3.4 percent late in 1969 to 6 percent in 1971, "but with no abatement in inflation," wrote Bob Hertzel in *The Monetary Policy of the Federal Reserve: A History*, a development which "created intellectual consternation among mainstream economists."[34] More concerned was Nixon, who feared that the Fed was sinking the economy in front of the 1972 election, in essence a repeat of the process that had forced Johnson out of the presidency. Nixon subsequently beat Hubert Humphrey by less than a million votes and thus worried that he could be vulnerable politically in a soft economy.

In early August, at the insistence of Treasury Undersecretary Paul Volcker, Nixon held a secret meeting at the Camp David retreat to discuss the crisis affecting the economy. Congress had given Nixon broad powers over wages and prices in 1970 via the Economic Stabilization Act, and Nixon was determined to use them. Treasury Secretary John Connally, who Nixon recruited for the Cabinet in 1970, laid out the plan to the assembled staff, including the wage and price controls, an import surcharge, and closing the gold window. Nixon admitted at the time that he was not sure of the impact of the decision to close the gold window. Fed Chairman Burns was against closing the gold window, but was in agreement with the other aspects of the Nixon NEP. Connally would say after the summit meeting that when Nixon announced the unilateral United States departure from Bretton Woods: "We have awakened forces that nobody is at all familiar with."

Chairman Burns, for his part, urged Nixon during the discussions not to close the gold window when he announced the other measures, feeling that these policy changes were more than sufficient to stop the outflow of gold. "If we close the window, other countries could double the price of gold. We are releasing forces that we need not release. I think that Paul Volcker should go ahead and start negotiating with other countries on a realignment of currencies," Burns argued and allowed that President Nixon could close the gold window later if these other measures did not restore confidence in the dollar. But Nixon was shrewd enough to know that if he announced his other policy moves that the markets would next anticipate a change in gold convertibility of the dollar. Paul Volcker did not want to close the gold window either, but also worried that speculators would drive up the price of gold. "We have to come up with a proposal to demonstrate gold is not that important," Volcker told the meeting. "Maybe we should sell some," echoing the thinking of Burns.[35]

The Return of Sovereign Borrowing

By leaving the gold standard in 1971, Nixon devalued the dollar for many of the same political reasons that drove FDR's decision in 1933, but Nixon was done in by the Watergate scandal and cover-up two years later. The difference between the two decisions was that the dollar was now the predominant means of exchange in the global economy. So while the United States could devalue its currency and borrow *in dollars* to fund internal spending and external deficits, other nations of the world with balance of payments problems were faced with devaluation—or taking on foreign currency debt.

The onerous debts imposed on Germany after WWI had been identified as an eventual cause of WWII. The framers of Bretton Woods saw the ill effects of currency inflation and commercialized lending or creating commercial claims against sovereign states after WWI. Loans to other nations were the chief causes of the conflict, but significant foreign borrowing by developing nations from commercial banks quickly came back into practice after Nixon's devaluation. The decision by President Nixon to devalue the dollar not only set the United States free of fiscal boundaries, but also set a very poor example for other nation states. As already noted, the flow of dollars into the global markets created a surfeit of greenbacks so large that they warranted a separate category—Eurodollars. And foreign nations began to borrow dollars in the same way as had occurred between the two great wars.

Walker Todd wrote in his classic monograph, "A History of International Lending," in 1991:

> The Bretton Woods framers never intended that such commercialized international lending resume—yet such loans were made increasingly after 1973. Thus there are some significant, still largely unexplained gaps in the logic of economists and policy makers who advocate a greater role for commercial banks' loans, ostensibly for development purposes. Somehow, in the mid-1970s, we leaped almost overnight from the supposedly desirable original environment, in which there was no development lending by commercial banks, to primary reliance on such lending.[36]

One of the chief rationales for adjustment lending in the 1970s at least among the political leaders of the major industrial countries, was the oil embargo in 1973. The weakness of the dollar and the sharp increase in energy costs imposed a heavy tax on the global economy in terms of lowered growth prospects. But equally harmful to many exporting nations was the steady decline in the value of the dollar, which had become unstable as early as 1967–1968 when gold flows from the United States increased. GDP growth in the U.S. was cut in half, unemployment rose, and the visible level of inflation also surged from low single-digits to twice those levels and more. David Gordon described the chaos and uncertainty caused by the final interment of Bretton Woods in 1994:

> When Bretton Woods was formally buried in 1973, the dollar was still apparently overvalued, resulting in a continuing decline of 2.9 percent per year in 1973–1979. No longer officially the world's key currency, the dollar's sharp decline underscored how artificially inflated its value had become at

the end of the boom years. The international hegemon had begun to seem more and more like a paper tiger.[37]

Paper tiger or not, the United States still had a vast advantage in the global marketplace compared to other nations. It could print money and issue debt in dollars, and essentially be indifferent to the movement of the currency. Other nations, however, including the largest industrial nations of Europe, were not so lucky. Generally speaking, in the 1970s a debtor nation other than the United States that came to have balance of payments problems had three choices:

1. Loans from and austerity measures imposed and supervised by the IMF. Present and future consumers in these nations would see living standards, and political unrest would ensue.
2. Overt default and devaluation, meaning an end to all foreign borrowing and the loss of access to even short-term credit to clear trade transactions. Cold turkey and an all cash economy. Political unrest would ensue.
3. In the case of less-developed countries, debt forgiveness by the creditor nations whose citizens (mostly the United States) would bear the losses. This was the preferred choice.

During the years of the Cold War, the default choice was always more lending, either from the IMF, the World Bank, and/or private lenders, because the alternative in the form of a harsh economic adjustment was politically unpalatable for the inhabitants of Washington of either political party and for the banks that lent money to the debtor nations. Concerns over the prospect of a left-wing swing in the nations of the Americas, Asia, or the Middle East were sufficient to propel more lending to the subject debtor nation. And even in the case of the largest countries, repayment was never assured or even likely. Indeed, Todd notes that over the past 150 years or so over the history of international lending, repayment of foreign loans almost never occurred.

Gerald O'Driscoll of the CATO Institute, who served on the President's Council of Economic Advisers, wrote in a 1984 paper that "[g]etting from where we are today to a resolution of who is, in fact, going to bear the losses is the key to restoring credibility to international lending."[38] These losses on foreign loans, O'Driscoll noted, had already occurred but were yet to be recognized. But this was precisely the point. These "loans" were never really meant to be repaid. Even Great Britain, once considered the second best sovereign credit risk after the United States, had defaulted on every foreign loan it contracted since the end of the Boer War in 1902, Todd notes. "Instead, every such loan has been subjected to major currency devaluation, rolled over, suspended, rescheduled, or otherwise restructured, repudiated, reduced, cancelled, or forgiven. The more drastic steps, leading to eventual, partial or complete cancelation of debt have been surprisingly frequent."[39]

The views of researchers such as Walker Todd and Gerry O'Driscoll on foreign lending are confirmed in the more recent work of Carmen Reinhart and Kenneth Rogoff, *This Time it is Different: Eight Centuries of Financial Folly*. The book is another monumental research effort in the fine tradition of Freidman and Schwartz's *Monetary History of the United States* and Allan Meltzer's updates of that work, albeit focused on the foreign debt component of the economic story.

Reinhart and Rogoff nicely document the fact that foreign lending between sovereign states or private parties has always been problematic, but in the post-WWII era the fiscal and external imbalances of the United States have become the key factor. While Reinhart and Rogoff set an inflation rate of 40 percent as the threshold for describing an inflationary "crisis," their work also suggests that since the 1970s a larger and larger percentage of nations have been captured by global financial crises. As the use of what Reinhart and Rogoff describe as repression of domestic markets and price controls ended in the 1970s and 1980s, and the U.S. deficit and debt grew, the frequency and number of nations affected by periodic economic crises also increased.[40]

From the closing of the Suez Canal in 1956, the United Kingdom and France had been the primary recipients of adjustment loans. Even in those times, the availability of dollars was so limited that it would have been difficult in a practical sense for foreign nations to incur large amounts of dollar debt. As late as December of 1973, the total of all U.S. bank claims on foreigners was just $20 billion—about in the same neighborhood as the U.S. budget deficit in that year—and one third of this amount was held against Japan. By the late 1980s, however, total U.S. claims on foreigners had risen to $388 billion, a 20-fold increase in dollar debts in less than 15 years.[41]

The return of international lending as a significant factor in the global economy in the 1970s and the explosion of foreign debt as a problem in the 1980s was at its roots no different from the neo-Keynesian economic policies that were being followed in the United States at the same time. Policy makers in the industrial countries, aided by armies of economists and bankers, pretended that foreign loans would be repaid. But the reality was that none of these dollar loans, particularly to the established industrial nations, would ever be repaid. The operative goal of Washington's foreign and economic policy was to keep the level of aggregate output in the non-Communist world rising, at least in nominal terms. Inside the United States, deficit spending, debt, and inflation were the primary means to keep growth on an upward-sloping curve, while internationally foreign loans, trade subsidies, and other means were used to maintain the appearance of output increases.

So long as the supply of dollars already very visible in the growth of Eurodollar deposits continued to expand and the United States was willing to run external deficits, political leaders in the industrial nations could claim that the collective economic pie represented by global trade and commerce was increasing. But once the assumption of constant growth and expansion of international output was questioned, then the United States and other nations were faced with a problem of distributing real income from a static or shrinking global economic pie. In that event, O'Driscoll and other researchers predicted decades ago, the world economy would be right back in the position of the 1930s, with a contraction of world economic output and reduced living standards in both debtor and creditor nations.[42]

By the end of the 1970s, with the second oil price shock, the use of debt to offset the decline in output and income caused by a quadrupling of energy prices had become as much a part of the established practice internationally as deficit spending was accepted as a domestic policy tool within the United States. Despite all of the work and study and discussion by generations of economists before and after WWII, the same problems of growth and debt dogged the United States and the other nations as the 1980s were beginning. The role of the dollar as the international reserve currency was in doubt, and none of the great thinkers and theorists of the day seemed to have a clear idea in what direction to head next.

The next three decades would see the problems of global debt and inflation intensify even as the growth potential of the United States and Europe seemed to wane, and all with little or no suggestion of a solution to get the global economy onto a less volatile, more stable footing. "I recently commented to some of my economist friends that I'm not aware of any large contribution that economic science has made to central banking in the last 50 years or so," Paul Volcker told Gary H. Stern of the Federal Reserve Bank of Minneapolis.[43]

Volcker would probably chuckle at the thought that central banking hasn't made any contribution to economic science, either. Perhaps the fact that little has changed in the issues and constraints facing the evolution of global economies is what makes the search for solutions so challenging.

Chapter 8

Leveraging the American Dream

With the 1971 decision by President Richard Nixon to end gold convertibility of the dollar, banks and dollar-based investors were irrevocably tied to the greenback as a means of exchange and store of value. Unlike the process leading up to the Bretton-Woods agreement, there were no meetings, no international consultations. The decision to end the gold convertibility of the dollar came down to just the unilateral calculus of the President of the United States, who was seeking to manage his domestic political—that is economic—problems. The end of convertibility allowed Nixon to avoid the embarrassment of seeing the Treasury run out of gold. The end of convertibility also cleared the way for increased deficit spending by Congress and commensurate monetary expansion by the Federal Reserve to accommodate it.

Fed Chairman Arthur Burns later said in a conversation with Richard Whalen that the choice to end gold convertibility was a "terrible decision" that should never have happened, but one that "had to happen." Treasury Secretary John Connally at first did not realize what Nixon had done, thinking that merely another dollar devaluation had occurred a la FDR. As Burns opposed the move and also Nixon's demands to stimulate the economy, but ultimately the political pressure for growth prevailed. In 1972, Fed Chairman Arthur Burns kept monetary policy sufficiently expansive to help Richard Nixon win reelection by a landslide, taking 60 percent of the popular vote. The quid pro quo to Burn's easy money posture had been Nixon's imposition of price controls the year before, which made inflation at least appear to be low compared to the official statistics. But the economy was weak, no matter what the figures suggested and Americans knew it.

"Once past the election, the price controls began to break down. Inflation jumped to 8.7 percent in 1973 and 12.3 percent in 1974," wrote Bruce Bartlett, who was a domestic policy adviser to President Ronald Reagan. "Another recession began in November 1973 and didn't end until March 1975. These poor economic conditions created fertile soil for Nixon's enemies when the Watergate scandal broke. Had the economy been stronger, Nixon probably would have survived it, just as a strong economy unquestionably helped former President Bill Clinton weather the Monica Lewinski scandal."[1]

The rising inflation and unemployment of the 1970s would come to be known as stagflation, standing for low growth and inflation, a description for something that many Americans had thought impossible. The modern day version of the American dream, as interpreted by FDR, LBJ, and Richard Nixon, was to use the government to deliver or at least promise a modicum of prosperity. This objective was not so different from the political goals and pretensions of American politicians of the past. But the consequences in terms of inflation and public debt were far greater now that America was given custody of the world's reserve currency and had created a global market for dollar-denominated Treasury debt. After Nixon's decision to abandon the gold standard in 1971, the basic role of the dollar remained the same, though the rules set by the industrial nations after WWII were no longer being followed.

When Gerald Ford took over the Presidency from Nixon on August 4, 1974, inflation was in double digits. Americans barely knew of Ford, a veteran congressman from Michigan who had worked his way up the Republican ladder to the position of leader. Ford is the only President who succeeded to the office without being elected. He was made Vice President under the terms of the 26th Amendment after the resignation of Spiro Agnew. The Constitution provides for the replacement of the Vice President when the office is made vacant by resignation or death. Ford then succeeded President Nixon.

Ford entered into a political and economic maelstrom that would test his character and humor, but at the end of the process Ford remained one of the most likable presidents in recent memory. "Nixonomics, the highly variable sequence of economic doctrines that left the country simultaneously overstimulated and underemployed has given way now to President Ford's economics of candor and moral uplift," wrote Leonard Silk in September 1974. "The time has clearly come to take a look at what is right with the economy."[2]

Few people of that time held Silk's optimistic view. Ford tried to hold the line on federal spending, but without success. Had he been able to prevent Congress from passing any additional legislation during his short tenure in office, the budget deficits would have climbed because of the actions of past governments. The rising red ink in Washington ultimately resulted in his defeat at the hands of former Georgia Governor Jimmy Carter. Ford wanted to cut taxes to stimulate the economy, but with estimates of a $35 billion deficit for the following year floating around the White House at the end of 1974, Ford did not have a lot of easy options. By March of 1975 the same aides inside the White House were projecting a deficit of $100 billion in the next fiscal year.

In Congressional testimony during that period, Treasury Secretary William Simon told Congress that the deficit for 1976 would come in around $80 billion, inclusive of a planned tax cut. A young assistant Director of the Office of Management and Budget named Paul O'Neill, who would later serve briefly as Treasury Secretary under George W. Bush, worried that many of the "temporary" emergency spending initiatives being put in place by the Congress in that year would become permanent. He was right. The Ford Administration, while asking for modest tax increases, attempted to convince Congress to slow fiscal stimulus efforts. But Senator Edmund Muskie (D-ME) dismissed the idea that Congress would ever pass anything like a budget with a $100 billion deficit. Muskie knew that the Ford Administration was right that the public was getting angry at these growing budget shortfalls. And he worried that "adding up our spending proposals we may find that we have already used up our options."

In the summer of 1974, the Federal debt was $475 billion, up a little over a hundred billion from the start of the Nixon Administration in 1969. The budget deficit would actually fall in that momentous year to just $7 billion, but would climb from that point to $70 billion by the time of the November 1976 election. In that year the government was going to spend about $390 billion and take in $291 billion, including a cut in taxes of about $25 billion. The chart in Figure 8.1 illustrates the federal government's spending in that period.

Ford had the bad luck of serving in the worst economy since the Great Depression. The mid-1970s were difficult years in the United States, with the oil shock and double-digit unemployment breaking the renewed sense of confidence that had prevailed in the post-WWII era. The fact that the fiscal deficits were rising at a time of slack economic demand made the public uneasy. Despite the fact that members of both political parties tacitly accepted the need for deficits, the public at large was still largely unaware of the change in the basic assumptions of government which had occurred during the Cold War. The boom

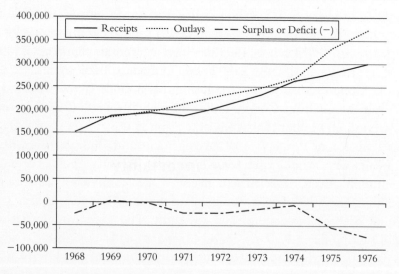

Figure 8.1   Federal Outlays, Receipts, and Balance (1968–1976) (Millions of $)
SOURCE: Office of Management and Budget.

years of the 1950s and 1960s gave way to the years of crisis and uncertainty of the 1970s. Competition from Japan and Europe put the U.S. into an unaccustomed position of being a trade debtor. This caused many Americans to question whether the country was headed in the right direction. The added factor of runaway inflation, which had only been a problem in wartime, complicated the political equation in a new and unfamiliar way.

President Nixon appointed Alan Greenspan as head of the Council of Economic Advisers in the summer of 1974, one of Nixon's last significant official acts prior to his resignation. Greenspan made it clear to the Nixon staff that any resort to further price controls would trigger his departure as well. "He stayed on after Nixon resigned in 1974 and Gerald Ford assumed the presidency," Bob Woodward wrote of Nixon during this period. "Greenspan thought that Ford was the bravest and most correct when he didn't meddle with free markets during the recession of 1974–1975, even at the risk of his own political future."[3]

Ford attempted to address the issue of inflation with a program of voluntary restraints on consumption that were meant to reduce demand. Millions of red and white buttons with the word "WIN"— for "Whip Inflation Now"—were produced in 1974 at the instructions of President Ford. The campaign was pretty much of a failure, but while it was clear that Ford was in political trouble, Americans could not help but sympathize with a man who had made a political career of being affable and honest. "Jerry Ford was the most decent man I ever encountered in public life," Greenspan said in a statement after Ford's death in 2006. "It was a great privilege to work for him. I will miss him."[4]

The New Uncertainty

In his excellent 1995 book on federal budget deficits, *Deficit Government: Taxing and Spending in Modern America*, Iwan Morgan divides the post-WWII periods into four segments:[5]

- The Age of Equilibrium, 1945–1960
- The Age of Activism, 1961–1968

- The Age of Uncertainty, 1969–1980
- The Age of Excess, 1981–1988

The years of Richard Nixon, Gerald Ford, and Jimmy Carter were uncertain times and the first hint that the years of "equilibrium" under the domination of the United States in the global marketplace were ending. None of the policymakers in Washington in either party had any idea what to do—except spend more money. The result was inflation rather than jobs and prosperity. Neither Ford nor Carter had any broad vision or ideas about finance or economics. Both men were mere accidents of history—yet again—in the proud and oftentimes peculiar story of the American presidency. Ford was a loyal friend and had stood with Nixon through the Watergate scandal. He would eventually grant him a presidential pardon in September 1974, sealing Ford's fate in the 1976 election. In that sense, the choice of Ford to deal with the aftermath of his resignation made sense for Nixon personally and was not a bad choice for the country. But the tragedy of the Watergate scandal was that Nixon had intended to appoint John Connally as Vice President when it became clear that Spiro Agnew was in serious trouble.

Agnew resigned as Nixon's vice president in 1973 after authorities learned he had taken bribes and kickbacks—including free groceries—going all the way back to his years as Maryland governor in Annapolis. The Watergate scandal would make the Connally scenario impossible, however, and left the presidency in the hands of a man with no clear agenda when it came to the economy. How different the American political and economic map might look today had Watergate never happened and Connally succeeded Nixon to the presidency in 1976.

Instead America got Jerry Ford and Nelson Rockefeller, the latter who had to wait four months until the Democratic Congress deigned to ratify his appointment as Vice President. Ford was a moderate Republican who, like Ronald Reagan, had a disarming personal charm and facility with people. He had a remarkable capacity to remember people and names, and would use this talent to great advantage in his dealings with Congress. Even during partisan battles, Ford maintained a level of personal decorum with all members of Congress that was and is still remarkable today. A former football star for the University of

Michigan, Ford understood the chemistry of teamwork and was always most proud of his athletic achievements.[6]

When he assumed office in the middle of a mid-term election in 1974, Ford was dealing with a Democratic and decidedly activist Congress that was emboldened by Watergate and the popular opposition to the Vietnam War. If the years under Richard Nixon had been the Imperial Presidency, then the brief tenure of Jerry Ford was decidedly non-royal and very down to earth. But still Ford was an appointed president. The addition of New York Governor Rockefeller made the Ford Administration one of the most superficially conservative since Dwight Eisenhower, but without Ike's strong sensibilities about avoiding budget deficits and unnecessary defense spending. Writer Richard Reeves noted that Rockefeller had to crawl—and worse—to get the VP slot with Ford, a process of political prostration to the right wing of the GOP that included using state troopers with guns blazing to put down the strike at Attica prison in New York. Many commentators mistakenly thought that the Ford-Rockefeller ticket in the 1976 election would be a winner, at least in the early days of the Ford Administration. Reeves, though, disagreed and predicted that 1976 would be a "pocketbook election"—and he was right. Reeves commented on the selection of Rockefeller in *New York Magazine* in 1974:

> Still, Rockefeller *was* the best choice for Ford, for the Republican party, for the country. It's a cruel world, the one the rest of us have to share with the Rockefellers, and Nelson Rockefeller is a very capable man. Capable of anything, perhaps, but whatever else he is, Rocky is a heavyweight. Despite all the talk about lists and sealed envelopes, I don't think the president seriously considered anyone but Rockefeller.[7]

During the years of the Vietnam War, many Democrats migrated to the anti-war, anti-defense spending camp, but John Kennedy had run against the Republicans in 1960 based on the Eisenhower Administration being soft on defense and not being prepared to resist a Russian missile onslaught. Eisenhower, for his part, dismissed the idea that war with Moscow was imminent and resisted bipartisan Congressional efforts to increase defense spending. This time Ike turned out to be right about the largely symbolic nature of the Cold War. But by 1974, the center of the Democratic Party was moving to the left—so much so that Southern conservatives would soon start to change parties. Ford and Rockefeller were only as far to the right of center as the mainstream Democrats were to the left—and the differences between the parties and among Americans were widening. Whereas in 1963 a Democratic Congress was pushing a tax cut to help stimulate the economy, by 1974 the political equation was again changing between the two major parties. The Democrats focused on spending and the Republicans resisting these initiatives from the position of a seemingly permanent minority.

In 1974, concerns about the rate of increase of expenditures for the Great Society programs and the cost of the Vietnam War forced Congress to pass the Congressional Budget and Impoundment Control Act. "The Act attempted to strengthen the congressional role in the making of the budget by beefing up and centralizing its budgetary capacity," noted a 1993 report by the *Joint Committee on the Congress*. "The House and Senate Budget Committees were created to coordinate the congressional consideration of the budget, and the Congressional Budget Office was established as a source of nonpartisan analysis and information relating to the budget and the economy. Indeed, perhaps the most important early role for CBO was to provide an alternate economic forecast to the Congress." Alice Rivlin was the first director, and she established a reputation for being neutral and objective.

It is generally agreed that the 1974 Act, while an important step forward in terms of organizing the annual budget process for Congress, was not a success in either reining in deficit spending or in helping the government do a better job of anticipating the revenues and expenditures of the Treasury, either immediately or in the longer term. The problem in 1974 was that nobody knew what was happening with the U.S. economy, oil prices, or the trends shaping the rest of the global marketplace. The Arab oil embargo largely fooled most contemporary forecasters when it came to anticipating the decrease in growth and increase in unemployment. The negative impact on employment of the increase in energy prices was felt for years thereafter and forced Americans to begin adjusting the way energy is consumed.

Forecasters from the Conference Board to Herbert Stein believed that unemployment would peak at or below 6 percent, but instead it came in over 7 percent. Nominal growth came in at 6.5 percent in 1974, but with visible inflation at 12 percent. The stunning actual result for the year was a real, inflation-adjusted *decline* in U.S. output of 5 percent.[8] As much as any year since the end of WWII, 1974 began to shake the public's belief in the ability of Washington to engineer a positive economic outcome. Paul Volcker recalled that when his predecessor Arthur Burns gave his valedictory speech in 1979, the Fed Chairman confessed to feeling helpless in the face of the powerful forces that seemed to be moving markets and prices. Volcker also repeated his view that leaving the gold standard in 1971 did not necessarily drive the subsequent inflation in the United States over the next decade. Soaring energy costs did.[9]

The problem faced by Presidents Ford and Carter was that the rate of inflation was higher than the growth in the money supply, forcing the central bank into a quandary. If the Fed expanded the growth of money to help boost demand, which had been the priority throughout the post-war period, then inflation would also be increased. Real money balances, which is the money stock divided by the inflation rate, had been falling during 1973 and 1974. This development was shocking to many observers because unlike in past periods when the growth in the money supply had slowed while prices remained stable, in the 1974–1975 period the opposite situation occurred with a stable money supply, lower velocity of money in terms of the turnover visible in the economy, but with double-digit inflation. The quadrupling of energy prices had rendered one-fourth of the U.S. economy obsolete and uneconomic to operate.

For the Democrats, the answer was more spending and more debt, while Ford made inflation his chief point of attack. The Republican platform in 1976 identified inflation as the number one obstacle in dealing with unemployment, but the Democrats, led by such luminaries as Edmund Muskie (D-ME) ridiculed Ford's 1977 budget and its $50 billion estimated deficit as inadequate. "The party's 1976 platform decreed full employment as the answer to the nation's problems," wrote Iwan Morgan, "on the grounds that the consequent boost to consumption would lead in turn to business expansion, higher profits, and greater investment."[10] But with low or no growth and already accommodative monetary policy, the notion of even more federal spending to spur the economy was not welcome at the Fed or among the Republicans in Congress.

By 1976, a real battle was brewing in the Republican Party between the Ford loyalists, who felt that the incumbent president deserved a chance to lead the party in an election, and the supporters of California governor Ronald Reagan, who wanted to make growth, big government, and the Democrats the issues in the election. Reagan was not shy about taking on the Democrats and the Great Society in 1976. He attacked "the erosion of freedom that has taken place under Democratic rule in this country, the invasion of private rights, the controls and restrictions on the vitality of the great free economy that we enjoy."

Nelson Rockefeller had been dumped from the ticket and Ford was looking for something or someone to energize his candidacy. Jimmy Carter was running away with the Democratic nomination and would later select Walter Mondale as his running mate. The former actor and paid TV commentator Reagan was written off early on, but came back late in the game with a series of primary wins that turned the Republican nomination process into a real contest. Though Jerry Ford was the favorite in the race, Reagan clearly was the man of the future by the time that the GOP delegates met in Kansas City. Ford actually considered Reagan as a running mate in 1976, but eventually picked Senator Bob Dole (R-KS)—fortunately for Reagan.

When Ford and Reagan did meet at the Republican convention, the incumbent president never asked Reagan to consider the vice presidency. Ford only asked if he had "any ideas," Reagan told Richard Whalen after his one-on-one private meeting with Ford. What some Republicans called the dream ticket of Ford and Reagan was not to be. At the end of the 1976 Republican convention, however, when President Ford, Senator Dole, and Nelson Rockefeller stood, with their spouses on the platform amid the applause from the delegates, Ford beckoned to Reagan to come down to the platform and join them.

The delegates gave Reagan a standing ovation as he delivered a crisp, six-minute statement of values, a call to action that asked what they were willing to do today to protect freedom that would be remembered at the tricentenial celebration of America's independence: "This is our challenge; and this is why here in this hall tonight, better than we have ever done before, we have got to quit talking to each other and about each other and go out and communicate to the world that we may be fewer in numbers than we have ever been, but we carry the message they are waiting for." And by inviting his adversary to share the platform with him that night, Jerry Ford fulfilled his stewardship as the unelected president and gave the future of the Republican Party to Ronald Reagan, whatever happened in the election that year.[11]

Even as the Ford–Dole ticket went down to a close defeat in 1976, with 297 electoral votes for Carter to 241 for Ford, the seeds of the Reagan revolution were already starting to grow. By the mid-term election in 1978, the insurgent conservatives in the Republican Party were beginning to effectively target liberal Democrats in Southern states with the basic Reagan message of tax cuts and smaller government. Only weeks before the election in 1978, a New York Congressman named Jack Kemp and Senator William Roth of Delaware won initial approval of a 25 percent across the board cut in tax rates, but the measure was dropped from the legislation. It would take four more years and the election of Ronald Reagan for the Kemp–Roth tax cut to be adopted by Congress.

Humphrey-Hawkins and Full Employment

The political reaction by the Democratic majority in Congress to the election of Jimmy Carter and Senator Fritz Mondale (D-MN) was to greatly increase federal spending. Among even mainstream Democrats, the answer to the years of uncertainty and unemployment during the 1970s was to embed in the law the right to full employment. Senator Hubert Humphrey (D-MN) and Congressman Gus Hawkins (D-CA) sponsored legislation in the early 1970s to do just that and in 1978 the Congress passed the Humphrey-Hawkins Full Employment and Balanced Growth Act.

The law established a maximum unemployment rate of 4 percent and did not mandate a government-paid job for anyone who sought one. It was described as the "the last gasp of the New Deal generation's struggle for economic justice," according to Randy Shannon, a progressive activist from Pennsylvania. "Its passage occurred at the beginning of the neo-liberal campaign to reverse the New Deal policies." In chronological terms this description is correct, but it also reflects the economic reality that was already visible in the slow-down of growth over the previous decade. After decades of recovery and expansion, the stagflation of the 1970s took a great deal of the momentum out of the popular confidence in the American dream. By 1978, the impact of high oil prices and the novel idea of an external constraint on American economic power created an enormous feeling of anxiety and uncertainty.

The fact that the Democrats, at this late date, were still fiddling around with the leftovers from the New Deal is a pretty tough indictment of the lack of creative thinking among the left of that era, economists or otherwise. When one pushes aside the rhetoric of the past half century and more since WWII, the United States had not managed to contribute anything more original to the sum total of thinking on the economic management than to create ever-more-ingenious forms of debt. Even the sacred "four freedoms" articulated by FDR depend upon the continuance of government in order to fulfill these promises.

In his state of the union address in 1941, FDR articulated "four freedoms," including:

- Freedom of speech and expression
- Freedom of religion
- Freedom from want
- Freedom from fear

These "four freedoms" were Roosevelt's way of reducing the bill of rights down to four simple objectives: mandates, and entitlements rather than rights and responsibilities. These "freedoms" were the promise of the corporate state and, indeed, FDR was offering these freedoms to all of the people of the world. Reflecting FDR's support for Wilson's vision of a unified community of nations, the four freedoms were the New Deal adapted for a global audience. Notice that the first two freedoms are taken from the Bill of Rights and are, in traditional American terms, rights that were extant even before the existence of government. The last two "freedoms," however, can be interpreted as statements of dependency. Freedom from want and freedom from fear are essentially the promises of safety made by the paternalistic welfare state, the very unfortunate situation in which hundreds of millions of people live today in Europe and Asia. The United Nations has adopted these goals as well.

While the American model of political economy saw free people free to live and worship as they choose, the model of the four freedoms is decidedly positivist and European in perspective. Isaiah Berlin, in his classic essay "Two Concepts of Liberty,"[12] defines negative liberty as being able to fulfill our projects without coercion, a direct analog to the American ethic of freedom or the American Dream being "life, liberty and the pursuit of happiness." Positive liberty, on the other hand, is defined by Berlin as the freedom afforded by a deterministic and oppressive regime much like the political configurations visible today in Europe and Asia. "Since liberalism has spent half a century trying to define itself against totalitarian ideologies," Stanley Hoffman observed in 1998, "these distinctions have been found very useful."[13]

The Soviets defined freedom as the right to support the Party and build Socialism. The four freedoms of FDR conjure up George Orwell's book, *1984*, where Big Brother is ever present and the reduction of vocabulary is used to limit dangerous thinking. Of course, most people forget or never knew that Orwell was hardly a conservative. In fact, he fought for the Republicans in Spain and agitated for an English socialist revolution during WWII. After the war, Orwell was a staunch supporter of the Labor Party, but always from a position that was keenly aware of the primacy of individual freedom. "The sin of nearly all left-wingers from 1933 onwards," Orwell wrote in his essay on Arthur Koestler, "is that they have wanted to be anti-Fascist without being anti-totalitarian." In a similar vein, most members of the political left in the European Union and United States do not appreciate or care that in order to "guarantee" anything resembling the four freedoms, you must embrace a totalitarian and fascist political and economic model.

Fortunately a majority of the Congress rejected the vision of Senator Humphrey and Representative Hawkins, two men who for decades made a career out of representing their respective communities in Washington. But despite their optimism about the government's ability to provide a living for any and all citizens, Humphrey–Hawkins was an attempt to legislate an economic reality that could not really be achieved. The fact that it occurred in 1978, as economic output was starting to stabilize in the United States, was not as remarkable as the fact that it took several years for the Congress to agree on the final legislation. The legislation started in 1974 as a firm and hard proposal to make the U.S. government the employer of last resort, but was altered and amended to compromise with Republicans and also President Carter.

Jimmy Carter was far more conservative and less "worldly" than the neo-Keynesian socialists who populated the Democratic Party at the end of the 1970s. The South was insulated from many social and intellectual currents prevalent in the Northern states until well into the twentieth century—among them the novel idea of deficit spending. Every state except Vermont has some form of balanced budget amendment, which is one reason why states often must cut back services dramatically in the event of a recession. State governors understood the idea of fiscal constraints, but these rules did not apply in Washington after the 1970s.

As former South Carolina Senator Ernest Hollings, who also served as governor of that state, recalled: "Every governor, every mayor, has got to pay next year's bill. He's figuring out how to keep his credit rating and pay the bills. But when we get to Washington, well, oh no, you become an economist and you've got a percent of the GNP."[14] Hollings also confirmed what politicians and economic analysts were only starting to suspect in the late 1970s, namely that the efficacy of fiscal stimulus is just about zero and that other means must be sought to encourage growth and employment. But such subjects were just starting to be discussed in a serious way as Jimmy Carter began his term as president.

When it came to spending, Jimmy Carter was far more cautious than the average for the Democratic Party in 1976. With a background as a child of the Depression and a U.S. Navy officer, he viewed deficits as a serious problem. But the harsh political realities of unemployment and gasoline rationing were making politicians in both parties on Capitol Hill desperate. At first he attempted to work with the Democrats in the Congress, but within only a matter of months

President Carter was making public his view that increased deficits would only further stoke the fires of inflation. His close friend and Budget Director, Bert Lance, was a fiscal conservative and powerful influence on Carter. Carter in his memoirs chastises himself for "the obvious inconsistency in my policy" of trying to craft further economic stimulus and also fight inflation at the same time. He would eventually resolve that "my major economic battle would be against inflation, and I would stay on the side of fiscal prudence, restricted budgets, and lower deficits."[15]

Carter was caught between the Democratic Congress and even the liberals within his own administration on the one hand, and the Federal Reserve Board under Arthur Burns on the other. The Fed had early on drawn a line regarding the trade-off between further fiscal stimulus financed with debt and higher inflation—and higher interest rates. In November of 1976, Burns said that he wanted to "cooperate" with the Carter Administration, but apparently his statement was interpreted as a warning to Carter that the Fed was prepared for a confrontation.

In so many words what Burns was saying was if the new Administration sought to promote a faster recovery by applying greater fiscal stimulus, then the Fed would raise interest rates further. From the easy money period of 1976, the Fed's tighter posture in 1977 generated tensions within the business and political communities as the tepid economic growth achieved in the previous few years began to ebb. Liberals called for increased spending and assailed the Fed for their excessive concern over inflation, but Carter stuck to his message of fiscal restraint and a focus on wasteful government spending—an almost Republican message from a former Democratic governor from Georgia.

With inflation continuing to rise, however, the debate over fiscal policy quickly began to change. After decades of Soviet-style ideology from the Democrats and their fellow travelers in the academic community in support of deficit spending, doubts were heard. Henry Hazlitt had published his classic book, *The Failure of the "New Economics": An Analysis of the Keynesian Fallacies*, in 1959, but it would take another 20 years or the reality of the link between deficit spending and inflation to become understood at a popular level.

Writer Richard Ebeling described Hazlitt's view of Keynes 35 years after the book's publication:

> The central flaw in Keynes's thinking, Hazlitt insisted, was his unwillingness to acknowledge that the high unemployment in Great Britain in the 1920s and the United States in the 1930s was caused by government intervention, including the empowering of labor unions, that made many prices and wages virtually "rigid." Political and special-interest power prevented markets from competitively re-establishing a balance between supply and demand for various goods. Hence, the market was trapped in wage and price distortions that destroyed employment and production opportunities, resulting in the Great Depression.[16]

America was and is a very young country. Until the 1970s, the United States only experienced sustained inflation during wars. There was and is even today a very limited appreciation for the link between how Washington manages or fails to manage its budget and the dollar, and the result in terms of employment and economic opportunities generally. Ford and Carter both were forced to confront this reality during a period of international upheaval and two oil price shocks.

The low-point for inflation in the United States during the 1970s would, ironically, be 1976, a fact that did not help the Ford–Dole ticket at the polls. In the years that followed the rate of price increase trended higher until inflation reached double digits in 1979. Ultimately, inflation continued to race ahead and unemployment was growing, leaving President Carter in the position of facing worsening inflation despite interest rates close to 20 percent. The deadly reality of stagflation, or growth rates below the level of inflation, brought a chilling new economic reality that would destroy the Carter presidency. (I predicted a few years ago that we would have snagflation, where the economy is just snagged at a slow growth rate, even as inflation creeps up. Now this is the new normal.)

Balanced Budgets and Inflation

In 1970 when Richard Nixon appointed Arthur Burns to succeed William McChesney Martin as head of the Federal Reserve Board, Burns was taking the reins from the Fed chairman most synonymous with sound money and monetary stability. After almost two decades at his post, Martin had done an enviable job in enhancing the standing and independence of the central bank, albeit during a time of stable economic growth and relatively low inflation. Only during the Vietnam War did Martin and the Fed Board give in to pressure from President Lyndon Johnson and the White House to keep interest rate policy easy in 1967, a decision that caused inflation to rise to over 6 percent by 1969 as Richard Nixon returned to Washington as President.

The 1950–1960s in the United States were years of torrid growth but still restrained financial markets, both domestically and internationally. The relationships between the public and private sectors, particularly between public and private debt, had also remained very stable for most of Martin's era with no crises or market scandals to disturb the appearance of Washington's intelligent design. But the artificial stability of the first two decades of the post-WWII period was about to end.

When Burns took over at the Fed in January 1970, there were already significant changes occurring in the U.S. economy and in global markets as well. But the fierce velocity and daunting breadth of the changes that occurred during the term of Arthur Burns at the Fed almost seemed the antithesis of the previous two decades under Chairman Martin. Burns had to deal with the end of the post-WWII economic order and the related changes to the U.S. economy. These changes were often not welcome to many Americans and certainly not to the major political parties.

During Chairman Burns's term at the Fed the amount of debt in the United States, both public and private, began to grow dramatically relative to the size of the real economy. Even though the amount of federal debt had grown during the Cold War, the U.S. economy had grown much faster. Initially the burden of servicing this debt actually shrank in real terms because of the high rates of economic growth. But in the 1970s the total of all non-financial debt, public and private, began to rise relative to the U.S. economy and would continue to rise in the decades that followed. Just as WWI was an important inflection point for America in its relationship with the rest of the world, the 1970s marked a point of departure for Americans in terms of how we understood and attempted to manage the changes in the economy.

When the term of Chairman Burns ended in March 1978, President Carter appointed G. William Miller, a successful businessman and investment banker who had served as the Chairman and CEO of Textron. Like Carter, Miller was a fiscal conservative but also a bit of a neo-Keynesian. He believed that the United States could grow its way out of a recession while also addressing inflationary pressures. Miller, in fact, was adopting the very "inconsistency" to which Carter would later refer in his memoirs, namely thinking you can fight inflation and grow public deficits at the same time. "Unlike his predecessor, Arthur F. Burns, who had tried to limit economic expansion in the belief that inflation was the far greater peril, Mr. Miller insisted that inflation and unemployment could be fought simultaneously," the *New York Times* observed.[17]

Within months it was clear to many that Carter made a mistake in putting Miller at the Fed. There was even a line of thinking at the time that perhaps President Carter had inadvertently picked the wrong Miller. The global markets were not impressed by Miller's talk of fighting inflation and unemployment at the same time, and the dollar dropped sharply during that fateful year. Roger Kubarych, who worked for Paul Volcker at the Federal Reserve Bank of New York, recalled the period in late 1978:

> The Carter people were beginning to realize that Miller was not fitting in. He was a CEO, not an academic collegial guy. It's like the TV ad with the firemen. The chief says: You want lower interest rates? Hands go up. Done in 15 minutes. So the Carter people approached the late Bob Roosa, of Brown Brothers Harriman and Treasury under-secretary under his pal Jack Kennedy. He said "You really should go to Volcker," then president of the Fed of New York. The White House had thought about Volcker before, but decided to go in a different direction. Miller was one of the few business CEOs who really took all of this corporate governance and responsibility seriously. He did a very fine job as secretary of the Treasury. Miller was not a bad guy, he just did not belong at the Federal Reserve Board.[18]

By July of 1979, rumors of a Cabinet reshuffling were flying around Washington and eventually appeared on the front page of the major newspapers. The dollar slumped in global markets. Gold passed $300 per ounce for the first time, illustrating just how far out of line was the official $35 per ounce gold price had become before Nixon ended convertibility only eight years earlier and a sobering indicator of the pace of inflation. The irony was that Carter's stand on reducing federal deficits in order to fight inflation may have been entirely erroneous. Because of Carter's consistent efforts to reduce federal spending, the deficit in 1979 was a mere $2.4 billion on an economy of almost $3 trillion in gross domestic product.

Whereas the inflation of the 1960s was arguably due to the fiscal policies of Presidents Kennedy and Johnson, the inflation of the 1970s was seemingly a function of external shocks from oil prices. Though few contemporary observers understood the problem at the time, the proper response to the external oil price shocks might have been a combination of fiscal stimulus, tax cuts, and oil conservation measures. The sad fact was that even if Carter had actually achieved a balanced budget, it might not have significantly reduced inflation.[19]

Carter's orthodox views on inflation and debt made it impossible for him to propose the obvious solution to the weak economy, namely tax cuts. He was so focused on balancing the budget, reflecting an almost Jacksonian obsession with purging the evil of debt and deficits. By taking a conservative line on deficits, Carter gave the issue of economic recovery to the Republicans. Carter had adopted the fiscal conventions of Gerald Ford without questioning the basic assumption that fiscal deficits were linked with inflation and in so doing associated federal deficits with rising prices.

While deficits and debt clearly had inflationary consequences, the United States and many other industrial nations were responding to the external shock of oil prices with monetary tightening and fiscal restraint, essentially the old economic playbook from the nineteenth century. With little or no consideration, Carter essentially did what conservatives had failed to do for decades, namely discredited the entire economic world of Keynesian mechanics. Iwan Morgan observed that Carter's failure to curb inflation meant that "he did not provide his party with a viable new political economy. All this worked to the advantage of his Republican opponent, who promised to replace the economics of misery with the economics of joy."[20]

At the end of July 1979, President Carter nominated Paul Volcker to become Chairman of the Federal Reserve Board. Such was the gravity of the situation in the financial markets that in just three weeks Volcker was confirmed by the Senate and sworn in on August 6, 1979. Kubarych recalled that on the day of his appointment by Jimmy Carter, Volcker kept a foreign visitor waiting for him for hours at the Federal Reserve Bank of New York. "Finally Volcker comes back apologizing profusely and meets with the visitor for a few minutes," he recalled. "Then he came out and said to me: 'Thanks for doing the meeting. We've got some work to do in the morning.' "[21]

Volcker's Shock Treatment

By October of 1979, the United States was facing its most serious economic crisis in generations. Inflation was rising and the dollar was falling. Saudi Arabia's finance minister said that his country was considering new cutbacks in oil production because of the eroding value of the dollar. Wall Street welcomed the appointment of Volcker, but the honeymoon would be especially short.

As Volcker moved from New York to Washington, statisticians at the Labor Department confirmed that over the previous six months the U.S. has experienced the steepest spiral of inflation in nearly 30 years. But more disturbing were the comments seen more and more in the media and in the political discourse of a nation living on the accumulated wealth of yesterday. Concerns about foreign trade and offshore competition were growing especially sharp in Washington during this period and would increase in the 1980s. In 1979 with the Iranian hostage crisis as a backdrop, Americans worried about losing their economic edge in the world; that the situation might be too far gone to correct. The income of the average American household had doubled during the 1970s, but real purchasing power had risen only one-tenth that amount. For many Americans, the reality of the two-income household was already becoming the norm.

The inflation of the dollar was widely seen as the villain in the global economic bust, which had seen a series of mini-crises erupt after the Nixon decision in 1971. The dollar slid dramatically over the decade prior to the appointment of Paul Volcker as Fed Chairman. He had been deeply involved in managing the process, first at Treasury and then at the Fed of New York. Bringing Volcker to Washington to lead the Federal Reserve Board was the perfect move at the right time, but one that occurred only because of the intervention of a number of people, including Tony Solomon. Kubarych relates how Tony Solomon, who served in the Treasury as Under Secretary for Monetary Affairs, was tasked by Mike Blumenthal and Charlie Schultz with convincing Jimmy Carter to appoint Paul Volcker to the Fed. Solomon succeeded and took over for Volker as President of the Fed of New York, a fitting culmination to a remarkable career of public service.[22]

The Volcker appointment also allowed President Carter to replace Treasury Secretary Michael Blumethal with Fed Chairman Miller, an arrangement that was far better suited to the latter's talents. Miller would lead the federal bailout for Chrysler. Miller was better suited for politics than the world of the central bank, which in those days was seen as being "above politics." This meant, of course, that the Fed was entirely political, but in a covert and nonconfrontational way. Miller was far too honest and direct for the world of central banking. In July 1979 just prior to his move to Treasury, he announced to the Congress that there would be no changes in monetary policy for the rest of the year. Volcker, on the other hand, was an economist and knew how to behave like one in public—namely, to be vague, non-committal, and inoffensive in a political sense.

Volcker needed all of his considerable credibility to convince the world that the United States had not lost its way. Since 1971, foreign nations had accumulated tens of billions of dollars in offshore deposits— Eurodollars—and they were anxious about further erosion in value. As already noted, under Fed Chairmen like Burns and even Martin, the Fed had responded to political pressure to lean in favor or ease at critical periods. Volcker had to do the opposite and govern monetary policy by a clearer set of rules in order to help the U.S. Treasury and the dollar regain the respect of the world markets.

In late August of 1979 the Federal Open Market Committee raised the federal funds rate from 10 percent to 10.5 percent, a record. The Fed would continue to keep policy tight, driving the U.S. economy into recession in 1980. The Fed paused in its efforts to throttle inflation prior to the 1980 election, but when prices started to again rise—by now inflation was 1 percent per month and mounting—Volcker and the Federal Open Market Committee took U.S. interest rates up until the Federal funds rate almost reached 20 percent. "It was only after the election, when Volcker knew that Carter had lost, that he really clamped down on the money supply," argues Bruce Bartlett. "This illustrates an important point: Presidents get the Fed policy they want, no matter how 'independent' the Fed may be."[23]

Independent or not, Volcker and the Federal Open Market Committee in 1980–1981 put the U.S. economy into a wrenching recession that would see unemployment soar into double digits. In heartland manufacturing states such as Indiana, Michigan, and Illinois joblessness reached into the teens. The U.S. economy was mired in recession for three years. This illustrated the level of adjustment that the two oil price increases of the decade, 1973 and 1979, required literally to squeeze the inflationary *increases* out of the system. The United States was unable to remove the impact of the oil shocks, but could merely slow the rate of increases in prices by brutally suppressing the economy.

In a 1982 memo from Paul Krugman and Larry Summers, who were both then working in the Reagan White House, to William Poole and Martin Feldstein, the two economists predicted that inflation would again begin to accelerate because the reduction in inflation engineered by the Fed was only temporary. But Summers, Krugman, and many other liberal economists were wrong. In fact the relentless rate squeeze by the Fed and a lot of positively coincidental and mostly external trends broke the inflation in the United States, but did not really instill fiscal sobriety. But Paul Volcker broke the momentum of inflation and also took sufficient demand out of the economy to give the crucial impression of price stability.

The underlying rate of inflation, represented by internal prices in the United States and the value of the dollar, remained high enough so that, in real terms, the cost of energy and particularly oil dropped for almost two decades to the end of the twentieth century. While the dollar rallied sharply from 1980 through 1985 because of the towering interest rate regime imposed by Volcker and the resulting rebound in U.S. standing with global investors, the overall trend continued to be one of steady inflation of the dollar and decreased purchasing power for U.S. consumers—except in the case of oil.

In fact, because of the dollar's gradual decline after 1985, in real terms adjusted for inflation, energy prices would not reach the levels of the early 1980s again until well into the 2000s. This decrease in the real cost of energy prices added a deflationary bias to this entire period of U.S. economic history, a rare positive factor at a time of secular consumer and producer price inflation. Indeed, the period after the mid-2000s, when real energy prices in the United States began to rise rapidly, may be an important reason for the sluggish economic growth and barren job market seen after the 2008 financial crisis.

The other important change that came about as Volcker took over at the Fed was the growing imbalance in the U.S. financial relationship with the world. Until the 1980s, the United States supplied as much capital to the world as foreigners invested in the United States, a remarkable balance that has been the subject of a great deal of scholarly research. Benjamin Friedman asked the key question coming out of this period in a March 1987 paper for the National Bureau of Economic Research, namely "Does the continuing large federal government deficit impair the economy's ability to undertake productive capital formation?"[24]

Economists on the left and the right would debate this issue during the 1980s, but it is fair to say that none of the political or financial observers in that period imagined that the imbalances between public and private debt, and between what the United States owes the world and American investments abroad, would grow so great. "The sharply changed relationship since 1980 between total debt and income in the U.S. economy—and, within the total, between the respective debt of the economy's public and private sectors—presents such a puzzle, and correspondingly provides an opportunity," Friedman concluded.[25]

"In 1981 Ronald Reagan entered the White House and immediately implemented a dramatic new economic policy agenda for the country that was dubbed 'Reaganomics,'" noted the CATO Institute in 1996. "Reaganomics consisted of four key elements to reverse the high-inflation, slow-growth economic record of the 1970s: (1) a restrictive monetary policy designed to stabilize the value of the dollar and end runaway inflation; (2) a 25-percent across-the-board tax cut enacted (The Economic Recovery Tax Act of 1981) designed to spur savings, investment, work, and economic efficiency; (3) a promise to balance the budget through domestic spending restraint; and (4) an agenda to roll back government regulation."[26]

Unfortunately, other than cutting taxes, the Reagan Administration did not accomplish any of these other objectives. The monetary policy followed by Paul Volcker was only restrictive until the visible rate of inflation was knocked back down to low single digits. Through the 1980s, the Fed continued to tolerate underlying inflation that was arguably mid-single digits per year. The Reagan promise to deregulate was fulfilled, but in the case of the financial services reforms created the circumstances for future financial crises. These crises were made inevitable because Reagan and the presidents who came before and after his eight years in office found it impossible to rein in spending. No amount of tax cuts will save American consumers from the ravages of inflation if Congress refuses to eliminate fiscal deficits. Even Ronald Reagan, with all of his rhetoric about scaling back the size of government, was reluctant to pay the political price of confronting Congress over spending. The bubble economy was simply passed to the next generation.

The Crisis Managers

Volcker, a self-described "Brooklyn Democrat" who was born in Cape May, N.J., was inherited by Ronald Reagan, a converted Democrat and former labor leader and California governor. Reagan understood the connection between money and inflation. During a talk to the Prosperity Caucus in Washington in the early 1990s, syndicated columnist Robert Novak revealed that Reagan's favorite economist was Fredric Bastiat, a nineteenth-century French economic philosopher and author of *The Law*. It was the fact of inflation that led to the defeat of Gerald Ford and Jimmy Carter, and created groundwork for the election of Ronald Reagan.

Such was the state of the U.S. economy in 1981 that, for the next several years, the Reagan White House wisely and expediently let Volcker take the heat on inflation, while advancing the conservative political agenda on Capitol Hill. The Kemp–Roth tax cuts, deregulation of the oil industry, and a tough attitude toward organized labor were all part of breaking the embedded public psychology of inflation. Paul Samuelson explained that many observers of the post-WWII period missed the importance of inflation in the American narrative, a story that was fundamental to the career of Paul Volcker and many other financial professionals with whom he worked:

> We have arrived at the end of a roughly half-century economic cycle dominated by inflation, for good and ill. Its rise and fall constitute one of the great upheavals of our time, though one largely forgotten and misunderstood. From 1960 to 1979, annual U.S. inflation increased from a negligible 1.4 percent to 13.3 percent. By 2001 it had receded to 1.6 percent, almost exactly what it had been in 1960. For this entire period, inflation's climb and collapse exerted a dominant influence over the economy's successes and failures. It also shaped, either directly or indirectly, how Americans felt about themselves and their society; how they voted and the nature of their politics; how businesses operated and treated their workers; and how the American economy was connected with the rest of the world.[27]

One of the symptoms of the increasing inflation visible in the United States in the 1970s and 1980s was volatility in the financial markets and, with this volatility, greater opportunities for financial crises and the failure of large banks. Because his institutional experience extended back to the Nixon Administration and the eventual surrender to the inflationary pressures that were already building, Volcker understood the monetary and fiscal roots of the crises that erupted during his tenure at the Federal Reserve. Volcker formed one of his most important relationships during those years with a young economist then at the Fed of New York named E. Gerald Corrigan. Corrigan would become Volcker's heir as crisis manager at the Fed and would succeed Tony Solomon as President of the Federal Reserve Bank of New York. Even after his departure from the New York Fed post in 1993, Corrigan would continue to exert great influence over the U.S. financial markets.

Corrigan's unlikely rise to the top of the American financial system started in 1976 when as corporate secretary of the New York Fed he was befriended by then-President Volcker. Other senior officers of the New York Reserve Bank still were a bit standoffish toward Volcker because of policy disagreements, most notably, after America's abandonment of gold for international settlements at Camp David in August 1971. Corrigan extended himself for the new Fed president and quickly became his trusted adviser and friend. Corrigan was the man doing the difficult jobs behind the scenes as Volcker attracted the public limelight as the supreme crisis manager.

When Volcker was appointed Fed Chairman late in the summer of 1979, Corrigan followed him to Washington as the chairman's aide and hands-on situation manager, although he remained on the New York Fed's payroll and was subsequently promoted. He was quickly thrown into the crisis control fray when Bunker and Herbert Hunt's attempt to manipulate the silver market blew up into a $1.3 billion disaster in 1980.

In May of that year, Chairman Volcker was compelled to make a statement about Fed awareness of the Hunt brothers' attempts to corner the silver markets, including an admission that the Fed had asked banks to cease "speculative lending." Volcker also confirmed that the Federal Open Market Committee had taken into account concern about speculation in silver and other commodities as part of its decision to tighten monetary policy further. Volcker's statement regarding the Hunt brothers was one of the first and most direct admissions by the Fed of an active interest in overseeing the financial markets, even though Volcker would go out of his way to disavow any particular interest in these modern-day successors to Jay Gould. The collapse of the Hunt brothers' commodity pool affected other legitimate enterprises and lenders. It was a side effect of the boom in metals that the inflation spawned and was one of the first modern "systemic" crises in the post-WWII era.

Corrigan managed the unwinding of silver positions, providing the moral suasion necessary to convince reluctant banks to furnish credit to brokers who made bad loans to the Hunts to finance their silver purchases. In 1982, when Drysdale Government Securities collapsed, Corrigan was again the man on the scene to do the cleanup job, working to avoid the worst effects of one of the ugliest financial debacles in the postwar period. Drysdale was the first in a series of shocks during the 1980s that included the Mexican debt default (1982) and the collapse of Penn Square Bank (1982) and Continental Illinois (1984).

Drysdale threatened not only the workings of the government securities market, but the stability of a major money center bank, Chase Manhattan, which saw its stock plummet when rumors began to fly as to the magnitude of losses. Volcker was a former employee of Chase and had spent a good bit of his early career as a research officer at the bank. Corrigan fashioned a combination of Fed loans of cash and collateral, and other expedients, to make the crisis slowly disappear, even as Volcker again received public credit for meeting the crisis.

The Latin Debt Crisis

In 1982 Mexico devalued its currency and defaulted on $80 billion in public sector debt, an event that almost caused the world financial system to collapse. The growth in foreign lending by U.S. banks, which was virtually nonexistent only a decade before, made these institutions vulnerable in a new and unexpected way. "Under the leadership of Fed Chairman Paul Volcker," researcher Walker Todd wrote in 1999, "a temporizing strategy was devised under which the bank lent new funds to the debtors, who then repaid the same amounts to lenders to cover interest payments falling due. Principal owed was never reduced (in fact, it usually increased)."[28]

Yet the cost of fixing the 1982 financial crisis was tiny, a couple billion dollars, petty cash compared to the looming default on tens of billions of dollars worth of hard currency obligations of private Mexican companies and banks. When Mexico defaulted in August 1982, the Reagan Administration immediately extended $2 billion in order to refloat the country's battered economy and insure a smooth political transition for the new government of Miguel de la Madrid. Another $2 billion came from the Commodity Credit Corp. and U.S. commitments to buy Mexican oil for the Strategic Petroleum Reserve.

Through the mid-1980s, foreign banks refused new money to Mexico and even pressed demands for repayment, although the IMF and other multilateral agencies continued to lend. A steady flow of new money loans from multilateral agencies, as well as direct investment flows, kept Mexico's single-party state afloat for the balance of the decade. By 1987, net flows of capital from Mexico back to its creditors in the industrial world were actually positive as it slowly repaid its hard currency debts. Unlike the United States, Mexico could not merely print money to fund its external obligations.

In 1987, Brazil declared a moratorium on foreign loans and Washington feared that Mexico would follow. The larger banks, led by Citibank and J.P. Morgan, reluctantly began to reserve against the eventual write-off of loans to Mexico and other debtor nations. Federal Reserve Chairman Paul Volcker, a fierce opponent of debt forgiveness and making the banks write down bad loans, left his post later that year. In the July 1988 elections, Carlos Salinas de Gortari was defeated by Cuauhtemoc Cardenas Solorzano. Through electoral fraud and another $1 billion "bridge loan" from Washington to the De la Madrid government in August of that year, Salinas prevented Cardenas, the son of nationalist hero General Lazaro Cardenas, from taking office and fulfilling his vow to repudiate Mexico's then $105 billion in foreign debt.

The impact of the debt crisis on American consumers was, very simply, more inflation. The Fed had to maintain an easy monetary stance through much of the period in order to help the largest banks regain profitability. It is interesting to note that none of the member banks in the New York Clearing House was able to issue new equity between 1982 and 1989, when Treasury Secretary Nicholas Brady put aside the policy of temporizing on Latin debt embraced by Chairman Volcker and Treasury Secretary James Baker.

In February 1989, food riots in Venezuela caused nervous bankers and their servants in Washington to capitulate on the issue of repayment and extend new loans. The abortive debt reduction plan named for then-Treasury Secretary Nicholas Brady was completed roughly a year later. It afforded Mexico little real debt relief, but did provide the first substantial new money in almost seven years. The Brady Plan was followed with a proposal for a "free trade" agreement by former CIA director and then-President George H.W. Bush.

More than 15 years before, when he worked in the oil business in Texas and Mexico, Bush had built a close personal relationship with Salinas and his father, Raul Salinas Lozano, the power behind the state oil monopoly, Pemex. There are those who believe that George Bush was in fact a CIA asset through all of his years in the oil business, his congressional campaigns, ambassadorships, and eventually as director of central intelligence. Thus his attention to Mexico and close political contacts in that country, and Bush's eventual pursuit of a free trade agreement with Mexico, make a great deal of geopolitical sense in terms of helping to stabilize that country.[29]

The Latin Debt crisis illustrates how Paul Volcker and many of his contemporaries laid the intellectual and practical foundations for policies such as "too big to fail" for the largest banks. The tendency to bail out large financial institutions and eventually whole countries in the 2008–2010 period dates from the late 1970s and the tenure of Paul Volcker at the Fed and James Baker at Treasury. Whether one speaks of the WWI and WWII loans to Europe or the bad foreign debts of the largest banks, Washington's tendency in the twentieth century was to paper over the problem with more debt and inflation.

The 1980s also illustrates that while many analysts in that era, including the author, despaired of Mexico, Brazil, and other "developing" nations such as Russia ending their dependence on foreign borrowing and loans from the IMF, in fact all of the debtor nations have repaid their debts or at least ended their reliance on new borrowing. Mexico, Brazil, China, and many of the emerging industrial nations today have no need to issue foreign debt or use the facilities of the IMF. Indeed, it is the older, more developed and less dynamic economies, such as the European Union and the United States, where debt and inflation are now chronic problems. Meeting the challenge of providing growth and managing a rising debt load in the United States is the task of a cadre of American officials who began their careers in the 1970s and 1980s fighting debt crises overseas.

By 1982 Volcker, who was by then supervising the unfolding Penn Square situation, pushed for Corrigan to take the open presidency of the Minneapolis Fed. Corrigan was president of the Minneapolis Federal Reserve Bank for four and a half years before moving to the New York Fed. Volcker later admitted wanting to keep the badly insolvent Penn Square open for fear of wider market effects, but the Federal Deposit Insurance Corporation closed down the now infamous Oklahoma bank, paying out only on insured deposits. Comptroller of the Currency C.T. Conover told Congress in December 1982 that

Penn Square bank's failure was inevitable, but the fact remains that Volcker, Corrigan, and other Fed officials would have rescued the badly insolvent lender.

In his 2010 book *Senseless Panic: How Washington Failed America*, former FDIC Chairman William Isaac confirms that Mike Bradfield, then general counsel of the Fed and until recently in the same position at the FDIC, demanded that the FDIC bail out Penn Square Bank, no doubt with the knowledge of Volcker and other Fed governors. Isaac responded that he would if the central bank shared the cost, but the Fed balked.[30]

As Volcker promoted Corrigan's career within the Fed, he took extraordinary measures to prevent the nomination or appointment of respected conservative economists and free market advocates like W. Lee Hoskins and Jerry L. Jordan to head other Reserve Banks. Both Hoskins and later Jordan were appointed to the Cleveland Reserve Bank's presidency after Volcker's departure as Chairman in 1987. Hoskins in particular was the antithesis of Volcker, an unrepentant exponent of conservative, sound money theory. Hoskins advocated making zero inflation a national goal. Volcker and the more liberal economists who had controlled the Fed for decades were against excessive inflation, but more than happy to tolerate visible inflation of two percent if it got the country close to full employment.

Hoskins left the Cleveland Fed in 1992 to become president of the Huntington Bank. He and other free market exponents believed that ill-managed banks should be allowed to fail and that federal deposit insurance hurts rather than protects the financial system by allowing banks to take excessive risks that are, in effect, subsidized by the American taxpayer. This free market perspective, which represented mainstream American economic thought before the New Deal, is at odds with the Volcker–Corrigan view of avoiding "systemic risk" via public subsidies for large banks and other, more generalized types of government intervention in the "private" marketplace.

Reagan Reappoints Volcker

In his book *Maestro*,[31] Bob Woodward describes how the Reagan inner circle believed that they needed to keep Volcker at the Fed in 1983 because of the turmoil in the financial markets caused over the previous year. But the actual reappointment of Volcker was a more problematic process than is generally appreciated. Volcker had a one-year head start on Reagan in terms of managing the economy. Nobody in the Reagan group was paying attention to the politics of the Fed and what the consequences of a V-shaped recession and likely 10 percent unemployment would be for a new president.

Some members of the Reagan kitchen cabinet periodically would meet with Volcker to better understand the timing of the inevitable recession and what the impact of the high anti-inflation interest rates would be on the economy. The general assumption in Washington in early 1980 was that Carter would be re-elected and that Reagan was, in Volcker's words, "just an actor." But Volcker was soon made aware of the fact that Reagan was going to win the election and that the Fed Chairman needed to start managing the expectations of the new political leadership.[32]

Volcker was crucially important to Reagan because he had been on the job fighting the key economic battle of the time. With the encouragement of several people around Reagan, Volcker decided to call Reagan long before the election decision and Reagan at once returned the call. The connection enabled Reagan to better appreciate how dire the economic situation really was and to direct his Cabinet to act accordingly. Former Regan adviser Richard Whalen recalls the inside politics of the appointment and re-appointment of Paul Volcker:

> The Volcker appointment was a source of great unhappiness to all kinds of people, including Donald T. Regan, who had been my first client as a consultant many years earlier when he was CEO at Merrill Lynch. Walter Guzzardi and I had both been assisting managing editors at *Fortune*. He became the inside guy at Merrill and I was the outside guy at Merrill. We guided Don Regan, who was an arrogant SOB, ex-Marine colonel, through the minefield of creating the SIPC and burying some of the bodies from various Wall Street firm failures that occurred during the 1970s. He called me one day in the 1980s and said "Dick, I've been asked to become Secretary of the Treasury." And I said, "I know, you're on the list." So he said, "What should I do?" And I said, "If you want it, take it, but for Christ's sake stay away from Nancy Reagan and do not mess around with the Fed. Those are my terms if you want my

help." So soon after Volcker had done this brilliant job of saving the economy and making it possible for Reagan to have a successful first term, [Don] Regan tried to impose Beryl Sprinkel as the new [Fed] chairman. I had to go around Don Regan to Senator Paul Laxalt (R–NV) to carry my recommendation to the President. It was just Laxalt, Reagan and the wives at Camp David. I urged Reagan to call Paul Volcker that Sunday night and ask him to accept reappointment as Chairman of the Fed. I gave Paul Laxalt the telephone number and the call occurred and Volcker stayed on at the Fed until 1987. Laxalt called me that Monday and thanked me for taking the initiative on this. And I thought is this the way these things always happen?[33]

Roger Kubarych noted that the group of Reagan conservatives who were in control of the administration by 1987, intended to get the Democrat Volcker next time. "And then we had 17 years of the good and the bad Alan Greenspan, Kubarych observed."

Volcker moved to protect his bureaucratic flank in 1984 when he nominated Gerald Corrigan as a replacement for Anthony Solomon as president at the New York Fed, an event that required almost as much lobbying as was later needed to block the appointment of Lee Hoskins to head the St. Louis Fed in 1986. The cigar-chomping Fed chairman, who was known for his affable nature, got on a plane to hold a rare Sunday meeting of the St. Louis Fed's board. He reportedly pounded the table and warned of being outnumbered by Reagan-era free market-zealots if the board picked Hoskins. Volcker, it seems, may have still expected to be re-nominated by Reagan. The St. Louis Fed's board caved in to Volcker's demands and Hoskins was passed over, although he would be appointed President of the Cleveland Fed in late 1987, after Volcker no longer was Federal Reserve Board Chairman.

Corrigan's impending selection as Fed of New York President late in 1984 caused several conservative line officers and research officials to flee the New York Reserve Bank. Roger Kubarych, who was one of the deputy heads of research in New York and a widely respected economist on Wall Street, actually resigned the day Corrigan's appointment was formally announced, fulfilling an earlier vow not to serve under Volcker's apprentice that symbolized earlier internal Fed disputes.

Following the 1985 Plaza Accord when the United States and other industrial nations attempted to depreciate the dollar, Corrigan would often appear in the domestic and foreign exchange trading rooms at all hours of the day or night during periods of market intervention. In the mid-1980s, the Fed of New York was open 24-7 because of the cash and clearing operations. The young traders and analysts in the foreign exchange and domestic trading function often worked round the clock. During the market intervention to push down the value of the dollar in 1985 known as the Plaza Accord, there were many times the author would see Corrigan on deck in the foreign exchange trading room at the crack of dawn to check market rates.

The Neverending Crisis

From the first day he took over as head of the New York Fed in 1985, Corrigan's chief priority was "managing" the Latin debt crisis and in particular its devastating effects on the New York money center banks. Even in the late 1980s, most scholars and government officials admitted that loans to countries like Brazil, Argentina, and Mexico would have to be written off, as J.P. Morgan did in 1989. But Corrigan continued to push for new lending to indebted countries in an effort to bolster the fiction that loans made earlier could still be carried at par or book value, 100 cents on the dollar. Even by the early 1990s, when some analysts declared the debt crisis to be over, the secondary market bid prices for Latin debt ranged from 65 cents for Mexico to 45 cents for Argentina and 25 cents for Brazil.

"Anything approaching a 'forced' write-down of even a part of the debt—no matter how well dressed up—seems to me to run the risks of inevitably and fatally crushing the prospects for fresh money financing that is so central to growth prospects of the troubled [less developed countries (LDCs)] and to the ultimate restoration of their credit standing," Corrigan wrote in the New York Fed *Quarterly Review* in 1988. "A debt strategy that cannot hold out the hope of renewed debtor access to market sources of external finance is no strategy at all."

And of course, in the case of Mexico, debt relief was followed by massive new lending and short-term investment, albeit to finance a growing external trade imbalance that was strikingly similar to the import surge that preceded the 1982 debt default. Likewise bankrupt Russia, which was supposedly cut off from new Western credit, received almost $18 billion in new Western loans in 1992–1993—loans guaranteed by the taxpayers of the G-7 countries and facilitated by Corrigan.

But in addition to pressing for new loans to LDC countries, Corrigan worked hard at home to manage the debt crisis, bending accounting rules, delaying and even intervening in the closing of bank examinations, resisting regulatory initiatives such as market value accounting for banks' investment securities portfolios, and initially promoting the growth of the interbank loans, swaps, and other designer "derivative" assets traded in the growing, unregulated over-the-counter (OTC) market. In particular, Corrigan played a leading role in affording regulatory forbearance to a number of large banks with fatal levels of exposure to heavily indebted countries in Latin America. But no member of the New York Clearing House received more special treatment than Citibank.

Former Citicorp chairman Walter Wriston said that sovereign nations don't go bankrupt, in response to questions about his bank's extensive financial risk exposure because of lending in Latin America. His supreme confidence in the eventual outcome of the Latin debt crisis was credible because he and other financiers knew that senior Fed officials like Volcker and Corrigan would do their best to blunt the impact of bad loans on the balance sheets and income statements of major banking institutions. In 1989, for example, as Wriston's successor, John Reed, was in Buenos Aires negotiating a debt-for-equity swap to reduce his bank's credit exposure in Argentina, Corrigan pressured bank examiners in New York to keep open the bank's examination for 14 months.

Corrigan's decision probably was made in order to avoid charges against earnings by forcing the bank to post higher reserves against its illiquid Third World loan portfolio, an action that would later be taken anyway as Argentina slid further down the slope of inflation and political chaos. It is significant to note that Corrigan and other officials pushed the Baker plan after 1985, essentially a new money lending program, to help buy time for commercial banks—as Volcker, the

Chase alumnus, did before him. Indeed, because of its debt-reduction aspects there remains doubt as to whether Corrigan even fully endorsed the abortive Brady Plan, which sought to reduce the debts of Latin nations through forgiveness and restructuring.

Paul Volcker has never been a hawk on bank regulation and especially with respect to the largest banks. His concern with the well being of the financial system essentially made the argument for bailing out particular banks. The good of the many, to borrow the old phrase, was more important than market discipline for the one failed institution, even if that meant embracing public subsidies and moral hazard writ large. In a very real sense, Paul Volcker and not Gerry Corrigan was the father of "too big to fail" with respect to the largest U.S. banks.

Apart from fighting inflation, Volcker's legacy to the Fed was to support and enhance the tendency of the central bank to bail out large banks. But the actions of both Volcker and Corrigan were driven by the growing reliance of America on inflation and debt; but they compounded the problem. When the Salomon Brothers market-rigging scandal erupted in the spring and summer of 1991, Corrigan was again the key man on the scene to manage the fallout from the debacle. Following 1986, when regulatory responsibility for the government bond market had been explicitly given to the SEC, the Fed, at Corrigan's instruction, largely curtailed its surveillance of the market for Treasury debt, particularly the informal "when-issued" market in Treasury paper before each auction.

When the Salomon scandal broke open, it was apparent that the hands-on "management" of markets publicly championed by Volcker and Corrigan failed to prevent one of the great financial scandals of the century. "Neither in Washington nor in New York did the Fed seem aware that the dangers of failure to supervise this market had grown exponentially in 1991," Martin Mayer wrote on the Salomon debacle in his 1993 book *Nightmare on Wall Street*. "Like the Federal Home Loan Bank Board in its pursuit of making the S&Ls look solvent in 1981–1982, the Fed had adopted tunnel-vision policies to save the nation's banks. And just as excessive kindness to S&Ls in the early 1980s had drawn to the trough people who should not have been in the thrift business, Fed monetary policies in the early 1990s created a carnival in the government bond business."[34]

The Salomon crisis was not the only problem facing the central bank in 1991. During December of 1990, the Federal Reserve Bank of New York, working in concert with several private institutions, fashioned a rescue package for Chase Manhattan Bank when markets refused to lend money to the troubled banking giant. While Chase officials vociferously denied that any bailout had occurred, the pattern of discount window loans during the period and off-the-record statements by officials at the Fed and several private banks suggest very strongly that Corrigan's personal intervention prevented a major banking crisis at the end of 1990 and the peak of the S&L crisis.

Rational observers would agree that the collapse of a major banking institution is not a desirable outcome, but the larger, more fundamental issue is whether any private bank, large or small, should be subject to the discipline of the marketplace. The same issues of moral hazard and "too big to fail" that have been the subject of fierce debate and reform legislation in the Congress during 2009 and 2010 have their roots in crises two decades earlier. In the case of Salomon Brothers, Citibank, Chase, and numerous other smaller institutions that received government help in the 1990s, when the question is asked: Should these banks have been allowed to fail? Corrigan, like Volcker before him, answered with a resounding "no" and thereby failed the public trust.

Volcker Exits, Volatility Returns

In June of 1987, Volcker's term was ending, much as it began, with the dollar weak and the world uncertain about the direction of the U.S. economy. While Volcker was able to get inflation under control, he was not able to stabilize the dollar or work out a better means for the management of global markets. "He was brought in to help stabilize the dollar," Lee Hoskins told the *Los Angeles Times* in 1987. "Now after record highs and a steep decline, he was leaving the dollar in the same condition in which he found it—weak. But he saw that the major issue was inflation, and he turned it around."[35]

During the Volcker era, budget deficits had been a fact of life, but the outstanding debt of the U.S. Treasury, inclusive of the obligations of the trust funds, was growing very rapidly, as shown in Figure 8.2.

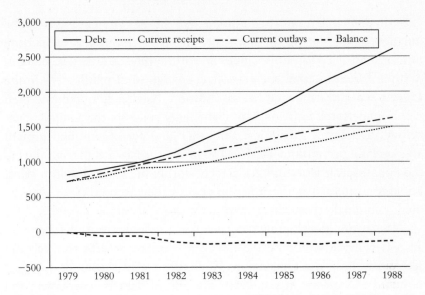

Figure 8.2 Federal Debt, Outlays, Receipts, and Balance (1979–1988)
(Millions of $)
Source: Office of Management and Budget.

The other factor that contributed to the growth in the total debt of the U.S. Treasury was the relatively high level of interest rates during much of this period, some years well into double digits. Since the United States never actually ran a surplus during the 1980s period to retire any debt and averaged deficits over $100 billion, the growth in the overall corpus of public and internal debt was greatly accelerated by these years of high interest rates.

The high inflation years of the 1980s and the growing public debt also produced greater and greater official sensitivity to the public's perception of inflation. "Government statistics are about the last place one should look to find inflation, as they are designed to not show much," investment manager David Einhorn argued in a May 26, 2010 *New York Times* commentary. "Over the last 35 years the government has changed the way it calculates inflation several times. According to the Web site Shadow Government Statistics, using the pre-1980 method, the Consumer Price Index would be over 9 percent, compared with about 2 percent in the official statistics today."[36]

One of the chief methods used by government officials to mask the true rate of inflation is to use estimates of the "core rate" of inflation, excluding volatile items such as food and energy. The net effect of the inflation of the late 1970s and really all of the 1980s was to increase official sensitivity to public disclosure of the rate of inflation, but this did not diminish either the rate of accumulation of public debt in the United States nor the true rate of inflation. As already noted, the high rate of underlying inflation kept real energy prices in the United States below 1973 levels for almost three decades. Real economic growth averaged 3.2 percent during the Reagan years versus 2.8 percent during the Ford–Carter years and 2.1 percent during the Bush–Clinton years, but this assumes that the inflation figures used to adjust the government's nominal economic growth statistics are accurate.

The major development during the 1990s under Fed Chairman Alan Greenspan would be the rise of private sector debt to levels not seen since the Great Depression. While the use of consumer debt had returned and grown in the 1950s, the use of debt by consumers and private businesses had been very restrained through the late 1970s. From 1947 through 1974, for example, total loans to consumers by all U.S. banks tracked by the Federal Reserve Board grew from $4 billion to just under $100 billion. Given the low level of private debt at the end of the war and the sharp increase in GDP over three decades, the growth rate is not that remarkable.

Over the next ten years the amount of outstanding consumer debt would double to over $200 billion and would double again between 1984 and 1994. More telling than the rise of consumer debt was the overall increase in the use of credit in the U.S. economy. From the appointment of Alan Greenspan to the Fed in 1987 through to the banking crisis in 2007, the total credit outstanding in the United States as a percentage of gross domestic product rose from a little over 100 percent to over 230 percent—more than the pre-Depression peak in 1929.[37]

The key drivers of this increase were the boom in the housing market and the related explosion in mortgage and consumer debt. But the more significant point is that debt was growing much faster than the economy, suggesting that future inflation will be significantly higher. "When I boil what I've learned all down to one factor that drives the markets and an economy, it is debt," Jerry Flum, CEO of Credit Risk Monitor observed. "Every dollar of debt moves a future purchase into the present. As credit grows we spend more of it now.[38]

So, if you look at debt versus gross domestic product, we are already at record levels. We can also look at incremental debt versus incremental gross domestic product. In the 1950s, it took $1.50 in debt to produce an incremental $1 of GDP. Today it takes more than $6 in debt to produce $1 of GDP, so we are approaching the end of the game."

From Excess to Delusion

Harvard professor Elizabeth Warren, in her book *The Two-Income Trap*,[39] describes part of the changes in the behavior of Americans that began in the late 1980s and accelerated into the 1990s, namely the use of two-family incomes to make better homes with better, safer schools and amenities possible for more Americans. The national obsession with home ownership began after WWII with the GI Bill. By the late 1970s, the housing industry began to evolve into a replacement for the defense industry as an engine of growth—and debt. Just as consumers were taught to want the better job or car or washing machine, the better home in the better neighborhood with the better school district became the new definition of the American dream.

This progression to "housing industrial complex" in wartime parlance started to mature in the 1980s, when the first major real estate bubble was revealed and burst by the Fed's tight interest rate policies. The combination of direct government support for affordable housing, active advocacy, and credit availability by government-sponsored enterprises such as Fannie Mae and Freddie Mac and intense lobbying and marketing efforts by the real estate, home building, banking, and mortgage lending industries, created the circumstances for the subprime bust of 2007–2010. That bust had its roots in the savings and loan crisis of the late 1980s and the end of the first modern real estate recession in the United States.

During a 2008 interview at the height of the financial crisis, Robert Feinberg, a veteran Washington consultant and observer of Capitol Hill, put the growth of the real estate lobby in historical context:

When I first started working on the Hill in the early 1970s, there was a conservative Democrat on the Education and

Labor Committee named Edith Green who coined the term
"Education and Labor Industrial Complex" to describe what
she was up against regarding education policy. Starting about that
same time there developed what I call the Homebuilder-Realtor-
Mortgage Banker Industrial Complex. They created a mythology
that said you could not have enough housing and it was up to the
government to make sure that happened. The home builders had
a quota of 2 million units that had to be constructed every year.
They really didn't care what happened to those homes once they
were built . . . You must remember that 95 percent of what you
hear in Washington is pure propaganda and is not even believed
by the people propagating it, so don't feel bad about hurt feelings.
People in Washington say that nobody saw this crisis coming, but
there were clear signs of trouble for anyone looking.[40]

The respected housing finance expert Josh Rosner told the story of
the real estate bust in September 2007:

The reasons for the boom in housing in the past decade come
from the structural changes in the housing industry over a decade before. Most of these changes were a result of the 1980s
recession. We came out of the economic slump and a lot of
the industry players had lost their shirts in the S&L crisis. We
saw Fannie Mae insolvent on a mark-to-market basis in 1986
and that was largely because of the portfolio of foreclosed real
estate. We saw housing in 1993 and 1994 with home ownership rates stagnant, in fact exactly where they were at the
beginning of the 1980s. Home ownership rates have consistently ranged in this country between 62 and 64 percent during the post-WWII period, and yet affordability had actually
locked people out.[41]

Rosner argues that the "problem" of home affordability saw the
creation of the largest public–private partnership to date, started as
the National Partners in Home Ownership in 1994. Supported by the
realtors, the home builders, Fannie, Freddie, the mortgage bankers,
and HUD, the push to make housing more affordable was a massive
effort, with more than 1,500 public and private participants.

The stated goal of the push for affordable housing was to reach all-time high home ownership levels by the end of the century. And the stated strategy proposal to reach that goal, says Rosner, was: "to increase creative financing methods for mortgage origination." He continues:

> By 1995 we saw home prices start to rise and home ownership levels also start to rise. How did we do that? There was no private label mortgage market at that point. We were really dealing in a world of government-sponsored debt from Fannie and Freddie. We saw most of the features of the subprime debacle, such as CDOs and structured assets, that we now see as atrocious or irresponsible or poor risk management, starting in the enterprise markets. We saw changes in the loan-to-value ratios, changes from manual underwriting to automated underwriting. The new, automated approval models used were easy to game. We saw reductions in documentation requirements. We saw changes for mortgage insurance requirements. We saw the perversion of the appraisal process and a move to automated appraisals. All of these "innovations," which we now look at and point our fingers at the subprime originators and say 'you bad boys,' all started with government-sponsored entities like Fannie Mae and Freddie Mac."[42]

Though the precursors of the problems in the housing industry are pretty obvious, what is not so apparent in either the accounts of Professor Warren or Josh Rosner is the underlying impact of inflation on the American pursuit of home ownership. Rising prices and falling purchasing power forced many American households to use the power of two wage earners to make the purchase of a home a reality. And many Americans through the mid-1990s through 2007 saw the value of their homes rise dramatically, in some cases more than 100 percent over that period, leading to many people thinking of homes as speculative investment vehicles instead of a place to live. But the most striking fact coming out of the housing crisis for this author is that despite the 25 to 35 percent drop in value for many homes in major metropolitan areas, the cost of replacing many existing homes is above the current market value—grim testament to the reality of the underlying rate of inflation in the United States.

The Greenspan Legacy

Contemporary observers writing accounts of the collapse of the sub-prime debt bubble blame Greenspan and the members of the Federal Open Market Committee for the crisis. The more accurate observation seems to be that the Greenspan-dominated Fed presided over a two-decade long increase in the financial leverage of the U.S. economy under two successive Republican presidents, followed by a conservative Democrat and an even more conservative Republican. This gradual change from at least paying lip service to deficit reduction to a formal and explicit embrace of inflation and debt as tools of economic policy represented a radical shift in economic thinking, a break which culminated in the great financial bust of 2007–2009.

The fact that the massive growth in public and private sector debt occurred during the tenure of Alan Greenspan is a little ironic, but only a little. While Greenspan is styled as a conservative, like many Republicans today he is really a fan of big government. The former disciple of author Ayn Rand did nothing to prevent the growth of government or the federal debt during his tenure. Greenspan occasionally criticized fiscal deficits during his years at the Fed, and had some notable exchanges with members of the Senate regarding the fiscal impact of Social Security, but he hardly confronted either Congress or the White House over fiscal policy. Likewise Greenspan said little when Democrats congratulated themselves in the 1990s for almost eliminating the federal deficit. Greenspan only modestly protested their accounting gimmickry of counting Social Security payments toward the true budget deficit.

In the Randian world view of Alan Greenspan, which is most easily understood as a European-style, "positive liberty" perspective versus the negative liberty, "libertarian" world view of pre-WWI America, the markets existed for private agents to exploit. The world of Rand is not a conservative utopia of the sort romantically described by American conservatives, but a state of institutionalized selfishness where government allocates freedom to individuals. Greenspan's focus on monetary policy and his belief in "self regulating" markets was partly a reflection of his views forged by long association with Rand. But it was also a passive recognition of the political tide in America and of the fact that the federal regulators have been captured by the banking industry.

While Big Government was rhetorically demonized by Ronald Reagan, government in fact continued to grow nonetheless. Greenspan made Americans believe that they could have a normal, stable economy despite the growing debt load and continuing red ink. Just as past Fed chairmen have given past Presidents their way with respect to monetary policy, Greenspan did so and more. He gave Americans what they wanted to see, namely the appearance of economic prosperity, without forcing Congress and successive presidents to address fiscal problems.

There was no need for Presidents Reagan, Bush, Clinton, or Bush to encourage Greenspan to provide easy money as Ronald Reagan and James Baker had done so bluntly with Paul Volcker in 1984. Greenspan was leading the easy-money parade from the outset. This fact simply proves the point made by the Fed's framers about the ill effects of putting the central bank in Washington or having a unitary central bank at all. The Fed merely encouraged and facilitated a trend toward a greater use of debt throughout the American economy.

While critics of Chairman Greenspan like to blame him for the subprime bubble, not nearly enough attention is paid to the fact that American presidents from Clinton forward allowed the Fed's Board of Governors to be dominated by Greenspan and to become narrowly focused on monetary policy. Chairman Greenspan may not have been a particularly good economic prognosticator or bank regulator, but he was an exceptional politician. In 1992, when President-elect Clinton invited Alan Greenspan to Little Rock, Greenspan jumped at the chance and quickly reintegrated himself back into the White House policy loop he knew so well.[43]

Greenspan largely ignored the effects of expansive fiscal and monetary policies on banks and markets, leaving such matters to staff and the other regulators. By accommodating the political concerns of the White House and of the banking industry, Greenspan gained effective control over the Fed Board and the selection of governors through his entire term, thus the Board and its staff tended to be focused almost entirely on monetary policy. Bank supervisory matters tended to be handled by the Board's staff and led by Corrigan until 1993. This tendency to give Greenspan virtual control over the appointment of Fed governors continued through the administration of George W. Bush. Successive Republican and Democratic governments and their supporters in the business community became very comfortable with the monetary policy of Chairman Greenspan. To paraphrase Mark Twain, we had the best government money could buy. After the October 1987 market breakdown, when the Fed showed itself willing to provide the credit and access to collateral required to get through the crack in confidence, there was no reason to replace him.[34]

The real cost of two decades of Alan Greenspan at the Fed will be measured in the successive decades ahead. The failure of Chairman Greenspan and other FOMC members to address the fiscal and monetary problems of the United States during his almost two decades at the Fed has left the United States on a trajectory for economic stagnation, hyperinflation, and the attendant political and social costs of such policies. But it it easy to go overboard in blaming Greenspan for the country's woes. Chances are that any Fed chairman would have served the White House and the banking industry, just as Ben Bernanke has since he replaced Alan Greenspan. History does repeat itself.

The institutionalized crisis affecting financial markets and the government's fiscal situation is inexorably moving the United States toward a more centralized and less democratic form of government. Without a change in the fiscal and monetary regimes of the United States, government will continue to be the central player in the economy, surrounded by a heavily regulated "private" market. Individual liberties and opportunities will become increasingly a function of administrative mechanisms, and decisions about major business transactions will be concentrated far beyond what was thought possible even two decades ago. This fundamental economic evolution, which has its roots in the Great Depression and the two World Wars, is occurring within the world's greatest democracy without an informed public debate. The United States has lurched away from the ideal democratic republic to that of an authoritarian, bureaucratic, socialist state run by a junta of mercantilist oligarchs. If the United States cannot summon the will to grapple with the twin demons of public debt and inflation, then it may be that America lost the Cold War after all.

Chapter 9

A New Monetary Order

In the course of our journey through two centuries of American monetary and political history, we examined a number of recurring themes that have become increasingly prominent as the decades passed. The reliance on public debt and the unwillingness of Americans to live within their means since WWII are some of the primary threads in the narrative of the American dream. The financial and economic trends since the 1980s have merely confirmed the pattern set in the preceding years, with public sector debt and other government obligations, and inflation, growing at a pace much faster than the real economy. As the ability of the private sector to generate jobs and real economic opportunities waned, the size of government and the public sector increased steadily. Indeed, today the average wage of public sector workers in America is twice that of workers in the private sector.

Many observers of the past several years of financial and economic crisis in the United States blame the calamity on the private sector, including greedy investment banks and mortgage companies, hedge funds, and anyone else who was seen to be profiting from the latest cycle of market inflation and deflation. But is it fair to blame private individuals for profiting from the foolish policies emanating from Washington? In a world awash with fiat paper dollars, a hedge fund may well be the most rational choice of free individuals as a means of preserving some modicum of real value from the ravages of the predatory state. The road paved with inflation and debt is also the road to authoritarianism.

Over the past decade, the political process of expanding the available pool of credit, driving up asset prices and nominal economic activity, and then deflating the resulting bubble, created the temporary impression of economic growth in the United States. The average American was once again enticed and seduced by the image of the gold rush, of making easy money today by borrowing from tomorrow. As James Grant wrote in *Money of the Mind*: "As the marginal debtor received the marginal loan, the extra car (or house, boat or corporation) was sold. All this worked to enlarge the national income."[1]

The American addiction to inflation and debt is one obvious theme that emerges from our inquiry, an addiction that had contributed to financial market crises and overall volatility. One need only consider the erosion in the purchasing power of the dollar since the Great Depression to appreciate just how much of the economic activity in the United States reported during this period was an illusion. Members of Congress and the public, for example, are horrified by the several trillion dollars worth of assistance provided to banks by the Fed and Treasury since the start of the subprime debt crisis. If one inflates the several billion in Fed purchases of securities between 1933 and 1936 using the GDP deflator, plus Treasury purchases of gold with newly minted greenbacks, the total in today's dollars goes into the double-digit billions, illustrating the huge currency inflation since the 1930s. Put another way, every $1 spent in fiscal and monetary assistance in the 1930s is worth almost $14 in today's inflated money using the GDP deflator and over $16 using the consumer price index as the inflation measure. And remember that both of these widely accepted, officially defined measures of inflation understate the true erosion in the real value of the dollar.

For several decades, analysts and authors have been predicting that the chronic dependency of the United States on inflation and public debt to stimulate the economy in the short run must eventually end in crisis and default. It may be time to consider another possibility, namely that the United States will continue to use currency inflation to reduce the relative burden of the total load of public and private debt. Far from being a new idea, this is precisely how the United States dealt with the relatively huge public debt load which existed immediately after the Civil War and WWII.

From over 100 percent of GDP in 1945, within a decade the size of the federal debt was cut to just 50 percent of GDP due to strong economic expansion and a brisk rate of inflation. Current estimates of future levels of public debt to GDP for the United States reach as high as 250 percent by 2050, with the chief drivers being Social Security, Medicaid, and Medicare. As Alan Greenspan told the Congress during an appearance on Capitol Hill while Fed Chairman, there is no question that Social Security recipients will get their checks. The question is: What will the dollars purchase?

The more important political point to ponder, though, is whether the American people are likely to embrace a regime of fiscal stringency if and when the other nations of the world demand it.[2] Americans are an instinctively self-reliant, isolationist people who might very well turn their backs on the world if given a free choice. The same progression that took President Theodore Roosevelt from blissful isolation of the American continent that he loved so well to the foreign expansionism of the big stick could be reversed given the right combination of circumstances and personalities. But it is the view of this author that the destiny of America lies in global engagement, in competition and leadership, in making real the words of Ronald Reagan that America is "the last best hope of man on earth."

All along the way, conservative economists and political figures have warned the American people about the dangers of inflation, but most Americans don't have sufficient wealth to worry about the value of the dollar next week, much less next year. Even were the United States to return to the gold standard tomorrow, the wizards of Wall Street would find a way to create new vehicles for leverage and speculation just as Gould, Fisk, and Cooke did more than a century ago. In a free society, the tendency of human beings to use debt, derivatives, and other forms of leverage to earn nominal profits discourages and defeats the most sincere efforts to protect the soundness of money. As L.J. Davis wrote in his classic 1981 book *Bad Money*:

> With the public currency rendered finite and expensive by the gold standard, private currency can be expected to flourish as the bankers and the businessmen seek to keep the marketplace as liquid as possible, bringing Gresham's Law into operation. Cheap money is more attractive than expensive money.[3]

The history of the ebb and flow of monetary policy and financial regulation in the United States suggests that politics is the short-term factor governing the probability of crises, but this evolution is set against the backdrop of an increased role for the state in money and banking generally. The degree of regulatory capture or better, cooperation, between the various parts of the financial community, the housing industry, the national Congress, and the regulators, seems to have made the most recent crisis inevitable. But even as Congress responds with legislation to reform the private financial services sector, the role of the public sector in all aspects of private banking and finance seems to be growing.

If inflation and debt are the obvious problems facing the United States, and if the American political class is unwilling to make changes in fiscal and monetary policy to address these problems, then what does the future hold for Americans and the nations who trade with and invest in the United States? For a start, at home the likelihood is for a continuing diminution of real living standards, asset values, and economic opportunities due to inflation. Recalling our earlier point about greenbacks and Treasury bonds both being forms of "debt" and therefore functionally equivalent, the trillions of dollars in U.S. public sector debt, guarantees, and contingent liabilities represent future inflation.

Today there seems to be no appetite on the part of Americans to address fiscal imbalances and the related problem of inflation in the way in which presidents such as Gerald Ford or Jimmy Carter attempted to do in the 1970s and 1980s. A steady, low double-digit increase in the cost of living, regardless of what the heavily manipulated official inflation statistics indicate, seems baked into the model of the U.S. economy for generations. But the major point of vulnerability for the United States may not be inflation per se but diminished economic growth and a gradually weaker dollar, both of which will diminish the influence of America in the world.

According to economist Bruce Bartlett:

> As long as the U.S. national debt is entirely denominated in dollars, there is no risk that we will run into the sort of financial crisis that small countries often run into. What gets them into trouble isn't the debt per se, but an inability to acquire sufficient foreign exchange with their own currency to service it. While the U.S. Treasury has never issued bonds denominated in foreign currencies, it is conceivable that it could be forced to do so if the dollar falls sharply and foreign demand for U.S. bonds wanes. That will be the point at which our debt problem becomes more than theoretical and we are really on the road to national bankruptcy.[4]

In addition to the fact of secular inflation in American economic life, the export of American jobs to other countries and the related decline in the dollar cost of many consumer goods have masked the true rate of inflation in the United States. Successive U.S. governments have managed to keep the value of the dollar artificially high because of the need to borrow hundreds of billions of dollars each year to finance chronic fiscal deficits. Just as the large federal spending deficits and debt represent future inflation, the equally persistent trade and current account deficits run by the United States are likewise a reflection of the degree to which the rest of the world finances the American economy and depends upon it for growth.

The subsidy provided to the United States by foreign nations depends upon America's willingness to borrow, which now seems to be waning. "It is always easier to borrow as long as someone will lend to you," observes Alex Pollock, resident scholar at American Enterprise Institute. "When the lenders stop lending, that's what forces the change. Witness Greece and the EU."[5]

The core issue facing the world in the future is how to generate economic growth in a world where the United States. is no longer the engine of expansion. "Lending to yourself only works if the newly created and borrowed money will be accepted by the rest of the world in exchange for real stuff," responds William Dunkelberg, chief economist for the National Federation of Independent Business. "We get huge trade deficits instead of inflation as long as this willingness persists."[6]

The Growth Challenge

As this book was being finalized in the summer of 2010, the price of gold was hitting new records. The Chinese government announced its intention to allow the yuan to gradually appreciate further against the dollar, suggesting that the government in Beijing is now willing to see the living standards of its people rise despite the continuing threat of domestic inflation. The European Union seems to be emerging from the disarray and severe market damage following the U.S. subprime crisis. China's stability remains in doubt in the near-term, but the economic ascendancy of Asia is a long-term trend and holds a profound warning for the United States. Just as a surging U.S. economy helped America surpass the nations of Europe in terms of wealth and economic vitality in the early 1900s, today China and the other industrial nations of Asia may be experiencing a similar evolution vis-à-vis the maturing U.S. political economy.

"We live in an amazing world," former Fed Chairman Paul Volcker noted recently. "Everybody has big budget deficits and big easy money, but somehow the world as a whole cannot fully employ itself. It is a serious question. We are no longer just talking about a single country having a big depression but the entire world. If the world as a whole cannot employ everyone who is ready and able to work, it raises some big questions."[7]

One of the issues facing the United States and the global economy when it comes to generating jobs and economic opportunities is the still-lingering effects of WWII. The Bretton Woods agreement was an arrangement defined by a victor in war that was agreed to by a world that lay in ruins. The children of the victors, the "greatest generation," are the chief factor in our narrative, the demographic bulge in the United States popularly known as the baby boom. For decades, the United States has been the engine of global growth in order to meet the wants and needs of the boomers, exchanging fiat paper dollars for real goods and services.

When Richard Nixon ended the link between the dollar and gold, the value of the dollar became a function of the political credibility of the United States. But as the growth potential of the U.S. economy wanes and the baby boomers reach retirement age, all the while refusing to rein in their insatiable desire for consumption, the ability of the American economy to fulfill the dreams of workers around the world is in doubt. How we deal with the uniquely American problem of a global fiat currency will define the destiny of America and the world in the next century and beyond.

One of the issues raised by the subprime housing crisis of 2007–2009 that is not often discussed in the media or economic circles is how the increasingly hollow U.S. economy will look without the positive effect of a constantly buoyant housing market. Josh Rosner believes that the positive influence of the baby boom in the decades following WWII is now becoming a serious drag on future U.S. economic growth. He explains:

There are three issues or "headwinds" as I like to describe them, factors that were once positives for the economy or tailwinds, but are now a drag on the economy. The first issue is the two-income household. Beginning in the inflation of the 1970s, as wages under-paced asset price increases, we moved from one- to two-income families. This boosted current growth and real estate prices for decades, but we have reached the limit of this "fix" to support employment and real estate prices. Now the tailwind of two-income families has become a headwind that is a drag on the economy. The shift has made household finances more fragile. It used to be if the family wage earner lost his/her job the other could replace some of that income. With spending rebalanced to two incomes there is less household margin of safety in case of job loss.

The second issue is the democratization of credit. Beginning in late 1970s the move from charge cards to consumer revolving debt issuance changed the consumption patterns of an entire nation. The monthly debt service cost, not the value of the good or service, became the criteria used for making a purchase. Beside just super-charging consumption it commoditized luxury goods. Remember when the family on your block that owned a Caddy or Mercedes really was financially more wealthy? By the 1980s, the consumption function had shifted upward because of the expanding availability of credit. That trend is now reversed as banks, individuals, and households are de-leveraging. The tailwind that drove consumption in the 1980–2007 period is now a big headwind.

The third headwind is demographic. Coming out of the recessions of the late 70s and 80s we were supported by the fact that the largest generation in U.S. history was coming to peak earnings potential. These boomers are now moving to become the largest tax on the social safety net. The largest generation in U.S. history will retire with less equity in what has historically been the largest retirement and intergenerational wealth transfer asset for most families—their homes. In many cases, these people will have no net personal savings when they reach the end of their working lives and will essentially become wards of the state. This increased burden on the U.S. Treasury, in a decade, is the largest unconsidered impact of the current crisis.[8]

Jobs versus Inflation

One of the major themes to take away from this book is that Americans need to develop new models and frameworks for distinguishing between real economic growth and the illusion of growth created by inflation and credit-driven speculation. Since the collapse of Bear, Stearns & Co. and Lehman Brothers in 2008, the Fed has kept interest rates at zero, ostensibly to help the banking sector recover from record credit losses. Since then, Fed interest rate policies have transferred trillions of dollars from savers to the shareholders of banks through low interest rates. Little of this largess has reached American households, however, because neither the banks nor the millions of residential mortgages now underwater have been restructured or refinanced by the banking industry, thwarting the Fed's reflation efforts.

The more interesting question raised by Fed policies since 2001 is whether the U.S. economy can generate positive real growth as and when interest rates in the United States return to something like normal levels. In 2001, when the U.S. economy experienced a "mini" recession, Fed Chairman Alan Greenspan and the FOMC responded by dropping interest rates to very low levels. Critics of Chairman Greenspan have subsequently lambasted the Fed for keeping rates too low for too long and thereby causing the bubble in real estate later in the decade. But what many observers fail to appreciate is that the Fed, operating in real time, was mostly concerned with deflation inside financial institutions, not with spurring growth.

"During the period after 2001, people in the Fed were worried about repeating the deflationary experience of Japan," concludes David Kotok, CEO of Cumberland Advisers. "They chose policies that were designed to blunt the risk of deflation, but they failed to appreciate the other risk, namely encouraging a bubble in the domestic real estate market. It is easy to criticize the Fed in hindsight, but the central bank operates in real time. In this case the perceived solution to one problem created another."[9]

Based upon the work done by my firm in analyzing and rating U.S. banks, it appears that the Fed's motivation in the early 2000s was not to create a bubble in the housing market, but to keep the level of nominal economic growth and employment above some acceptable minimum level. Large consumer lenders such as Citigroup, a bellwether of an economy where the average borrower is subprime, experienced significant increases in credit losses during the 2001–2003 period, losses far above the bank's peers and also higher than many market analysts expected. The Federal Open Market Committee took the federal funds rate from 5 percent at the end of 2000 down to just above zero by the end of 2003, yet concerns remained. These concerns caused officials at the central bank to consider new policy alternatives for operating in an environment of very low nominal interest rates.[10] That is precisely where the United States is today. Or as a senior Fed official said in June 2010, "Go back to the 1990s and count the number of quarters where we have not had fiscal stimulus or expansionary Fed interest rate policy or both."

Had Chairman Greenspan and the Federal Open Market Committee raised interest rates sooner, the bubble in the housing market might not have been nearly as large, but the U.S. economy might well have weakened rapidly because of a basic lack of economic strength, a problem that continues to the present day. The trend in the United States going back to the late 1960s has been for Americans to focus more and more spending on consumption and less on investment; thus the weakness seen today in the U.S. job market is no surprise. Whereas in the years immediately after WWII the United States had modest inflation but still higher levels of growth, today the situation is reversed, with persistent inflation and negative real levels of economic growth.

"A nation that spends on itself is not spending on physical plant and equipment," observes Vincent Reinhart, former director of the Federal Reserve Board's Division of Monetary Affairs. "I don't think it's an accident that high savings rates and low deficits were associated with fast growth. We forgot that lesson in the 1960s. Financial innovation also made it easier for the government and households to spend more."[11]

Changing Places

Former Fed Governor Alan Blinder famously said in 1994: "The last duty of a central banker is to tell the public the truth." But this, of course, assumes that our political leaders and central bankers know the truth in the first place. The basic question the Fed, the Congress, and the American people need to consider is whether the current load of public and private debt, combined with an over-valued dollar, makes stable, non-inflationary growth and job creation impossible. How will the economy and job market perform if the Fed and Treasury are ever forced to defend the dollar with higher interest rates?

It is important to recall that the average maturity of the $11 trillion in U.S. federal debt is only about five years, meaning that the entire corpus of debt must be refinanced each decade or so, this in addition to the new incremental debt issued each year. This precarious position for the Treasury was created by Undersecretary Peter Fisher, who in October of 2001 announced that the Treasury would suspend issuing 30-year Treasury bonds. Fisher's decision, made at a time when receipts to the Social Security system were masking the overall federal deficit and the Fed was driving rates down, shortened the duration of the outstanding public debt of the United States. The arrogance and ignorance that would allow any official of the Treasury to make such a short-sighted decision is a commentary on us all.

Up until 2001, as much as one third of total Treasury debt issuance had been in 30-year bonds, but now the Treasury is issuing mostly short-term debt in an ill-considered effort to conceal the increase in the overall federal deficit. In a 2001 statement, Fisher said: "We do not need the 30-year bond to meet the government's current financing needs, nor those that we expect to face in coming years. Looking beyond the next few years, as I already observed, we believe that the likely outcome is that the federal government's fiscal position will improve after the temporary setback that we are now experiencing." By 2008, however, Fisher, who by then had gone to work for BlackRock, opined that the Treasury should start to issue 100-year debt.

In an environment where the United States is forced to respond to demands from foreign investors either to pay higher rates to compensate for risk or issue foreign-currency denominated debt, the United States could face a situation similar to the one confronted by Chairman Volcker and the Fed in the 1970s. Only this time, instead of being focused on restraining *domestic* inflation, the U.S. central bank and Treasury may instead find themselves fighting to placate angry foreign creditors by maintaining the value of the dollar and access to the international capital markets. This would place the United States in a position similar to that experienced by Mexico, Brazil, Russia and other former crisis-ridden debtor nations.

During the 1980s and early 1990s, for example, Mexico was forced to pay double-digit interest rates on T-bills in order to finance its deficits. When Mexico and other heavily indebted nations ran into problems in decades past, currency devaluations and IMF-administered fiscal austerity measures were imposed as a condition of gaining access to new credit. Some of the debtor nations followed these prescriptions, others did not, but one of the remarkable facts of the twenty-first century is that the United States and the EU have now taken the place of these emerging nations as potential subjects for structural adjustment due to excessive debt. As mentioned previously, Mexico, Brazil, China, and other major debtor nations of decades ago are now self-sustaining, without the need of assistance from the IMF. The question facing both the United States and the EU is which of these older, more developed economic blocs will be the first to get their fiscal and monetary house in order.

A combination of historical and more recent political factors has forced the United States into a potentially disastrous financial and economic trap. The first step in escaping this situation is for Americans to accept that the social and economic impact of the two world wars and the Cold War that followed are still driving U.S. policy. The solution to this predicament involves a combination of old and new approaches, but ultimately comes down to a change in U.S. policy in three crucial areas: fiscal deficits, global trade, and the dollar.

In the wake of the crisis that hit the EU in 2010 with the near-default of Greece, many American observers have predicted that the EU will disintegrate and the common European currency will fail. Misery, after all, loves company. EU nations from Germany to Great Britain are attacking their fiscal imbalances with a degree of seriousness and purpose that puts their American counterparts to shame. U.S. Treasury Secretary Timothy Geithner has advised the finance ministers of the EU member states to increase spending, but such advice seems to be falling on deaf ears.

America's leaders, reflecting their consumer-oriented bias, continue to believe that global deflation remains the greatest risk to the world economy, a world economy in which the United States occupies the central position. The nations of Europe, led by Germany, however, have decided that fiscal responsibility and global competitiveness are the correct priorities, much like the leaders of China and other Asian nations.

Looking forward over the next decade and beyond, Americans should ask themselves how the global competitive position of the United States will be affected if the EU is successful in restructuring itself before the United States even begins that same process. Instead of disintegration of the EU, we may instead see a resurgent Europe, expanded to 30 or more nations that are united in a desire to be a relevant, prosperous, and competitive part of the global economy. For years there has been speculation about how and when the U.S. dollar might lose its status as the world's reserve currency, but the fact is that the migration process is already underway. The euro, the Chinese yuan, and even the Canadian dollar are all gaining attractiveness for investors who want to avoid the risk of devaluation and default as the United States wallows in self indulgence and indecision.

If you compare the response by U.S. leaders to the subprime debt crisis and the response by leaders in Europe and other nations to their debt problems, the divergence in how we define the problems and the solutions is striking. It is often said that no other nation wants the job of being the global reserve currency, but as financial adviser David Kotok reflected, "this is not a job you look for. It is a job that finds you."

"The Greek crisis was a gift," continued Kotok, who published a bullish book on the EU just before the Greek crisis exploded. He remains unrepentant and is even more bullish. "My view is that the euro will emerge battle tested from the Greek crisis. European governments are making rapid movement in favor of closing fiscal deficits. The EU will expand to include Poland and Czechoslovakia. Over the next ten to twenty years we will see a larger Eurozone that will provide an alternative reserve currency to the dollar."[12]

Triffin's Dilemma and the Dollar

A reckoning long foreseen is at hand. "Nearly 50 years ago, Yale University economist Robert Triffin identified the inevitable future deterioration of the dollar in his book, *Gold and the Dollar Crisis: The Future of Convertibility* (1960)," wrote researcher Walker Todd in a December 2008 article. "Essentially, Triffin argued, under the Bretton Woods system in which the U.S. dollar was the world's principal reserve currency (instead of gold, for example), the United States had to incur large trade deficits in order to provide the rest of the world with the liquidity required for the functioning of the global trading system."[13]

Returning to the point with respect to the soaring cost of imported energy, the fact that the dollar continues to trade at current levels versus other currencies reflects the reality that as the global means of exchange, the dollar cannot be easily replaced. One reason for this is that the global trade in petroleum and other hydrocarbons is so large that it requires an equally large currency to accommodate it. If you recall the phenomenon of the greenback slowly rising back to parity with gold after the Civil War, the demand for a means of exchange is a powerful force and one that seemingly is indifferent to inflation, at least in the short-run. This is the essence of "Triffin's Dilemma."

Just as most American consumers are naturally too focused on jobs and family to concentrate on the erosion of the dollar's value in real terms, the major exporting nations likewise live in the present and are focused on maximizing national income today. For years analysts have predicted that other nations would one day shun the dollar in favor of some alternative money, but this eventuality has been slow to arrive. Although America and the world could probably continue to live with the current global currency system for many years to come, the question for U.S. policymakers is whether this serves the national interest. Experience teaches that so long as American politicians believe that they can borrow to paper over fiscal deficits, they will do so. Thus dealing with the role of the dollar in the global economy ultimately is linked to fiscal and political reform in the United States.

Conventional wisdom says that there is no way out of the current situation of having the dollar as the global reserve currency. A study published in June 2010 by the Council on Foreign Relations quoted Luo Ping, a director-general at the China Banking Regulatory Commission, on the issue of the reserve currency status of the dollar:

> Except for U.S. Treasuries, what can you hold? Gold? You don't hold Japanese government bonds or United Kingdom bonds. U.S. Treasuries are the safe haven. For everyone, including China, it is the only option. . . . We know the dollar is going to depreciate, so we hate you guys, but there is nothing much we can do.[14]

One means of dealing with this issue would be to go back to the original framework for the Bretton Woods agreement and fashion a new global currency mechanism, one that no longer affords the dollar a monopoly and no longer gives American politicians a free ride when it comes to fiscal discipline. If we start with the fact that Bretton Woods was as much about propping up Great Britain and the other bankrupt nations of Europe after WWII as it was an effort to create a truly balanced international monetary system, then the path for a new system should be focused on helping the United States restructure its public debt and other fiscal obligations to avoid an outright default, essentially a twenty-first century Marshall Plan in reverse.

The first phase should involve an agreement among the largest trading partners of the United States, most likely within the Group of 20 industrial nations, to implement a managed devaluation of the dollar to decrease America's external deficits and boost demand for U.S. exports. This approach would essentially reverse the roles of the industrial nations and would seek to place the United States in a slight surplus position as the other nations of the world stimulated domestic demand and went into deficit. The United States would agree to substantial cuts in spending and changes in tax policy to increase revenue and make taxes more focused on consumption rather than income—for example, a value added tax. This is pretty close to the policy that U.S. officials have been trying for decades to implement through bilateral negotiations with nations such as China, but would instead be pursued in a multilateral framework.

As part of this new international financial order, the world would gradually but deliberately replace the dollar as the sole international reserve currency and include at least two other currencies, the euro and the Chinese yuan. These currencies would gradually take a larger and larger share of international financial and commercial flows, and force the United States to manage its fiscal and monetary policies in a more responsible fashion. Instead of the dollar as the sole means of exchange for global commerce, there would now be three large reserve currency blocs built around Europe, North America, and Asia that would essentially compete in terms of encouraging growth and maintaining fiscal discipline.

In a historical sense, creating a means for the United States to transition away from bearing the full burden of serving as the reserve currency for the world economy would truly mark the end of the Cold War period and, more broadly, the recovery of the world from the two world wars. Just as it has taken nearly a century for the social and demographic effects of WWI and WWII to work their way through the U.S. political economy, the economic effects of these terrible upheavals are still being felt in the huge fiscal imbalances and inflation visible in the United States today.

Capital markets veteran James Rickards put the tactical and strategic situation facing the United States in the global payments system succinctly:

> We have been operating in a dollar world for decades. Notwithstanding the demise of Bretton Woods in 1971, it's still a dollar system. All of the world's expectations, all of its productive capacity, all of its allocations of capital are built around that system. When the caretakers of that system allow weeds in the garden and for the system to disintegrate and fall apart, which is what I see happening in the U.S., the immediate reaction is first confusion, then panic and then self help. This gets to the heart of the national security implications of the financial crisis. Initially other nations were content to wait for the U.S. response, but now I see nations like China, Russia and Germany increasingly willing to act on their own. The trend in the amount of global trade priced in dollars has been going down for decades. This brings us today to the key question, which is what is the U.S. plan? Fed Chairman Bernanke wakes up every morning and tries to trash the dollar with quantitative easing, zero interest rates and swaps lines with the central banks. But it has not been working. The Fed has never taken it to the next step and asked what happens when quantitative easing does not work.[15]

Americans face a decision as we approach an inevitability: One day the other nations such as China and the EU will want an equal share of the global monetary franchise that has belonged solely to the United States since WWII. As Nouriel Rubini said in his book *Crisis Economics*,[16] Adam Smith and other economists spent their time focused on why markets work, not why they falter. We are witnessing the slow demise of the dollar system, just as the currency system based on the English pound declined before it. How America transitions from holding a monopoly on the world's money to being merely one large player in an equal exchange among nations will be a test of its national character.

In meeting this challenge, Americans will do what they do best: adjust, adapt, and excel in a way that no other people on earth can.

The most important question facing Americans is: Do we want to make this necessary adjustment at a time and at a pace of our choosing? Or do we prefer to wait for events to force change upon us in a time of crisis or worse? Do Americans have the honesty to talk about limiting our national wants and needs to our national income? Do we have the courage to lead another global discussion with other nations about the dollar and America's infatuation with inflation and debt? I believe that the answer to these questions is yes.

Notes

Preface

1. Adams, James Truslow, *The Epic of America* (New York: Little Brown, 1931), 404.

Chapter 1

1. Sylla, Richard, "Financial Foundations: Public Credit, the National Bank, and Securities Markets," National Bureau of Economic Research (NBER), (February 8, 2010): 4-7.

2. Homer, Sidney and Sylla, Richard Eugene, *A History of Interest Rates* (Piscataway, NJ: Rutgers University Press, 1996), 274.

3. McCullough, David, *John Adams* (New York: Simon & Schuster 2001), 171.

4. Chernow, Ron, *Alexander Hamilton* (London: Penguin Press, 2004), 346.

5. History of the Bank of New York, Bank of New York Mellon Corporation.

6. McCullough, 428.

7. Dunn, Susan, "When America was Transformed," *New York Review of Books*, March 25, 2010, 30. Dunn reviewed Gordon Wood's *Empire of Liberty: A History of the Early Republic 1789–1815* (New York: Oxford University Press US, 2009).

8. Catteral, Ralph Charles Henry, *The Second Bank of the United States* (University of Chicago Press, 1903), 9.

9. Byrd, Robert C. *The Senate, 1789–1989* (Washington, DC: U.S. Government Printing Office, 1988), 66.

10. Ibid., 67.

11. Dunn, 29.

12. Myers, Margaret G., *A Financial History of the United States* (New York: Columbia University Press, 1970), 143.

13. Kennedy, James, *The Exchange Artist: A Tale of High-Flying Speculation and America's First Banking Collapse* (London: Viking Penguin, 2008).

14. Grinath III, Arthur; Wallis, John; and Sylla, Richard, "Debt, Default and Revenue Structure: The American State Debt Crisis in the Early 1840s," Historical Paper 97, NBER (March 1997), 3.

15. Foulke, Roy A., *The Sinews of American Commerce* (New York: Dunn & Bradstreet, 1941), 151.

16. Grinath, 4.

17. Schweikart, Larry, *Banking in the American South from the Age of Jackson to Reconstruction* (Louisiana State University Press, 1987), 167.

18. Grinath, 26–27.

19. Dunbar, Willis F. and May, George, *Michigan: A History of the Wolverine State* (Grand Rapids: Wm Erdmans 1995), 230.

20. Specie refers to metal coins, bullion coins, hard money, commodity metals, and other hard stores of value that are also used as a means of exchange.

21. Byrd, 105.

22. "President Jackson's Veto Message Regarding the Bank of the United States" (July 10, 1832), Yale Law School.

23. Taylor, George Rogers, *Jackson Versus Biddle: The Struggle over the Second Bank of the United States* (Boston: CD Heath, 1949), viii.

24. Ibid.

25. James, Marquis, *The Life of Andrew Jackson* (Camden: Haddon Craftsmen, 1938), 583.

26. James, 601.

27. James, 664.

28. James, 729.

29. "1995 Annual Report: A Brief History of Our Nation's Paper Money," *Annual Report*, Federal Reserve Bank of San Francisco, 1995.

30. History of the U.S. Treasury, U.S. Department of the Treasury, Washington, DC.

31. Webster, Daniel, *The Works of Daniel Webster, Vol. III* (Boston: Little Brown, 1881), 394.

32. Margo, Robert A., "Wages in California During the Gold Rush," NBER Historical Working Paper No. 101* (June 1997).

33. Brands, H.W., *The Age of Gold: The California Gold Rush and the New American Dream* (New York: Anchor Books, 2003), 488.

34. For an interesting discussion of the New York clearinghouse, see Ida M. Tarbel, "The Hunt for a Money Trust," *American Magazine*, Volume LXXVI, July 1913 to December 1913, (New York: Phillips Publishing Co.), 42.

35. Timberlake, Richard H., *Monetary Policy in the United States: An Intellectual and Institutional History* (Chicago: University of Chicago Press, 1978), 213. Timberlake provides an overview of Goodhart's views of the clearinghouse function.

Chapter 2

1. Bloom, Harold, "The Central Man," *The New York Review of Books,* July 19, 1984.

2. Phillips, Kevin, *The Cousins' War* (New York: Basic Books, 2009), 459.

3. Canova, Timothy, "Lincoln's Populist Sovereignty: Public Finance Of, By, and For the People," PAPER NO. 09-38, Chapman Law Review, Vol. 12, 2009, 561–562 (http://ssrn.com/abstract=1489439).

4. McNally, Terrence, "Exposing the Secrets of the Temple: How the Federal Reserve Makes Money Out of Thin Air," *Alternet*, May 12, 2010.

5. Janeway, Elliot, *The Struggle for Survival* (New York: Weybright & Talley, 1951), 15–16.

6. Paul, Ron, *End the Fed* (New York: Grand Central Publishing (2009), 1.

7. Hornberger, Jacob G., "Legal Tender and the Civil War," *Freedom Daily* (Fairfax, VA: Future of Freedom Foundation, November 2000).

8. Rothbard, Murray Newton, *A History of Money and Banking in the United States* (Auburn, AL: Ludwig von Mises Institute, 2002), 122-123.

9. Phillips, 389.

10. Dubois, W.E.B., *The Suppression of the African Slave Trade in the United States of America 1638–1870* (New York: Social Science Press, 1954), 123.

11. Ibid., 424-425.

12. Byrd, 247.

13. Bloom, Harold, "The Central Man," *NY Review of Books* (July 19, 1984).

14. David Kinley, "The Independent Treasury of the United States and its Relations to Banks in the Country," National Monetary Commission, U.S. Government Printing Office (1910), 97.

15. Rothbard, 123.

16. Ibid., 124.

17. Byrd, 253.

18. Hixson, William F., *Triumph of the Bankers: Money and Banking in the Eighteenth and Nineteenth Centuries* (Westport CT: Praeger Publishers, 1993), 143.

19. Josephson, Matthew, *The Robber Barons* (New York: Harcourt Brace & Co., 1934), 36.

20. Rothbard, 133.

21. Wilkeson, Samuel, "How Our National Debt May Be A National Blessing" (Philadelphia: M'Laughlin Brothers Printers, 1865).

22. *History of the Treasury,* Secretaries of the Treasury: William P. Fessenden, U.S. Department of the Treasury web site (www.ustreas.gov).

23. Hixson, 136.

24. Myers, 175.

25. History of the Treasury, Secretaries of the Treasury: Salmon Chase.

26. Rothbard, 152–153.

27. Swanberg, W.A., *Jim Fisk: The Career of an Improbable Rascal* (New York: Longmans, 1960), 123.

28. Hoyt, Edwin P., *The Goulds: A Social History* (New York: Weybright & Talley, 1969), 49.

29. Swanberg, 123.

30. Ibid., 145.

31. It has been suggested in several published works that Gould and Fisk, in fact, were in league even as Gould seemed to be profiting at his confederate's expense, and that the two men divided the profits on the gold market operation afterward.

32. Rothbard, 138–139.

33. Hoyt, 61.

34. Ibid., 126–132.

35. *The Campaign Text Book*, National Democratic Committee (1880), 169-171.

36. Josephson, 167.

37. McDill, Kathleeen and Sheehan, Kevin, "Sources of Historical Banking Panics: A Markov Switching Approach," FDIC Working Paper 2006-01, 4. The authors provide a good review of scholarship regarding the causes and attributes of financial crises.

38. Rothbard, 161.

39. Ibid., 163.

40. Holdsworth, John Thom, *Money and Banking* (New York: D. Appleton and Co., 1922), 30.

41. McFeely, William, *Grant: A Biography* (New York: WW Norton & Co., 2002), 397.

42. Byrd, 321.

43. Faulkner, Harold, *Politics, Reform and Expansion: 1890–1900* (New York: Harper & Row, 1959), x.

44. Adams, 316.

45. Byrd, 348.

46. Myers, 212.

Chapter 3

1. Twain, Mark and Warner, Charles Dudley, *The Gilded Age: A Tale of To-Day* (Hartford: American Publishing Company, 1874), v.

2. Mintz, Steven, (2007). Digital History (www.digitalhistory.uh.edu/), viewed March 6, 2010.

3. Friedman, Milton and Schwartz, Anna, *A Monetary History of the United States, 1867–1960*, NBER (1965), 138.

4. Rothbard, 167. See also Friedman and Schwartz, 106.

5. Rothbard, 168.

6. See "The Reading Receivership," *The Nation*, Vol. 56, No. 1445, The Evening Post Publishing Co., New York (1893), 174.

7. See "New Hope for Financial Economics: Interview with Bill Janeway," *The Institutional Risk Analyst*, (November 17, 2008).

8. "The Reading Receivership," 175.

9. Batchelor, 17.

10. Kleppner, Paul, *The Third Electoral System 1853–1892: Parties, Voters, and Political Cultures* (Charlotte, NC: University of North Carolina Press, 1979), 291–296. Murray Rothbard prepared an excellent summary of Kleppner's work and the evolution of the American political system after 1896 in his *History of Money and Banking in the United States* (Auburn, AL: Ludwig von Mises Institute, 2002), 169–179.

11. Nevins, Allan and Comanger, Henry Steele, *A Short History of the United States (Fifth Edition)*, Knopf, New York (1966), 378.

12. History of the United States Senate, "Adlai Ewing Stevenson, 23rd Vice President (1893–1897)," Senate Historical Office, U.S. Senate web site (www.senate.gov).

13. Rothbard, 168–169.

14. Kleppner, 291–296.

15. Ibid.

16. Goodwyn, Lawrence, *The Populist Moment: A Short History of the Agrarian Revolt in America* (London: Oxford University Press, 1978), 236–238.

17. Myers, 218–219.

18. White House Profile (www.whitehouse.gov/about/presidents/williammckinley).

19. "Report of the Monetary Commission of the Indianapolis Convention," Hollenbeck Press, Indianapolis (1900).

20. Ibid., 77.

21. Goodwyn, 282–283.

22. Theodore Roosevelt Association.

23. Myers, 221.

Chapter 4

1. Jones, Eliot, *The Trust Problem in the United States* (New York: The MacMillan Co, 1921), 198–201.

2. Pound, Arthur, and Moore, Samuel Taylor, *They Told Barron: The Notes of Clarence W. Barron* (New York: Harper Brothers, 1930), 85–86.

3. Magie, David, *Life of Garret Augustus Hobart: Twenty-Fourth Vice-President of the United States* (New York: G.P. Putnam's Sons, 1910), 53.

4. Ibid., 41.

5. See United States Senate History, "Garret Augustus Hobart, 24th Vice President (1897–1899)."

6. See "Timeline," The Roosevelt Association (www.theodoreroosevelt.org/life/timeline.htm).

7. Pound and Moore, 21.

8. Josephson, 446.

9. Myers, 256.

10. Pound and Moore, 80.

11. Harrison, Robert, *Congress, Progressive Reform, and the New American State* (New York: Cambridge University Press, 2004), 250.

12. Josephson, 450–451.

13. Faris, Ralph, *Crisis and Consciousness* (Amsterdam: BR Gruener Publishing, 1977), 21.

14. Byrd, 374–375.

15. *Autobiography of Theodore Roosevelt* (Blacksburg, VA: Wilder Publications, 2008), 210–211.

16. Speech at Quincy, Illinois, April 29, 1903. See Theodore Roosevelt, Elisha Ely Garrison, *The Roosevelt Doctrine: Being the Personal Utterances of the President on . . .* (New York: Robert Greier Cooke, 1904), 153.

17. Theodore Roosevelt and Andrew Carnegie, *The Roosevelt Policy: Speeches, Letters and State Papers, Relating to Corporate Wealth and Closely Allied Topics* (New York: The Current Literature Publishing Company, 1908), 667.

18. Freidman and Schwartz, 181.

19. Ibid., 163.

20. See *Watson's Jeffersonian Magazine*, Volume 5, Thomas Edward Watson, Editor (July 1910), 1050. See also W.F. McCaleb, *Theodore Roosevelt*, (New York: A&C Boni, 1931), 242.

21. Grant, 119.

22. "Beyond the Crisis: Reflections on the Challenges," Remarks by Terrence J. Checki, Executive Vice President Federal Reserve Bank of New York, at the Foreign Policy Association Corporate Dinner, New York, NY, Tuesday, December 2, 2009.

23. Batchelor, 18–19.

24. Gordon, John Steele, "A Short Banking History of the United States," *Wall Street Journal* (October 10, 2008).

25. Steffens reference to Aldrich as "the boss of the United States" is found in his book, *The Struggle for Self Government*, (New York: S.S. McClure Co., 1904), 120.

26. "Eager To Testify On Money Trust; Members of National Citizens' League So Inform Congress Committee," *New York Times* (March 20, 1912), 14.

27. Warburg, Paul M., *The Federal Reserve System Its Origin and Growth: Reflections and Recollections Vol. II* (New York: The MacMillan Company, 1930), 117.

28. "Money Trust Investigation: Investigation of Financial and Monetary Conditions in the United States Under House Resolutions Nos. 429 and 504: 1912–1913," FRASER, Federal Reserve Bank of St Louis.

29. "Think Money Inquiry Forced Chase Sale," *New York Times*, (January 7, 1913), 1.

30. "Oppose Reopening of Money Inquiry; Wilson and Underwood Also Against Embodying Pujo Remedies in Currency Bill," *New York Times*, (May 31, 1913), 13.

31. Rothbard, Murray, *The Case Against the Fed* (Auburn, AL: Ludwig von Mises Institute, 1994), 116.

32. Gilbert, Clinton, *The Mirrors of Wall Street* (New York: Putnam & Sons, 1933), 14. Originally published anonymously.

33. Byrd, 412.

34. Goodwyn, 269.

35. "Carter Glass, 88, Dies in Capital," *New York Times*, (May 29, 1946), 1.

36. Chernow, Ron, *The House of Morgan: An American Banking Dynasty and the Rise of Modern Finance* (New York: Grove Press, 2001), 182.

37. Ibid., 149.

38. President Theodore Roosevelt, *Theodore Roosevelt: An Autobiography* (New York: Macmillan, 1913).

39. Todd, Walker F., "The Federal Reserve Board and the Rise of the Corporate State, 1931–1934," *Economic Education Bulletin*, Vol. XXXV, No. 9 American Institute for Economic Research, Great Barrington, Massachusetts (September 1995).

40. Goodwyn, 267.

41. Gilbert, 9–10.

42. Ibid., 15.

43. Todd, "The Federal Reserve Board and the Rise of the Corporate State," 42.

Chapter 5

1. "Historical Debt Outstanding," US Treasury web site (www.treasurydirect .gov). The totals for debt outstanding provided by the U.S. Treasury include all physical dollars or "legal tender notes," and any silver and gold certificates that are still in existence. All of the paper issued by the Treasury, either currency or in the form of notes and bonds, are essentially debt, even if the former is not convertible into gold upon demand. This is why conservative, hard-"money" exponents are so violently against fiat money because it is essentially debt, which promises value but which is never redeemed.

2. Tansill, Charles Callan, *America Goes to War* (Boston: Little Brown and Co., 1938), 69, n7.

3. Ibid., 73–75.

4. Ibid., 79.

5. Barron, Clarence W., *The Audacious War* (New York: Houghton Mifflin Co, 1915), ix.

6. "This War's Finance," *New York Times* (May 12, 1915), 12.

7. Tansill, 87–90.

8. *Federal Reserve Bulletin*, (November 1, 1916) 591.

9. House, Edward Mandell and Seymour, Charles, *The Intimate Papers of Colonel House* (Cambridge: Houghton Mifflin, 1926), 412.

10. "Baruch Demands Hearing on Charge," *New York Times*, (March 5, 1924), 1.

11. Grant, 145.

12. Miron, Jeffrey A., "The Founding of the Fed and the Destabilization of the Post-1914 Economy," NBER Working Paper No. 2701, *National Bureau of Economic Research* (February 1990), 3. Miron provides an excellent overview of the research on the economic impact of the creation of the Fed on the direction of the U.S. economy since 1914.

13. Gilbert, 24.

14. Freidman and Schwartz, 190.

15. Ibid., 194.

16. Interview with Walker Todd, April 12, 2010.

17. Hoff, Joan, *A Faustian Foreign Policy from Woodrow Wilson to George W. Bush* (New York: Cambridge University Press, 2008), 72–73. Regarding the eventual loan default by France and Britain, Hoff notes that the loans to the Allies were not really "business transactions" because the countries were insolvent at the time of WWI and very clearly could not repay their debts.

18. Seymour, Charles, *Woodrow Wilson and the World War: A Chronicle of Our Own Times*, (New Haven, CT: Yale University Press, 1921), 183.

19. Ibid., 185.

20. Minton, Bruce and Stuart, John, *The Fat Years and the Lean* (New York: International Publishers, 1940), 3.

21. Timeline, Theodore Roosevelt Association.

22. "Gompers Assails Harding Position," *New York Times* (September 27, 1920), 5.

23. Calvin Coolidge, White House history.

24. Chernow, 254.

25. "Tell Why Aamerica is Now Unpopular," *New York Times* (May 12, 1920), 2.

26. For example, Henry Ford is credited not only with using mass production methods to make his products less expensive, but with instituting the $5 per day wage in 1914, when many Americans could barely survive. More recent research suggests that, in fact, James Couzens, the general manager of Ford and later the Senator from Michigan was the man who actually pressed Ford to increase wages for workers. See Harry Bernard, *Independent Man: The Life of James Couzens*, (Detroit: Wayne State University Press, 2002).

27. Graham, Benjamin and Dodd, David, *Securities Analysis* (New York: McGraw Hill, 1934), 307.

28. On April 13, 2010, the Federal Deposit Insurance Corporation issued a proposal that would change the calculation of deposit insurance assessments for "large" or "highly complex" institutions. Pursuant to the proposal, the FDIC would replace fundamentals based ratings and certain financial measures currently used with a "scorecard" consisting of well-defined financial measures that are more forward looking.

29. Minton and Stewart, 184.

30. Malone, Michael Shawn, *The Future Arrived Yesterday: The Rise of the Protean Corporation and What it Means to You* (New York: Crown Publishing, 2009), 54–55.

31. The author has written and researched most of a book on the corporate history of Ford.

32. Calder, Lendol, *Financing the American Dream: A Cultural History of Consumer Credit* (Princeton: Princeton University Press, 1999), 6.

33. Ibid., 18–20.

34. GMAC company history, GMAC web site (www.ally.com/about/company-structure/history/index.html).

35. Graham and Dodd, 309.

36. Sowell, 15–16.

37. Marshall, Peter H., *William Godwin* (Yale University Press: 1984).

38. Reis, Bernard J. and Flynn, John, *False Security: The Betrayal of the American Investor* (New York: The Stratford Press, 1937), 1. A facsimile of the original book was republished by Kessinger Publishing.

39. Ibid., 134.

40. Friedman and Schwartz, 244.

41. See Meltzer, Alan, *The Federal Reserve System: An Encyclopedia*, R.W. Hafer, Editor, (Westport: Greenwood Press, 2005) 243.

42. Robins, Lionel, *The Great Depression*, (London: Macmillan, 1934), 50–62.

43. "Mr. Coolidge's Farewell Warning," *The Literary Digest* (December 15, 1928), 5.

44. Byrd, 447.

45. Beaudreau, Bernard, *Making Sense of Smoot-Hawley, Technology and Tariffs* (Lincoln, NE: iUniverse, 2005).

46. Sparling, Earl, *Mystery Men of Wall Street: The Power Behind the Market* (New York: Greenberg, 1930), 17.

47. Friedman and Schwartz, 257.

48. Ibid., 259–264.

49. McGrattna, Ellen R., and Prescott, Edward C., "The Stock Market Crash of 1929: Irving Fisher Was Right!," NBER Working Paper No. 8622 (December 2001).

50. Friedman and Schwartz, 247.

51. "The Subprime Crisis & Ratings: PRMIA Meeting Notes," *The Institutional Risk Analyst* (September 24, 2007).

52. Galbraith, John Kenneth, *The Great Crash* (New York: Houghton Mifflin, 2009), vii.

53. "Roosevelt Attacks Theories of Hoover," *New York Times* (November 2, 1928), 11.

54. Ibid., 65.

55. Jones, Jesse and Angly, Edward, *Fifty Billion Dollars: My Thirteen Years at the RFC* (New York: MacMillan, 1951), 64–65.

56. Jones, 55.

57. Barnard, Harry, *Independent Man: The Life of Senator James Couzens* (Detroit: Wayne State University Press, 2002), 286.

58. Hoover, Herbert. *The Great Depression* (New York: Macmillan, 1952), 207.

59. Ibid., 354.

Chapter 6

1. Hoover, 359.

2. Minton and Stewart, *The Fat Years and the Lean*, 284.

3. Hoover, 355-356, n4.

4. Sowell, T. *A Conflict of Visions.*

5. Janeway, Eliot, *The Struggle for Survival* (New York: Weybright & Talley, 1951), 10–11.

6. Steel, Ronald, *Walter Lippmann and the American Century* (New York: Little Brown, 1980), 292–293.

7. Whalen, Richard, *The Founding Father: The Story of Joseph P. Kennedy* (New York: New American Library, 1964), 118–129.

8. "The SEC," *Fortune* (June 1940).

9. "The First Fifty Years: A History of the FDIC 1933–1983," FDIC, 37.

10. Cassell, Gustav, *The Downfall of the Gold Standard* (New York: Augustus Kelley, 1966 [1936]), 118–19.

11. "Sound Money and Balanced Budget Only Way to Revival, Says Baruch; Inflation the 'Road to Ruin,'" *New York Times* (February 14, 1933), 1.

12. Ibid.

13. Bovard, James, "Money: The Great Gold Robbery," *The Freeman* (June 1999).

14. Hoover, 407.

15. Ibid, 353.

16. Steel, 304.

17. Todd, 2.

18. Higgs, Robert, "How FDR Made the Depression Worse," *The Free Market*, Ludwig von Mises Institute (February 1995) Volume 13, Number 2.

19. Keynes, John Maynard, "National Self-Sufficiency," *The Yale Review*, Vol. 22, No. 4 (June 1933).

20. Keynes, John Maynard, *Treatise on Money: The Pure Theory of Money, Volume 1,* (London: Cambridge University Press, 1976).

21. Keynes, John Maynard, *The General Theory of Employment, Interest, and Money* (New York: Harcourt, Brace, 1936).

22. The Unofficial Observer, *The New Dealers* (New York: Simon and Schuster, 1934), 104.

23. Dallek, Robert, *Franklin D. Roosevelt and American Foreign Policy, 1932–1945* (New York: Oxford University Press, 1981), 38.

24. Cohen, Adam, *Nothing to Fear: FDR's Inner Circle and the Hundred Days that Created Modern America* (New York: The Penguin Press, 2009), 237.

25. *The New Dealers,* 131.

26. The Unofficial Observer, 131.

27. Baruch, B., *The Public Years*, 257.

28. Hoover, 398–399.

29. Warburg, James P., *The Money Muddle* (New York: Alfred A. Knopf, 1934), 159.

30. Smith, Rixey, and Beasley, Norman, *Carter Glass* (New York: Ayer Publishing, 1970), 358–359.

31. Ibid., 353.

32. Lippmann, Walter, *The Good Society* (Boston: Little Brown & Co, 1937), 48–49.

33. Todd, 11.

34. Byrd, 471–472.

35. Chernow, Ron, "Where is Our Ferdinand Pecora?" *New York Times* (January 5, 2009).

36. Both quotations come from a paper by Pollock, Alex, "Reprivatizing Credit: Remarks at a Federalist Society Conference on 'The Financial Services Bailout'," Washington, DC, (March 19, 2009).

37. Calomiris, Charles W., *United States Bank Deregulation in Historical Perspective* (London: Cambridge University Press, 2000), 200.

38. Holcombe, Randall G., "Federal Government Growth Before the New Deal," *The Freeman* (September 1, 1997).

39. Powell, Jim, *FDR's Folly: How Roosevelt and His New Deal Prolonged the Great Depression* (New York: Three Rivers Press, 2003), ix.

40. Ibid., back cover.

41. Interview with Ezra Klein, "Galbraith: The Danger Posed by the Deficit 'is Zero'," *Washington Post* (May 12, 2010).

42. Hoover, 9.

43. Jones, 84.

44. Ibid., 85–86.

45. Baruch, 250.

46. Todd, 15.

47. Chernow, 348.

48. Rothbard, *America's Great Depression*, 298.

49. Hoover, 214.

50. Schlesinger, Arthur, *The Politics of Upheaval, 1935–1936: The Age of Roosevelt* (New York: Houghton Mifflin Harcourt, 2003), 55–56.

51. Smith and Beasley, 341–343.

52. Todd, 23.

53. Ibid.

54. Todd, 43.

55. See Todd, citing Olson in "Rise of the Corporate State . . .," 36.

56. Ibid., 36.

57. Schlesinger, Arthur, *The Coming of the New Deal, 1933–1935* (New York: Houghton Mifflin, 2003), 433.

58. Oklahoma Historical Society (http://digital.library.okstate.edu/encyclopedia/entries/T/TH008.html).

59. Todd, 42.

60. Greider, William, *Secrets of the Temple* (New York: Simon and Schuster 1989), 310.

61. Meltzer, Allan H., *A History of the Federal Reserve: 1913–1951*, 465.

62. Ibid., 478.

63. Greider, 308–309.

64. D'Arista, Jane, *The Evolution of U.S. Finance: Federal Reserve Monetary Policy, 1915–1935* (Armonk, NY: ME Sharpe, 1994), 192.

65. Bernanke, Benjamin, *Essays on the Great Depression* (Princeton, NJ: Princeton University Press, 2000), 253.

66. Manchester, William, *The Glory and the Dream: A Narrative History of America, 1932–1972* (New York: Bantam, 1984), 289–295.

67. Regarding FDR's advance knowledge of the Japanese strike on Pearl Harbor in 1941, see C.L. Sulzberger, "Foreign Affairs: The Dim-Witted Machines," *New York Times* (December 8, 1966).

68. Keynes, John Maynard, "How to Pay for the War: A Radical Plan for the Chancellor of the Exchequer," (1940).

69. Skidelski, Robert, *Keynes: The Return of the Master* (New York: Public Affairs, 2009), 74.

70. Tansill, Charles Callan, *Back Door to War: Roosevelt Foreign Policy 1933–1941*, 588.

71. Freidman and Schwartz, 546.

72. Ibid., 553–555.

73. Ibid., 596.

74. Gardner, Richard, *Sterling-Dollar Diplomacy in Current Perspective* (New York: Columbia University Press, 1980), xxx.

75. Sicherman, Harvey, "America and the West: Lessons from the Marshall Plan," *Foreign Policy Research Institute*, Volume 1, Number 3 (January 1998).

76. Gardner, 195–245.

Chapter 7

1. Manchester, *Glory and the Dream,* 349.

2. Myers, 361.

3. Santoni, G.J., "The Employment Act of 1946: Some History Notes," Federal Reserve Bank of St. Louis, (November 1986).

4. Interview with Richard Whalen, April 30, 2010.

5. "Opinion of the Week," *New York Times* (June 17, 1962).

6. Higgs, Robert, "Regime Uncertainty: Why the Great Depression Lasted So Long and Why Prosperity Resumed after the War," *The Independent Review*, Vol. I, No. 4 (Spring 1997), 561–590.

7. Ibid., 564.

8. Hetzel, Robert L. and Leach, Ralph F., "The Treasury-Fed Accord: A New Narrative Account," *Economic Quarterly* (Winter 2001), 33–34.

9. Ibid., 35–37.

10. Ibid., 50–54.

11. Hetzel and Leach.

12. Hazlitt, Henry, *Will Dollars Save the World?* (New York: D. Appleton Century Co., 1947).

13. Friedman and Schwartz, 5.

14. Reinhart, Carmen, "This Time Is Different Chartbook: Country Histories on Debt, Default, and Financial Crises," NBER Working Paper 18815, March 2010, Figure 66c, 119.

15. Friedman, Benjamin, "Postwar Changes in the American Financial Markets," NBER Working Paper No. 458, March 1981, Issued in March 1981.

16. Whalen, Richard J., "The Shifting Equation of Nuclear Defense," *Fortune* (June 1, 1967).

17. Morgan, Iwan, *Deficit Government: Taxing and Spending in Modern America* (Chicago: Ivan R. Dee, 1995), ix.

18. Taleb, Nassim, *The Black Swan: The Impact of the Highly Improbable* (New York: Random House, 2008).

19. Baldwin, Robert E., *The Changing Nature of U.S. Trade Policy Since WWII* (University of Chicago Press, 1984), 5–7.

20. Lake, David, *The International Political Economy of Trade*, Vol. I, (Cheltenham: Edward Elgar Publishing, 1993), 8–10.

21. *The United States in World Affairs: The World Economy in 1951*, Council on Foreign Relations, 225–229.

22. Higgins, Matthew and Klitgaard, Thomas, "Viewing the Current Account Deficit as a Capital Inflow," *Current Issues*, Federal Reserve Bank of New York (December 1998), 4.

23. Barton, John H., Fisher, Bart S. and Malloy, Michael P., "Regulating International Investment," *International Trade and Economic Negotiation*, 6 (2006).

24. Hazlitt, Henry, *From Bretton Woods to World Inflation: A Study of Causes and Consequences* (Auburn, AL: Ludwig von Mises Institute, 2009), 7.

25. Bluestein, Paul, *The Chastening: Inside the Crisis that Rocked the Global Financial System, and Humbled the IMF* (New York: Basic Books, 2003), 16.

26. Jones, James R., "Why LBJ Bowed Out," *The Los Angeles Times* (March 30, 2008).

27. Whalen, Richard J., *Catch the Falling Flag: A Republican's Challenge to His Party* (New York: Houghton Mifflin, 1972), 6.

28. Manchester, 1251–1252.

29. Yergin, Daniel and Stanislaw, Joseph, *The Commanding Heights* (New York: Simon & Schuster, 1997), 60–64.

30. North, Gary, "The Lesser of Two Evils Rarely Is," www.LewRockwell.com (June 8, 2007).

31. Sidey, Hugh, "The Economy: Nixon's Grand Design for Recovery," *Time* (August 30, 1971).

32. Whalen, *Catch the Falling Flag*, 266.

33. Abrams, Burton A. 2006. "How Richard Nixon Pressured Arthur Burns: Evidence from the Nixon Tapes." *Journal of Economic Perspectives*, 20: 4 (Fall): 177–88.

34. Hertzel, Bob, *The Monetary Policy of the Federal Reserve: A History* (London: Cambridge University Press, 2008), 77.

35. Safire, William, *Before the Fall* (New York: Doubleday, 1975), 513–515.

36. Todd, Walker, "A History of International Lending," *Research in Financial Services Private and Public Policy*, Vol. 3. (Greenwich, CT: JAI Press, 1991), 203.

37. Gordon, David M., "Chickens Come Home to Roost: From Prosperity to Stagnation in the Postwar Economy," *Understanding American economic decline* (London: Cambridge University Press, 1994), 54.

38. O'Driscoll, Gerald, "Restoring Credibility to International Lending," CATO Journal, Vol. 4, No. 1 (Spring/Summer 1984), 131.

39. Todd, 205.

40. Reinhart, Carmen and Rogoff, Kenneth, *This Time is Different: Eight Centuries of Financial Folly* (Princeton, NJ: Princeton University Press, 2009), 205.

41. *Federal Reserve Bulletin*, 1990, A64.

42. O'Driscoll, 132.

43. "Interview with Paul A. Volcker In Conversation with Gary H. Stern," Federal Reserve Bank of Minneapolis, July 15, 2009.

Chapter 8

1. Bartlett, Bruce, "(More) Politics at the Fed? Greenspan Should Tighten A.S.A.P.—For His and the Country's Good," *NRO Financial* (April 28, 2004).

2. Silk, Leonard, "There's a Brighter Side; . . ." *New York Times,* September 18, 1974, 55.

3. Woodward, Bob, *The Maestro: Greenspan's Fed and the American Boom* (New York: Simon & Schuster, 2000), 35.

4. Grutsinger, Martin, "Ford WIN Buttons Remembered," *The Associated Press* (December 28, 2006).

5. Morgan, Iwan, *Taxing and Spending in Modern America* (London: Iwan Dee, 1995).

6. Mieczkowski, Yanek, "The Secrets of Gerald Ford's Success . . . 30 Years After He Became President It's Time to Consider What Made Him Tick," *History News Network*, George Mason University (August 2, 2004).

7. Reeves, Richard, "The City Politic: The Nationwide Search for Nelson Rockefeller," *New York Magazine* (September 2, 1974), 8.

8. Roesch, Susan R., "The FOMC During 1974: Monetary Policy During Economic Uncertainty," Federal Reserve Bank of St. Louis (April 1975), 2.

9. Interview with Paul Volcker, March 18, 2010.

10. Morgan, 127.

11. Anderson, Martin, *Revolution: The Reagan Legacy* (Stamford: Hoover Press, 1990), 69.

12. Berlin, Isaiah, "Two Concepts of Liberty," an inaugural lecture delivered before the University of Oxford on 31 October 1958, London: Clarendon Press, 1958.

13. Hoffman, Stanley, *Redeeming American Political Thought* (University of Chicago Press, 1998), 111.

14. "Do a Good Job: Interview With Senator Ernest Hollings," *The Institutional Risk Analyst,* May 3, 2010.

15. Carter, Jimmy, *Keeping Faith: memoirs of a president* (Little Rock: University of Arkansas Press, 1995), 82.

16. Ebeling, Richard M., "Henry Hazlitt and the Failure of Keynesian Economics," *The Freeman* (November 2004), 17.

17. McFadden, Robert, "G. William Miller, 81, Former Top Economic Official, Dies," *New York Times* (March 20, 2006).

18. "Fed Chairmen and Presidents: Roundtable with Roger Kubarych and Richard Whalen," *The Institutional Risk Analyst* (October 30, 2008).

19. Morgan, 133.

20. Ibid., 134.

21. "Fed Chairmen and Presidents."

22. Ibid.

23. Bartlett, Bruce, "Warriors Against Inflation: Volcker *and* Reagan got the job done," National Review Online (June 14, 2004).

24. Friedman, Benjamin, "New Directions in the Relationship between Public and Private Debt," *National Bureau of Economic Research*, Working Paper No. 2186 (March 1987).

25. Ibid.

26. Niskanen, William A. and Moore, Stephen, "Supply-Side Tax Cuts and the Truth about the Reagan Economic Record" (Washington: CATO Institute, October 22, 1996).

27. Samuelson, Paul, "Lessons From the Great Inflation: Paul Volcker and Ronald Reagan's Forgotten Miracle Created a Quarter Century of Prosperity—and a Dangerous Bubble of Complacency," *Reason Magazine*, January 2009.

28. Todd, Walker, "Latin America, Asia & Russia: Have the Lessons Been Learned?", *Research in Financial Services* (Stamford, CT: JAI Press, 1999), 116–117.

29. Whalen, Christopher, "Going South," *The Nation*, (January 23, 1995).

30. Isaac, William, *Senseless Panic: How Washington Failed America* (Hoboken, NJ: John Wiley and Sons, 2010), 30–31.

31. Woodward, Bob, *Maestro: Greenspan's Fed and the American boom* (New York: Simon & Schuster, 2001).

32. "Fed Chairmen and Presidents."

33. Ibid.

34. Mayer, Martin, *Nightmare on Wall Street: Salomon Brothers and the Corruption of the Marketplace* (New York: Simon & Schuster, 1993). Quotation taken from book draft in "Gone Fishing: E. Gerald Corrigan and the Era of Managed Markets" (Herbert Gold Society, 1993), 12.

35. "Volcker Won the War against Inflation, but Dollar Again Weak," *Los Angeles Times* (June 7, 1987).

36. Einhorn, David, "Easy Money, Hard Truths," *New York Times* (May 26, 2010).

37. Reinhart, 119.

38. "So What About the Real Economy? Interview with Credit Risk Monitor," *The Institutional Risk Analyst,* October 26, 2009.

39. Warren, Elizabeth and Tyagi, Amelia, *The Two Income Trap* (New York: Basic Books, 2003).

40. "GSE Nation: Interview with Robert Feinberg," *The Institutional Risk Analyst,* (March 17, 2008).

41. Interview with Josh Rosner, June 2010.

42. Ibid.

43. Woodward, 95.

44. Whalen, Christopher, "I am Superman: The Federal Reserve Board and the Neverending Crisis," *Networks Financial Institute of Indiana State University,* August 2010.

Chapter 9

1. Grant, 5.

2. Morgan, Iwan, *The Age of Deficits* (Lawrence, KS: University Press of Kansas, 2009), 257.

3. David, L.J., *Bad Money* (New York: St. Martin's Press, 1982), 92.

4. Bartlett, Bruce, "America's Foreign Owned Debt," *Forbes*, March 12, 2010.

5. "Talking the Economy: Alex Pollock, Bruce Bartlett and Josh Rosner," *The Institutional Risk Analyst,* June 21, 2010.

6. Conversation with William Dunkelberg, June 2010.

7. Interview with Paul Volcker, March 18, 2010.

8. Interview with Josh Rosner, June 2010.

9. Interview with David Kotok, June 22, 2010.

10. Federal Open Market Committee, Briefing on Monetary Policy Alternatives, October 28, 2003.

11. Interview with Vincent Reinhart, May 29, 2010.

12. Kotok interview.

13. Todd, Walker, "Triffin's Dilemma, Reserve Currencies, and Gold," *American Institute for Economic Research* (December 31, 2008).

14. Sender, Henny, "China to Stick with U.S. Bonds," *The Financial Times* (February 11, 2009).

15. "Paper Gold vs. the Dollar? Interview with James Rickards," *The Institutional Risk Analyst* (July 7, 2010).

16. Roubini, Nouriel and Mihm, Stephen, *Crisis Economics* (New York: Penguin, 2010).

Selected References

Adams, J.T. (1932). *The Epic of America*. New York: Little Brown.

Barron, C.W. (1915). *The Audacious War*. New York: Houghton Mifflin Co.

Baruch, B. (1957). *The Public Years*. New York: Holt.

Bernard, H. (2002). *Independent Man: The Life of James Couzens*. Detroit: Wayne State University Press.

Brands, H.W. (2003). *The Age of Gold: The California Gold Rush and the New American dream*. New York: Anchor Books

Byrd, R.C. (1988). *The Senate, 1789–1989*. Washington, DC: U.S. Government Printing Office.

Calder, L. (1999). *Financing the American Dream: A Cultural History of Consumer Credit*. Princeton, NJ: Princeton University Press,

Catteral, R.C.H. (1903). *The Second Bank of the United States*. Chicago: The University of Chicago Press.

Chernow, R. (1990). *The House of Morgan: An American Banking Dynasty and the Rise of Modern Finance*. NY: Grove Press.

Chernow, R. (2004). *Alexander Hamilton*. New York: Penguin Press.

Clinton, G. (1933). *The Mirrors of Wall Street*. NY: Putnam & Sons.

Dubois, WEB (1954). *The Suppression of the African Slave Trade in the United States of America 1638–1870*. New York: Social Science Press.

Dunbar, Willis F. and May, George (1995) *Michigan: A History of the Wolverine State*. Grand Rapids, MI: Erdmans Publishing.

Federal Reserve Bank of San Francisco (1995). "1995 Annual Report: A Brief History of Our Nation's Paper Money."

Foulke, R.A. (1941). *The Sinews of American Commerce.* New York: Dunn & Bradstreet.

Friedman, M. and Schwartz, A. (1965). *A Monetary History of the United States, 1867–1960.* New York: National Bureau of Economic Research.

Galbraith, J.K. (1997). *The Great Crash 1929.* NY: Houghton Mifflin.

Goodwyn, L. (1978). *The Populist Moment: A Short History of the Agrarian Revolt in America.* London: Oxford University Press.

Graham, B. and Dodd, D. (1934). *Securities Analysis,.* New York: McGraw Hill.

Grant, J. (1992). *Money on the Mind.* New York: Macmillan.

Grinath, A., Wallis, J. and Sylla, R. (March 1997). "Debt, Default and Revenue Structure: The American State Debt Crisis in the Early 1840s," Historical Paper 97, National Bureau of Economic Research.

Hayek, F.A. (1990). *Denationalisation of Money—The Argument Refined: An Analysis of the Theory and Practice of Concurrent Currencies.* 3rd ed. London: Institute of Economic Affairs.

Higgs, R. (February 1995). "How FDR Made the Depression Worse," *The Free Market,* Auburn, AL: Ludwig von Mises Institute.

Hixon, W.F., (1993). *Triumph of the Bankers: Money and Banking in the Eighteenth and Nineteenth Centuries.* Westport: Praeger Publishers.

Homer, S. and Sylla, R. (1963). *A History of Interest Rates.* Rutgers University Press.

Hoover, H. (1952). *The Great Depression.* New York: Macmillan.

Hornberger, J.G., November 2000. "Legal Tender and the Civil War," *Freedom Daily,* Future of Freedom Foundation.

Jackson, A. (1832). "Veto Message Regarding the Bank of the United States," Yale Law School.

James, M. (1938). *The Life of Andrew Jackson.* Camden, NJ: Haddon Craftsmen.

Janeway, E. (1951). *The Struggle for Survival.* New York: Weybright & Talley.

Jones, J. and Angly, E. (1951). *Fifty Billion Dollars: My Thirteen Years at the RFC.* New York: Macmillan.

Josephson, M. (1934). *The Robber Barons.* New York: Harcourt Brace & Co.

Kamensky, J. (2008). *The Exchange Artist: A Tale of High-Flying Speculation and America's First Banking Collapse.* New York: Viking Penguin.

Keynes, J.M. (June 1933). "National Self-Sufficiency," New Haven: *The Yale Review.*

Lippmann, W. (1937) *The Good Society.* Boston: Little Brown & Co.

McCullough, D. *John Adams (2001).* New York: Simon & Schuster

McDill, K.M. and Sheehan, K.P. (2006). "Sources of Historical Banking Panics: A Markov Switching Approach." FDIC Working Paper 2006-01.

Meltzer, A.H. (2003). *A History of the Federal Reserve: 1913–1951.* Chicago: University of Chicago Press.

Minton, B. and Stuart, J. (1940). *The Fat Years and the Lean.* New York: International Publishers.

Miron, J.A. (February 1990). *The Founding of the Fed and the Destabilization of the Post-1914 Economy.* New York: National Bureau of Economic Research.

Myers, M.G. (1970). *A Financial History of the United States.* NY: Columbia University Press.

Nevins, A and Comanger, H.S. (1996) *A Short History of the United States.* New York: Knopf.

Phillips, K. (2009). *The Cousins' War.* New York: Basic Books.

Pollock, A. (2009). "Reprivatizing Credit: Remarks at a Federalist Society Conference on 'the Financial Services Bailout'." Washington, DC. March 19.

Pound, A. and Morse, S. (1930). *They Told Barron: The Notes of Clarence W. Barron.* New York: Harper Brothers.

Powell, J. (2003). *FDR's Folly: How Roosevelt and His New Deal Prolonged the Great Depression.* New York: Three Rivers Press.

Reinhart, C. and Rogoff, K. (2009). *This Time is Different: Eight Centuries of Financial Folly.* Princeton, NJ: Princeton University Press.

Roosevelt, T. (2008). *Autobiography of Theodore Roosevelt.* Blacksburg, VA: Wilder Publications.

Rothbard, M. (2002). *A History of Money and Banking in the United States.* Auburn, AL: Ludwig von Mises Institute.

———. (1994). *The Case Against the Fed.* Auburn, AL: The Ludwig von Mises Institute.

Safire, W. (1975). *Before the Fall.* New York: Doubleday.

Schlesinger, A. (2003). *The Politics of Upheaval, 1935–1936: The Age of Roosevelt.* New York: Houghton Mifflin Harcourt.

Schweikart, L. (1987). *Banking in the American South from the Age of Jackson to Reconstruction.* Baton Rouge, LA: Louisiana State University Press.

Smith, R., and Beasley, N. (1970). *Carter Glass.* New York: Ayer Publishing.

Sowell, T. (2007). *A Conflict of Visions: Ideological Origins of Political Struggles.* New York: Basic Books.

Sparling, E. (1930). *Mystery Men of Wall Street: The Power Behind the Market.* New York: Greenberg.

Steel, R. (1980). *Walter Lippmann and the American century.* New York: Little Brown.

Swanberg, W.A. (1960). *Jim Fisk: The Career of an Improbable Rascal.* New York: Longmans.

Tansil, C.C. (1938). *America Goes to War.* Boston: Little Brown and Co.

Taylor, G. (1949). *Jackson Versus Biddle: The Struggle over the Second Bank of the United States.* Boston: CD Heath.

The Unofficial Observer (1934). *The New Dealers,* New York: Simon and Schuster.

Timberlake, R.H., (1978). *Monetary Policy in the United States: An Intellectual and Institutional History.* Chicago: University of Chicago Press.

Todd, W.F. (1991). A History of International Lending." *Research in Financial Services, Private and Public Policy.* Volume 3, Stamford, CT: JAI Press Inc.

———. (1993). "FDICIA's Emergency Liquidity Provisions." Federal Reserve Bank of Cleveland *Economic Review* (3rd quarter).

——. (1995). "The Federal Reserve Board and the Rise of the Corporate State, 1931–1934," *Economic Education Bulletin*, Great Barrington, MA: American Institute for Economic Research

Warburg, P.M. (1930). *The Federal Reserve System, Its Origins and Growth: Reflections and Recollections*. Vol. II. NY: The Macmillan Company.

Warren, E. (2004) *The Two Income Trap*. New York: Basic Books.

Whalen, R.J. (1972). *Catch the Falling Flag: A Republican's Challenge to His Party*. New York: Houghton Mifflin.

Whalen, R.J. (1964) *The Founding Father: The Story of Joseph P. Kennedy*. New York: New American Library.

Wilkeson, S. (1865). *How Our National Debt May Be A National Blessing*. Philadelphia: M'Laughlin Brothers Printers.

Woodward, B. (2000). *The Maestro: Greenspan's Fed and the American Boom*. New York: Simon & Schuster.

About the Author

R. Christopher Whalen is co-founder of Institutional Risk Analytics, the Los Angeles-based provider of bank ratings, risk management tools, and consulting services for auditors, regulators, and financial professionals. He leads IRA's risk advisory practice and consults for global companies on financial and regulatory issues.

Christopher currently edits *The Institutional Risk Analyst*, a weekly news report and commentary on significant developments in and around the global financial markets. Christopher has testified before the Congress and the Securities and Exchange Commission on a range of financial issues and contributes articles and commentaries to publications such as *American Banker, Bank Credit Analyst*, and Reuters.

Christopher is a Fellow of the Networks Financial Institute at Indiana State University. He is a member of the Professional Risk Managers International Association and volunteers as a member of the steering committee for PRMIA's Washington, DC chapter. Christopher is a member of the Economic Advisory Committee of the Financial Industry Regulatory Authority (FINRA).

Christopher was born in 1959 in Richmond, Virginia. He grew up in Washington, DC and attended St. John's College High School and Villanova University (1981). Christopher and his wife Pamela live at the top of Red Hill in the Village of Croton-on-Hudson, New York. For more information, go to www.rcwhalen.com.

Index